A REVIEW AND REFERENCE GRAMMAR

Dirk O. Hoffmann
Colgate University

Agnes Domandi Langdon
Colgate University

HOLT, RINEHART AND WINSTON, INC.

New York / Chicago / San Francisco / Philadelphia / Montreal / Toronto / London / Sydney / Tokyo

Publisher   Ted Buchholz
Sr. Acquisitions Editor   Jim Harmon
Production Manager   Annette Dudley Wiggins
Cover Art   Matthias Duwel
Cover & Text Design   Off Broadway Graphics
Editorial & Production Services   Michael Bass & Associates
Illustrations   Duvan Hoffmann, Wolfgang Schütz, Per-Henrik Gürth
Photo Research   Rona Tuccillo
Illustration Credit   Page 43, Apple Computer, Inc.

Library of Congress Cataloging-in-Publication Data

Hoffmann, Dirk O., 1942–

Alternativen, a review and reference grammar / Dirk O. Hoffmann, Agnes Domandi Langdon.

p.   cm.

Includes index.

ISBN 0-03-003733-6

1. German language—Grammar—1950–   2. German language—Textbooks for foreign speakers—English.   I. Langdon, Agnes Domandi.
II. Title.
PF3112.H58 1989   88–19100
438.2′421—dc19   CIP

Address Editorial Correspondence To: 301 Commerce Street, Suite 3700, Fort Worth, TX 76102

Address Orders To: 6277 Sea Harbor Drive, Orlando, FL 32887
1-800-782-4479, or 1-800-433-0001 (in Florida)

Printed in the United States of America

0 1 2 3   039   9 8 7 6 5 4 3 2 1

Holt, Rinehart and Winston, Inc.
The Dryden Press
Saunders College Publishing

Preface

ALTERNATIVEN is a set of three integrated books for the study of intermediate German: a REVIEW AND REFERENCE GRAMMAR, a READER of culture and literature texts, and a WORKBOOK-LAB MANUAL. When used together, these three components make up a year's course (two semesters or four quarters with four class hours a week).

The ALTERNATIVEN principle gives instructors a great deal of choice in how to use the books. Each component of the package may be used by itself. The GRAMMAR volume alone serves as a one-semester review course of German grammar, or as a reference work. When it is used with the WORKBOOK-LAB MANUAL, it offers extensive study of grammatical phenomena in the classroom and the language laboratory plus vocabulary building, chapter by chapter. The GRAMMAR can also be used with the READER because the additional exercises in the grammar are coordinated with the READER vocabulary.

The READER volume alone serves as a third or fourth semester introduction to German literature and culture. It could be used with the WORKBOOK-LAB MANUAL if the students know their grammar although they may need a little work in certain areas. It is also possible to use only parts of the READER in conjunction with the GRAMMAR and/or WORKBOOK-LAB MANUAL since individual sections in each volume are coordinated.

As evident from the above, the integration of the three component volumes is achieved by way of vocabulary. The exercises in each GRAMMAR chapter feature the active vocabulary from the respective READER chapter. The WORKBOOK exercises not only work up the active vocabulary from the coordinated READER chapter but reflect much of the chapter texts' subject matter. The LAB MANUAL lessons work up the active vocabulary from the respective READER chapter and feature dictations, dialogues, and comprehension exercises based directly on READER texts.

The grammar has been designed to facilitate learning:

- Individual grammar points are immediately practiced by CHECK AND PRACTICE sections which are distinctly marked. In these CHECK AND PRACTICE sections the exercises are often very simple structural exercises which drill a grammar point independently from a semantic context — the students are asked to focus on a structural point. Because many students need to approach language acquisition in a step-by-step manner, these simple exercises are active paradigms (additional examples which the students have to do themselves).

- Relevant cross-references have been added for quick checking. The index in back gives more detailed information.

- Each chapter concludes with the section ADDITIONAL EXERCISES which reviews the major grammar points of that chapter and puts the grammar points in a context. The section ADDITIONAL EXERCISES is subdivided into two parts to give the teacher real flexibility. These parts begin with few new thematic words from the reader (A, B, C text, as specified in the headings) to help with vocabulary building. Instructors can use all exercises or just one or the other group, because the grammar points covered are identical.

The ALTERNATIVEN principle also allows different methods of language teaching. For example, instructors who wish to stress grammar review may start with the active vocabulary and assign a grammar chapter, or part thereof, for review. Then they can simultaneously practice the grammar points and the new vocabulary by doing the ADDITIONAL EXERCISES in class and by assigning WORKBOOK drills as homework. Students should then find the texts fairly easy because they have already learned the active vocabulary. The laboratory work could be assigned before or during classroom discussions of themes, and doing the activities.

Instructors who wish to further their students' communicative and reading skills may wish to start with the READER texts, the questions, themes and activities including the laboratory lessons. Then they could move to the grammar review. The students would be able to concentrate on grammatical phenomena, and do the ADDITIONAL EXERCISES in the GRAMMAR and the drills in the WORKBOOK with some ease because they are familiar with the vocabulary and the link with READER topics the drills offer.

Finally, an instructor may vary the approach chapter by chapter, emphasizing or deemphasizing individual sections in the GRAMMAR, the READER or the WORKBOOK-LAB MANUAL.

Acknowledgments

Every grammar is indebted to numerous grammars and textbooks written before. Although it is impossible to list all of them which influenced the present volume, special acknowledgment should be given to G. Helbig and J. Buscha, *Deutsche Grammatik*; C. Pollard's contribution "The Weak Verb — How to Recognize it in the Infinitive" in *The Teaching of German — Problems and Methods*; W.F.W. Lohnes, F.W. Strothmann, and W.E. Petig, *German — A Structural Approach*.

Special thanks go to Patti Voss for supervising the vocabulary list and the many students who worked with the present grammar and whose suggestions have been incorporated.

We would like to thank the following colleagues who reviewed the manuscript during its various stages of development: James Ronald Bartlett, University of Mississippi; Brigitte Bradley, Barnard College; Maria-Louise Caputo-Mayr, Temple University; Jerry L. Cox, Furman University; Wolfgang Dill, Oregon State University; Bruce Duncan, Dartmouth College; Henry Gerlach, University of Illinois, Champaign; William Keel, University of Kansas; Harvey Kendall, California State University; Valda Melngailio, Boston College; Harry Paulin, San Diego State University; William Petig, Stanford University; Karen Ready, Indiana University of PA; Conrad Schaum, University of Notre Dame; Tim Sellner, Wake Forest University; Elfriede W. Smith, Drew University; Marion Sonnenfeld, Fredonia State University; Patricia Stanley, Florida State University; Norman Watt, St. Olaf College; Kathleen Webb, University of Pennsylvania; Peter Winkel, Trenton State.

Contents

VERBS (Part One)

PRINCIPLES OF TENSE FORMATION

General Survey

1 German utilizes *two simple tenses*   PRESENT TENSE
                                                 SIMPLE PAST TENSE
       and *four compound tenses,*   PRESENT PERFECT TENSE
            which are formed   PAST PERFECT TENSE
            with the addition   FUTURE TENSE
            of auxiliaries.   FUTURE PERFECT TENSE

2 German and English tense forms resemble each other, yet they are used differently. [For usage, see § 38ff.]

SIMPLE TENSES

Present Tense	ich	**lerne**	*I learn*
Simple Past Tense	ich	**lernte**	*I learned*

COMPOUND TENSES

Present Perfect Tense	ich	**habe gelernt**	*I have learned*
Past Perfect Tense	ich	**hatte gelernt**	*I had learned*
Future Tense	ich	**werde lernen**	*I will learn*
Future Perfect Tense	ich	**werde gelernt haben**	*I will have learned*

3 In addition to these tense forms, English also uses:

1. the progressive (I am waiting; I was waiting; I have been waiting; I had been waiting);
2. the emphatic (I do wait; I did wait).
   German does not have these tense forms.

Basic Verb Forms

4 1. All German verbs have three basic forms, which are called the *principal parts* of the verb. From these all verb forms can be derived.

Basic Verb Forms	INFINITIVE	SIMPLE PAST	PAST PARTICIPLE
	lernen	**lern**te	ge **lern**t
	STEM ENDING	STEM ENDING	PREFIX STEM ENDING

2. In addition, the auxiliaries **werden, haben,** and **sein** are used to create compound tenses.

CHECK AND PRACTICE

Identify the tense.

1. Ich **werde** erst 1995 nach München **kommen.**
2. Ich **fahre** gern mit dem Zug.
3. Ich **habe** gestern viel **gekocht.**
4. Früher **reiste** ich oft ins Ausland.
5. Ich **hatte** gerade eine Fahrkarte am Bahnhof **gekauft,** als das Unglück **passierte.**
6. Ich **glaube,** ich **werde** ihm den Blödsinn wohl **gesagt haben.**
7. Peter, gestern **habe** ich ein Kleid **genäht.**
8. Ich **hole** dir gleich noch ein Glas Bier.
9. Paul **lachte** und **lachte.**
10. Morgen **werde** ich meinen alten Wagen **verkaufen.**

You don't need to know the meaning of the words. Just look at the forms and compare them with those in table § 2.

Verb Classification: Weak or Strong

5 German verbs are classified as either *weak* or *strong*, based on their forms only, not their function.

For weak verbs, see § 10ff.   For strong verbs, see § 17ff.

6 Weak verbs 1. form the *past tense* with the suffix **-t-** following the stem;
   2. form the *past participle* with the prefix **ge-** and the suffix **-t** following the stem.

BASIC VERB FORMS

Infinitive	Past Tense	Past Participle
zeigen	zeigte	**ge**zeig**t**

7   Strong verbs change the stem vowel in the past tense and the past participle. They

1. have no suffix in the *past tense;*

2. form the *past participle* with the prefix **ge-** and the suffix **-en.**

fliegen	flog	**ge**flog**en**

8   EXCEPTION: Some verbs, both weak and strong, omit the **ge-** prefix in the past participle. These are verbs which are not stressed on the first syllable. There are two classes:

1. verbs ending in **-ieren.**

Infinitive	reservieren
Past Participle	reserviert

2. verbs which have an inseparable prefix. [See § 68ff.]

Infinitive	besuchen	beginnen
Past Participle	besucht	begonnen

You don't need to know the meanings of the words.

CHECK AND PRACTICE

Look at the basic forms, then identify each verb as weak or strong.

1.	bauen	baute	gebaut
2.	kaufen	kaufte	gekauft
3.	beginnen	begann	begonnen
4.	lassen	ließ	gelassen
5.	brauchen	brauchte	gebraucht
6.	liegen	lag	gelegen
7.	studieren	studierte	studiert
8.	rufen	rief	gerufen
9.	hören	hörte	gehört
10.	versuchen	versuchte	versucht

9   It is not always possible to tell from the infinitive if a verb is weak or strong. However, there are some general rules:

1. The following suffixes signal that a verb is weak:

lächel**n**	beteu**ern**	kündi**gen**	verniedl**ichen**	marsch**ieren**

-ier-lich-er   Ig-el

2. The following table of stem vowels shows which verbs tend to be weak and which verbs tend to be strong:

VERBS WHICH TEND TO BE

Weak			Strong
äu ö ä		i	e ei ie
eu au ü		a	in + consonant
o			im + consonant
u			

a. There are over 200 verbs with an umlauted vowel in the stem. With very few exceptions they are all weak (e.g., **lösen** *to solve,* **hüten** *to guard,* **säugen** *to nurse,* **vergällen** *to embitter*). Important exceptions are **schwören** *to swear,* **lügen** *to lie,* **betrügen** *to deceive.*

b. Almost all verbs with the diphthong **eu** or **au** in the stem are weak (e.g., **beugen** *to bend,* **bauen** *to build*). The only common exception is **laufen** *to walk.*

c. There are about 45 verbs with the stem vowel **o** (e.g., **holen** *to get,* **wohnen** *to reside*) and 45 verbs with the stem vowel **u**. All are weak except **kommen** *to come,* **stoßen** *to push,* **rufen** *to call* and **tun** *to do.*

d. The majority of the verbs with the stem **i** are weak (e.g., **schicken** *to send*). Important exceptions are **wissen** *to know,* **bitten** *to ask a favor,* **sitzen** *to sit.*
   BUT verbs with **m** or **n** plus a consonant are strong (e.g., **schwimmen** *to swim,* **singen** *to sing*).

e. Out of 145 verbs with the stem vowel **a** (e.g., **sagen** *to say,* **danken** *to thank*) only about 20 are strong [see § 20].

f. Verbs with the stem vowels **e**, **ei**, or **ie** tend to be strong (e.g., **lesen** *to read,* **reiten** *to ride,* **fliegen** *to fly*). An important exception is **zeigen** *to show.*

Basic Verb Forms of Weak Verbs

10   Most weak verbs form the past tense with the suffix –**t** [see also §6]. For reasons of pronunciation, some add the suffix –**et** instead of –**t**. –**et** is found in verbs:

1. whose stems end in –**t** or –**d**;

INFINITIVE	PAST TENSE	PAST PARTICIPLE	
arbeit–en	arbeit–**et**–e	gearbeit–**et**	*to work*
wart–en	wart–**et**–e	gewart–**et**	*to wait*
red–en	red–**et**–e	gered–**et**	*to talk*

2. whose stems end in –**m** or –**n** preceded by a consonant other than **h, l,** and **r**.

ö**ffn**–en	ö**ffn**–**et**–e	geö**ffn**–**et**		wohn–en	wohn–te	gewohn–t
to open				*to reside*		
re**chn**–en	re**chn**–**et**–e	gere**chn**–**et**	BUT	film–en	film–te	gefilm–t
to calculate				*to film*		
re**gn**–en	re**gn**–**et**–e	gere**gn**–**et**		turn–en	turn–te	geturn–t
to rain				*to do gymnastics*		

CHECK AND PRACTICE

Give the past tense and past participle of the following verbs:

1. arbeiten	2. weinen	3. fühlen	4. kaufen	5. bauen
6. blühen	7. führen	8. lachen	9. zählen	10. drücken
11. wählen	12. legen	13. wünschen	14. wechseln	15. glauben
16. lernen	17. wohnen	18. warten	19. melden	20. pflanzen

BASIC VERB FORMS OF SPECIAL WEAK VERBS

haben

Note the irregular change in stem consonant.

11   The special weak verb **haben** is used most of the time as an auxiliary.

INFINITIVE	PAST TENSE	PAST PARTICIPLE
haben	hatte	gehabt

"Hybrid" Verbs

12 1. There are a few verbs that are classifiied as weak because of their past tense and past participle formation. However, the stem vowel changes like a strong verb. Therefore, they are sometimes called 'hybrid verbs.' Note the change from **e** to **a** in the following:

INFINITIVE	PAST TENSE	PAST PARTICIPLE	
brennen	brannte	gebrannt	*to burn*
kennen	kannte	gekannt	*to know*
nennen	nannte	genannt	*to call, to name*
rennen	rannte	gerannt	*to run*
senden	sandte	gesandt	*to send*
wenden	wandte	gewandt	*to turn*

2. Two verbs of this group also have a regular weak form. These forms are not wholly interchangeable and imply, especially for **senden**, a change of meaning:

senden	sandte	gesandt	*to send*
	sendete	gesendet	*to broadcast*
wenden	wandte	gewandt	*to turn*
	wendete	gewendet	

13 Two very common but irregular weak verbs, **bringen** and **denken**, have a stem vowel change to **a** as well as a consonant change.

bringen	bra**ch**te	gebra**ch**t	*to bring*
denk**en**	da**ch**te	geda**ch**t	*to think*

CHECK AND PRACTICE

Which form is this? Identify it as infinitive, past tense, or past participle. Give the two missing forms.

1. haben	2. reisen	3. gerannt	4. erinnerte	5. besucht
6. gekocht	7. reserviert	8. kennen	9. danken	10. denken
11. geregnet	12. brachte	13. fühlte	14. brannte	15. erklärt
16. nennen	17. gehören	18. fragen	19. beobachtete	20. senden

14 The stem vowel of the verb **wissen** *to know* changes from **i** to **u** in the past tense and past participle. [For the present tense forms, see § 29]

INFINITIVE	PAST TENSE	PAST PARTICIPLE
wissen	wußte	gewußt

Modal Auxiliaries

15 The model auxiliaries also show a peculiarity. The umlaut of the infinitive, if there is one, disappears in the past tense and past participle. [For the present tense forms, see § 29. For usage, see § 78ff.]

dürfen	durfte	gedurft
können	konnte	gekonnt
müssen	mußte	gemußt
sollen	sollte	gesollt
wollen	wollte	gewollt

16 In the case of the modal **mögen**, the umlaut omission is accompanied by a consonant change. [See also § 29]

mögen	mochte	gemocht

CHECK AND PRACTICE

Which form is this? Identify it as infinitive, past tense, or past participle. Give the two missing forms.

1. wußte	2. sollte	3. gemußt	4. mögen	5. dürfen
6. gebrannt	7. gehustet	8. schicken	9. gewollt	10. konnte
11. haben	12. vermuten	13. denken	14. kochte	15. brachte
16. grüßte	17. danken	18. korrigiert	19. geturnt	20. heiraten

Basic Verb Forms of Strong Verbs

17 *Vowel changes* occurring in the past tense and past participle of strong verbs [see §7] can be arranged into three groups:

Pattern I	1	2	2
	bleiben	blieb	geblieben
	fliegen	flog	geflogen
Pattern II	**1**	**2**	**3**
	beginnen	begann	begonnen
	singen	sang	gesungen
	sprechen	sprach	gesprochen
Pattern III	**1**	**2**	**1**
	geben	gab	gegeben
	fahren	fuhr	gefahren
	schlafen	schlief	geschlafen

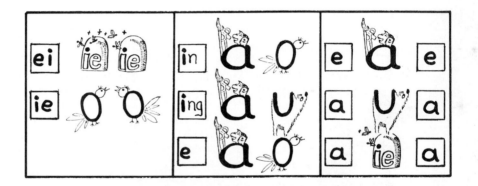

18 Group I has the pattern:

INFINITIVE	PAST TENSE	PAST PARTICIPLE
1	2	2

The past tense and the past participle have the same vowel, whereas the vowel of the infinitive varies. Almost all strong verbs with the stem vowel **ei** and **ie**, and a few strong verbs with **ö** and **ü** are in this group. Most verbs with an umlaut as a stem vowel are weak [See § 9.2.a.]

	INFINITIVE	PAST TENSE	PAST PARTICIPLE	
ēi īe īe	bleiben	blieb	**ist** geblieben	*to remain*
	entscheiden	entschied	hat entschieden	*to decide*
	preisen	pries	hat gepriesen	*to praise*
	scheinen	schien	hat geschienen	*to seem*
	schreiben	schrieb	hat geschrieben	*to write*
	schreien	schrie	hat geschrie(e)n	*to cry*
	schweigen	schwieg	hat geschwiegen	*to be silent*
	steigen	stieg	**ist** gestiegen	*to ascend*
ēi ĭ ĭ	beißen	biß	hat gebissen	*to bite*
	greifen	griff	hat gegriffen	*to seize*
	pfeifen	pfiff	hat gepfiffen	*to whistle*
	reißen	riß	hat gerissen	*to tear*
	reiten	ritt	**ist** geritten	*to ride*
	schleichen	schlich	**ist** geschlichen	*to sneak*
	schneiden	schnitt	hat geschnitten	*to cut*
	schreiten	schritt	**ist** geschritten	*to stride*
	streichen	strich	hat gestrichen	*to stroke, paint*
	streiten	stritt	hat gestritten	*to argue*
	vergleichen	verglich	hat verglichen	*to compare*

EXCEPTION	**heißen**	**hieß**	**hat geheißen**	*to be called*

	INFINITIVE	PAST TENSE	PAST PARTICIPLE	
īe ō ō	biegen	bog	hat gebogen	*to bend*
	fliegen	flog	**ist** geflogen	*to fly*
	fliehen	floh	**ist** geflohen	*to flee*
	frieren	fror	hat gefroren	*to freeze*
	schieben	schob	hat geschoben	*to push*
	verbieten	verbot	hat verboten	*to forbid*
	verlieren	verlor	hat verloren	*to lose*
	wiegen	wog	hat gewogen	*to weigh*
īe ŏ ŏ	fließen	floß *floss*	**ist** geflossen	*to flow*
	genießen	genoß	hat genossen	*to enjoy*
	gießen	goß	hat gegossen	*to pour*
	schießen	schoß	hat geschossen	*to shoot*
	schließen	schloß	hat geschlossen	*to close*

EXCEPTION	**liegen**	**lag**	**hat gelegen**	*to lie*

	INFINITIVE	PAST TENSE	PAST PARTICIPLE	
ȫ ō ō	schwören	schwor	hat geschworen	*to swear*
ǖ ō ō	betrügen	betrog	hat betrogen	*to deceive*
	lügen	log	hat gelogen	*to lie*

[For the use of **haben** or **sein**, see § 32ff.]

19 Group II has the pattern:

INFINITIVE	PAST TENSE	PAST PARTICIPLE
1	2	3

Each one of the basic verb forms has a different vowel. Almost all strong verbs with the stem vowel **i** and many strong verbs with the stem vowel **e** are in this group.

ĭ ă ŏ	• beginnen	begann	hat begonnen	*to begin*
+ m/n	• gewinnen	gewann	hat gewonnen	*to win*
	• schwimmen	schwamm	**ist** geschwommen	*to swim*
ĭ ă ŭ	binden	band	hat gebunden	*to bind*
+ m/n + additional consonant	• finden	fand	hat gefunden	*to find*
	gelingen	gelang	**ist** gelungen	*to succeed*
	klingen	klang	hat geklungen	*to sound*
	ringen	rang	hat gerungen	*to struggle*
	schwingen	schwang	hat geschwungen	*to swing*
	• singen	sang	hat gesungen	*to sing*
	• springen	sprang	**ist** gesprungen	*to jump*
	stinken	stank	hat gestunken	*to stink*
	• trinken	trank	hat getrunken	*to drink*
	zwingen	zwang	hat gezwungen	*to force*
ĭ ā ē	• bitten	bat	hat gebeten	*to request*
ē ā ō	— befehlen (ie)	befahl	hat befohlen	*to command*
	⌒• empfehlen (ie)	empfahl	hat empfohlen	*to recommend*
	⌒ stehlen (ie)	stahl	hat gestohlen	*to steal*
ē ā ŏ	⌒• nehmen (i)	nahm	hat genommen	*to take*
ē ā ŏ	⌒• brechen (i)	brach	hat gebrochen	*to break*
	— erschrecken (i)	erschrak	**ist** erschrocken	*to become frightened*
	— • helfen (i)	half	hat geholfen	*to help*
	• sprechen (i)	sprach	hat gesprochen	*to speak*
	— stechen (i)	stach	hat gestochen	*to prick*
	⌒• sterben (i)	starb	**ist** gestorben	*to die*
	⌒• treffen (i)	traf	hat getroffen	*to meet, hit*
	⌒ werfen (i)	warf	hat geworfen	*to throw*

NOTE The vowel changes given in parentheses are the forms for the second and third person present tense. [See § 27]

CHECK AND PRACTICE

Give the missing forms.

1. schnitt	2. springen	3. schwimmen	4. gefroren	5. heißen
6. gewogen	7. geholfen	8. gesungen	9. lügen	10. schrieb
11. fließen	12. nahm	13. trank	14. liegen	15. ritt

20   Group III has the pattern:

INFINITIVE	PAST TENSE	PAST PARTICIPLE
1	2	1

The infinitive and the past participle have the same vowel, whereas the vowel of the past tense varies. A few strong verbs with the stem vowel **e**, most strong verbs with the stem vowels **a** (including **hängen**, whose older form is **hangen**), **au**, **u**, and **o** are in this group.

ē	ā	ē	geben	(i)	gab	hat gegeben	*to give*
			geschehen	(ie)	geschah	**ist** geschehen	*to happen*
			lesen	(ie)	las	hat gelesen	*to read*
			sehen	(ie)	sah	hat gesehen	*to see*
			treten	(i)	trat	**ist** getreten	*to step*
ĕ	ā	ĕ	essen	(i)	aß	hat gegessen	*to eat*
			fressen	(i)	fraß	hat gefressen	*to eat (of animals)*
			messen	(i)	maß	hat gemessen	*to measure*
			vergessen	(i)	vergaß	hat vergessen	*to forget*

EXCEPTION	**heben**	**hob**	**hat gehoben**	*to lift*

ā	ū	ā	einladen	(ä)	lud ein	hat eingeladen	*to invite*
			fahren	(ä)	fuhr	**ist** gefahren	*to drive*
			graben	(ä)	grub	hat gegraben	*to dig*
			schlagen	(ä)	schlug	hat geschlagen	*to strike*
			tragen	(ä)	trug	hat getragen	*to carry*
ă	ū	ă	schaffen		schuf	hat geschaffen	*to create*
			wachsen	(ä)	wuchs	**ist** gewachsen	*to grow*
			waschen	(ä)	wusch	hat gewaschen	*to wash*
ā	ie	ā	blasen	(ä)	blies	hat geblasen	*to blow*
			braten	(ä)	briet	hat gebraten	*to roast*
			raten	(ä)	riet	hat geraten	*to advise*
			schlafen	(ä)	schlief	hat geschlafen	*to sleep*
ă	ie	ă	fallen	(ä)	fiel	**ist** gefallen	*to fall*
			halten	(ä)	hielt	hat gehalten	*to hold*
			lassen	(ä)	ließ	hat gelassen	*to let*
ă	ĭ	ă	fangen	(ä)	fing	hat gefangen	*to catch*
ă	ĭ	ă	hängen		hing	hat gehangen	*to hang (trans.)*
au	ie	au	laufen	(äu)	lief	**ist** gelaufen	*to run*

EXCEPTION	**saufen** (äu)	**soff**	**hat gesoffen**	*to drink (of animals)*

ū	ie	ū	rufen		rief	hat gerufen	*to call*
ō	ie	ō	stoßen	(ö)	stieß	hat gestoßen	*to push*
ŏ	ā	ŏ	kommen		kam	**ist** gekommen	*to come*

NOTE   The vowel changes given in parentheses are the forms for the second and third person present tense. [See § 27]

[handwritten margin notes:] Something hanging on the wall — for someone hangs — Er hängte das Bild

21   In a few cases, the vowel change is accompanied by a consonant change.

ziehen	zog	gezogen	*to pull*	• stehen	stand	gestanden	*to stand*
				• tun	tat	getan	*to do*
• sitzen	saß	gesessen	*to sit*	• gehen	ging	gegangen	*to go*

BASIC VERB FORMS OF SPECIAL STRONG VERBS

22   The verbs **sein** *to be* and **werden** *to become*, which are used also as auxiliaries, have special forms. [For the present tense form, see § 28]

INFINITIVE	PAST TENSE	PAST PARTICIPLE
sein	war	gewesen
werden	wurde	geworden

CHECK AND PRACTICE

Give the missing forms.

1. geben	2. sah	3. gekommen	4. gehen	5. vergessen
6. heben	7. schlief	8. werden	9. stand	10. schlug
11. blies	12. hing	13. tat	14. laufen	15. gemessen
16. sein	17. waschen	18. saß	19. saufen	20. treten
21. gelesen	22. rufen	23. ziehen	24. gewachsen	25. stieß

TENSE FORMS

Present Tense

REGULAR FORMS

23   The *present tense* is formed by adding the personal endings **–e, –st, –t, –en** to the stem of the verb. These personal *endings are the same* whether the verb is weak (e.g., **sagen** *to say*) or strong (e.g., **fliegen** *to fly*).

	SINGULAR				PLURAL		
Person	Pronoun	Weak	Strong	Person	Pronoun	Weak	Strong
1st	ich	sage	fliege	**1st**	wir	sagen	fliegen
2nd	du	sagst	fliegst	**2nd**	ihr	sagt	fliegt
	Sie	sagen	fliegen		Sie	sagen	fliegen
3rd	er sie es	sagt	fliegt	**3rd**	sie	sagen	fliegen

There are three German equivalents to the English *you*:

1. The forms **du** and **ihr** (2nd person singular and plural) are used as familiar forms to address children, relatives, close friends, and pets. They are not capitalized except in letters. In addition, God is addressed with **Du**.

2. The **Sie** form (2nd person singular and plural) is the formal or polite form and is always capitalized. *The verb form is identical with the 3rd person plural.*

24   1. The plural verb form of the first and third person (**wir, sie**) and the polite form **Sie** are identical with the *infinitive*. If the infinitive ends in **–en**, these forms end in **–en**; if the infinitive ends in **–n** (as in the verbs **sammeln, wandern,** and **tun**), these forms end in **–n** also.

Infinitive		**sammeln** *to collect*	**wandern** *to hike*	**tun** *to do*
	wir	sammeln	wandern	tun
	sie	sammeln	wandern	tun
	Sie	sammeln	wandern	tun

2. Verbs ending in **–eln** or **–ern** often omit the **e** before **l** or **r** when an inflectional **e** is added.

ich samm(e)**le**   ich wand(e)**re**

CHECK AND PRACTICE

Give the present tense forms of the verbs in parentheses.

1. ich (bezahlen)	2. ihr (danken)	3. er (führen)
4. wir (beginnen)	5. er (trinken)	6. du (gewinnen)
7. Sie (helfen)	8. sie *pl.* (rauchen)	9. wir (verlieren)
10. du (singen)	11. ich (erklären)	12. ihr (holen)
13. sie *sg.* (bleiben)	14. du (folgen)	15. ich (radeln)
16. sie *sg.* (plaudern)	17. wir (ändern)	18. du (schreiben)

25 To facilitate pronunciation, some verbs add an **–e–** in the 2nd and 3rd person singular and the 2nd person plural; i.e., before the **–st** and **–t** endings [same principle as was seen in § 10]. These are:

1. Verbs with *stems ending in* **–t** *or* **–d**. Exceptions are the verbs which show a vowel change in the present tense singular [see § 27].

Infinitive		reiten	warten	reden		senden		halten
		to ride	*to wait*	*to talk*		*to send*		*to hold*
Singular	du	reit**est**	wart**est**	red**est**		send**est**	BUT	hält**st**
	er, sie, es	reit**et**	wart**et**	red**et**		send**et**		hält
Plural	ihr	reit**et**	wart**et**	red**et**		send**et**		halt**et**

2. Verbs with *stems ending in* **–m** *or* **–n** preceded by a consonant other than **h**, **l**, or **r**.

Infinitive		öffnen	rechnen	begegnen		wohnen	filmen	lernen
		to open	*to calculate*	*to meet*		*to live*	*to film*	*to learn*
Singular	du	öff**n**est	rech**n**est	bege**gn**est	BUT	woh**n**st	fil**m**st	ler**n**st
	er, sie, es	öff**n**et	rech**n**et	bege**gn**et		woh**n**t	fil**m**t	ler**n**t
Plural	ihr	öff**n**et	rech**n**et	bege**gn**et		woh**n**t	fil**m**t	ler**n**t

26 Verbs with *stems ending in* –s, –ss, –ß, –z, –tz *omit* the –s of the 2nd person singular –st ending; i.e., the forms for 2nd person and 3rd person singular are identical.

Infinitive		reisen	hassen	heißen	stürzen	sitzen
		to travel	*to hate*	*to be called*	*to fall*	*to sit*
Present T.	du	reist	haßt	heißt	stürzt	sitzt
	er, sie, es	reist	haßt	heißt	stürzt	sitzt

CHECK AND PRACTICE

Give the *du–*, *er–*, and *ihr–* forms.

1. verletzen   2. genießen   3. turnen   4. begegnen   5. beobachten
6. arbeiten   7. halten   8. verbinden   9. leiden   10. rechnen
11. baden   12. hetzen   13. warten   14. zeichnen   15. wohnen

FORMS WITH A VOWEL CHANGE

27 Almost all strong verbs with the stem vowel –a– and most with the stem vowels –e–, –au–, and –o– show a vowel change in the present tense in the 2nd and 3rd person singular. [See the forms given in parentheses in the tables § 18–20]

a > ä	e > ie	e > i	au > äu	o > ö
to drive	*to see*	*to give*	*to run*	*to push*
ich fahre	ich sehe	ich gebe	ich laufe	ich stoße
du fährst	du siehst	du gibst	du läufst	du stößt
er fährt	er sieht	er gibt	er läuft	er stößt
fahren	befehlen	brechen	laufen	stoßen
fallen	geschehen	essen		
fangen	lesen	fressen		
halten	sehen	geben		
lassen	stehlen	nehmen		
raten	NO CHANGE	sprechen		
schlafen	gehen	sterben		
schlagen	stehen	treffen		
tragen	heben	treten		
wachsen		vergessen		
waschen		werfen		

CHECK AND PRACTICE

Give the *du–* and *er–* forms.

1. brechen	2. lesen	3. sehen	4. befehlen	5. sterben
6. empfehlen	7. helfen	8. vergessen	9. essen	10. schlafen
11. erschrecken	12. nehmen	13. fahren	14. sprechen	15. tragen

IRREGULAR FORMS

sein, haben, werden

28   The verbs **sein**, **haben**, and **werden**, which are also used as auxiliaries, have irregular present tense forms.

SINGULAR				PLURAL			
ich	bin	habe	werde	wir	sind	haben	werden
du	bist	hast	wirst	ihr	seid	habt	werdet
er							
sie	ist	hat	wird	sie	sind	haben	werden
es							

CHECK AND PRACTICE

Supply the correct forms of the verbs in parentheses.

1. (haben) du Geld?
2. Er (werden) Lehrer.
3. (sein) ihr müde?
4. Wir (werden) krank.
5. (sein) du müde?
6. Ich (haben) kein Geld.
7. (haben) ihr Hunger?
8. Sie *sg.* (sein) in Deutschland.
9. (sein) sie *pl.* reich?
10. Es (sein) dunkel.

Modal Auxiliaries and *wissen*

29   Other verbs with irregular forms are the *modals* and the verb **wissen**. [For principal parts, see § 14f. For usage of the modals, see § 78 ff.]

Infinitive							
	dürfen	können	mögen	müssen	sollen	wollen	wissen
Singular							
ich	darf	kann	mag	muß	soll	will	weiß
du	darfst	kannst	magst	mußt	sollst	willst	weißt
er							
sie	darf	kann	mag	muß	soll	will	weiß
es							
Plural							
wir	dürfen	können	mögen	müssen	sollen	wollen	wissen
ihr	dürft	könnt	mögt	müßt	sollt	wollt	wißt
sie	dürfen	können	mögen	müssen	sollen	wollen	wissen

CHECK AND PRACTICE

Supply the suggested forms.

1. er (müssen)
2. ihr (wollen)
3. du (können)
4. wir (mögen)
5. ich (können)
6. du (wissen)
7. du (müssen)
8. er (dürfen)
9. du (sollen)
10. ihr (dürfen)
11. ihr (müssen)
12. ihr (wissen)

Simple Past Tense

30   In the simple past tense, the *personal suffixes* for weak and strong verbs vary slightly. A zero suffix (i.e., no ending) is used in strong verbs, 1st and 3rd person.

	WEAK					**STRONG**	
Singular							
ich	reiste	hatte	wurde	wußte	mußte	fuhr☐	war☐
du	reistest	hattest	wurdest	wußtest	mußtest	fuhrst	warst
er							
sie	reiste	hatte	wurde	wußte	mußte	fuhr☐	war☐
es							
Plural							
wir	reisten	hatten	wurden	wußten	mußten	fuhren	waren
ihr	reistet	hattet	wurdet	wußtet	mußtet	fuhrt	wart
sie	reisten	hatten	wurden	wußten	mußten	fuhren	waren

31 Strong verbs whose past tense stem ends in **–s** or **–ß** omit the **–s** in the 2nd person singular ending [see also § 26]. Therefore, the singular and plural forms look alike.

Infinitive	heißen		Past Tense	Singular	du hießt
				Plural	ihr hießt

CHECK AND PRACTICE

Give the simple past tense forms.

1. ich (fahren)
2. sie *sg.* (wissen)
3. ich (sein)
4. du (reisen)
5. er (können)
6. sie *sg.* (setzen)
7. er (gehen)
8. ihr (arbeiten)
9. wir (geben)
10. wir (kommen)
11. wir (müssen)
12. du (heißen)
13. ihr (werden)
14. sie *pl.* (sagen)
15. ihr (finden)

Present Perfect and Past Perfect Tense

USE OF *haben*

32 The *present perfect* and *past perfect* are compound tenses. The first component is the present or past tense form of the auxiliary **haben** or **sein**, with personal endings. The second component is the *past participle of the main verb*, positioned at the end of the clause. [For word order, see § 289ff. For present perfect forms of modals, see § 48 and 95]

		CONJUGATED AUXILIARY	PAST PARTICIPLE OF MAIN VERB
Perfect	ich	habe	gegessen / gelacht
	ich	bin	gelaufen / gereist
Past Perfect	ich	hatte	gegessen / gelacht
	ich	war	gelaufen / gereist

33 All *transitive verbs* are conjugated with **haben**. A transitive verb is a verb that is followed by a direct object.

Transitive	Paul	bemalt	die Wand.	
		VERB	DIRECT OBJECT	
Intransitive	Es	regnet.		
		VERB	NO DIRECT OBJECT	

CHECK AND PRACTICE

Give the present perfect and past perfect forms of the verbs in parentheses. Place the correct form of *haben* or *hatten* where the verb in parentheses is, and put the past participle at the end of the sentence.

Example

Ich **(wissen)** das.
Ich **habe** das **gewußt.**
Ich **hatte** das **gewußt.**

1. Wir (haben) das.
2. Er (treffen) sie.
3. (holen) ihr das?
4. Sie *pl.* (vergessen) es.
5. (merken) du das?
6. (verkaufen) du es?
7. Sie (sagen) das.
8. Sie *sg.* (schlagen) ihn.
9. Sie *sg.* (verlassen) ihn.
10. Ich (riechen) es.
11. Ich (kennen) ihn.
12. Wir (rufen) sie.
13. (treffen) ihr ihn?
14. Er (retten) ihn.
15. (sehen) du ihn?
16. Ich (lesen) es.
17. (zeichnen) er es?
18. Wir (gewinnen) es.
19. Ich (trinken) es.
20. (glauben) ihr das?

USE OF *sein*

34 Most *intransitive verbs* also use **haben** (e.g., **es hat geregnet**). Some intransitive verbs, however, are conjugated with **sein** in the perfect tenses. These are:

1. verbs denoting motion:

ich **bin** gegangen **war**	*I have gone had*	ich **bin** gefallen **war**	*I have fallen had*
ich **bin** gereist **war**	*I have traveled had*	ich **bin** gekommen **war**	*I have come had*

2. verbs expressing a change in condition:

er **ist** gestorben **war**	*he has died had*	es **ist** geschehen **war**	*it has happened had*

3. **sein, werden** and **bleiben**:

er **ist** gewesen **war**	*he has been had*	er **ist** geworden **war**	*he has become had*
er **ist** geblieben **war**	*he has stayed had*		

CHECK AND PRACTICE

Give the present perfect and past perfect forms of the verbs in parentheses.

1. Es (regnen).
2. Wir (helfen) ihm.
3. Ich (reden) mit ihm. habe geredet
4. (kommen) ihr?
5. Wir (schwimmen). sind
6. (werden) du Lehrer?
7. Er (fallen).
8. Er (sein) krank.
9. Sie *sg.* (antworten) ihm. geantwortet
10. Ich (laufen) viel.
11. (fahren) ihr mit dem Zug?
12. Sie *sg.* (lügen).
13. Sie *pl.* (danken) ihnen.
14. Wir (rechnen).
15. (bleiben) du?
16. Er (reiten) oft.
17. Ich (fliegen) nach Deutschland.
18. Sie *sg.* (turnen) gern.
19. (gehen) er mit dir?
20. Sie *pl.* (sterben).

35   Some verbs can be used either intransitively or transitively, thus requiring **sein** in one instance, **haben** in the other. The presence or absence of a direct object is the deciding factor.

INTRANSITIVE	TRANSITIVE
Paula went by train.	*Paul drove the train.*
Paula **ist** <u>mit dem Zug</u> gefahren.	Paul **hat** <u>den Zug</u> gefahren.
PREPOSITIONAL PHRASE	**DIRECT OBJECT**

The verb **fahren** is a motion verb. In the first sentence, there is a prepositional phrase (preposition and its object), **mit dem Zug**, which explains how the change of location came about. There is no direct object. The verb **fahren** is therefore being used intransitively, and **sein** is the correct auxiliary.

In the second sentence, using the same verb, there is a direct object, **den Zug**, which indicates what object was driven by **Paul**. The verb is being used transitively. Therefore, **haben** is the correct auxiliary.

CHECK AND PRACTICE

Supply the auxiliary in the following sentence.

Example

Wir _____ nach Berlin gefahren.   Wir _____ den Wagen gezogen.
Wir **sind** nach Berlin gefahren.   Wir **haben** den Wagen gezogen.

1. Sie _____ die Maschine selbst geflogen.   2. _____ ihr mit dem Wagen gefahren?
3. _____ du das Auto deines Vaters gefahren?   4. Sie _____ nach Berlin gezogen.
5. Wir _____ nach Europa geflogen.

Future and Future Perfect Tense

36   German has two future tenses corresponding to the English "I will sing" and "I will have sung." The future in German is formed by using the present tense of **werden** as an auxiliary and the infinitive of the main verb. The infinitive always goes at the end of the sentence. [For word order, see § 289ff.]

CONJUGATED AUXILIARY		INFINITIVE OF MAIN VERB
Ich	**werde** ohne euch nach Deutschland	**fliegen.**
I will fly to Germany without you.		

37 The *future perfect* is formed by using the present tense of **werden** as auxiliary with the past participle of the main verb plus the infinitive of **haben** or **sein**. This combination of the past participle of the main verb and the infinitive of **haben** or **sein** is called the *perfect infinitive of the main verb*. The perfect infinitive always goes at the end of the sentence. [For word order, see § 289f. For usage see § 53 ff.]

CONJUGATED AUXILIARY		INFINITIVE OF MAIN VERB
Ich **werde**	den Brief bald	**geschrieben haben.**
Soon I will have finished the letter.		

CHECK AND PRACTICE

Restate in the future tense. Put the auxiliary in the place of the inflected verb. The infinitive of the verb goes at the end of the sentence.

1. Ich zeige dir mein Haus.
2. Tust du das für mich?
3. Nichts geschieht.
4. Helft ihr uns?
5. Erklärt er das?
6. Bleibt er in Berlin?
7. Das Konzert beginnt bald.
8. Das machen wir.
9. Bleibt ihr zu Hause?
10. Ihr verdient viel Geld.

Restate in the future perfect tense. Put the auxiliary in the place of the inflected verb. The perfect infinitive goes at the end of the sentence.

11. Hast du den Brief bis heute abend geschrieben?
12. In einer Stunde haben wir alles gegessen.
13. Vor nächster Woche habt ihr das schon verstanden.
14. Bis morgen habt ihr es wieder vergessen.
15. In drei Minuten habe ich ihn gezeichnet.

Give the indicated tense.

FUTURE TENSE	PRESENT PERFECT TENSE	PAST PERFECT TENSE
16. es (gelingen)	17. er (fahren)	18. wir (sein)
19. wir (beginnen)	20. sie *sg.* (bleiben)	21. er (fliegen)
22. du (lachen)	23. ihr (haben)	24. sie *pl.* (tanzen)

PRESENT TENSE	FUTURE PERFECT TENSE	PAST TENSE
25. er (geben)	26. wir (gewinnen)	27. ich (wechseln)
28. du (sprechen)	29. es (geschehen)	30. ihr (nehmen)
31. wir (kommen)	32. sie *pl.* (sterben)	33. du (stehen)

I. VOCABULARY FOR REVIEW (A AND B TEXTS FROM READER, CHAPTER I)

Verbs

benutzen	to use
besichtigen	to visit, inspect
ein·steigen ie, ie (+ sein)	to get in
erleben	to experience
halten (ä) ie, a	to stop
herum·fahren (ä) u, a (+ sein)	to travel around
weiter·fahren (ä) u, a (+ sein)	to drive on
kennen·lernen	to meet
übernachten	to spend the night
überqueren	to cross over
unterbrechen (i) a, o	to interrupt

Nouns

der **Aufenthalt, —e**	stay
die **Auskunft, ˙˙e**	information
das **Ausland**	(land) abroad
der **Bahnsteig, —e**	platform
der **Führer, —**	guide, leader
die **Grenze, —n**	border, bound
die **Landkarte, —n**	map
die **Landschaft, —n**	landscape
der **Paß, ˙˙sse**	passport
die **Strecke, —n**	route, section

ADDITIONAL EXERCISES (A AND B TEXTS FROM THE READER)

Reisen sie gern?

Respond with appropriate present tense verb forms.

1. Halten alle Züge hier? Nein, der Expreß _____ hier nicht.
2. Fahren Sie mit? Nein, ich _____ gern allein ins Ausland.
3. Benutzen Sie ein Interrailticket? Nein, meine Frau _____ das auch nie.
4. Wird sie die Reise unterbrechen? Ja, sie _____ die Fahrt oft.
5. Muß sie viel Gepäck tragen? Nein, der Führer _____ das für sie.
6. Werdet ihr viele Kirchen besichtigen? Ja, meine Tochter _____ gerade den Dom.

Insert the appropriate present tense verb forms.

7. _____ ihr diesen Sommer in die Schweiz? (reisen)

8. Wo _____ ihr die Alpen? (überqueren)

9. _____ ihr wirklich manchmal auf dem Bahnsteig? (übernachten)

10. Wo _____ ihr Aufenthalt? (machen)

11. _____ ihr wirklich die Reise? (unterbrechen)

Tell the story in the past tense.

12. Österreich ist immer ein schönes Reiseland.

13. Wir nehmen die Landkarte und suchen eine gute Reisestrecke.

14. Wir fragen auch bei der Auskunft.

15. Dann gehen wir auf den Bahnsteig und steigen in den Zug ein.

16. Wir verbringen ein paar Tage in der schönen Landschaft.

Answer in the present perfect, using the suggestions.

Example

Warum haben Sie die Reise unterbrochen? (wir/in Basel übernachten)
Wir haben in Basel übernachtet.

17. Wie sind Sie gereist? (wir/Interrailtickets kaufen)

18. Wo haben Sie übernachtet? (wir/im Nachtzug schlafen)

19. Haben Sie die Alpen überquert? Ja, (wir/eine gute Straße benutzen)

20. Was haben Sie in der Schweiz gemacht? (schöne Städte besichtigen)

21. Fanden Sie das interessant? Ja, (wir/viel kennenlernen)

Answer in the past perfect, using the suggestions.

Example

War Inge auf dem Bahnsteig? Nein, sie (schon weiterfahren)
Nein, sie war schon weitergefahren.

22. Fanden Sie gute Plätze im Zug? Ja, denn wir (Platzkarten/kaufen)

23. Warum konnten Sie nicht ins Ausland fahren? Wir (keine Pässe bekommen)

24. Warum bliebt ihr so lange in Zürich? Wir (nette Leute/kennenlernen)

25. Konntet ihr im Hotel übernachten? Nein, wir (kein Zimmer/finden)

26. Warum fuhrt ihr so schnell weiter? Wir (schon alles/besichtigen)

Respond with the future tense forms, using the suggestions.

Example

Erzählen Sie mir bitte von der Reise! Nein, (ich/nicht)
Nein, ich **werde** nicht von der Reise **erzählen!**

27. Was **machen** Sie diesen Sommer? (ich/eine Reise ins Ausland)

28. **Fahren** Sie wirklich irgendwo **herum**? Ja, (ich/in ganz Österreich)
29. **Machen** Sie auch in Tirol **Aufenthalt**? (wir/drei Tage/dort)
30. Wann **sind** Sie wieder zuhause? (ich/in drei Wochen)
31. **Geben** Sie dann das Interrailticket **ab**? Nein, (ich/nie)

Respond with the future perfect tense forms, using the suggestions.

Example

Haben Sie auf der Reise viel **erlebt**? (Bis Ende der Reise)
Bis Ende der Reise **werden** wir viel **erlebt haben**.

32. Habt ihr schöne Landschaften **kennengelernt**? (Bevor wir zurückfahren,)
33. Haben Sie Auskunft **bekommen**? Nein, (aber bis heute abend)
34. Habt ihr auch die Schweiz **besichtigt**? (Vor August)
35. Seid ihr an der Grenze **gewesen**? (Vor nächster Woche)
36. Hast du schon Fahrkarten **gekauft**? (Vor heute abend)

II. VOCABULARY FOR REVIEW (C AND D TEXTS FROM READER, CHAPTER I)

Verbs

ab·fahren (ä), u, a (+ sein)	to leave *to depart*
ab·warten	to wait
bewohnen	to occupy
hinauf·gehen i, a (+ sein)	to go up
hinunter·gehen i, a (+ sein)	to go down
hinunter·kommen a, o (+ sein)	to come down
verlassen (ä) ie, a	to leave *Something beh...*
verschwinden a, u (+ sein)	to disappear
vorbei·kommen a, o (+ sein)	to pass by
weiter·gehen i, a (+ sein)	to go on
zurück·kehren (+ sein)	to return

Nouns

der **Eingang, ¨-e**	entry
das **Einzelzimmer, -**	single room
der **Gast, ¨-e**	guest
das **Gasthaus, ¨-er**	inn
die **Gaststube, -n**	restaurant
die **Handtasche, -n**	handbag
die **Wanderschaft**	journeying
der **Wirt, -e**	innkeeper

ADDITIONAL EXERCISES (C AND D TEXTS FROM THE READER)

Auf der Reise, im Gasthaus und in Hotels

Restate as informal questions.

Example

Haben Sie schon eine Fahrkarte?
Hast du schon eine Fahrkarte?

1. Wo sind Sie geboren?
2. Sind Sie wirklich Schweizerin?
3. Reisen Sie gern in den Alpen?
4. Warum verlassen Sie das Land?
5. Besitzen Sie viel Gepäck?
6. Wann fahren Sie ab?
7. Verschwinden Sie immer so schnell?

Respond with the suggested interrogatives.

Example

Wir gehen jetzt hinauf. (Warum? schon)
Warum geht **ihr** schon hinauf?

8. Ich nehme ein Einzelzimmer. (Warum?)
9. Der Wirt geht mit mir hinauf. (Wer?)
10. Die anderen Gäste warten den Morgen ab. (Wo?)
11. Ich sitze in der Gaststube. (Wie lange?)
12. Wir gehen an diesem Eingang vorbei. (Warum?)
13. Dieser Gast verläßt das Gasthaus. (Wann?)
14. Aber er kehrt bald zurück. (Warum?)

Respond with present tense forms using the suggested phrases.

Example

Wann sind die Gäste in die Gaststube gekommen? (sie/jeden Morgen)
Sie kommen jeden Morgen in die Gaststube.

15. Hat der Gast ein Einzelzimmer genommen? (dieser Mann/oft)
16. Haben sie Doppelzimmer bewohnt? (diese Gäste/nie)
17. Hat der Wirt abends am Eingang gestanden? (er/immer)
18. Ist der Wirt schon aus der Gaststube verschwunden? (er/nie so früh)
19. Ist der Junge schon auf Wanderschaft gegangen? (er/morgen)

Restate with past tense forms.

Example

Er **bewohnt** ein Haus am Hafen.
Er **bewohnte** ein Haus am Hafen.

20. Seit Montag bewohnen sie ein Haus in diesem Hotel.
21. Abends gehen wir früh hinauf.
22. Die anderen Gäste kommen oft in die Gaststube hinunter.
23. Sie kommen am Eingang vorbei und gehen weiter.
24. Der Wirt verläßt das Gasthaus und kehrt nicht zurück.

Answer using the perfect tense forms.

Example

Nimmst du meine Handtasche? Nein, (der junge Mann schon)
Nein, der junge Mann **hat** die Handtasche schon **genommen.**

25. Wann fährt unser Schiff? Es (schon vor zwei Minuten)
26. Wartet ihr auf neue Gäste? Nein, (gestern)
27. Trägt der Wirt unser Gepäck? Nein, wir (selbst)
28. Steht immer ein junger Mann im Eingang? Ja, nur (gestern nicht)
29. Bewohnst du diesmal ein Einzelzimmer? Ich (früher auch)
30. Wann verläßt der Wirt die Gaststube? Er (schon vor einer Stunde)

Restate in the future.

Example

Natürlich **kaufe** ich eine Fahrkarte.
Natürlich **werde** ich eine Fahrkarte **kaufen.**

31. Bewohnst du wieder ein Einzelzimmer?
32. Und wer trägt unser Gepäck?
33. Es verschwindet bestimmt nicht.
34. Treffen wir uns am Eingang?
35. Gehen wir dann in die Gaststube?

Restate in the future perfect.

Example

Er **hat** große Sehnsucht **gehabt.**
Er **wird** große Sehnsucht **gehabt haben**.

36. Bis morgen hat er die Handtasche zurückgegeben.
37. Bevor du zurückkehrst, bin ich verschwunden.
38. Die anderen Gäste sind auch schon abgefahren.
39. Sie haben bestimmt die Stadt verlassen.
40. Vielleicht sind sie auf Wanderschaft gegangen.

VERBS (Part Two)

TENSE USAGE

38 The German usage of tense often differs significantly from the English. There are some instances where the grammatical tense does not correspond to the real time referred to in the sentence; for example, when the present tense can express the future.

Present Tense   [For forms, see § 23ff.]

GERMAN VERSUS ENGLISH

39 1. Since German has neither a progressive nor an emphatic form, a single present tense form may have any of three English equivalents.

> Sie **raucht**. *She is smoking.*
> *She smokes.*
> *She does smoke.*

2. The context generally indicates which meaning is applicable. In some instances, an adverb resolves possible ambiguities.

Action In Progress	Er schreibt **gerade** einen Brief.
	He is (at this moment) writing a letter.
Emphasis	Ist dieses Bild nicht toll? Er zeichnet **wirklich** gut.
	Isn't this picture great? He (really) does draw well.

CHECK AND PRACTICE

Translate into German.

1. Adam (*is eating*) einen Apfel. (essen)
2. Die Mutter (*is reading*) gerade die Zeitung. (lesen)
3. Der Vater (*is fixing dinner*) in der Küche. (das Abendessen kochen)
4. Er (*does work*) gut, wenn er will. (arbeiten)
5. Ich glaube, er (*does like*) mich _____. (gern haben)
6. Hier (*snows*) es immer viel im Winter. (schneien)
7. Es (*rains*) jeden Tag. (regnen)

GERMAN PRESENT TENSE FOR ENGLISH PRESENT PERFECT

40 1. In contrast to English, German employs the present tense if an action *has begun in the past and continues.* English uses the present perfect or present perfect progressive form in such instances.

	Time Phrase	
Wir **wohnen schon**	**immer**	in Berlin.
*We **have always lived** in Berlin.*		
	Time Phrase	
Paul **wartet (schon)**	**seit fünf Uhr**	auf den Zug.
*Paul **has been waiting** for the train **since five o'clock**.*		

As the German speaker is dealing with a *present* situation, he uses the *present tense.* If this present situation is modified by a time phrase, the adverb **schon** is used to indicate that we are referring to a period extending into the past. The adverb **schon** can only be omitted if this reference is clearly indicated by another part of speech, e.g., the preposition **seit** *since.*

2. If the action ends at the time of speaking, there is a choice. Either the present or the perfect tense can be used.

Da bist du ja endlich.   Ich **warte schon** drei Stunden lang.
Ich **habe (schon)** drei Stunden lang **gewartet.**
There you are. I've been waiting for three hours.

CHECK AND PRACTICE

Using the German cues, translate the phrases in parentheses.

1. Das Haus (*has been burning*) neun Stunden lang. (brennen)
2. Die alte Frau (*has been sitting*) seit heute morgen beim Fenster. (sitzen)
3. Die Eltern (*have been waiting*) jahrelang auf ihren Sohn. (warten)
4. Wie lange (*have you been studying*) Deutsch? (lernen)
5. Ich (*have been studying*) seit einem Jahr. (lernen)

PRESENT TENSE FOR FUTURE TIME

41 Often the present tense has *future meaning* in German, particularly when the sentence contains an adverb indicating future time or begins with **wann** or **wenn**.

Morgen <u>**fährt**</u> Paul mit dem Auto.
*Paul **will go** by car tomorrow. Paul is going by car tomorrow.*

Inge, <u>wann</u> **bist** du in Deutschland?
*Inge, when **will** you **be** in Germany?*

<u>Wenn</u> Paul nach Frankfurt kommt, **besuchen** wir ihn.
*When Paul comes to Frankfurt, we **will visit** him.*

CHECK AND PRACTICE

Use the cues given to translate the phrases in parentheses.

1. Wann (*will you travel*) nach Deutschland? (reisen)
2. Wir (*will give*) ihm 300 Mark, wenn er die Wette gewinnt. (geben)
3. Wir (*will meet*) ihn nächste Woche. (treffen)

PRESENT TENSE FOR PAST TIME

42 The "historical present" expresses a past occurrence very vividly by using the present tense. In these instances the present tense is interchangeable with the past tense (as in English).

Denk dir nur, ich **gehe** gestern in die Stadt und **treffe** meinen alten Lateinlehrer.
*Just imagine, I **go** downtown yesterday and **meet** my old Latin teacher.*

---

43 The present tense instead of the past tense is also found in headlines.

POLIZIST **GEWINNT** EINE MILLION
*POLICEMAN **WINS** ONE MILLION*

---

44 In chronicles and history books, the present tense has purely a recording function.

---

7. Dezember 1970   Willy Brandt **besucht** Polen
*December 7, 1970   Willy Brandt **visits** Poland*

Simple Past and Present Perfect Tense

DIFFERENCES IN USAGE   [For forms, see 30ff.]

45 The simple past and the present perfect tenses are both used to report events or scenes which occurred in the past. But, whereas the simple past tense can be regarded as the narrative tense of German fiction, the present perfect tense is the predominant tense of conversation.

SIMPLE PAST TENSE — the tense of narration

Es **war** einmal ein Mann, der **hatte** so viele Kinder, daß er ihnen nicht genug zu essen geben **konnte.** Also **ging** er in die Welt, um Hilfe zu finden. Auf seinem Weg **begegnete** er einem alten Mann. Das **war** der liebe Gott . . .

*Once upon a time, there **was** a man who **had** so many children that he was not **able** to feed them. Therefore, he **went** away to find help. On his way, he **met** an old man. It **was** God . . .*

PRESENT PERFECT TENSE — the tense of conversation

Was **hast** du gestern **gemacht?**	*What **did** you **do** yesterday?*
Zuerst **habe** ich meine Hausaufgaben **gemacht,**	*At first I **did** my homework,*
dann **sind** wir ins Kino **gegangen.**	* then we **went** to the movies.*

PRESENT PERFECT TENSE — the tense which links the past with the present

Ich **bin** gerade von der Arbeit **gekommen.**	IMPLIED *And I am still wound up.*
I just returned from work.	
Ich **habe** gut **geschlafen.**	IMPLIED *And I am rested now.*
I slept well.	

CHECK AND PRACTICE

Give the correct verb forms and translate them into English. Compare English and German.

Paul und Inge
Eine Liebesgeschichte

1. Als Paul durch Deutschland _____, _____ er ein Mädchen. (reisen) (treffen)
2. Sie _____ Inge, _____bei BMW und _____ gern in Cafés. (heißen) (arbeiten) (gehen)
3. Paul _____ auch nicht nur Museen. (besuchen)
4. Und so _____ er ihr eines Nachmittags zwischen zwei Stücken Schwarzwälder Kirschtorte. (begegnen)

5. Sie _____, _____ und _____. (kommen) (sehen) (siegen)

6. Bald darauf _____ sie. (heiraten)

7. {Gestern _____ ich meinen Onkel _____.} (besuchen)

8. {Peter und Paul _____ im letzten Jahr zwei Monate lang durch ganz Europa _____.} (reisen)

9. {Ich _____ gerade das Buch _____. Es ist toll!} (lesen)

10. {Nichts _____.} (geschehen)

11. {Er _____ Arzt _____.} (werden)

12. {Meine Großmutter _____ heute _____.} (sterben)

13. {Gestern abend _____ wir ins Theater _____.} (gehen)

14. {Ich _____ um drei Uhr _____.} (ankommen)

15. {Sie _____ gerade nach Berlin _____.} (ziehen)

GERMAN VERSUS ENGLISH

46 1. English uses the past tense for reporting repetitive events if they occurred over a period of time in the past. The present perfect is used if the time period in which these events occur is not yet over.

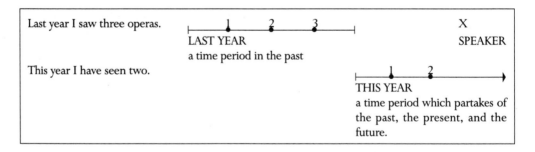

Last year I saw three operas.	1 2 3 X
	LAST YEAR SPEAKER
	a time period in the past
This year I have seen two.	1 2
	THIS YEAR
	a time period which partakes of the past, the present, and the future.

2. German uses the same tense (past or present perfect) in both instances. It distinguishes between the two time periods with the help of adverbs of time such as **bisher** *up to now*, which then appears usually in the front field, or adverbs such as **noch nicht** *not yet*, **schon** *already*, and **erst**, **nur** *only*.

Letztes Jahr habe ich drei Opern gesehen.
Bisher habe ich dieses Jahr zwei Opern gesehen.
Dieses Jahr habe ich noch keine Opern gesehen.   (**noch** *is used for negations*)
Dieses Jahr habe ich schon zwei Opern gesehen.   (IMPLIED *more times than expected*)
Dieses Jahr habe ich erst zwei Opern gesehen.   (IMPLIED *fewer times than expected*)

CHECK AND PRACTICE

Translate the phrases in parentheses. Remember to place the inflected verb in second position and the participle in end position.

1. Letztes Jahr (*I was*) viermal in Berlin.
2. Dieses Jahr (*I have been*) erst einmal in Berlin.
3. 1989 (*won*) Steffi viele Tennisspiele. (gewinnen)
4. Bisher (*has received*) Monika nur gute Noten. (bekommen)
5. Diese Woche (*we have had*) schon vier Examen.
6. Heute (*has disturbed*) Paul mich noch nicht. (stören)

ENGLISH *"WOULD"* AND THE GERMAN PAST TENSE

47 Just as the present tense refers to habitual actions or to general truths, so the simple past and the present perfect tenses can refer to such actions which occurred in the past. English uses *used to* and *would*.

> Sie **kam** immer in die Küche, **las** die Zeitung und **trank** Bier.
> Sie **ist** immer in die Küche **gekommen**, **hat** die Zeitung **gelesen** und Bier **getrunken**.
> *She **would** always **come** into the kitchen, **read** the newspaper and **drink** beer.*

CHECK AND PRACTICE

Translate the phrases in parentheses.

1. Früher (*Paul used to work a lot*), aber in letzter Zeit sitzt er nur noch in Bars.
2. (*My dog would always come*), wenn ich ihn rief.
3. (*His uncle would visit him each year*), bis er in die Vereinigten Staaten zog.
4. Als sie noch jünger war, (*my aunt used to write many letters*).
5. Peter und Inge (*would always play*) mit den Kindern, wenn sie uns besuchten.

MODAL AUXILIARIES AND *sein* AND *haben*

48   1. The past of the modals and of the verbs **sein** and **haben** is usually expressed by the simple past tense, seldom by the present perfect tense.

Usually	Ich **wollte**	ins Kino gehen,	aber ich **hatte** kein Geld.
Seldom	Ich **habe**	ins Kino gehen **wollen**,	aber ich **hatte** kein Geld.
	I wanted to go to the movies but I had no money.		
Usually	Frau Meyer **war** gestern in Köln.		
Seldom	Frau Meyer **ist** gestern in Köln **gewesen**.		
	Mrs. Meyer was in Cologne yesterday.		

2. The present perfect tense of the modals tends to be used in contexts where English would also use the present perfect rather than the simple past. This occurs, for example, with the time expressions **noch nie**, **schon oft**, and **schon immer**.

	Ich **habe** ihm **schon oft** bei den Hausaufgaben **helfen müssen**.
Instead of	Ich **mußte** ihm **schon oft** bei den Hausaufgaben **helfen**.
	I have often had to help him with the homework.

CHECK AND PRACTICE

Complete the sentences.

1. Wo _____ du? Ich _____ in der Bibliothek. Ich _____ noch ein Buch lesen.
   (sein) (sein) (müssen)
2. Warum _____ du gestern nicht _____? Ich _____ keine Zeit. (kommen) (haben)

PRESENT PERFECT TENSE FOR FUTURE TIME

49   Just as the present tense can imply an action in a future time [see § 41], so the present perfect tense can imply completion of an action in a future time (a future perfect meaning). Because such statements are intended to convey assurance, adverbs such as **bestimmt**, **gewiß**, **sicherlich** *certainly* are usually added.

	Morgen **habe** ich den Brief bestimmt **geschrieben haben**.
Instead of	Morgen **werde** ich den Brief bestimmt **geschrieben haben**.
	Tomorrow I will have written the letter for certain.

Past Perfect Tense

[For forms, see § 32ff.]

50 The past perfect tense, like the English equivalent, is used to indicate that one action or event happened *before another past action* or event. Here is the standard construction with **nachdem** *after*:

Nachdem ich **gegessen hatte**, fuhr ich zur Universität. *After I **had eaten**, I drove to the university.*	
ACTION 1 expressed by PAST PERFECT TENSE	**ACTION 2** expressed by SIMPLE PAST TENSE

CHECK AND PRACTICE

Transform into sentences with *nachdem*.

Example

Zuerst machte er seine Hausaufgaben; dann ging er spazieren.
Nachdem er seine Hausaufgaben **gemacht hatte**, ging er spazieren.

1. Zuerst aß er; dann zog er den dunklen Anzug an.
2. Wir setzten uns; dann bestellten wir Wein.
3. Sie gab ihm ihr Buch, und er las es.
4. Die Musiker kamen zuerst; später erschien der Dirigent.

Future Tense

[For forms, see § 36]

51 As in English, the future tense is used for actions or events that take place in the future. However, if the context makes it clear that the action or event will occur in the future, the present tense is normally used in German. [See § 41]

Ich **werde** zu Hause **bleiben.** *I'll **stay** home.*	Morgen **bleibe** ich zu Hause. *Tomorrow I **am staying** home.*

52 The future tense is also used to express a supposition or probability referring to present or future time. Adverbs such as **wohl, wahrscheinlich** *probably*, **vielleicht** *perhaps*, and **sicher, bestimmt, gewiß** *certainly* add emphasis. The future is then interchangeable with the present tense, which has to have one of the above-mentioned adverbs of modality.

Er **wird** (wohl) krank **sein**. *He **is** probably sick.*   Er **ist wohl** krank.

CHECK AND PRACTICE

Express probability using the future tense.

1. Das Mädchen gefällt dir bestimmt.
2. Hans versteht dich schon.
3. Paul liest wohl gerade dein Buch.
4. Eva ist sicher zu Hause.
5. Hörst du das Singen? Das ist wohl Paula.
6. Uwe schläft wahrscheinlich noch.

Future Perfect Tense   [For forms, see § 37]

53 The future perfect tense is generally used to express probability or supposition about an action in the past, often reinforced by adverbs like **wohl, wahrscheinlich, sicher, bestimmt**, and **gewiß**. It is interchangeable with the perfect tense when the latter is combined with one of the above-mentioned adverbs.

Ihr **werdet** (wohl) in der Stadt **gewesen sein**, als wir euch **anriefen**.
*You **were** probably downtown when we **called** you up.*

Ich **werde** (gewiß) die Prüfung **bestanden haben**.
Ich **habe** gewiß die Prüfung **bestanden**.
*I most probably **passed** the exam.*

---

54 The future perfect is rarely used in its original function: to express the completion of a future action by some point in time in the future. In modern usage, the perfect is preferred [see § 49]. In both instances the future is expressed by an adverb or an adverbial phrase of time.

In einer halben Stunde **werde** ich den Brief bestimmt **geschrieben haben**.
In einer halben Stunde **habe** ich den Brief bestimmt **geschrieben**.
*In half an hour I'll **have written** the letter.*

IMPERATIVE

55 The *imperative* form of a verb is used to express commands, requests, or directives. It can also be used to make suggestions, or even to wish someone well. Depending on their usage, imperative sentences end with an exclamation mark or, if there is no special emphasis, with a period.

Command	Gehen Sie hinaus! *Go out.*
Request	Schlagen Sie bitte die Bücher auf. *Please open your books.*
Directive	Fahren Sie geradeaus. *Drive straight ahead.*
Suggestion	Probieren Sie diesen Wein. *Try this wine.*
Wish	Kommen Sie gut nach Hause. *Get home well.*

Second Person Imperative

56 1. There are *three second-person imperatives* in German, corresponding to the three pronouns for *you*. As in English, the subject pronoun is omitted in the two informal German imperatives. In the formal imperative, **Sie** follows its verb form.

INFORMAL	SINGULAR **du** PLURAL **ihr**	Hans, **sprich** lauter! *Hans, **talk** louder.* Kinder, **sprecht** lauter! *Children, **talk** louder.*
FORMAL	SINGULAR and PLURAL **Sie**	Herr Braun, **sprechen Sie** lauter! Meine Herren, *Mr. Brown,* ***talk** louder.* *Gentlemen,*

2. In very emphatic speech the pronouns **du** and **ihr** might appear when a contrast between the person addressed and someone else is established.

Sprich **du** mit ihm!	*Do speak with him.* (**You** *go speak with him.* Implied: *I won't.*)
Kümmert **ihr** euch darum!	*Take care of that.*

CHECK AND PRACTICE

Mark the sentences which contain an imperative.

1. Am Morgen sind Sie wohl immer müde.
2. Stehen Sie bitte auf.
3. Gehen Sie viel spazieren. Das ist gesund.
4. Paul, fahr bitte etwas langsamer.
5. Nach dem Essen schlafen sie oft.
6. Bitte lesen Sie den Abschnitt auf Seite 45.
7. Oft gehen Sie schon um 3 Uhr nach Hause. Das ist zu früh.
8. Lernt eure Vokabeln.
9. Morgen lernt ihr den Imperativ.
10. Redet nicht soviel.

Du-IMPERATIVE

Regular Forms

57   1. With most verbs, the **du-***imperative* is based on the present-tense stem of the verb. If the verb stem ends in **-d, -t, -ig,** or awkward consonant clusters, **-e** must be added; otherwise, the addition is optional.

PRESENT TENSE STEM		INFORMAL IMPERATIVE *du*-FORM	
mach-	Peter,	**mach(e)** das Fenster zu!	*close the window.*
komm-		**komm(e)** doch her!	*come here.*
lauf-		**lauf(e)** schneller!	*run faster.*
werd-		**werde** bald gesund!	*get well soon.*
entschuldig-		**entschuldige** bitte!	*excuse me.*
öffn-		**öffne** die Tür!	*open the door.*

2. a. In colloquial speech, **e** is usually omitted after **d** or **t**. The omission is often indicated by an apostrophe.

   b. Verbs which end in **-eln** or **-ern** have a variety of forms.

STANDARD		
schütt**eln**	Inge, schütt**le** die Flasche.	*Inge, shake the bottle.*
kich**ern**	Peter, kich**ere** nicht.	*Peter, don't giggle.*
COLLOQUIAL		
schütt**eln**	Inge, schütt**el** die Flasche.	
kich**ern**	Peter, kich**re** nicht.	
	Peter, kich**er** nicht.	

Verbs With Vowel Change

1. The strong verbs showing vowel change from **e** to **i** or **e** to **ie** in the 2nd person singular of the present tense (with the exception of **werden**) form their imperative from those forms by dropping the personal ending [see § 27].

PRESENT TENSE		**INFORMAL IMPERATIVE**	
du-FORM		**du**-FORM	
du gibst	Peter,	**gib** mir die Zeitung!	*give me the newspaper.*
du liest		**lies** das Buch!	*read the book.*

2. Note that the changes from **a** to **ä**, **au** to **äu**, and **o** to **ö** do *not* occur in the imperative.

Schlaf(e) gut!

sein

The verb **sein** adds no **e** in the informal imperative [see also § 462.2. and 490].

sei-	Anna, **sei** vorsichtig!	*be careful.*
	Herr Schulz, **seien Sie** vorsichtig!	*be careful.*

Ihr-IMPERATIVE

60 The **ihr**-*imperative* is always the usual **ihr**-form of the verb.

PRESENT TENSE ihr-FORM		INFORMAL IMPERATIVE ihr-FORM
ihr macht	Peter und Inge,	**macht** das Fenster zu!
ihr kommt		**kommt** doch her!
ihr lauft		**lauft** schneller!
ihr werdet		**werdet** bald gesund!
ihr entschuldigt		**entschuldigt** bitte!
ihr öffnet		**öffnet** die Tür!
ihr seid		**seid** vorsichtig!
ihr gebt		**gebt** mir die Zeitung!
ihr lest		**lest** das Buch!

CHECK AND PRACTICE

Restate the imperative according to the person addressed.

1. Nimm das Buch! (Herr Braun)
2. Tun Sie das! (mein Kind)
3. Arbeiten Sie schneller! (Hans)
4. Gehen Sie in den Garten! (Kinder)
5. Essen Sie die Banana! (Claudia)
6. Sprich nicht so laut! (meine Herren)
7. Hilf mir! (Fräulein Heim)
8. Geben Sie mir die Zeitung! (Vater)
9. Schlaf nicht! (Hans und Inge)
10. Entschuldigen Sie! (Inge)

First Person Imperative

61 In addition to second person imperatives, there is also an *imperative of the first person plural* (in English "Let's go!"). It is formed by placing the pronoun **wir** after the second person plural present tense form of the verb.

> **Gehen wir** nach Hause! *Let's* go home.

Lassen in Imperative Forms

62 Sometimes a construction with **lassen** is used (as *let's* is used in English).

Gabi,	**laß uns**	nach Hause **gehen.**	***Let's*** *go home.*
Gabi und Franz,	**laßt uns**	nach Hause **gehen.**	
Fräulein Erhardt,	**lassen Sie uns**	nach Hause **gehen.**	
Meine Damen,	**lassen Sie uns**	nach Hause **gehen.**	

Infinitive as Imperative

63 The impersonal imperative is expressed by an infinitive without **zu**.

Passive as Imperative

64 Another impersonal way of expressing a request or command is the use of passive constructions without a subject [see § 525 and 532].

> Jetzt wird geschlafen! *It's time to go to sleep now (or else!)*

Future Tense as Imperative

65 For emphasis in spoken German, one might also encounter the **du-** and **ihr-** forms of the future tense. The personal pronoun may appear after or before the verb.

> Du wirst jetzt schlafen gehen! *Go to sleep now. (You shall go to sleep now . . . or else!)*
>
> Werdet ihr still sein! *Will you be quiet!*

Past Participles as Imperative

66 Primarily in the military, past participles are used for commands.

| Stillgestanden | *Attention!* |

PREFIXES

67 The basic meaning of a verb can be altered by the addition of prefixes. There are three kinds: *inseparable*, *separable*, and *two-way* prefixes.

 ## Inseparable Prefixes

68 Inseparable prefixes are *never separated* from the verb and always remain *unstressed*.

| Das Kind bekam einen Ball. | *The child got a ball.* |

69 Verbs with inseparable prefixes form the past participle without the normal **ge-** prefix [see § 8.2]

70 The most common inseparable prefixes are listed here with verb stems:

bekommen *to get*	**er**klären *to explain*	**miß**trauen *to mistrust*
empfangen *to receive*	**ge**fallen *to please*	**ver**stehen *to understand*
entscheiden *to decide*		**zer**reißen *to tear up*

CHECK AND PRACTICE

Give the correct forms in the present and present perfect tense.

Example

PRESENT
   Paul (verstehen) Deutsch.
   Paul **versteht** Deutsch.

PERFECT
   Paul (verstehen) Deutsch.
   Paul **hat** Deutsch **verstanden.**

1. Wir (bekommen) Besuch.
2. Sie (verlieren) Geld.
3. Ich (besuchen) die Eltern.
4. Ulla (mißverstehen) den Text.
5. Du (zerreißen) das Papier.
6. Die Arbeit (gelingen).
7. Er (vergessen) den Paß.
8. Der Lehrer (erklären) die Aufgabe.
9. Paul (entscheiden) die Sache.
10. Der Ober (empfehlen) das Schnitzel.

Separable Prefixes

71 Many English verbs complete their meaning by using complements (e.g., *to turn **off***) whose position in a sentence may vary (*He turned off the light./He turned the light off.*). In German such complements are often attached to the infinitives as prefixes; only in the present tense and simple past tense may they be separated from the verb stem:

1. *In main clauses,* the separable prefix stands in last position, *separated* from its verb stem [see § 289ff.].

2. *In dependent clauses,* in which the inflected verb stands in last position, the separable prefix *rejoins* its verb stem.

Infinitive	*to turn **off***	**aus**schalten
Main Clause	*He **turned off** the light.*	Er **schaltete** das Licht **aus.**
Dependent Clause	*I saw him when he turned **off** the light.*	Ich sah ihn, als er das Licht **aus**schaltete.

72 In contrast to inseparable prefixes [see § 68], separable prefixes are *always stressed.*

ánfangen

73 The past participle of verbs with separable prefixes is formed by attaching the separable prefix before the **ge-** prefix of the participle.

INFINITIVE	PAST PARTICIPLE
anfangen	an**ge**fangen

CHECK AND PRACTICE

Give the correct forms in the present and perfect tense of the following verbs (all with separable prefixes).

1. Paul (ankommen) heute.
2. Frau Meyer (anfangen) mit dem Unterricht.
3. Inge (anrufen) oft.
4. Der Besucher (ansehen) das Bild.

74   Some of the most common separable prefixes are:

ab·fahren *to leave*	**her·**bringen *to bring (here)*	**vor·**schlagen *to suggest*
an·kommen *to arrive*	**hin·**bringen *to take (there)*	**weg·**gehen *to go away*
auf·stehen *to get up*	**los·**lassen *to let go*	**weiter·**lesen *to read on*
aus·steigen *to get out*	**mit·**nehmen *to take along*	**zu·**hören *to listen*
ein·steigen *to get in*	**nach·**eilen *to hurry after*	**zurück·**kehren *to return*
fort·fahren *to leave*	**nieder·**brennen *to burn down*	**zusammen·**fassen *to summarize*

CHECK AND PRACTICE

Rewrite the sentences in the tenses suggested.

*The dot is **not** part of the spelling of the infinitive; it is used only to identify separable prefixes.

1. Der Zug wird um 9 Uhr abfahren. (PRESENT TENSE)
2. Wann wird der Winter anfangen? (PRESENT TENSE)
3. Sie wird das Fenster aufmachen. (PERFECT TENSE)
4. Sie haben viel Geld ausgegeben. (PAST TENSE)
5. Der Herr wird wahrscheinlich eintreten. (PAST PERFECT TENSE)
6. Er ist fortgegangen. (FUTURE TENSE)
7. Sie kommt nicht her. (PERFECT TENSE)
8. Wir gingen dort hin. (FUTURE TENSE)
9. Wann seid ihr losgefahren? (PRESENT TENSE)
10. Was wirst du mitbringen? (PERFECT TENSE)
11. Er kommt sicher nach. (FUTURE TENSE)
12. Der Polizist hat ihn niedergeschlagen. (PAST TENSE)
13. Sie schlug eine Reise vor. (PAST PERFECT TENSE)
14. Der Zug wird schon weggefahren sein. (PERFECT TENSE)
15. Wir arbeiten das ganze Jahr weiter. (FUTURE TENSE)
16. Die Frau machte die Tür sofort zu. (PAST PERFECT TENSE)
17. Mein Vater wird schon längst zurückgekehrt sein. (PERFECT TENSE)
18. Das hat mit unserem Plan zusammengehängt. (PAST TENSE)

75 The separable prefixes are mostly prepositions or adverbs, but verbs, nouns and adverbs derived from adjectives are also common as separable prefixes.

PREPOSITION	PREFIX
Anna hat das Bier **aus** der Küche geholt. *Anna got the beer **from** the kitchen.*	Er hat das Licht **aus**gemacht. *He turned **off** the light.*
ADVERB	**PREFIX**
Sein Geld ist **fort.** *His money is gone.*	Sie ist **fort**gegangen. *She left.*
zusammen fahren *to ride together*	**zusammen**fahren *to start back in alarm*
Wir fuhren einst **zusammen** tagtäglich mit der "Zehn", jetzt **fahren** wir **zusammen,** wenn wir uns wiedersehn! (Heinz Erhardt)	*We used to ride together each day with the tram no. 10, now we start back in alarm when we see each other again.*
VERB	**PREFIX**
Herr Meyer hat Paul **gekannt.** *Mr. Meyer **knew** Paul.*	Er hat sie **kennen**gelernt. *He **got to know** her.*
NOUN	**PREFIX**
Anna hatte früher ein **Rad.** *Anna had a **bike** some time ago.*	Sie ist viel **rad**gefahren. *She used to **bicycle** often.*
ADVERB derived from an adjective	**PREFIX**
Inge hat heute wirklich **schlecht** gesungen. *Inge sang really **badly** today.*	Ihr ist es **schlecht**gegangen. *She was in a **bad** way.*

76 Double Prefixes

Verbs with two prefixes are normally treated in accordance with their first prefix:

1. INSEPARABLE + SEPARABLE PREFIX **sich verabschieden** *to say goodbye*

Ich verabschiede mich von ihr. *I'm saying goodbye to her.* Ich habe mich von ihr verabschiedet. *I said goodbye to her.*

2. SEPARABLE + INSEPARABLE PREFIX **anvertrauen** *to entrust*
    Unlike other verbs with separable prefixes, these verbs have *no* **-ge-** in the past participle.

> Et vertraut mir sein Geheimnis an. *He entrusts his secret to me.*
> Er hat mir sein Geheimnis anvertraut. *He entrusted his secret to me.*

3. INSEPARABLE + INSEPARABLE PREFIX **mißverstehen** *to misunderstand*
    When **miß-** is attached to a verb with another inseparable prefix, then it carries the stress; otherwise, it is unstressed as all other inseparable prefixes.

> mißverstehen *to misunderstand*   mißáchten *to disregard*

Two-Way Prefixes

77 Two-way prefixes are separable or inseparable. In general, the prefix is used as a separable prefix when it retains its literal meaning, whereas figurative usage causes the prefix to be inseparable. As noted earlier [see § 68 and 72], the separable prefix is stressed and the inseparable prefix is unstressed.

dúrchbrechen	Er brach den Ast nicht ganz durch.
	He didn't quite break the branch through.
durchbréchen	Sie durchbrach ihre Grundsätze.
	She violated her principles.
überlegen	Sie legte sich eine Decke über, weil es so kalt war.
	She covered herself with a blanket because it was so cold.
überlégen	Paul überlegte sich, was er tun sollte.
	Paul pondered what he should do.
úmschreiben	Sie schrieb ihren Artikel nochmals um.
	She rewrote her article once again.
umschréiben	Sie umschrieb seine Aufgaben in wenigen Worten.
	She outlined his tasks briefly.
únterschlagen	Er hat die Beine beim Sitzen immer untergeschlagen.
	He always sits with his legs crossed.

unterschlágen	Er hat viel Geld unterschlagen. *He embezzled a lot of money.*
wiéderholen	Paul kam und holte sein Buch wieder. *Paul came and got his book back.*
wiederhólen	Wir wiederholen die Grammatik. *We are reviewing the grammar.*

CHECK AND PRACTICE

Complete the statements in the simple past tense, using verbs with separable or inseparable prefixes, as determined by meaning.

1. (durchfahren)
   a. Sie _____ bis Wien _____. *(to travel non-stop)*
   b. ein Schreck _____ ihn _____. *(to pass through)*
2. (übersetzen)
   a. Das Boot _____ die Leute _____, da es keine Brücke gab. *(to ferry across)*
   b. Die Sekretärin _____ den Text _____. *(to translate)*
3. (überlaufen)
   a. Die Milch _____. *(to flow over)*
   b. Ein schreckliches Gefühl _____ mich _____. *(to overcome)*

USE OF MODALS   [For forms, see § 15, 29. For tense use, see § 48]

78 *Modal verbs* are grouped together because they have a common function. They modify the main verbal action and indicate the "mode" in which it takes place.

One can distinguish between an objective and a subjective use of modals.

OBJECTIVE USE	SUBJECTIVE USE
Expresses the facts of life; unavoidable necessities. Alle Menschen **müssen** sterben. *All men **must** die.*	**Expresses personal judgment.** Ich **muß** unsterblich sein. *I **must** be immortal.*

Reference Chart

79 The following table summarizes the most basic, general meaning of the modals. Further treatment is given in the referenced paragraphs. Because of their idiomatic usage, translations into English are not exact and meanings overlap in many cases.

OBJECTIVE USE	SUBJECTIVE USE
Permission dürfen [see § 80–81]	**Probability**
to be allowed to *can* *may* (negative) *must not* *may not*	*to do / be probably*
Darf der Patient schon aufstehen? *Is the patient **allowed** to get up?*	Er **dürfte** inzwischen gesund sein. *He **is probably** healthy by now.*
Ability können [see § 82–84]	**Possibility**
can *to be able to* *to know how* *to master*	*can* *may*
Mary **kann** gut Deutsch sprechen. *Mary **can** speak German well.*	Das Bild **kann** ein Original sein. *The picture **may** be an original.*
Inclination mögen [see § 85–87]	**Possibility**
to like to *to care to*	*may*
Paul **mag** keine Tomaten. *Paul does not **like** tomatoes.*	Das **mag** wohl sein. *That **may** be so.*
Compulsion müssen [see § 88–89]	**Assumption**
to have to *must*	*must*
Sie **muß** am Sonntag arbeiten. *She **has to** work on Sunday.*	Sie **muß** sehr klug sein. *She **must be** very intelligent.*
Obligation sollen [see § 90–91]	**Supposition**
to be expected to *shall* *to be supposed to*	*to be said to*
Du **sollst** Peter anrufen. *You **are supposed to** call Peter.*	Sie **soll** sehr klug sein. *She is **said to be** very intelligent.*
Desire wollen [see § 92–93]	**Claim**
to want to *to intend to*	*to claim to*
Sie **wollte** nach Hause gehen. *She **wanted** to go home.*	Er **will** Deutsch können. *He **claims** to know German.*

Modals in Detail

dürfen

80   1. The basic meaning of **dürfen** in the objective usage is permission. **Nicht dürfen** expresses a strong warning or prohibition: *must not*.

> **Darfst** du kommen? ***Are you allowed*** *to (can you) come?*
> Das **dürfen** wir **nicht** tun. *We **mustn't** do that.*

2. Although **dürfen** is often replaced by **können** [see § 83], it is still used in situations in which permission is referred to in a more general sense or in which advice is implied.

> **Darf** hier geraucht werden? ***May*** *one smoke here?*

81   1. When used subjectively, **dürfen** expresses probability, supposition, or assumption. Often the subjunctive form **dürfte** is used.

> Ich **darf** wohl annehmen, daß nun alle die Regel verstanden haben.
> *I **suppose I may assume** that all understood the rule now.*
> Erika **dürfte** jetzt schon in Mainz sein. *Erika **is probably** already in Mainz by now.*

2. **dürfen** is also used as an expression of politeness.

> Wir **dürfen** Ihnen heute mitteilen, daß Ihr Auftrag eingetroffen ist.
> *Please **allow us** to inform you that your order has arrived.*

können

82   The objective meaning of **können** is ability.

> Peter **kann** gut singen. *Peter **can** (is able to) sing well.*
> Inge **kann** gut Tennis spielen. *Inge **knows how** to play tennis well.*

83   Often, it is used instead of **dürfen** for expressing permission.

> **Kann** ich mit ins Kino gehen? ***Can*** *I come along to the movies?*

84   When used subjectively, **können** expresses a possibility.

> **Kann** das dort drüben Frau Fischer sein? ***Can*** *that be Mrs. Fischer over there?*

CHECK AND PRACTICE

1. „Nein! Du _____ heute nicht ins Kino," sagt die Mutter.
   „No. You are not allowed to go to the movies today," says mother.
2. Die Aufgabe ist viel zu schwer! Ich _____ sie nicht machen.
   The problem is much too difficult. I can't do it.

mögen

85   When used in its objective meaning, **mögen** expresses an inclination; but its use is very restricted. It usually is used by itself (most of the time with **nicht** or some other negative to express dislike or reluctance) and *takes an accusative object.*

> Ich **mag** so etwas nicht. *I **dislike** that kind of thing.*

86   In contrast to the indicative forms of **mögen**, the subjunctive form **möchte** *would like* is frequently used by itself or together with another verb. It is also used as a polite form.

> Ich **möchte** das nicht.   *I don't **want** that.*
> Er **möchte** einen Roman schreiben.   *He **would like** to write a novel.*
> Ich **möchte** gern Arzt werden.   *I **would like** to become a doctor.*
> **Möchtest** du noch etwas Kaffee?   ***Do you care** for some more coffee?*

87   When used subjectively, **mögen** denotes possibility, doubt.

> Er **mag** sehr klug sein, aber trotzdem hat er viele Fehler gemacht.
> *He **may be** very intelligent, but he still made many mistakes.*

müssen

88   The objective meaning of **müssen** expresses a compulsion. Usually, **müssen** is negated by **nicht brauchen** (plus infinitive with **zu**).

> Sie **müssen** mir alles sagen, was Sie wissen. *You **must** tell me everything you know.*
> Sie **müssen** mir **nicht** alles sagen, was Sie wissen.
> Sie **brauchen** mir **nicht** alles **zu** sagen, was Sie wissen.
> *You don't need to tell me everything you know.*

89 Used subjectively, **müssen** expresses an assumption.

> Paula hat einen teuren Sportwagen. Ihre Eltern **müssen** reich sein.
> *Paula has an expensive sportscar. Her parents **must** be rich.*

sollen

90 The objective use of **sollen** expresses an obligation. In conversational German it is often used in questions expressing a suggestion.

> Ich **soll** Ihnen mitteilen, daß Sie entlassen sind. *I'm **obliged** to tell you that you are dismissed/fired.*
> Du **sollst** nicht töten. *Thou **shalt** not kill.*
> **Soll** ich Ihnen einen Stuhl bringen? ***Shall** I bring you a chair?*

91 Used subjectively, **sollen** expresses a supposition.

> Dieser Film **soll** sehr gut sein. *This film **is said to be** very good.*

wollen

92 In its objective usage, **wollen** expresses a desire. In conversational German **wollen** is frequently used together with **gerade** or **eben** in the sense of *was on the point of* or *was (just) about to.*

> Die Touristen **wollen** in die Schweiz fahren. *The tourists **want** to travel to Switzerland.*
> Ich **wollte** gerade gehen. *I **was just about** to leave.*

93 When used subjectively, **wollen** assumes the meaning *to claim.*

> Er **will** ein guter Tennisspieler sein. *He **claims to be** a good tennis player.*

CHECK AND PRACTICE

1. Die armen Studenten! Jeden Tag _____ sie viele Stunden arbeiten.
   These poor students! Each day they have to work for many hours.
2. Gott sagt, du _____ seinen Namen nicht mißbrauchen.
   God says you ought not to misuse his name.
3. _____ du Fisch?
   Do you like fish?

4. Was ＿＿＿ ihr machen, wenn ihr mit der Arbeit fertig seid?
   What do you want to do when you are finished with your work?

5. Lisa ＿＿＿ Rechtsanwalt werden. Ja, das ＿＿＿ sie schon als kleines Kind.
   Lisa would like to become a lawyer. Yes, she wanted to do that already when she was a small child.

6. Man ＿＿＿ nicht vergessen, daß Herr Müller schon 80 Jahre alt ist.
   You mustn't forget that Mr. Müller is already 80 years old.

7. Sie ＿＿＿ abends keinen Kaffee mehr trinken.
   You mustn't drink coffee at night any more.

Use of Modals with Dependent Infinitives

94 When a modal verb modifies an action, it functions as an inflected auxiliary. The original main verb appears in its infinitive form at the end of the clause without **zu**. In this case the infinitive of the main verb is called a "dependent infinitive."

	MODAL		DEPENDENT INFINITIVE
Lisa	**darf**	heute abend ins Kino	**gehen.**
Lisa	*may go*	*to the movies tonight.*	

95 When used with a dependent infinitive, the form of the modal verbs in the three perfect tenses changes. Instead of the past participle (e.g., **gedurft**), the infinitive of the modal (e.g., **dürfen**) is used. Such constructions are usually avoided in spoken German [see § 48]. They are called double infinitives and both infinitives are positioned at the end of the sentence.

PERFECT TENSE		Verb Infinitive	Modal Infinitive
Auxiliary			
Paul	**hat** gestern abend ins Kino	**gehen**	**dürfen.**
*Paul **was allowed to go** to the movies last night.*			

96

	MODALS ALONE			WITH DEPENDENT INFINITIVE			
Present	ich **kann**			ich **kann**		sehen	
Past	**konnte**			**konnte**		sehen	
Perfect	habe	**gekonnt**		habe		sehen	**können**
Past Perfect	hatte	**gekonnt**		hatte		sehen	**können**
Future	werde		**können**	werde		sehen	**können**
Future Perfect	werde	**gekonnt**	haben	werde	haben	sehen	**können**

[For word order, see § 310]

CHECK AND PRACTICE

Add the modal. Pay attention to the tenses.

1. Wir gingen einkaufen. (wollen)   2. Sie holt Frau Meier ab. (sollen)
3. Ich laufe gut Ski. (können)   4. Warum wirst du zu Hause bleiben? (müssen)
5. Wir haben das nicht gegessen. (mögen)

Use of Modals without Dependent Infinitives

97 When the main verb is clearly understood from the context, dependent infinitives need not be repeated. This is particularly true of verbs of motion.

Ich **will** nach Hause.	*I want to go home.*
Sie **darf** ins Theater.	*She is allowed to go to the theater.*
Du **mußt** sofort ins Bett.	*You have to go to bed immediately.*
Er **soll** fort.	*He is supposed to go away.*
Wir **können** jetzt los.	*We can start now.*

98 If modals are without a dependent infinitive, they use the regular past participle in the three perfect tenses.

Hast du nach Hause **gewollt?**   *Did you want to go home?*

CHECK AND PRACTICE

Translate.

1. Do you have to go home already? Yes, our children have to go to bed.
2. Do you want this book?

3. He can speak German.
4. She is allowed to go to the theater.
5. I must go to the library.

Review the tenses. Express the sentences in the tenses cued. Use additional time expressions if given.

6. Ich darf mit seinem Wagen fahren. (PRESENT PERFECT) (schon oft)
7. Er darf es nie. (PRESENT PERFECT) (noch nie)
8. Peter will eine Woche bei uns bleiben. (PAST PERFECT)
9. Diesen Wein mag wohl niemand. (FUTURE)
10. Wir müssen auf Frau Müller warten. (PRESENT PERFECT) (schon oft)
11. Sie müssen es nie. (PRESENT PERFECT) (noch nie)
12. Niemand kann Paul helfen. (PAST PERFECT)
13. Du kannst es auch nicht. (PAST PERFECT)
14. Doch wir können es. (FUTURE)

I. VOCABULARY FOR REVIEW (A AND B TEXTS FROM READER, CHAPTER II)

Verbs

sich aus·ruhen	to rest
fern·sehen	to watch TV
frei·haben	to have off
Sport treiben, ie, ie,	to do sports
zusammen·zählen	to add up

Nouns

der **Alltag, -e**	everyday life
der **Ausflug, ·̈e**	excursion
die **Bewegung, -en**	movement
der **Druck**	pressure, stress
die **Einrichtung, -en**	establishment
die **Entspannung, -en**	relaxation

die **Erholung, -en**	recreation
der **Feiertag, -e**	holiday
die **Freizeit, -en**	leisure time
der **Fußball**	soccer
das **Kegeln**	German bowling
der **Kegler, -**	bowler
die **Mannschaft, -en**	team
das **Mitglied, -er**	member
zu Ostern	at Easter
zu Pfingsten	at Whitsun, Pentecost
das **Schwimmbad, ̈-er**	swimming pool
die **Sportart, -en**	type of sport
die **Unterhaltung**	entertainment
der **Verein, -e**	club
das **Vergnügen, -**	amusement, pleasure
die **Wanderung, -en**	hike
das **Wochenende, -n**	weekend

ADDITIONAL EXERCISES (A AND B TEXTS FROM THE READER)

Translate the questions into German and answer in German to observe the contrast in present tense usage.

1. When will you rest? (*in my leisure time*)
2. What are you going to do now? (*watch television*)
3. Do you do sports? (*Yes, we do*)
4. Will you be at home at Whitsun? (*Yes, we'll be . . .*)
5. Do you always go to the club at Easter? (*We always do . . .*)
6. Are you going to play soccer tonight? (*No, but tomorrow*)

Translate into English. Explain the contrast in present tense usage.

7. Die meisten Menschen arbeiten fünf Tage in der Woche.
8. Wir sind schon drei Tage auf dieser Wanderung.
9. Die Freizeit-Industrie macht schon immer große Profite.
10. Am Tag arbeiten wir; aber abends brauchen wir Unterhaltung.
11. Ruhen Sie sich am Feiertag nicht aus? Doch, wir ruhen uns aus.

Ostern bei den Meinkes

Tell the story in the simple past.

12. Herr und Frau Meinke schauen aus dem Fenster. 13. Sie können ihren Garten sehen. 14. Sie müssen jeden Tag dort arbeiten. 15. Aber heute ist Ostern, da wollen sie sich ausruhen. 16. Sie haben das ganze Wochenende frei; das ist ein großes Vergnügen für sie.

Sport in der Freizeit

Translate into English. Explain the contrast in the usage of past tenses.

17. In allen Dörfern gab es Fußballplätze.
18. Die Leute interessierten sich seit Jahren für diesen Sport.
19. Die Nationalmannschaft stand immer unter großem Druck.
20. Habt ihr selbst keinen Sport getrieben? Doch, wir waren Schwimmer.
21. Wir mußten immer arbeiten, während ihr freihattet.

Was haben Sie am Feierabend gemacht?

Single actions are expressed in the perfect. Answer the questions accordingly.

22. Was haben Sie am Feierabend gemacht? (ich/nach Hause/gehen)
23. Wie kamen Sie denn nach Hause? (ich/mit dem Bus/fahren)
24. War Ihre Frau schon zu Hause? Nein, (sie/später/kommen)
25. Mußten Sie lange auf sie warten? Ja, aber (ich/fernsehen)
26. War das eine Erholung für Sie? Ja, ich (sich ausruhen)

Abends bei Bergers

Respond with the past perfect to indicate that the event in the answer happened before the (past action) question.

Example

Kegelten alle Klubmitglieder gut? Ja, denn (sie/kegeln/lernen)
Ja, denn sie hatten kegeln gelernt.

27. Waren Herr und Frau Berger beide im Zimmer? Ja, (sie/gleichzeitig/nach Hause kommen) *Sie waren .... gekommen*
28. Warum aß Herr Berger nichts? (er/schon/im Gasthaus essen) *Er hatte ... gegessen*
29. Wünschte er Unterhaltung? Ja, denn (er/den ganzen Tag/nur arbeiten)
30. Warum war seine Frau so müde? Sie (im Schwimmbad/sein) *Sie war...gewesen*
31. Konnte Herr Berger nicht kegeln? Nein, er (es/nicht lernen)

Frau Berger kommandiert ihren Mann herum

Example

Emil, _____! (in der Küche/helfen)
Emil, hilf in der Küche!

32. ein nettes Wochenende planen
33. früh nach Hause kommen
34. interessante Beschäftigungen vorschlagen
35. mit mir auf einen Ausflug gehen
36. mehr Zeit mit deiner Frau verbringen

Mutter sagt den Kindern, was sie tun sollen

Example

nicht schreien
Kinder, schreit nicht!

37. nicht so rastlos sein
38. nicht immerzu fernsehen
39. die Freizeit besser benutzen
40. bald Erwachsene werden
41. regelmäßig Sport treiben

Ein paar Arbeiter besprechen, was sie in der Freizeit tun wollen

Use *wir*- and *laß(t) uns*- imperatives.

Example

das Schwimmbad benutzen (Oskar) (Leute)
Oskar, benutzen wir das Schwimmbad!
Oskar, laß uns das Schwimmbad benutzen!
Leute, laßt uns das Schwimmbad benutzen!

42. ins öffentliche Schwimmbad gehen (Mark)
43. Kegler werden (Hans)
44. Vereinsmitglieder bleiben (Freunde)
45. einen Ausflug machen (Kollegen)
46. Ostern mit der Familie feiern (Leute)

Restate the commands informally, in the singular or plural as suggested by the names.

Example

Machen Sie Ordnung im Garten! (Emil)
Emil, mach Ordnung im Garten!

47. Helfen Sie mir in der Küche! (Renate)
48. Machen Sie sich mehr Bewegung! (Robert und Richard)
49. Geben Sie mir den Fußball! (Peter)
50. Sprechen Sie nicht gleichzeitig! (Hans und Peter)
51. Werden Sie Mitglied bei uns! (Monika)

Respond in the present tense without auxiliary verbs.

Example

Möchten Sie einen Ausflug **machen**? Ja, (ich gern)
Ja, ich mache gern einen Ausflug.

52. Wer soll diese neuen Einrichtungen ansehen? (Herr Burger)
53. Kann man sich dort vom Streß erholen? Ja,
54. Wird es dort auch ein Schwimmbad geben? Ja,
55. An welchen Tagen möchten Sie im Verein sein? (ich/jeden Tag)
56. Wollt ihr jetzt ausruhen? Nein, (wir/später)

Respond in the present perfect tense without modal verbs.

Example

Wann soll der Zug **abfahren?** (schon)
Der Zug ist schon **abgefahren.**

57. Wollt ihr zu Ostern zu Hause bleiben? Wir (zu Ostern/noch nie)
58. Möchtet ihr diese neue Einrichtung sehen? Wir (sie/schon)
59. Mußt du auch am Feierabend lernen? Ja, (früher/manchmal)
60. Wann kannst du endlich Mitglied werden? Ich (schon letztes Jahr)
61. Wer will eine Wanderung machen? Wir (letztes Wochenende)

Respond with the modal verb required by the context.

62. Wer geht ins Schwimmbad? Nur unsere Mitglieder _____ es benutzen.
63. Hast du Angst vor dem Wasser? Ja, denn ich _____ nicht schwimmen.
64. Warum treiben Sie Sport? Der Arzt sagt, ich _____ es tun.
65. Kommt ihr mit auf den Ausflug? Nein, wir _____ arbeiten.
66. Interessierst du dich für unseren Verein? Ja sehr, ich _____ Mitglied werden.

Translate into English, observing the meaning of the modal verbs.

67. Unser Verein mag wirklich zu teuer sein.

68. Das Kegeln soll entspannend sein.

69. Hans will ein guter Turner sein, stimmt das?

70. Du mußt doch noch nicht gehen, es ist noch so früh.

71. Wir dürfen heute nicht zum Kegeln.

72. In meiner Freizeit möchte ich gute Unterhaltung.

73. Hans soll sehr gut Fußball spielen, glaubst du das?

II. VOCABULARY FOR REVIEW (C AND D TEXTS FROM READER, CHAPTER II)

Verbs

auf·geben (i), a, e	to give up
aus·rechnen	to figure out, calculate
sich betrinken, a, u	to get drunk
betrügen, o, o	to deceive
fordern	to demand
genießen, o, o	to enjoy
grüßen	to greet
klagen	to complain
lächeln	to smile
nicken	to nod
rauchen	to smoke
verbrauchen	to consume
zu·schauen	to watch

Nouns

die **Kellnerin, -nen**	waitress
das **Pech**	bad luck
die **Spielregel, -n**	rule of game
der **Verlierer, -**	loser
der **Verlust, -e**	loss

Others

erfolgreich	successful
gleich	right away
neugierig	curious

ADDITIONAL EXERCISES (C AND D TEXTS FROM THE READER)

Beim Kartenspiel

Answer and translate into English to observe the contrast in present tense usage.

1. Wann beginnt das Spiel? (pünktlich um fünf)

2. Schauen Sie gleich zu? Nein, (erst später)

3. Bezahlt er jetzt? Ja, (immer gleich)

4. Wann bist du wieder da? (gleich)

5. Schaut er immer nur zu? (nach sieben Uhr nicht mehr)

Translate into English. Explain the contrast in present tense usage.

6. Die Spieler rechnen ihre Verluste aus.

7. Uns betrügt ihr nicht!

8. Das nächste Mal betrinke ich mich nicht wieder.

9. Das interessiert mich nicht.

10. Du magst das Spiel wohl nicht? Doch, ich genieße es.

11. Morgen haben Sie auch Pech!

The simple past is the narrative tense. Tell the story.

12. Er ist kein Kartenspieler. 13. Aber er geht jeden Tag ins Gasthaus und schaut dem Spiel zu. 14. Er grüßt den Wirt und die Kellnerin sehr freundlich. 15. Aber er sagt nichts, er lächelt nur. 16. Er raucht nicht und er trinkt nicht. 17. Wir wissen nicht, ob er das Kartenspiel versteht. 18. Vielleicht hat er Angst vor Pech.

Single actions are expressed in the present perfect. Respond to the statements.

Example

Sieht er heute dem Spiel **zu**? Nein, er (gestern)
Nein, er **hat** gestern dem Spiel **zugesehen.**

19. Betrügt hier jemand? (ein Spieler/im letzten Spiel)

20. Glauben Sie, die Verlierer klagen? (natürlich)

21. Fordern sie Revanche? Ja,

22. Kannst du etwas über die Spielregeln erfahren? Ich, (etwas)

23. Rauchst du vielleicht zuviel? Ich (nur bei einem Spiel)

Translate into English. Explain the contrast in the use of past tenses.

24. Immer verbrauchte er zuviel Geld.

25. Während er über sein Pech klagte, mußten wir lächeln.

26. Er hatte schon seit Jahren Verluste.

27. Früher war er erfolgreich.

28. Früher spielte er jeden Tag Karten.

Respond with the past perfect to indicate that the action in the answer happened before the past action.

Example

Warum **aß** er denn nichts? (schon)
Weil er schon **gegessen hatte**.

29. Bezahlten die Verlierer, als sie weggingen? Nein, (schon vorher)

30. Wer sollte denn alles ausrechnen? (die Kellnerin/schon) die Kell. hatte schon ausgerechnet

31. Wer sprach von seinem Pech? Er selbst (davon) er hatte selbst davon gesprochen

32. Warum rauchten die Spieler nicht? (schon/zuviel)

33. Warum fragte niemand nach den Verlusten? Die Spieler (schon) hatten gefragt

• SPEAKER

Die Spieler reden miteinander

Form informal imperatives in the singular.

Example

nicht so neugierig sein (Peter)
Peter, sei nicht so neugierig!

34. ein bißchen lächeln *Peter, lächele ein bißchen*
35. nicht immer den Kopf schütteln *Schüttle nicht immer den Kopf*
36. das Spiel nicht aufgeben *Gib das Spiel nicht*
37. dein Geld fordern *Fordere dein Geld*
38. die Spielregeln lernen

Ein Spieler sagt den anderen, was sie tun sollen

Form informal imperatives in the plural.

Example

die Regeln lernen (Freunde)
Freunde, lernt die Regeln!

39. nicht soviel rauchen
40. Geld von den Verlierern fordern *Fordert Geld von den Verlieren*
41. vorsichtiger spielen
42. die Ausgaben ausrechnen
43. das Spiel genießen

Die Spieler besprechen, was sie nun tun

Use *wir-* and *laß(t) uns-* imperatives.

Example

Sollen wir weiterspielen? Ja, (Freunde)
Ja, Freunde, spielen wir weiter!
Ja, Freunde, laßt uns weiterspielen!

44. Wollen wir unsere Verluste ausrechnen? Nein, (Freunde/später)
45. Sollen wir neue Regeln erfinden? Ja, (Kollegen)
46. Sollen wir unsere Partner betrügen? Nein, (niemals)

Restate the commands informally, in the singular or plural as suggested.

47. Geben Sie mir Feuer! Hans,

48. Seien Sie doch kein Pechvogel! Otto,

49. Nicken Sie doch nicht immer mit dem Kopf! Susanne,

50. Grüßen Sie bitte die Familie! Amanda und Manfred,

51. Fordern Sie bitte nicht zu viel Geld! Peter und Erwin,

52. Geben Sie sofort das Rauchen auf! Elisabeth,

Respond in the present tense.

Example

Möchten Sie heute mal **zuschauen?** Ja, (gern)
Ja, ich **schaue** gern **zu.**

53. Darf man über seine Verluste klagen? Ja, ich (immer)

54. Habt ihr euch gestern wirklich betrunken? Wir (doch nie)

55. Will Herr Kurt das Kartenspiel aufgeben? Nein, er (nie)

56. Möchte er heute zusehen? Ja, ich glaube, er (heute)

57. Sollen wir der Kellnerin helfen? Nein, Hans (ihr)

Respond in the present perfect.

Example

Wann soll denn der Zug **abfahren?** (schon um drei Uhr)
Der Zug **ist** schon um drei Uhr **abgefahren.**

58. Geben wir das Spiel jetzt auf? Wir nicht, aber die Verlierer

59. Ich möchte unsere Verluste ausrechnen. Die Kellnerin (schon)

60. Herr Kurt wollte kein Geld verbrauchen. Er (gestern/zu viel)

61. Wer kann so ein Spiel genießen? Wir (es/viele Jahre)

Translate, observing the German meaning of each modal verb.

62. Anna mag sich betrunken haben.

63. Jetzt soll sie als Kellnerin in einem Gasthaus arbeiten.

64. Er will ein guter Verlierer sein, aber ich glaube ihm nicht.

65. Man darf nie über sein Pech klagen.

66. Du mußt nicht immer den Kopf schütteln, du kannst auch mal lächeln.

67. Auch wenn ich das Kartenspiel nicht mag?

In der Bar

Respond, using the modal verb required by the context.

Example

Das stimmt doch nicht; ich _____ über so eine Erzählung lächeln.

ich muß über so eine Erzählung lächeln.

68. Geben Sie mir Feuer! Nein, Sie _____ hier nicht rauchen.
69. Wünschen Sie etwas, meine Dame? Ja, ich _____ ein Glas Wein.
70. Aber dieser Wein schmeckt nicht gut, ich _____ ihn gar nicht.
71. _____ ich Ihnen einen anderen geben?
72. Dieser Rheinwein hier _____ am besten sein, stimmt das?
73. Den _____ Sie zum halben Preis haben.
74. Also gut, den _____ ich bestellen.
75. Sie _____ ihn aber kalt trinken.
76. Wenn ich den Wein nicht bezahlen _____, _____ mein Mann dafür bezahlen.

3 NOUNS AND ARTICLES
(Part One)

99 A noun is a word denoting a person, place, thing, quality or act. In German, all nouns are capitalized in the written language.

GENDER

Gender as a Grammatical Category

100 German nouns have three *genders:*   MASCULINE
                                           FEMININE
                                           NEUTER

101 While German nouns themselves do not typically show gender, the articles, pronouns and adjectives that modify the nouns do reflect gender.

---

der Löffel *the spoon*   **die** Gabel *the fork*   **das** Messer *the knife*

MASCULINE   **FEMININE**   **NEUTER**

---

102 Gender is a linguistic and not a biological category, although words for male and female beings usually show natural gender.

---

der Mann *the man*   **die** Frau *the woman*

---

103 Many German nouns consist of two or more nouns strung together. These are called *compound nouns*, and their gender is determined by the last element.

---

das Auto + **der Schlüssel** = **der** Auto**schlüssel**
the car   the key   the car key

---

104 There are several ways to determine the gender of nouns. The most common classifications are:
1. gender according to form   [see § 105–107]
2. gender according to meaning   [see § 108–110]

Although these classifications help one to remember a noun's gender, they are not foolproof. Nouns should, therefore, always be learned with their articles.

Gender According to Form

105   MASCULINE NOUNS

1. Most nouns ending in **-er** (especially nouns denoting an animate *agent* as well as by analogy most instruments or inanimate agents; nouns denoting *home, town, or region,* some nouns of nationality); nouns ending in **-en** if they are not derived from an infinitive. [See § 107.3].

2. Nouns ending in **-or, -eur (-ör), -ant,** and nouns denoting an *agent* ending in **-ent.** [See also § 107.5].

-er	der Bäck**er** *the baker*		**-or**	der Profess**or** *the professor*	
	der Sportl**er** *the sportsman*			der Mot**or** *the motor*	
	der Weck**er** *the alarm clock*		**-eur**	der Fris**eur** *the barber*	
	der Berlin**er** *citizen of Berlin*		**-ör**	der Lik**ör** *the liqueur*	
	der Österreich**er** *the Austrian*		**-ant**	der Fabrik**ant** *the manufacturer*	
				der Konson**ant** *the consonant*	
			-ent	der Konsum**ent** *the consumer*	
-en	der Wag**en** *the car*				
	der Reg**en** *the rain*		**EXCEPTION**		
	der Gart**en** *the garden*		**das Restaurant**		

3. Nouns ending in **-ig, -ich, -ling**

4. Nouns ending in **-us.**

-ig	der Kön**ig** *the king*		**-us**	der Vir**us**
-ich	der Tepp**ich** *the carpet*			der Terroris**mus**
-ling	der Früh**ling** *the spring*			

106   FEMININE NOUNS

1. Most nouns ending in unaccented **-e**

2. Nouns ending in **-in:** feminine forms for professions, titles, nationalities (sometimes with umlaut)

-e	die Supp**e** the soup	-in	die Lehrer**in** *teacher*
			die König**in** *queen*

IMPORTANT EXCEPTIONS
der Kollege *colleague*
der Biologe *biologist*
der Psychologe *psychologist*
der Deutsche *German*
der Pole *Pole*
der Grieche *Greek*
der Franzose *Frenchman*
der Käse *the cheese*
der Name *the name*
das Auge *the eye*
das Ende *the end*
Nouns derived from adjectives:
das Böse *the evil*

die Biolog**in** *biologist*
die Psycholog**in** *psychologist*
die Ärzt**in** *doctor*
die Rechtsanwält**in** *lawyer*
die Pol**in** *Pole*
die Griech**in** *Greek*
die Französ**in** *French woman*
die Ausländer**in** *foreigner*
die Freund**in** *girl friend*
die Tourist**in** *tourist*

3. Nouns ending in **-heit, -keit, -ei, -ung, -ur, -schaft, -ie, -ik, -ion, -tät**

-heit	die Frei**heit** *the freedom*	-ung	die Zeit**ung** *the newspaper*	-ie	die Iron**ie** *irony*	BUT das Gen**ie**
-keit	die Neuig**keit** *the news*	-ur	die Nat**ur** *nature*	-ik	die Mus**ik** *music*	
-ei	die Bücher**ei** the library	-schaft	die Freund**schaft** friendship	-ion	die Nat**ion** *nation*	
				-tät	die Universi**tät** *university*	

107   NEUTER NOUNS

1. Diminutives ending in **-chen, -lein**   2. Most nouns ending in **-tum, -nis**

-chen	das Mäd**chen** *the girl*	-tum	das König**tum** *the kingdom*
-lein	das Männ**lein** *little man*	-nis	das Gefäng**nis** *the jail*
	(The natural gender is overruled by grammatical gender.)		

EXCEPTIONS
der Irrtum *error*
der Reichtum *wealth*
die Erlaubnis *permission*

3. Infinitives used as nouns [see § 114]   4. Most nouns beginning with **Ge-**

das **Rauchen** *smoking*	**Ge-** das **Ge**richt *the court*
das **Denken** *thinking*	das **Ge**bäude *the building*
	das **Ge**birge *the mountains*

> **EXCEPTIONS**
> die Geschichte *history*
> die Gefahr *the danger*
> der Gedanke *the thought*
> der Gesang *the singing*

5. Nouns ending in **-ment, -(i)um, -eau (-o),** and most words ending in **-ing** derived from English

-ment	das Argu**ment**		**-eau**	das Bur**eau**, Büro
-(i)um	das Stud**ium**		**-o**	das Aut**o**
	das Alb**um**		**-ing**	das Jogg**ing**

CHECK AND PRACTICE

Give the correct article for the following nouns. (You may not know all the words, but you do know the genders. Look at the endings!)

die 1. Störung   *der* 2. Rettich   *der* 3. Schmetterling   *die* 4. Höhe

die 5. Schule   *die* 6. Bildung   *der* 7. Keller   *die* 8. Nase

das 9. Leben   *die* 10. Freundlichkeit   *das* 11. Dokument   *die* 12. Fabrik

der 13. Finger   *die* 14. Peripherie   *das* 15. Geheimnis   *der* 16. Student

die 17. Politik   *das* 18. Studium   *das* 19. Hearing   *das* 20. Geschäft

das 21. Gedicht   *die* 22. Herrschaft   *die* 23. Kanalisation   *die* 24. Kultur

der 25. Fremdling   *der* 26. Honig   *der* 27. Schwimmer   *der* 28. Musikant

das 29. Gehirn   *der* 30. Amateur   *der* 31. Redner   *der* 32. Pfennig

Use color index cards:
BLUE for masculine nouns
RED for feminine nouns
GREEN for neuter nouns

Gender According to Meaning

108 *MASCULINE*

1. Male beings (natural gender)	**der Vater** *the father* **der Hahn** *the rooster*
2. The days of the week, division of the day, months, seasons	**der Sonntag** *Sunday* **der Abend** *the evening* EXCEPTION die Nacht *the night* **der Mai** *May* **der Herbst** *the fall*
3. Most rocks, precious stones	**der Stein** *the stone* **der Felsen** *the rock* **der Diamant** *the diamond*
4. Weather, compass terms	**der Regen** *the rain* **der Westen** *the west* **der Horizont** *horizon*
5. Professional and national designations [see also § 106.2]	**der Arzt** *the doctor* **der Amerikaner** *the American*
6. Most foreign rivers	**der Mississippi**

109 *FEMININE*

1. Female beings (natural gender)	**die Mutter** *the mother* **die Henne** *the hen*	EXCEPTION das Weib *the woman*
2. Most fruits, trees, flowers	**die Birne** *the pear* **die Tanne** *the fir tree* **die Rose** *the rose*	EXCEPTION der Apfel *the apple*
3. Most German rivers	**die Elbe**	EXCEPTIONS der Rhein der Main der Neckar
4. Numbers	**die Zwölf** *twelve*	
5. Names of ships	**die Bremen**	

110   NEUTER

1. Young living beings	**das Kind** *the child* **das Küken** *the chick*

2. Continents, countries, states, islands, cities.

These do not use articles except with a modifier.

These always use an article.

das alte Europa **das südliche Bayern** **das unbekannte China** **das schöne Sizilien** **das mittelalterliche Rothenburg**	

EXCEPTIONS	die Schweiz
	die Normandie
	die Tschechoslowakei
der Balkan	die Türkei
	die USA
	die USSR

3. Metal <br> chemical elements

das Silber *the silver* **das Chlor** *chlorine*	EXCEPTIONS der Stahl *steel* der Kalk *lime* der Schwefel *sulfur*

4. Adjectival nouns not referring to people

das Gute
 das Blau   des Himmels   *the blue of the sky*

5. Letters

das ABC   **das Alpha**

6. Many words of foreign origin

das Taxi
 das Mikrophon
 das Büro

CHECK AND PRACTICE

Give the articles for the following nouns:

der 1. Vater   *der* 2. Mittwoch   *der* 3. Granit   *die* 4. Elizabeth I.

die 5. Kuh   *die* 6. Eins   *das* 7. Blei ~lead   *der* 8. Dezember

die 9. Donau (*Danube*)   *das* 10. moderne China   *der* 11. Mensch   *die* 12. Pflaume

der 13. Akademiker   *das* 14. Y (Ypsilon)   *die* 15. Frau   *das* 16. Kino

das 17. Telefon   *das* 18. geteilte Berlin *das*   *der* 19. Schnee   *das* 20. Uranium

der 21. Beamte   *der* 22. Morgen   *das* 23. Risiko   *das* 24. Gold

Lisk

NOUN DERIVATION

111   Nouns can be derived from almost all word categories. However, two groups are especially important: adjectives and verbs.

From Adjectives

112   Adjectives can be made into nouns when they refer to "man," "woman," "people," or "thing" [see § 222ff.]:

der **alte** Mann	⟩	der **Alte**	*the old man*
die **alte** Frau	⟩	die **Alte**	*the old woman*
die **alten** Leute	⟩	die **Alten**	*the old people*
		das **Alte**	*the old things, the past*

From Verbs

113   Nouns can be derived from the *present participle*, which is formed in German by adding **-d** to the verb infinitive, and from the *past participle*. They are capitalized and follow the adjective declension [see § 221ff.].

INFINITIVE	PRESENT PARTICIPLE	NOUN	
ertrinken	ertrinken**d**	der Ertrinken**de**	*person drowning*

INFINITIVE	PAST PARTICIPLE	NOUN	
ertrinken	ertr**unken**	der Ertr**unkene**	*drowned person*

114   *Infinitives* can also be used as nouns. They are capitalized and always neuter. They usually occur in the singular and follow the strong declension [see § 134ff.].

lachen	⟩	das Lachen	*the laughter*

115   One-syllable verbal nouns are derived from the *infinitive stem*, the *past tense stem*, or the *stem of the past participle*. They are masculine and follow the strong declension [see § 134ff.].

sitzen	der **Sitz**	**klang**	der **Klang**	ge**gang**en	der **Gang**
to sit	*the seat*	*sounded*	*the sound*	*gone*	*the gait*

116 Nouns ending in **-er (-erin** for feminines) are derived from the *infinitive stem* and denote agency. Those in **-er** belong to the strong declension [see § 134ff.], and those in **-erin** to the weak declension [see § 138ff.].

rauchen	der **Rauch**er	die **Rauch**erin
to smoke	*the smoker*	

ARTICLES

Function of Articles

117 Articles are always followed by a noun which, in turn, may be modified either by adjectives, or by other parts of speech.

ARTICLE	NOUN MODIFICATION	NOUN
der		**Lehrer**
der	alte	**Lehrer**
der	ihm von früher bekannte	**Lehrer**

118 Articles indicate the   GENDER
                               NUMBER
                               CASE   of the following noun. In addition to the definite and the indefinite article, the so-called **der**-words and **ein**-words function as articles. [For the declension of articles, see § 132]

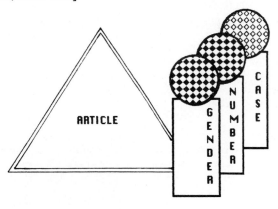

DEFINITE ARTICLE				INDEFINITE ARTICLE			
der			MASCULINE	ein			
die	}	*the*	FEMININE	eine	}	*a, an*	
das			NEUTER	ein			

der-words				**ein**-words			
(Declension like **der**)				(Declension like **ein**)			
dieser	*this*	[see § 119–120]	kein	*no, not a, not any* [see § 127]			
jener	*that*	[see § 119–120]					
jeder	*every, each*	[see § 121]	mein	*my*		unser	*our*
alle	*all (plural of **jeder**)*		dein	*your*		euer	*your*
mancher	*many a*	[see § 123]	Ihr	*your (formal)*			
solcher	*such, such a*	[see § 124–125]	sein	*his, its*		ihr	*their*
welcher	*which*	[see § 126]	ihr	*her*			

CHECK AND PRACTICE

Give the correct article. Use the cues in parentheses.

Dieser 1. (*This*) Mann ist sehr alt.

Jener (Der) 2. (*That*) Junge arbeitet gut.

Jeder 3. (*Each*) Schüler mußte eine Arbeit schreiben.

alle 4. (*All*) Kinder sahen dem Festzug zu.

Manche 5. (*Some*) Gäste tranken zuviel.

Solche 6. (*Such*) Bilder sind recht beliebt.

Welcher 7. (*Which*) Film gefiel dir am besten?

Mein 8. (*My*) Fahrrad ist leider kaputt.

deine 9. Paul, (*your*) Freundin hat mich gestern besucht.

Sein 10. (*His*) Paß ist noch immer bei der Polizei.

Ihre 11. Wo wohnt (*her*) Tante?

Unsere 12. (*Our*) Reise war ein großartiges Erlebnis.

euer 13. Kinder, (*your*) Onkel hat gerade angerufen.

Ihre 14. (*Their*) Freude war groß.

Keine 15. Sie hat (*no*) Angst.

16. Das ist (*not a*) gute Entschuldigung.

keine

Articles in Detail

119 **dieser** *this,* **jener** *that*

dieser and **jener** are sometimes used together to express a contrast; **jener** is rarely used except in combination with **dieser.** When no contrast is expressed, **der . . . da** or **dieser . . . da** is used instead of **jener.**

> **Dieser** Wagen ist billig. *This car is inexpensive.*
> Ich kenne sowohl **diese** Fotografie als auch **jenes** Bild. *I'm familiar with **this** photo and **that** picture.*
> **Jene** Kirche   ist der Kölner Dom. *That church is the Cologne Cathedral.*
> **Die** Kirche **da** ist der Kölner Dom.

120 In conversational German, the accented definite article is often used instead of **dieser.** In print, the letters are sometimes spaced to indicate this stress.

> **Dieses** Mädchen möchte ich kennenlernen. *I'd like to meet **this/that** girl.*
> **D a s**   Mädchen möchte ich kennenlernen.

121 **jeder** *every, each* (plural: **alle** *all*)

> **Jeder** Teilnehmer erhielt eine Urkunde. *Each participant received a certificate.*
> **Alle** Passagiere haben ihre Fahrkarten. *All passengers have their tickets.*

122 1. In contrast to the other **der**-words, **alle** can precede other articles. In these instances, the stem **all** is often used without ending.

> **All(e) diese** Busse fahren nach Berlin. *All these buses drive to Berlin.*
> **All(e) meine** Freunde wollen nach Deutschland reisen. *All my friends want to go to Germany.*

2. Certain forms of **alle** are used also in the singular:

> **Aller** (= Jeder) Anfang ist schwer. *Starting is always difficult.*

123   **mancher** and **manch ein** *many a* (plural: *some, quite a few*)

For **mancher**, primarily the plural forms are used. In the combination **manch ein**, only **ein** is declined.

> Wenn **mancher** Mann wüßte, wer **mancher** Mann wär',
> gäb' **mancher** Mann **manchem** Mann manchmal mehr Ehr'. (Sprichwort)
> *If **many a** man knew who **many a** man were*
> *then sometimes, **many a** man would give **many a** man more respect. (proverb)*
>
> Er faßte **manch einen** guten Vorsatz. *He had **many a good** intention.*

solcher / solch ein / ein solcher / so ein / ein so *such, such a*

124   **solcher** means *that kind of* or *such a degree of* and is mostly used in the plural. Usually no adjective follows it.

> Ich will mit **solchen** Menschen nichts zu tun haben. *I won't have anything to do with **such** people.*
> Warum bist du denn immer in **solcher** Eile? *Why are you always in **such** a hurry?*

125   1. More common than the inflected singular forms of **solcher** is the use of **so ein** and **ein so.** But whereas **so ein** *may* be followed by an adjective, **ein so** *must* be followed by an adjective.

> **So ein** (intelligentes) Mädchen weiß, was sie will.   *Such an (intelligent) girl knows what she wants.*
> **Ein so** intelligentes Mädchen weiß, was sie will.

   2. **solch ein** and **ein solcher** are less frequently used than **so ein** and **ein so.** In **solch ein**, only **ein** is declined. In **ein solcher,** *both* words are declined; the second one is declined like a preceded adjective.

   3. The plural of **so ein / ein so** is **so** followed by an adjective with strong endings. [For strong adjective declension, see § 181ff.]

> Ich wußte gar nicht, daß er noch **so** kleine Kinder hat. *I didn't know that his children are still **so** little.*

126   **welcher**   *which*

The interrogative **welcher** has its structural **ein**-equivalent in the phrase **was für ein** *what kind of.* **welcher** and **was für ein** should, however, not be confused with each other.

Welches Auto gehört Ihnen?	Was für ein Auto fahren Sie?
Which car is yours?	*What kind of a car do you drive?*
Das Auto mit der langen Antenne.	Ich fahre einen Sportwagen.
The car with the long antenna.	*I drive a sportscar.*

1. In the phrase, **was für ein, für** does not function as a preposition and has no effect on the case of the following noun. The phrase **was für ein** may be followed by:

Nominative	Was für **ein Auto** ist das? *What **sort of car** is that?*
Accusative	Was für **einen Ball** hast du gekauft? *What **kind of ball** did you buy?*
Dative	In was für **einem Restaurant** eßt ihr? *In what **sort of** restaurant are you going to eat?*

2. **welcher** is not synonymous with **welch ein**, which means *what a*. **welch** may also be used in this way by itself before any adjective. **was für ein** is even more frequently used in such exclamations.

| **Welch ein** Pech! ***What a** pity!* |
| **Welch** schönes Wetter! ***What** great weather!* |
| **Was für ein** herrlicher Schuß! ***What a** magnificent shot!* |

kein *no, not a, not any*

127 1. **kein** is a negative indefinite article. It precedes either a predicate nominative [see § 151] or an object.

Das ist **ein** Magazin.	Das ist **kein** Magazin.
*That's **a** magazine.*	*That's **not a** magazine.*
Ich habe Zeit.	Ich habe **keine** Zeit.
I have time.	*I have **no** time. / I don't have **any** time.*
Sie hat Papier.	Sie hat **kein** Papier.
She has paper.	*She **doesn't** have any paper. / She has **no** paper.*
Sie liest Romane.	Sie liest **keine** Romane.
She reads novels.	*She **doesn't** read novels. / She reads **no** novels.*
Er hat **eine** Katze.	Er hat **keine** Katze.
*He has **a** cat.*	*He has **no** cat. / He **doesn't** have a cat.*

2. **nicht ein** is used occasionally for emphasis and may mean *not one but more than one* and *not a single one.*

Ich sah **nicht einen** Mann, sondern drei hereinkommen. *I did**n't** see **one** but three men come in.*

Ich trinke auch **nicht ein** Glas Wein mehr. *I will **not** drink **another** glass of wine.*

Es fährt auch **nicht ein** Bus heute abend nach Reinheim. *There's **not a single** bus to Reinheim tonight.*

---

3. Nouns in the function of verbal complements which complete the meaning of the main verb can be negated by either **kein** or **nicht.**

Sie spielt Klavier.   Sie spielt **kein** Klavier.
                        Sie spielt **nicht** Klavier.

Use of Articles

128   1. In contrast to English usage, the *definite article* is used in German before abstract nouns when the quality as a whole (as an individualized and familiar concept) is referred to or envisaged.

Die Zeit vergeht. *Time passes.*   Im Heer wächst **die** Angst. *In the army fear is growing.*

BUT In proverbs and set phrases and as a verbal complement, the definite article is omitted.

Zeit ist Geld. (proverb) *Time is money.*   Er hat Angst. *(verbal complement) He is afraid.*

Ich fürchte **das** Alter.
I fear old age.
Alter schützt vor Torheit nicht.
Age is no proof against folly. (proverb)

The use of the definite article with abstract nouns is one of the most elusive parts of German grammar and usage, and some "Sprachgefühl" is essential. If in doubt, it is usually safer to put in the definite article.

NOTE In a direct address, the definite article before an abstract noun has a possessive meaning.

Du mußt versuchen, **die** (=deine) Angst zu überwinden. *You must try to overcome your fear.*

---

2. The definite article is also used with parts of the body or clothing, instead of the possessive **ein**-words.

> Er wäscht sich **die** Hände. *He washes his hands.* [See also § 266]

3. It is used with the words **Mensch** *man,* **Leute** *people,* and relatives.

> **Der** Mensch ist sterblich. *Man is mortal.*

4. It is used before **meist.**

> **Die** meisten meiner Freunde sind in den Ferien. *Most of my friends are on vacation.*

5. The definite article is used before modified proper names.

> **der** junge Goethe   *(the) young Goethe*

6. Other uses of the definite article include: names of streets and names of countries that are feminine.

> Wo ist die Goethestraße? *How do I get to Goethe Street?*
> Die Schweiz liegt in Europa, die Türkei liegt in Kleinasien. [See § 110.2.] *Switzerland is in Europe, Turkey is in Asia Minor.*

7. As in English, the definite article is used with country names in the plural.

> Ich wohne in den Vereinigten Staaten von Amerika. *I live in the United States.*

8. The definite article is also used with many adverbial phrases of time, all times of day, days of the week, names of months, seasons, parts of the day, and daily meals.

> Mit der Zeit geht alles besser. *With time, everything will be better.*
> Am Sonntag kommt Besuch. *Visitors are coming on Sunday.*
> Peter arbeitet spät in der Nacht. *Peter works late at night.*
> Zum Nachtisch essen wir immer Joghurt. *For dessert we always eat yogurt.*
>
> BUT   zu Beginn *in the beginning*   Anfang Januar *at the beginning of January*

NOTE **am = an dem, zum = zu dem**

9. Finally, it is used with certain adverbial phrases of manner and place.

in der Regel *as a rule*	im (= in dem) Bett *in bed*
mit der Hand *by hand*	mit dem Flugzeug *by plane*
vor der Schule *before school*	zum (= zu dem) Beispiel *for example*
in der Schule *in / at school*	zum (= zu dem) Schluß *in conclusion*
ins (= in das) Bett *to bed*	zur (= zu der) Kirche *to church*

BUT In set phrases and as a verbal complement, the definite article is omitted [see
§ 129] where in English, the definite article may be used.

bei Tisch   *at the table, during the meal*
zu Fuß gehen   *to walk, go on foot*
zu Mittag essen   *to have lunch*

CHECK AND PRACTICE

Complete the sentences, using the cues in parentheses.

1. Er wechselt _____ Hemd.   *(He changes his shirt.)*
2. _____ Leben ist schwer.   *(Life is hard.)*
3. Wir lieben _____ Freiheit.   *(We love freedom.)*
4. Er fühlte _____ Liebe für sie.   *(He felt love for her.)*
5. Er ruft _____ Mutter.   *(He calls mother.)*
6. _____ Leute meinten, er sei verrückt.   *(People thought him crazy.)*
7. _____ spielen gerne Fußball.   *(Most boys like to play soccer.)*

129 In contrast to English, the *definite* and *indefinite articles* are *omitted* in German in the following situations:

1. before verbal complements [see § 290.1].

Er fährt Auto. *He drives a car.*	Sie spielt Klavier. *She plays the piano.*
Ich habe Eile. *I'm in a hurry.*	Er hat Fieber. *He has a fever.*

NOTE Nouns used as verbal complements have lost their specificity; they refer not to an
individual object but the general idea expressed in the noun.

Er spielt Tennis.   *He plays tennis.*

COMPARE

Er fährt Auto.	Er fährt das Auto seines Vaters.
NO SPECIFIC CAR	A VERY SPECIFIC CAR
	the car of his father

---

2. before unmodified nouns indicating nationality, profession, religious affiliation, or social status.

Ich bin Deutscher.   *I'm a German.*
Er arbeitet als Maurer.   *He works as a bricklayer.*   BUT Er ist ein guter Maurer. *He is a good bricklayer.*
NOUN
MODIFIER

---

3. The German equivalent of "the Wagners," etc.

Wagners haben Gäste. *The Wagners have guests.*   Wir waren bei Meyers. *We were at the Meyers.*

CHECK AND PRACTICE

Add an article if necessary, and translate the phrases in parentheses.

1. Herr Müller ist (*by car*) gekommen.
2. _____ Mai ist gekommen. (*May has come.*)
3. Ich habe _____ Kopfweh. (*I have a headache.*)
4. Er kannte nicht nur _____ moderne Italien gut, sondern auch _____ alte Rom. (*He knew not only modern Italy well but also old Rome.*)
5. _____ Tschechoslowakei ist ein wunderschönes Land. (*Czechoslovakia is a wonderful country.*)
6. Herr Braun ist _____ Witwer. (*Mr. Brown is a widower.*)
7. Du mußt jetzt (*go to school*).
8. Er ist _____ Mohammedaner. (*He's a Muslim.*)
9. _____ Frühling ist endlich da. (*Spring is finally here.*)
10. _____Mittagessen war heute sehr gut. (*Lunch was very good today.*)
11. Letzten Sonntag war Frau Meyer nicht (*at church*).
12. Er ist _____ Zahnarzt. (*He's a dentist.*)

10. Hans **pflegt** die **Kranken** gut. Er ist ein guter _____.

11. Ursula will **Medizin** studieren. Sie will _____ werden.

12. Ich will niemand **richten**. Dann kannst du nicht _____ werden, Ursula.

13. **Zeichnest** du gern? Ja sehr; ich möchte _____ werden.

14. Herr Kunz **arbeitet** wirklich gut. Ja, er ist ein guter _____.

15. Kann Inge **schwimmen**? Jan, sie ist eine schnelle _____.

16. Du kommst doch nicht aus **Frankfurt**? Doch, ich bin _____.

17. Woher ist Robert, aus **England**? Ja, er ist _____.

18. Warum studierst du **Biologie**? Ich möchte als _____ arbeiten.

19. Seid ihr gut in **Naturwissenschaft**? Ja, wir wollen _____ werden.

In your answer substitute the phrase in bold print with the phrase suggested by the _der_-words in parentheses.

Example

Kann man dieses Fach **an der Hochschule** studieren? Ja, (_each_ . . .)
Ja, man kann dieses Fach an **jeder** Hochschule studieren.

20. **Welche Schülerin** will Medizin studieren? (_that . . . there_)

21. Strengen sich **die Forscher** wirklich an? Ja, (_all_ . . .)

22. Brauchen **alle Krankenpfleger** eine lange Ausbildung? (_no, only some_ . . .)

23. Kennen Sie **diese Musik?** Ja, (_such_ . . .)

24. Wir sollten Sozialwissenschaften studieren! (_which subject?_)

25. Haben Sie auch naturwissenschaftlich ausgebildete **Schüler** hier? Ja, (_we have such_ . . .)

26. **Unsere Gruppe** arbeitet im Freien. (_which_ . . . ?)

27. Suchen Sie **eine Anstellung** als Biologin? Ja, (_I need such_ . . .)

28. Können Sie **diese Situation** verstehen? (_not only this_ . . . _but all_ . . .)

29. Stimmten **die Tatsachen?** (_not all_ . . . _but some_ . . .)

Wem gehört was? Wer gehört zu wem?

Respond with the possessive required by the context.

Example

Wem gehört dieser Laden? Ihnen, Herr Müller? (Ja)
Ja, das ist mein Laden.

30. Wer kommt da? Hans und _____ Chef.

31. Wen hat denn der Chef im Büro angestellt? _____ Sohn und _____ Tochter.

32. Wie hoch ist ihr Stundenlohn? _____ Stundenlohn? Das weiß ich nicht.

33. Darf ich bitte _____ Führerschein sehen, Herr Meyer? Ach, ich habe _____ Führerschein zu Hause gelassen!

34. Wo sind unsere Führerscheine? _____ Führerscheine sind hier, meine Herren.

35. Hast du _____ ganzen Stundenlohn ausgegeben?

36. Kollegen, zeigt doch mal _____ Zeichnungen!

37. Frau Doktor, haben Sie _____ Untersuchungen fertig gemacht?

38. Darf ich in eurem Laden arbeiten? Natürlich, arbeite in _____ Laden!

II. VOCABULARY FOR REVIEW (D AND E TEXTS FROM READER, CHAPTER III)

Verbs

auf·springen a, u (+ sein)	to jump up
aus·sprechen (i) a, o	to express
ein·treten (i) a, e (+ sein)	to enter
ersetzen	to substitute
gebrauchen	to use
überlegen	to ponder
sich vor·stellen	to introduce oneself
wiederholen	to repeat

Nouns

die **Aufmerksamkeit, -en**	attention
der **Auftrag, ̈-e**	order
die **Begegnung, -en**	encounter
die **Bemerkung, -en**	remark
der **Blick, -e**	look
der **Chef, -s**	boss
der **Doppelgänger, -**	double
der **Ersatz (-es)**	substitute
die **Fähigkeit, -en**	capability
die **Haltung, -en**	attitude
die **Herstellung, -en**	production

der **Keller, -**	cellar
der **Knopf, ̈e**	button
der **Maurer, -**	mason
die **Probe, -n**	rehearsal
der **Roman, -e**	novel
der **Schriftsteller, -**	writer
der **Stellvertreter, -**	deputy
die **Versammlung, -en**	meeting
der **Verstand**	reason

ADDITIONAL EXERCISES (D AND E TEXTS FROM THE READER)

Nouns from the active vocabulary, and familiar basic nouns from the texts:

Aufmerksamkeit, Auftrag, Ausdruck, Ausländer, Aussicht, Begegnung, Bemerkung, Blick, Chef, Doppelgänger, Einfluß, Ersatz, Erzählung, Fähigkeit, Freundlichkeit, Gefängnis, Geschwindigkeit, Haltung, Herstellung, Höhe, Keller, Knopf, Masse, Maurer, Probe, Roman, Schriftsteller, Schritt, Stellvertreter, Störung, Versammlung, Verstand, Wesen, Zeile, Theater, Zeichen, Krieg, Soldat, Jahr, Werk, Erfolg, Mensch, Heimat, Arbeiter, Schüler, Leben, Buch, Sprache, Zeit, Fuß, Alter, Mitte, Gesicht, Hand, Sessel, Besuch, Stimme, Geschichte, Maschine, Fabrik, Geheimnis, Herz, Strom, Beispiel, Gespräch, Wetter, Film, Sport, Geschäft, Person, Grund, Zimmer, Herr, Maß, Tat, Wort, Kino, Haus, Name, Raum, Wand, Not, Brief, Stern, Gefahr.

1. **Are there any nouns which must be masculine or neuter because of their meaning? Read them and give their plurals.**
2. **Are there any nouns which must be feminine because of their form? Read them and give the plural which applies to them all.**
3. **Are there any nouns which must be neuter because of their form? Check your text for correctness. Give their plurals.**
4. **Use familiar noun suffixes to make nouns of the following words. Check your text or vocabulary for the correct forms.**
   aufmerksam, begegnen, bemerken, erzählen, fähig, freundlich, gefangen, geheim, geschwind, halten, herstellen, stören, überlegen, vertreten, versammeln, vorstellen, wiederholen.
5. **Using no suffixes, make nouns from the following verbs. Check text or vocabulary for correctness, then give the articles and the plurals.**
   auftragen, ausdrücken, blicken, ersetzen, schreiten, verstehen, leben, besuchen.

6. **Give the definite article for each noun (pay attention to the suffixes).**
Aufmerksamkeit, Ausländer, Begegnung, Bemerkung, Denker, Doppelgänger, Erzählung, Fähigkeit, Freundlichkeit, Gefängnis, Geschwindigkeit, Haltung, Herstellung, Höhe, Keller, Masse, Maurer, Probe, Schriftsteller, Stellvertreter, Störung, Versammlung, Zeile, Theater, Zeichen, Arbeiter, Schüler, Leben, Sprache, Alter, Mitte, Sessel, Stimme, Geschichte, Maschine, Fabrik, Geheimnis, Wetter, Zimmer.

Konversation über Literatur

Respond with any *der*-word(s) fitting the context.

Example

Warum springt diese Sekretärin immer auf?
Alle Sekretärinnen springen auf, wenn Besucher kommen.

7. Ein Roman war sehr wichtig für mich. Interessant, _____ Roman denn?

8. Denken Sie oft über Literatur nach? Ja, besonders über _____ Roman hier!

9. Sind die Erzählungen dieses Schriftstellers beliebt? Ja, aber nur _____ Erzählungen.

10. Er erzählt spannend. Ja, _____ Fähigkeit erklärt seinen Erfolg.

11. Was hat Hans gegen die Literatur? Oh, er findet _____ Schriftsteller zu lang und _____ Schriftsteller zu kurz, und er sagt, _____ Autoren sind zu langweilig für ihn.

12. Erzählen Sie von den Autoren! _____ Autor mögen Sie? Haben _____ Autoren die gleichen Fähigkeiten? Mit _____ Autor arbeiten Sie gern zusammen? Ist _____ alte Mann ein beliebter Autor? Ich habe gehört, daß _____ Schriftsteller nicht nett sind. _____ Gruppe von Autoren ist wohl besser als _____ Gruppen?

13. Dieser Schriftsteller ist hundert Jahre alt geworden. Wirklich? _____ langes Leben!

14. Gibt es viele Maurer, die Romane lesen? Bei _____ Maurern kann man viele Bücher finden. Z. B. bei _____ Maurer, der sich gerade vorgestellt hat.

15. Sie sagen, alle Autoren gebrauchen einen Stellvertreter? Nein, nicht _____ Autoren, aber _____ Autoren kann man ersetzen.

16. Was haben Sie da gesagt? Bitte wiederholen Sie _____ Bemerkung!

17. Sehen Sie mich nicht so an! _____ Blicke erschrecken mich.

18. Was sagen Sie, wenn Sie die vielen Menschen sehen? _____ Masse!

19. Alle Autoren hier haben Doppelgänger. Wirklich, _____ Autor hat einen?

Im Büro

Respond with the possessive required by the context.

Example

Können Sie **Ihre** Bemerkungen wiederholen, **Herr Kühn**?
Ich wiederhole **meine** Bemerkungen nie!

20. Wie fanden Sie die Versammlung heute morgen? _____ Ende fand ich sehr schlecht.

21. Ich kann nicht so schnell gehen wie mein Chef. _____ Schritte sind zu lang.

22. Wie heißt deine Chefin? _____ Chefin heißt Müller.

23. Kommt deine Chefin heute ins Büro? Nein, sie sendet _____ Stellvertreter.

24. Wo habt ihr euren Verstand gelassen? _____ Verstand?

25. Bitte treten Sie ein! In _____ Büro, Frau Seifert?

26. Herr Müller, Sie sind schon zurück? _____ Versammlung hat wohl nicht so lange gedauert?

27. Wer ist dieser Mann? _____ Blick ist so unfreundlich.

28. Kollegen, ich erwarte jetzt _____ Aufmerksamkeit.

29. Kennen Sie mich noch? Natürlich, ich erinnere mich gut an _____ Begegnung.

NOUNS AND
ARTICLES (Part Two)

DECLENSION OF ARTICLES AND NOUNS

Function of Case in German

130   The *case* of a German noun *indicates its function* in the sentence, unlike English, where the function of nouns is indicated by the noun's position in the sentence. Notice that because of case, German word order is freer than in English.

SUBJECT (AGENT) **Nominative**	PREDICATE (ACTION) **Verb**		OBJECT OF ACTION **Accusative**	
Der Junge	ißt	immer	den Nachtisch,	aber nie das Gemüse.
Den Nachtisch OBJECT OF ACTION **Accusative**	ißt PREDICATE (ACTION) **Verb**		der Junge SUBJECT (AGENT) **Nominative**	immer, aber nie das Gemüse.
The boy always eats the dessert, but never the vegetables.				

131   German has *four cases*:   NOMINATIVE
                                            ACCUSATIVE
                                            DATIVE
                                            GENITIVE

Case, like gender, is primarily reflected in the endings of the articles and adjectives which accompany most nouns.

Declension of Articles

132   The declension of the **der**-words and of the **ein**-words is identical except in three instances: NOMINATIVE MASCULINE AND NEUTER
                                ACCUSATIVE   NEUTER.

ein, of course, does *not* exist in the *plural*. The endings of the possessive **ein**-words (**mein**, etc.) correspond to the endings of **kein**. [For a list of articles, see § 118]

	SINGULAR			PLURAL
	MASCULINE	**FEMININE**	**NEUTER**	
Nominative	der	die	das	die
	dieser	diese	dieses	diese
	ein☐	eine	ein☐	
	kein☐	keine	kein☐	keine
Accusative	den	die	das	die
	diesen	diese	dieses	diese
	einen	eine	ein☐	
	keinen	keine	kein☐	keine
Dative	dem	der	dem	den
	diesem	dieser	diesem	diesen
	einem	einer	einem	
	keinem	keiner	keinem	keinen
Genitive	des	der	des	der
	dieses	dieser	dieses	dieser
	eines	einer	eines	
	keines	keiner	keines	keiner

NOTE The **-er** of **euer** and **unser** is often reduced to **-r** when an ending is added.

> Wo ist eu(e)re Wohnung? Uns(e)re Wohnung ist gleich um die Ecke.
> *Where is your apartment? Our apartment is just around the corner.*

REMEMBER Depending on the gender of the noun it modifies, the German equivalent of *its* is **sein-** or **ihr-**.

> Der Fehler und **seine** Folge sind zum Glück unbedeutend.
> *The mistake and **its** consequence are fortunately of no importance.*
> Die Maschine und **ihr** Erfinder kommen zur Messe.
> *The machine and **its** inventor will come to the fair.*

CHECK AND PRACTICE

Give the case endings. The gender is given in parentheses.

NOMINATIVE

1. Mein___ Wagen fährt schnell. (der)   2. Unser___ Wohnung ist alt. (die)

ACCUSATIVE

3. Paul liest dein___ Roman. (der)
5. Sie liebt ihr___ Kind. (das)

4. Peter traf sein___ Freunde. (der)
6. Wir sahen ihr___ Mutter. (die)

DATIVE (+ ACCUSATIVE)

7. Renate schenkt ihr___ Freund ihr___ Bild. (der)(das)
8. Wir gaben unser___ Lehrerin unser___ Hausaufgaben. (die)(die)

GENITIVE

9. Das Zimmer mein___ Bruders ist klein. (der)
10. Das Dach sein___ Hütte ist kaputt. (die)
11. Der Titel d___ Novelle ist lang. (die)
12. Der Turm d___ Schlosses ist hoch. (das)

Noun Declension

TYPES

133   The dictionary entries for German nouns usually include the gender and *three forms*, from which all other forms can be derived.

German nouns belong to one of four declension classes: STRONG
WEAK
MIXED
SPECIAL

and the three basic forms indicate which declension a noun belongs to.

STRONG NOUN DECLENSION

Reference Charts

134

Dictionary Entry	**Buch,**	-(e)s,	¨-er,	n
	NOMINATIVE SINGULAR	GENITIVE Buch**(e)s** SINGULAR	NOMINATIVE Bücher PLURAL	GENDER **das** Buch

135 In the strong noun declension:

1. The dative masculine and neuter of monosyllables may add **e** in the singular. In present-day German, however, it is generally omitted.

2. The dative plural adds **n** to all nouns (**den Kindern**) unless the plural ends in **-n** (e.g., **die Betten,** nominative plural; **den Betten,** dative plural).

3. Masculine and neuter nouns add **s** in the genitive singular (e.g., **des Kinds**); the monosyllables may add **s** or **es. es** is mandatory with all nouns that end in **s, ß, z, x** (e.g., **des Glases, des Grußes, des Gesetzes, des Reflexes**).

4. Feminine nouns *never* take an ending in the singular.

	SINGULAR		
	MASCULINE	**FEMININE**	**NEUTER**
Nominative	der Stuhl	die Bank	das Bild
Accusative	den Stuhl	die Bank	das Bild
Dative	dem Stuhl**(e)**	der Bank	dem Bild**(e)**
Genitive	des Stuhl**(e)s**	der Bank	des Bild**(e)s**

	PLURAL		
	MASCULINE	**FEMININE**	**NEUTER**
Nominative	die Stühle	die Bänke	die Bilder
Accusative	die Stühle	die Bänke	die Bilder
Dative	den Stühle**n**	den Bänke**n**	den Bilder**n**
Genitive	der Stühle	der Bänke	der Bilder

As you see, there are really only *two* cases with an ending:
GENITIVE SINGULAR   FOR MASCULINE AND NEUTER NOUNS
DATIVE PLURAL   FOR ALL NOUNS

The only forms you have to learn are the *plural forms.* The following general survey may be an aid.

Plural Formation

Plural forms of strong nouns of ONE syllable

136 1. The majority of masculine, and a few feminine nouns, and some neuter nouns add **-e.**

2. Most neuter nouns, and a few masculine nouns (no feminine nouns), and the polysyllabic nouns ending in **-tum** add **-er.**

MASCULINE	FEMININE	NEUTER
-e *or sometimes* **·e**	**-e** *or if possible* **·e**	**-e**
der Sohn, ·e der Tag, -e *also compounds whose second element* *has only one syllable, e.g.,* der Blei**stift**, -e	die Nacht, ·e die Luft, ·e die Maus, ·e	das Jahr, -e das Ding, -e das Stück, -e
-er *or if possible* **·er**		**-er** *or if possible* **·er**
der Mann, ·er der Wald, ·er der Reichtum, ·er		das Kind, -er das Buch, ·er das Fürstentum, ·er

Plural forms of strong nouns of TWO or MORE syllables

137 1. Most masculine and neuter nouns ending in **-(e)n, -el, -er**; two feminine nouns ending in **-er**; and neuter nouns with the endings **-chen** and **-lein** *add no* ending.

2. Most other masculine and neuter nouns add **-e** (often nouns of foreign origin with end stress); some masculine nouns also add umlaut. Nouns ending in **-nis** double the **s** when the plural **e** is added. [For feminine nouns, see § 140.1.]

	MASCULINE	FEMININE	NEUTER
	— *or sometimes* ··	··	— *or sometimes* ··
-(e)n **-el** **-er**	der Wagen, — der Mantel, ·· der Vater, ·· der Amerikaner, —	die Mutter, ·· die Tochter, ··	das Leben, — das Viertel, — das Fenster, — das Kloster, ··
	EXCEPTIONS		

<table>
<tr><td colspan="4" align="center">EXCEPTIONS
der Bauer, -n [belongs to § 140 and § 141]
der Vetter, -n [belongs to § 141]</td></tr>
</table>

	MASCULINE	FEMININE	NEUTER
-chen **-lein**			das Mädchen, — das Fräulein, —
	-e *or sometimes* **·e**		**-e**
	der Anzug, ·e der Versuch, -e der Offizier, -e		das Paket, -e das Problem, -e das Gefängnis, -se

CHECK AND PRACTICE

Give the plural forms.

1. der Morgen	2. der Freund	3. der Apfel	4. die Nuß	5. das Land
6. das Gewitter	7. das Papier	8. der Onkel	9. der Bahnhof	10. das Dach
11. der Bruder	12. das Stück	13. die Gans	14. das Haus	15. die Hand

WEAK NOUN DECLENSION

138

Dictionary Entry	**Frau,**	—,	**-en,**	**f**
	NOMINATIVE SINGULAR	GENITIVE Frau SINGULAR	NOMINATIVE Frau**en** PLURAL	GENDER **die** Frau

139 Because of the predominance of the ending **-n**, nouns of the weak declension are also often called **N**-nouns.

SINGULAR	MASCULINE	FEMININE
Nominative	der Herr	die Dame
Accusative	den Her**rn**	die Dame
Dative	dem Her**rn**	der Dame
Genitive	des Her**rn**	der Dame

PLURAL	MASCULINE	FEMININE
Nominative	die Her**ren**	die Dame**n**
Accusative	die Her**ren**	die Dame**n**
Dative	den Her**ren**	den Dame**n**
Genitive	der Her**ren**	der Dame**n**

140 This group includes:

1. almost all polysyllabic feminine nouns (nouns with the ending **-in** have double **n** in the plural); a few monosyllabics (e.g., **die Frau**);

2. a few masculine nouns (a few monosyllabics); nouns ending in an unstressed **-e**; many nouns of foreign origin accented on the last syllable.

FEMININE NOUNS	MASCULINE NOUNS		
die Kirche, -n *church*	der Mensch, -en *man*	der Junge, -en *boy*	der Planét, -en *planet*
die Frau, -en *woman*	der Herr, -en *gentleman*	der Hirte, -n *shepherd*	der Kommandánt, -en *commandánt*
die Ärztin, -nen *female doctor*	der Graf, -en *count*	der Franzose, -en *Frenchman*	der Student, -en *student*

[For adjectival nouns, see § 221ff.]

CHECK AND PRACTICE

Give the case and/or plural endings, as needed.

1. Die Mensch___ beherrschen die Welt. (N)
2. Herr Schulz half seinem Kollege___ bei der Abeit. (D)
3. Der Mann ging mit seiner Frau___ spazieren. (D)
4. Viele Soldat___ starben im letzten Krieg. (N)
5. Fräulein Müller gab den Herr___ einen Brief von Herr___ Meyer. (D)
6. Paul stellte seinen Freund auf die Probe___. (A)
7. Frau Schmidt hat eine schöne Stimme___. (A)
8. Der Bus hatte Platz für 40 Person___. (A)
9. Die Tourist___ kauften viele Geschenke ein. (N)
10. Die Mutter las ihrem Junge___ eine Geschichte vor. (D)

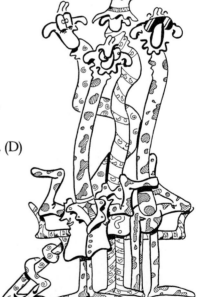

MIXED NOUN DECLENSION

141 1. In one small group of nouns which includes *no feminine nouns*, the singular forms use the strong declension, while the plural forms use the weak declension.

	SINGULAR (strong)		PLURAL (weak)	
	MASCULINE	**NEUTER**	**MASCULINE**	**NEUTER**
Nominative	der Motor	das Bett	die Moroten	die Betten
Accusative	den Motor	das Bett	die Motoren	die Betten
Dative	dem Motor	dem Bett	den Motoren	den Betten
Genitive	des Motors	des Betts	der Motoren	der Betten

2. Some nouns belong to the weak declension as well as to the mixed declension, e.g., **der Bauer, -n/-s, -n, der Nachbar,-n/-s, -n.**

142 In a second even smaller group of nouns which includes many masculine nouns ending in **-e** and a few neuter nouns (but *no feminine nouns*), all forms *but the genitive singular* use the weak declension. *The genitive singular adds the strong* **-s** *ending to the weak* **-n** *ending.*

	SINGULAR		PLURAL	
Nominative	der Name	das Herz	die Namen	die Herzen
Accusative	den Namen	das Herz	die Namen	die Herzen
Dative	dem Namen	dem Herzen	den Namen	den Herzen
Genitive	des Namens	des Herzens	der Namen	der Herzen

CHECK AND PRACTICE

Add the correct endings, using the information given in parentheses.

1. Wieviele Staat___ gibt es auf der Welt? (A) (der —, -(e)s, -en)
2. Die Aktentasche des Doktor___ ist immer sehr schwer. (G) (der —, -s, -en)
3. Er kannte alle Buchstabe___ des griechischen Alphabets. (A) (der —, -ns/-n, -n)
4. Man soll dem Jungen seinen Wille___ lassen. (A) (der —, -ns, -n)
5. Seines Glaube___ wegen war er ins Gefängnis gekommen. (G) (der —, -ns, -n)

6. Schließe deine Auge___ und schlafe jetzt. (A) (das —, -s, -n)

7. Der Kragen seines Hemd___ ist besonders schmutzig. (G) (das —, -(e)s, -en)

8. Die Kinder lagen noch um neun Uhr in ihren Bett___. (D) (das —, -(e)s, -en)

9. Die Ohr___ eines Hasen nennt man Löffel. (A) (das —, -(e)s, -en)

10. Am Ufer des See___ saßen viele Angler. (G) (der —, -s, -n)

11. Sie saß in Gedanke___ versunken am Schreibtisch. (A) (der —, -ns, -en)

12. Ihr flogen alle Herz___ der Zuhörer zu. (N) (das —, -ens, -en)

13. Anstatt des Schmerz___ fühlte er nur Glück. (G) (der —, -es, -en)

SPECIAL NOUN DECLENSION

143 The nouns in this group — primarily foreign words, e.g., **das Restaurant** and names, e.g., **die Leica** (a brand name which became a generic name for cameras) — follow the strong declension in the singular but have an **-s** ending in all plural cases.

	SINGULAR			PLURAL		
	MASCULINE	**FEMININE**	**NEUTER**	**MASCULINE**	**FEMININE**	**NEUTER**
Nominative	der Park	die Kamera	das Auto	die Parks	die Kameras	die Autos
Accusative	den Park	die Kamera	das Auto	die Parks	die Kameras	die Autos
Dative	dem Park	der Kamera	dem Auto	den Parks	den Kameras	den Autos
Genitive	des Parks	der Kamera	des Autos	der Parks	der Kameras	der Autos

NOUN DECLENSION VARIATIONS

144 Some nouns of foreign origins have special plurals:

SINGULAR	PLURAL	SINGULAR	PLURAL
der Rhythmus	die Rhythmen	das Verb	die Verben
der Hymnus	die Hymnen	das Museum	die Museen
der Virus	die Viren	das Zentrum	die Zentren
das Drama	die Dramen	das Studium	die Studien
das Epos	die Epen	das Thema	die Themen
		das Datum	die Daten

145 Some nouns occur only in the singular:

der Ärger	die Polizei	das Gold	
der Zorn	die Feuerwehr	das Silber	
	die Wut	das Blei	
	die Milch	das Vieh	NO PLURAL
	die Butter	das Wild	
	die Mathematik		
	die Politik		
	die Thematik		

146 Some nouns occur only in the plural:

	die Eltern
	die Ferien
NO SINGULAR	die Geschwister
	die Leute
	die Kosten

147 If used as a modifier to another noun, one feminine noun **die Mark** and all masculine and neuter terms of weight, measure, and currency use the singular form in the plural. [See also § 168.2.]

> Ein Pfund Butter kostet 1,50 DM, zwei Pfund Margarine kosten aber nur 2,50 DM.

148 Nouns ending in **-mann** form their plural with **-leute** when the noun refers to a profession or rank; otherwise, they form their plural with **-männer**. Some nouns can have either plural form, depending on whether or not the profession is emphasized (e.g., the plural **Dienstmänner** refers to a group of individuals; **Dienstleute** refers to the profession as such).

SINGULAR	PLURAL	
der Kaufmann	die Kaufleute	*businessman*
der Hauptmann	die Hauptleute	*captain*
der Edelmann	die Edelleute	*noble(man)*
der Schneemann	die Schneemänner	*snowman*
der Hampelmann	die Hampelmänner	*jumping jack*
der Staatsmann	die Staatsmänner	*statesman*
der Ehemann	die Ehemänner	*husband*
	BUT die Eheleute = das Ehepaar *married couple (husband and wife)*	
der Feuerwehrmann	die Feuerwehrleute OR die Feuerwehrmänner *fire fighter*	

149   Some nouns look alike in the nominative singular, but have different genders and usually vastly different meanings. These nouns tend to form different plurals and belong to different declension categories:

der **Band,** -es, ⸚e	*volume*	der **Leiter,** -s, -	*leader*
das **Band,** -es, ⸚er	*ribbon*	die **Leiter,** -, -n	*ladder*
der **Erbe,** -n, -n	*heir*	der **See,** -s, -n	*lake*
das **Erbe,** -s	*inheritance*	die **See,** -, -n	*sea*
der **Gehalt,** -(e)s, -e	*content*	der **Tau,** -(e)s	*dew*
das **Gehalt,** -(e)s, ⸚er	*salary*	das **Tau,** -(e)s, -e	*rope*
der **Heide,** -n, -n	*heathen*	der **Teil,** -(e)s, -e	*part*
die **Heide,** -, -n	*heath, heather*	das **Teil,** -(e)s, -e	*part*
der **Hut,** -(e)s, ⸚e	*hat*	der **Tor,** -en, -en	*fool*
die **Hut,**	*guard*	das **Tor,** -(e)s, -e	*gate*
der **Kunde,** -n, -n	*customer*	das **Wort,** -(e)s, ⸚er	*word (taken singly)*
die **Kunde,** -, -n	*news*	das **Wort,** -(e)s, -e	*word (meaning units)*

Ein **Wörter**buch *is a list of individual, isolated words.*
Er sagte ein paar nette **Worte**. *He said a few nice words.* (*Words* here mean *remarks.*)

CHECK AND PRACTICE

Add the correct case endings.

1. Herr Meyer war Mitglied in vielen Klub___. (D)
2. In dieser Stadt gibt es viele Hotel___. (N)
3. Dic Firma hatte Büro___ in der ganzen Stadt. (A)
4. Wieviele Chef___ hattest du schon? (A)
5. Hast du die unregelmäßigen Verb___ gelernt? (A)
6. Er sollte ein Kilogramm___ Zucker und fünf Kilogramm___ Mehl kaufen. (A)

CASE USAGE

Nominative

150 The *subject* of a sentence is in the nominative case. The subject denotes the actor or initiator of the action.

SUBJECT
Nominative

Der Junge ißt. **The boy** *is eating.*

---

151 The verbs **sein, werden, bleiben,** and **heißen** are incomplete as utterances; therefore, they need a complement. If this complement is a noun, it is in the nominative. It is called a *predicate nominative.*

SUBJECT Nominative		**Predicate** Nominative	
Der Junge	ist	**ein guter Schüler.**	*The boy is **a good student.***
Paula	wird	**Lehrerin.**	*Paula will become a **teacher.***
Die Atombombe	bleibt	**eine Gefahr.**	*The atomic bomb remains **a danger.***
Der Professor	heißt	**Herr Meyer.**	*The professor is called **Mr. Meyer.***

---

152 When two things are compared using **wie** or **als**, they are both the subject, usually, and can be interchanged in position. Consequently, both nouns are in the nominative.

Nominative		**Nominative**	
Sie	singt wie	**eine Nachtigall.**	*She sings like **a nightingale.***

CHECK AND PRACTICE
Complete the sentences with nominatives, as cued.

1. _____ macht ihre Hausaufgaben. (das Mädchen)
2. Er ist _____. (ein alter Kunde)
3. Er sieht aus wie _____. (ein netter Mann)
4. Sie wird _____. (die Ärztin) [See § 129.2]
5. Er will _____ werden. (ein guter Krankenpfleger)
6. Das bleibt _____. (der beste Beruf)

Accusative

ACCUSATIVE FOR DIRECT OBJECT

153 The accusative case is used after transitive verbs, which require a *direct object*. It denotes a person or thing acted upon. The direct object of a sentence answers the question "whom?" or "what?"

	DIRECT OBJECT **Accusative**
Der Junge ißt	**den Kuchen.**

154 *Double accusative* constructions occur after **nennen, heißen** *to call someone something,* **finden** *to consider, think someone something* as well as **lehren** *to teach* and **kosten** *to cost.* Word order is fixed in this situation: the accusative of the person (whom?) is followed by the accusative of the thing (what?).

		ACCUSATIVE 1	**ACCUSATIVE 2**	
Peter	nannte hieß fand	seinen Freund	einen Dummkopf.	*Peter called his friend a fool.* *Peter thought his friend a fool.*
Sie	lehrte	den Jungen	viele Lieder.	*She taught the boy many songs.*
Es	kostete	den König	den Kopf.	*It cost the king his head.*

155 After **bitten** and **fragen,** double accusative constructions are possible *only when the object of the request is expressed in general terms;* otherwise, for specific requests a preposition is required (e.g., **um, nach**).

	ACCUSATIVE OF PERSON	ACCUSATIVE OF THING	
Er bat	ihn	etwas.	*He asked him for something.*
Er fragte	ihn	etwas.	*He asked him something.*
Darf ich	Sie	um das Salz bitten?	*Please, pass the salt.* *(May I ask you for the salt.)*
Sie fragte	ihn	nach seinem letzten Roman.	*She asked him about his last novel.*

CHECK AND PRACTICE

Complete the sentences with accusatives, as cued.

1. Sie sah gestern _____. (ein Marsmensch)
2. Wir nannten _____ _____. (der Chef / ein Meister des Erfolgs)

3. Unser Nachbar hat _____. (ein Hund)

4. Die Studenten machten _____. (die Schlußprüfung)

ACCUSATIVE IN ADVERBIAL PHRASES

156   The accusative is used in certain adverbial phrases:

1. to express definite time and duration; [For indefinite time, see § 169]

Nächsten Samstag fahren wir nach Bonn. *Next Saturday, we'll go to Bonn.*
Sie blieb **den ganzen Tag** zu Hause. *She stayed home **all day.***

---

2. to denote weight, measure, value, space traversed, extent, especially with such adjectives as **breit** *wide*, **dick** *thick*, **hoch** *high*, **lang** *long*, and **tief** *deep*.

Der Graben ist **einen Meter** tief. *The trench is **one meter** deep.*

ACCUSATIVE AFTER CERTAIN PARTS OF SPEECH

157   Certain prepositions govern the accusative [See § 349ff. and § 413].

158   Certain adjectives used as verbal complements are preceded by an accusative.

---

gewohnt	Er ist **das kalte Wasser** nicht **gewohnt.**
to be used to	*He is **not used to the cold water.***
los	Endlich bin ich **diese Krankheit los.**
to be rid of	*I'm finally **rid of this disease.***
wert	Das Auto ist **diesen Preis wert.**
to be worth	*The car is **worth its price.***
	(= *to have a certain [money] value*) [For another meaning of **wert**, see § 173]

CHECK AND PRACTICE

Give the correct case of the adverbial phrases.

1. Inge putzt _____ das Wohnzimmer. (jeder Tag)

2. Die Lehrerin unterrichtet _____ in diesem Zimmer. (jede Woche)

3. Wir bleiben _____ in München. (dieser Montag)

4. Sie war _____ im Kino. (jeder Abend)

5. Paul und Peter wohnen _____ weit von hier. (ein Kilometer)

6. Hans ist _____ gewohnt. (dieser Ärger)

7. Der Sack wog _____. (ein Zentner)

8. Jetzt seid ihr _____ sicherlich los. (der Auftrag)

9. Diese Arbeit ist _____ wert. (kein Pfennig)

Dative

DATIVE FOR INDIRECT OBJECT

159   The dative is used to express the *indirect object*, the person (or thing)

1. to whom something is done: English often (but not always) supplies "to";

2. to whom the action refers; English usually supplies "for" (in some instances, a paraphrase with **für** followed by the accusative is also possible in German).

INDIRECT OBJECT
Dative

| Sie gibt | **ihrem Bruder** | ein Buch. | *She gives* | ***her brother*** *a book.* |
| | | | *She gives the book* | ***to her brother.*** |

Er trägt **seiner Frau** den Koffer. *He carries the suitcase **for his wife**.*
Dieser Tag ist **mir** viel zu kalt. *Today is much too cold **for me**.*

ETHICAL DATIVE

160   The dative always emphasizes the party who is (or should be) interested in the action. In spoken German, this function is especially obvious in impersonal constructions such as **Mir ist kalt** *I am cold* and in imperatives. The dative in imperatives states explicitly the person most interested in the result of the order. This dative is called the dative of interest or "ethical" dative.

Mir ist schlecht. *I don't feel well.*
Macht **mir** aber keinen Lärm! *Don't make any noise.*

---

161   In the same way, a possessive adjective might be, and usually is, replaced by a dative. This is especially true in sentences where the direct objects are part of the body or articles of clothing. [See § 266]

> Hast du **mein** Frühstück gemacht? *Did you prepare breakfast **for me**?*
> Hast du **mir** das Frühstück gemacht?

CHECK AND PRACTICE

Put the words in parentheses into the dative.

1. Ich gebe _____ ein Geschenk. (mein Mann)
2. Sie erzählt _____ die Geschichte. (ihre Mutter)
3. Er trägt _____ das Gepäck. (das Mädchen)
4. Schreibst du _____ einen Brief? (dein Vater)

Translate.

5. How are you?
6. Thank you, I am fine.

VERBS GOVERNING THE DATIVE

162   A small number of verbs always govern a dative object.

Unfortunately, not all English verbs give a hint that the equivalent German verbs require the dative case. For this reason, you have to memorize which verbs take the dative in German. You might think in terms of to give . . . to:
antworten *to give an answer to*

antworten *to answer*	gehorchen *to obey*	schmeicheln *to flatter*
begegnen *to meet*	gelingen *to succeed*	trauen *to trust*
danken *to thank*	glauben *to believe*	vergeben *to forgive*
dienen *to serve*	gleichen *to be like*	verzeihen *to forgive*
drohen *to threaten*	gratulieren *to congratulate*	weh tun *to hurt*
einfallen *to occur to one's mind*	helfen *to help*	widersprechen *to contradict*
entfliehen *to flee (from)*	imponieren *to impress*	winken *to wave to*
folgen *to follow*	mißfallen *to displease*	zustimmen *to agree with*
gefallen *to please*	mißtrauen *to mistrust*	zuvorkommen *to forestall*
gehören *to belong to*	schaden *to harm*	

Der Schüler **antwortete dem Lehrer.** *The student **answered the teacher.***

DATIVE AFTER OTHER PARTS OF SPEECH

163   Certain prepositions govern the dative. [See § 371 and § 413]

164 Some adjectives also govern the dative, in which case the dative form precedes the adjective.

ähnlich	*similar*	dankbar	*grateful*	schädlich	*harmful*
angenehm	*pleasant*	fremd	*unfamiliar*	treu	*loyal*
bekannt	*known*	gleich	*same*	unheimlich	*mysterious*
benachbart	*contiguous*	gleichgültig	*indifferent, of no importance*	zuwider	*contrary*
böse	*angry at*	parallel	*parallel*		

Der Mann ist **mir** gleichgültig.	*The man means nothing to **me.***
	I am indifferent to the man.

CHECK AND PRACTICE

Add the correct case endings.

1. Paul begegnete sein___ Freund in der Stadt.
2. Die Straße läuft d___ Fluß parallel. (*runs parallel to*)
3. Die Bilder gefallen d___ Lehrer nicht. (*literally: are not pleasing to*)
4. Plötzlich fiel d___ Frau der Name wieder ein.
5. Du hast dein___ Bruder weh getan.
6. Dieses Buch gehört ein___ Kollege___.
7. Wir müssen unser___ Professor antworten.
8. Ich glaube d___ Autor nicht.
9. Kannst du d___ Leute___ verzeihen?
10. Das Mädchen sieht ihr___ Schwester ähnlich.
11. Alle Arbeiter waren d___ Chef dankbar.

Genitive

GENITIVE AS AN INDICATOR FOR POSSESSION

165 1. The basic function of the genitive case is to *indicate possession*. A noun or pronoun in the genitive case is governed by another noun, which is the thing possessed. For example:

Peters Auto *Peter's car*	das Auto **meines Vaters** *my father's car*

2. The rules for word order are:

The genitive a. of proper names precedes the thing possessed;
                 b. of other nouns usually follows the thing possessed.

166   The genitive **-s** is added to proper names regardless of gender. When the proper name ends in an **s**-sound (**s, ß, z, tz**) no **-s** is added to the name. The omission is indicated by an apostrophe.

> Peter**s** Onkel   Maria**s** Vater   Thomas' Tante

167   Often the German uses the genitive where a phrase with "of" is used in English.

> der Titel **meines Romans**   *the title **of my novel***

OMISSION OF GENITIVE (GERMAN VERSUS ENGLISH)

168   In contrast to English:

1. proper names and names of months which are preceded by "of" in English are *not* in the genitive but in the same case as the nouns governing them;

> | | |
> |---|---|
> | die Stadt München | *the city of Munich* |
> | Anfang Januar | *beginning of January* |
> | Ende April | *end of April* |

2. nouns of weight and measure do not govern the genitive. [See also § 147]

> | | |
> |---|---|
> | ein Glas Wein | *a glass of wine* |
> | eine Tasse Kaffee | *a cup of coffee* |
> | drei Stunden Unterricht | *three hours of instruction* |

GENITIVE DENOTING INDEFINITE TIME

169   The genitive is also used for expressions of indefinite time.

> | | |
> |---|---|
> | **eines Tages** | *one day/someday* |
> | **eines Abends** | *one evening* |
> | **eines schönen Morgens** | *one beautiful morning* |
> | **eines Nachts** | *one night* (parallel construction to masculine genitive with **-s**). (**Nacht** is the only feminine noun in this group. [For gender, see § 108.2]). |

CHECK AND PRACTICE

Give the genitive.

1. Die Sprache (*of my mother*) habe ich nie gelernt. (meine Mutter)
2. Das Studierzimmer (*of my father*) ist klein. (mein Vater)
3. (*Mr. Meyer's*) Haus liegt im Grünen. (Herr Meyer)
4. Sie kam Mitte (*of February*). (Februar)
5. Herr Müller kaufte (*a pound of butter*). (ein Pfund) (die Butter)
6. Der Name (*of our town*) kommt aus dem Lateinischen. (unsere Stadt)
7. Das Ende (*of my novel*) war ganz toll. (der Roman)
8. Die Bewegungen (*of the doll*) waren steif. (die Puppe)
9. (*One day*) kam der Briefträger und brachte ein großes Paket. (ein Tag)

GENITIVE AFTER CERTAIN PARTS OF SPEECH

170   The genitive is used after certain prepositions. [See § 442ff.]

171   A few verbs in German require a genitive object. Because many of these verbs have an archaic or poetic ring to them, they are avoided in everyday speech. Some of them have an alternate form with a fixed preposition which is used instead (e.g., **sich entsinnen an** instead of **sich entsinnen; sich erinnern an** instead of **sich erinnern**).

sich jemandes (einer Sache) annehmen *to take care of*	sich erbarmen *to take pity on someone*
sich bedienen *to help oneself*	sich erinnern *to remember*
bedürfen *to need*	gedenken *to think of*
sich befleißigen *to apply oneself to*	gewahr werden *to catch sight of*
sich bemächtigen *to get hold of*	sich rühmen *to boast of*
sich enthalten *to refrain from*	sich schämen *to be ashamed of*
sich entsinnen *to remember*	sich vergewissern *to make sure of*

Sie rühmt sich immer ihrer Geschicklichkeit beim Skilaufen. *She always boasts of her skiing skills.*
Gedenke meiner. *Think of me. (more commonly:* Denke an mich.)
Erbarme dich unser. *Have mercy on us. (used in prayers)*

172   Genitives are found with an adverbial function (of manner), and in a few set phrases.

Sie reisten immer **zweiter Klasse**. *They always traveled **second class**.*
Ich bin **derselben Meinung**. *I'm **of the same opinion**.*

sich seines Lebens freuen *to enjoy one's life*
seines Amtes walten *to perform one's functions*
der Ruhe pflegen *to take a rest*

173 Certain adjectives govern the genitive. Note that the phrase in the genitive precedes the adjective. The most common such adjectives are:

bewußt *conscious of*	habhaft *in possession of*	sicher *sure of*
fähig *capable of*	müde *tired of*	wert *worth of*
gewahr *aware of*	schuldig *guilty of*	*[For* wert *(+ acc.), see § 158]*
		würdig *worthy of*

Paul war sich seines Irrtums bewußt. *Paul was aware of his error.*
Er war keiner Antwort fähig. *He was not capable of an answer.*
Das ist nicht der Rede wert. *It is not worth talking about!*

I. VOCABULARY FOR REVIEW (A AND B TEXTS FROM READER, CHAPTER IV)

Verbs

auf·räumen	to tidy up
auf·wachsen (ä), u, a (+ sein)	to grow up
erziehen, o, o	to educate
sich kümmern um	to take care of
mit·nehmen (i), a, o	to take along
sich scheiden lassen (ä) ie, a	to get divorced
schieben o, o	to push
verzichten auf	to renounce

Nouns

die **Bevölkerung**	population
das **Einzelkind, -er**	only child
der **Elternteil, -e**	parent
das **Gericht, -e**	(law) court
die **Geschwister** *(pl.)*	siblings
die **Heirat, -en**	marriage
der **Jugendliche, -n**	youth
der **Kinderwagen, -**	baby carriage
die **Scheidung, -en**	divorce
das **Verhältnis, -se**	relationship
der **Vetter, -n**	cousin
der **Vorname, -n**	first name
die **Witwe, -n**	widow
der **Witwer, -**	widower

Others

geschieden	divorced
getrennt	separated
kinderlos	childless
kinderreich	with many children
ledig	single
selbständig	independent
verheiratet	married
verwitwet	widowed

ADDITIONAL EXERCISES (A AND B TEXTS FROM THE READER)

Meine Familie

Complete the introduction of your family members with the predicate nominative.

1. Das ist _____. *(my father and my mother)*
2. Sie sind _____. *(a happy couple)*
3. Hier kommen _____. *(my siblings — my brothers and my sisters)*
4. Dieser Jugendliche hier ist _____. *(our nephew)*
5. Meine Nichte freut sich, _____ zu sein. *(our relative)*
6. Mein Vetter wächst als _____ auf. *(a single child)*
7. Mein Großvater ist schon lange _____. *(a widower)*
8. Unser Onkel möchte _____ bleiben. *(a youth)*

Familientag

Tell who is coming on your excursion, completing each statement with the direct object.

9. Wir nehmen _____ mit. *(our relatives, uncles and aunts)*
10. Sollen wir denn auf _____ verzichten? *(our grandfather, our cousin Ernst, and all couples)*
11. Deine Großmutter kommt mit, ja? Wie heißt sie? Ich weiß _____ nicht mehr. *(her first name)*
12. Dieser Jugendliche heißt Hans, er will _____ heiraten. *(my niece)*
13. Herr Kühn und seine Frau haben schon _____. *(a son)*
14. Wer schiebt denn _____? *(the baby carriage)*
15. Und wer erzieht _____? *(our brothers and sisters)*

Answer affirmatively, using the accusative of definite time. (Adjective endings will be -en.)

16. Machen wir **am nächsten Sonntag** einen Spaziergang?

17. Heiratet deine Tante **am siebten April?**

18. Gibst du dem Kind **an jedem Morgen** ein neues Spielzeug?

19. Müssen Ehepaare **im nächsten Monat** mehr Steuern zahlen?

20. Gibt es **in diesem Winter** mehr geschiedene Leute?

Answer each question with the accusative of duration. (Adjective endings will be -en.)

21. Wie lange seid ihr denn schon verheiratet? *(one month)*

22. Wie lange leben deine Eltern schon getrennt? *(one summer)*

23. Arbeitest du immer so lange? Ja, *(the entire evening)*

24. Bleibt Ihre Nichte lange im Büro? Ja, *(the entire morning)*

25. Wie lange dauerte der Spaziergang? *(the entire long day)*

Supply the indirect object to each statement.

26. Wir kaufen _____ ein Spielzeug. (unser Neffe)

27. Schenkt ihr _____ etwas Nettes? (euer Großvater)

28. Du mußt _____ das Verhältnis erklären. (deine Geschwister)

29. Sie sollten _____ ein paar Worte sagen! (die Verwandten)

30. Ich sollte _____ alles berichten. (das Gericht)

31. Zeigen Sie _____ Ihre Anerkennung! (beide Elternteile)

32. Großmutter, erzähl _____ eine Geschichte! (wir Kinder)

33. Erzählen wir _____ von der Heirat! (unsere ledigen Freunde)

34. Wir wollten _____ einen neuen Ehemann suchen. (die Witwe)

35. Gebt _____ einen schönen Vornamen! (eure Tochter)

Replace the underlined pronoun object with the given phrase in the dative.

36. Glaubt <u>ihm</u> nicht! (dieser Jugendliche)

37. Wann bist du <u>ihr</u> begegnet? (die Witwe)

38. Das ist <u>mir</u> gut gelungen. (unsere Familie)

39. Was ist <u>euch</u> denn passiert? (euer Vetter)

40. Hilf <u>ihm</u>! (alle Einzelkinder)

das **Verhalten**	behavior
die **Wärme**	warmth

Others

enttäuscht	disappointed
lächerlich	ridiculous
merkwürdig	strange

ADDITIONAL EXERCISES (C TEXT FROM THE READER)

Über Herrn Schwamm

Complete each statement with the predicate nominative.

1. Herr Schwamm ist _____ *(the best father)*
2. Das stimmt nicht! Das ist _____. *(a deception)*
3. Er ist nur _____. *(the most ridiculous fellow)*
4. Und hier scheint er _____ zu sein. *(a stranger)*
5. Er will gern _____ werden. *(an educator)*
6. Das ist und bleibt _____. *(his responsibility)*

Herr Schwamm kommt im Hotel an

Complete each statement with the direct object given.

7. Zuerst mußte er _____ ausfüllen. *(the papers)*
8. Der Portier wollte ihm _____ geben. *(a double room)*
9. Er bedauerte _____ an Einzelzimmern. *(the lack = der Mangel)*
10. Der Gast versuchte, _____ zu beeinflussen. *(the innkeeper)*
11. Der Wirt wollte _____ nicht betrügen. *(Mr. Schwamm)*
12. Er bedauerte _____ des Gastes. *(the unfriendly behavior)*
13. Schwamm sah _____ des Fremden. *(the shoulder)*
14. Aber er konnte _____ nicht erblicken. *(the fellow)*
15. Er haßte _____ im Zimmer. *(his presence = seine Gegenwart)*
16. Endlich fand er _____. *(his bed)*
17. Er spürte _____ in seinem Körper. *(a nice warmth)*
18. Die zwang _____ einzuschlafen. *(the man)*

Wann ist das alles passiert?

Answer with the accusative of definite time.

19. Wann fuhr der Vater in die stadt? *(each Monday)*

20. Wann erwachte der Kleine? *(every morning at 7 o'clock)*
21. Hat der Junge wirklich gewinkt? Ja, *(many a day)*
22. Winkte manchmal auch jemand zurück? Ja, *(this afternoon)*
23. Konnte der Junge schnell einschlafen? *(one evening, no night)*

Wie lange hat alles gedauert?

Answer with the accusative of duration. (Adjective endings will be -en.)

24. Wie lange blieb der Vater in der Stadt? *(only one night)*
25. Mußte der Junge lange auf den Zug warten? Ja, *(the whole morning)*
26. Verzweifelte er wirklich? Ja, aber *(only one moment)*
27. Weint der kleine Kerl manchmal? Ja, *(often the entire afternoon)*
28. Wie lange dauerte dieses Elend? *(the entire summer)*

Was Herr Schwamm alles tut

Supply the indirect object to each statement.

29. Er sagte _____, er wollte ein Einzelzimmer. (der Nachtportier)
30. Aber der Mann gab _____ keine Antwort. (Herr Schwamm)
31. Er setzte sich und schrieb _____ einen Brief. (seine Frau)
32. Er erzählte _____ die Geschichte des Fremden. (seine Partnerin)
33. Er gab _____ die ganze Verantwortung. (der Nachtportier)
34. Später ging er und kaufte _____ ein Spielzeug. (sein Enkel)
35. Letztes Jahr hatte er _____ ein Radio geschenkt. (das Kind)
36. _____ hatte er Geschenke mitgebracht. (seine Geschwister)
37. Er wollte _____ eine Freude machen. (sein Neffe)
38. Er versuchte, _____ Gerechtigkeit zu zeigen. (auch dieser Kerl)
39. Er winkt _____. (alle Kinder)
40. Abends liest er _____ die Zeitung vor. (seine Großeltern)

Ein Fremder

Replace the underlined pronoun object with the given phrase in the dative.

41. Gefällt <u>dir</u> diese Erzählung? (die Studenten)
42. Ein Fremder drohte <u>uns</u> mit der Faust. (meine Brüder und Schwestern)
43. Er winkte <u>ihr</u> vom Auto. (das Mädchen)
44. Er schämte sich nicht, <u>ihnen</u> ins Hotel zu folgen. (mein Onkel und meine Tante)
45. Sie zögerten, <u>ihm</u> zu helfen. (der Kerl)

Translate into English to observe German usage of the ethical dative.

46. Zögere mir nicht so lange, ich habe wenig Zeit!

47. Fallen Sie mir nur nicht über das Gepäck!

48. Daß uns niemand den Jungen beeinflußt!

49. Nun verzweifle mir doch nicht gleich!

Complete the answers with the genitive.

50. Besitzt Herr Schwamm **ein Hotel?** Ja, er ist Besitzer _____.

51. Hat Frau Schwamm **einen Sohn?** Ja, sie ist Mutter _____.

52. Kommt **der Brief** von dem Sohn? Ja, er ist der Schreiber _____.

53. Hat **das Kind** schon einen Namen? Ja, der Name _____ ist Mark.

54. Hat **sein Vater** ein großes Haus? Ja, das Haus _____ ist groß.

Complete the questions with the genitive.

55. **Ein Kind** muß Eltern haben. Sind Sie Eltern _____?

56. **Meine Mutter** arbeitet im Büro. Wo ist denn das Büro _____?

57. **Die Hotels** müssen Vorschriften haben. Ich hasse die Vorschriften _____!

58. **Die Welt** soll gerecht sein. Glaubst du an die Gerechtigkeit _____?

59. **Manche Menschen** leben im Elend. Denke an das Elend _____!

Replace the possessive adjective with the given phrase in the genitive.

Example

Ist das **sein** Koffer? (Peter) (dieser Herr)
Ist das **Peters** Koffer?
Ist das der Koffer **dieses Herrn?**

60. Alles passiert auf **seine** Verantwortung. Ist das _____? (Herr Meyer) (der Wirt)

61. Ruf **unseren** Vertreter an! Ruf! (Robert) (die Firma)

62. Hier kommen **meine** Eltern. Hier kommen (Marlene) (meine Freundin)

63. Das ist **dein** Zimmer. Das ist (Mutter) (die alte Tante)

64. Sprechen wir mit **euren** Erziehern! Sprechen wir mit! (Renate und Ingrid) (eure Töchter)

Wann wird das passieren?

Answer with the genitive of indefinite time.

65. Wird er nie enttäuscht werden? Doch, (ein Tag)

66. Hast du nie Mitleid gefühlt? Doch, (ein Abend)

67. Hat er sich noch nie geschämt? Doch, (eine Nacht)

68. Glaubst du, sie bedauert ihr Verhalten? Vielleicht (ein Tag)

ADJECTIVES
(Part One)

FUNCTION OF ADJECTIVES

174   Adjectives are words that modify a noun by limiting it, qualifying it, or making it more specific. German adjectives function in two ways:

1. They can be a complement to **sein, werden** and a few other verbs for which **sein** can be substituted. In this function they remain undeclined and are called *predicate adjectives.* This is parallel to English usage.

> Das Essen ist **verbrannt.** *The meal is **burned.***
> Der Tag wurde **warm.** *The day became **warm.***
> Er fühlte sich **krank.** *He felt **sick.***
> (= **ist**)

2. They can immediately precede the nouns they modify. In this case they are called *attributive adjectives* and are declined.

> Lisa ißt gern **frisches** Brot. *Lisa likes to eat **fresh** bread.*

CHECK AND PRACTICE

Choose the correct form.

Example

Peter liest ein _____ Buch. (dick / dickes)
Peter liest ein **dickes** Buch.

1. Erika hat _____ Angst. (groß / große)
2. Die Antwort war _____. (falsch / falsche)
3. Der Apfel schmeckt _____. (gut / gute)
4. Die _____ Arbeit dauerte lang. (schwer / schwere)
5. Dein Arm ist nicht sehr _____. (stark / starke)
6. Gib mir ein _____ Geschenk. (schön / schönes)

175   Some adjectives may be negated (or their opposite expressed) by using the prefixes **un-** for German words or **in-** for foreign words.

> höflich **un**höflich *im*polite   kompetent **in**kompetent *in*competent
> wichtig **un**wichtig *un*important

176 Adjectives are not capitalized unless they are part of an official title or name.

---

ein **deutscher** Politiker   BUT   das **Deutsche** Museum

---

177 1. Adjectives derived from names of cities are formed by adding **-er**; no further endings are ever added. They are always capitalized.

Alle Politiker lesen die **Berliner** Zeitung.   *All politicians read the **Berlin** newspaper.*

---

2. Adjectives derived from names are capitalized if they refer to a personal achievement or property.

---

die **Goethischen** Gedichte   *the poems by **Goethe***
die **Einsteinsche** Relativitätstheorie   ***Einstein's** theory of relativity*
das **Ohmsche** Gesetz   ***Ohm's** law*

---

3. Adjectives are not capitalized if they refer in a general sense to the achievement of a person or refer to something else named in honor of this person.

Gedichte von **goethischer** Klarheit   *poems of **Goethean** clarity*
fast **einsteinsche** Theorien   *theories almost like **Einstein's***
der **ohmsche** Widerstand   ***ohmic** resistance for electrical currents*

CHECK AND PRACTICE

Give the opposite.

1. möglich	2. endlich	3. geschickt	4. ruhig	5. akzeptabel
6. zufrieden	7. diskret	8. entbehrlich	9. glücklich	10. schuldig

Add the missing adjective. Use the cues in parentheses.

11. Ich esse gern _____ Schnitzel. (Wien)

12. Die _____ Verträge wurden nach dem Krieg geschlossen. (Potsdam)

ADJECTIVE DECLENSION

Weak Adjective Declension

178   There are three adjectival declensions in German: weak, strong and mixed. An adjective takes a weak ending **-e** or **-en** whenever it is preceded by an article (a definite or indefinite article, a **der**-word or an **ein**-word) which gives all the necessary information about number, gender, and case.

	MASCULINE			SINGULAR FEMININE			NEUTER		
Nominative	der	alt**e**	Löffel	die	alt**e**	Gabel	das	alt**e**	Messer
	see § 184			eine	alt**e**	Gabel	see § 184		
Accusative	den	alt**en**	Löffel	die	alt**e**	Gabel	das	alt**e**	Messer
	einen	alt**en**	Löffel	eine	alt**e**	Gabel	see § 184		
Dative	dem	alt**en**	Löffel	der	alt**en**	Gabel	einem	alt**en**	Messer
	einem	alt**en**	Löffel	einer	alt**en**	Gabel	einem	alt**en**	Messer
Genitive	des	alt**en**	Löffels	der	alt**en**	Gabel	des	alt**en**	Messers
	eines	alt**en**	Löffels	einer	alt**en**	Gabel	eines	alt**en**	Messers

	PLURAL ALL GENDERS		
Nominative	die	alt**en**	Löffel
	keine	alt**en**	Gabeln Messer
Accusative	die	alt**en**	Löffel
	keine	alt**en**	Gabeln Messer
Dative	den	alt**en**	Löffeln
	keinen	alt**en**	Gabeln Messern
Genitive	der	alt**en**	Löffel
	keiner	alt**en**	Gabeln Messer

179   In a series of adjectives preceded by an article, each one will show the same weak ending.

> Solche dumm**en**, unwichtig**en** Fehler sollte man nicht machen.
> *One shouldn't make such silly, unimportant mistakes.*

180   1. Compound adjectives like **derselbe** and **derjenige** are declined as if they were two words: the first element (the definite article) follows the strong declension [see § 132]; the second element follows the weak declension.

NOMINATIVE	ACCUSATIVE
Wirklich, es war derselb**e** Mann, . . .	Sie sah denselb**en** Mann am Bahnhof.
Really, it was the same man . . .	*She saw the same man at the train station.*

2. **derselbe** is written as one word unless the first syllable — the definite article — is contracted with a preceding preposition:

> Erika und Paul haben **denselben** Lehrer.
> Erika und Paul haben auch **im selben** Klassenzimmer Unterricht.

3. **derselbe** indicates identity, **der gleiche** indicates similarity.

> Peter und Paul benutzen **das gleiche** Textbuch.

Peter has a textbook of his own, and so does Paul. If they shared the same textbook, then one would say:

> Peter und Paul benutzen **dasselbe** Textbuch.

CHECK AND PRACTICE

Give the correct ending: -e or -en

1. Der bekannt__ Filmstar besuchte Frankfurt.
2. Kennst du den Titel des best__ Films von 1930?
3. Die Kinder spielten auf der breit__ Straße.
4. Er trug immer seine alt__ braun__ Schuhe.

5. Jeden Tag sahen wir dieselb___ dick___ Frau.

6. Er schlug mich mit einem dünn___ Stock.

7. Anna sah den alt___, krank___, müd___ Mann nie wieder.

8. Er gab diesem brav___, klein___ Kind ein Stück Schokolade.

9. Der Lehrer lobte den ernst___ Jungen.

10. Sie gab immer die falsch___ Antwort.

11. Sie aß das fett___ Fleisch nur ungern.

12. Dieses flach___ Dach ist unpraktisch.

13. Herr Meyer dankte seinen fleißig___ Mitarbeitern.

14. Jene alt___ Kirche muß renoviert werden.

15. Alle weiß___ Hemden waren schmutzig.

16. Die Abende der heiß___ Sommertage waren angenehm.

17. Haben Sie diese deutsch___ Zeitung schon gelesen?

18. Das Spielzeug des klein___ Kindes war kaputt.

19. Inge trug den kurz___ Rock sehr gern.

20. Er brachte die leer___ Flaschen ins Geschäft zurück.

Strong Adjective Declension

181   When an adjective modifies a noun but is *not* preceded by an article, it is declined like the definite article. The exception is the genitive singular masculine and neuter which take **-n,** not **-s** [for declension review, see § 132]. These endings are called strong endings. The reason for the strong endings is the need for German nouns to express number, gender and case via their modifiers.

Der Wein ist teuer.	ARTICLE + NOUN
Alt**er** Wein ist teuer.	ADJECTIVE + NOUN

	SINGULAR			**PLURAL**
	Masculine	**Feminine**	**Neuter**	
	cold tea	*cold milk*	*cold water*	*cold drinks*
Nominative	kalt**er** Tee	kalt**e** Milch	kalt**es** Wasser	kalt**e** Getränke
Accusative	kalt**en** Tee	kalt**e** Milch	kalt**es** Wasser	kalt**e** Getränke
Dative	kalt**em** Tee	kalt**er** Milch	kalt**em** Wasser	kalt**en** Getränken
Genitive	kalt**en** Tees	kalt**er** Milch	kalt**en** Wassers	kalt**er** Getränke

182 Adjectives ending in **-el** (and often those that end in **-er**) lose the **e** in these syllables when endings are attached. Similarly, the adjective **hoch** loses the **c** when endings are attached.

Die Zimmer sind dunk**el**.	Diese Bücher sind teu**er**.	Diese Berge sind ho**ch**.
The rooms are dark.	*These books are expensive.*	*These mountains are high.*
Das sind dunk**le** Zimmer.	Das sind teu**re** Bücher.	Das sind ho**he** Berge.
These are dark rooms.	*These are expensive books.*	*These are high mountains.*

183 In a series of adjectives without an article, each adjective will show the same strong ending.

Kalt**er** alt**er** rot**er** Wein schmeckt gut.
Cold old red wine tastes great.

CHECK AND PRACTICE

Replace the underlined der-words with the appropriate forms of the adjectives in parentheses.

1. Trinken Sie diesen Tee gern? (chinesisch)
2. Dieser Wein ist immer gut. (alt)
3. Bei solchem Wetter bleiben wir zu Hause. (schlecht)
4. Das Aroma dieses Kaffees füllte den Raum. (frisch)
5. Er ißt dieses Brot am liebsten. (schwarz)
6. In dieser Bibliothek findet man alle Zeitungen. (ausländisch)
7. Mit dieser Milch schmeckt der Kuchen noch besser. (heiß)
8. Lisa hatte solches Glück. (groß)
9. Sie hörte solche Musik gern. (leis, romantisch)

Insert the adjectives in parentheses.

10. Siehst du dort das _____ Gebäude? (hoch)
11. Das _____ Wetter schien nicht enden zu wollen. (miserabel)
12. Er schüttete die _____ Milch weg. (sauer)

Mixed Adjective Declension

184 In the masculine nominative and the neuter nominative and accusative, the indefinite article and the **ein**-words have lost their endings [see § 132]. Adjectives following these articles, therefore, must show strong endings in these three instances so that the number, gender and case of the noun is indicated. The other forms correspond to the weak declension [see § 178].

	MASCULINE	NEUTER
Nominative	ein☐ alt**er** Löffel	ein☐ alt**es** Messer
Accusative		ein☐ alt**es** Messer

CHECK AND PRACTICE

Give the correct adjective endings. In a few instances, case and/or gender are given in parentheses.

1. Interessant___ Fernsehprogramme sind selten.
2. Erika hatte ein dick___ Buch mit viel___ Bildern von selten___ Vögeln (D).
3. Er war ein kräftig___ Mann mit schwarz___ Haar (D/n), dick___ Hals (D/m), kurz___ Nase (D/f) und klein___ Händen.
4. Sie wußte auch keine wirklich___ Lösung zu den wichtig___ Problemen (D), über die sie in der neuest___ Zeitung (D) gelesen hatte.
5. Paul nannte seiner Freundin nicht den Preis des teur___ Geschenks, das er an ihrem letzt___ Geburtstag in einer toll___ Boutique gekauft hatte.
6. Frisch___ Fleisch (n) kauft man beim Metzger.
7. Welche Städte haben heute noch sauber___ Luft? (f)
8. Groß___ Gott, wir loben dich!
9. Jugendliche lieben laut___ Musik.
10. Offen___ Feuer kann gefährlich sein. (n)
11. Wir wünschen uns gut___ Wetter. (n)
12. Kalt___ Tee ist gut. (m)
13. Frau Meyer sammelt selten___ Briefmarken.
14. Peter schlief gern in einem sehr weich___ Bett.
15. Wahr___ Freunde helfen immer.
16. Hast du trocken___ Handtücher?
17. Hunde sind treu___ Freunde.

18. Steh nie am Rand eines tief___ Lochs.
19. Eine Flasche alt___ Weins ist sehr teuer.
20. Herr Heim mag keinen süß___ Tee.

Summary of Adjective Declension

185

ARTICLES AND ADJECTIVES			
Singular			
	NO ENDING	STRONG ENDING	WEAK ENDING
MASCULINE			
Nominative	ein	der / alter / alter	alte	Löffel
Accusative		den / einen / alten	alten / alten	Löffel
Dative		dem / einem / altem	alten / alten	Löffel
Genitive		des / eines	alten / alten / alten	Löffels
FEMININE			
Nominative		die / eine / alte	alte / alte	Gabel
Accusative		die / eine / alte	alte / alte	Gabel
Dative		der / einer / alter	alten / alten	Gabel
Genitive		der / einer / alter	alten / alten	Gabel

Cardinal Numbers

188 The German system is quite similar to English. From 0 to 12, each number has its own name; from 13 on, the numbers are either compounded or are derived from the basic set 1–9. Note that from 21 to 29, 31 to 39, etc., German reverses the English pattern: *twenty-one* becomes **einundzwanzig.** Numbers from 1 to 999,999 are written as one word, including the conjunction **und**.

> *forty-three*
> dreiundvierzig
>
> Im letzten Semester studierten etwa **fünfundsiebzig** Studenten Deutsch.

189 The numbers **Million** (1 000 000), **Milliarde** (1 000 000 000), **Billion** (1 000 000 000 000), etc., are feminine nouns, forming their plurals with **-(e)n:**

> eine Million   eine Milliarde
> zwei Million**en**   zwei Milliard**en**

German-speaking Countries	USA
BILLION	TRILLION
MILLIARDE	BILLION
MILLION	MILLION

> Es gibt über **eine Million fünfhunderttausend** Menschen in dieser Stadt.
> *There are over one million five hundred thousand inhabitants in this city.*

190 Numbers in German are written out in most of the same situations as in English. One significant difference is in stating an *approximation.* English uses numbers; *German writes them out.*

> Ich habe zehn Bücher.   *I have ten books.*
> Ich fahre um 10.00 ab.   *I'm leaving at 10:00.*
>
> Es gibt **über zehntausend** Angestellte in dieser Fabrik.
> *There are **over 10,000** employees in this factory.*

191 Commas are used in German where a decimal point is used in English, and a space or a period is used in German where commas are used in English.

> 1,30 DM = eine Mark dreißig   *1.30 marks*
> -,22 DM = zweiundzwanzig Pfennig   *.22 marks*
> 1 500 000   *1,500,000*
> 1.500.000

CHECK AND PRACTICE

Say and write the following numbers in German:

1.	54	2.	45	3.	38
4.	83	5.	77	6.	166
7.	321	8.	692	9.	711
10.	956	11.	1 030	12.	13 174
13.	335 728	14.	1 000 000	15.	21 000 345
16.	602 464 212	17.	1 000 000 003	18.	998 437 241 561
19.	735 527 139 422 853	20.	921 348 012 273 987	21.	521 382 213

192   With the exception of **eins**, cardinal numbers are usually not declined.

> Sie hatte **zwei** Bleistifte, **drei** Bücher, **vier** Hefte und **fünfundzwanzig** Blatt Papier.
> *She had **two** pencils, **three** books, **four** notebooks and **twenty-five** pieces of paper.*

193   When used with a noun, the number **eins** drops the **-s** and is declined in the same manner as the indefinite article [see § 132]. If preceded by a **der**-word (e.g., the definite article or **dieser**, etc.), **eins** drops the **-s** and takes weak endings.

> Der Lehrer mußte zwei Schülerinen eine Vier und **einem** Schüler sogar eine Fünf geben.
> *The teacher had to give two students a D and **one** student an F.*
> *(In German schools, the grading system is: 1, 2, 3, 4, 5, where 1 = A and 5 = F.)*

> Der Lehrer gab dem ein**en** Schüler, der nach der Klasse nicht gleich weggegangen war, ein Buch.
> *The teacher gave a book to the **one** student who had not left right away after class.*

194   Since numerals are regarded as adjectives, the adjectives that follow them take strong or weak endings depending on whether or not the numerals are preceded by articles.

UNPRECEDED	STRONG ENDINGS	Er kauft		grü**ne** Hemden.
				zwei grü**ne**
PRECEDED	WEAK ENDINGS	Er kauft	die	grü**nen** Hemden.
			die zwei grü**nen**	

195   Instead of **zwei**, the adjective **beide** *(both)* can be used if it refers to two persons or things already mentioned and seen as a group. **beide** is declined like all other adjectives, but adjectives following **beide** without an article can either have the same strong endings as **beide**, or—not very frequently— weak endings as if **beide** were an article.

Die beid**en** jung**en** Mädchen tragen ein rotes Kleid.   *Both young girls wear a red dress.*
   Beid**e**   jung**e**   Mädchen tragen ein rotes Kleid.
   Beid**e**   jung**en** Mädchen tragen ein rotes Kleid.

CHECK AND PRACTICE

Give the endings.

1. Die drei_____ müd_____ Arbeiter gingen nach Hause.
2. Er kaufte seiner Freundin fünfundzwanzig_____ rot_____ Rosen.
3. Inge schrieb fünf_____ Briefe an Peter und ein_____ Postkarte an Robert.
4. In Herrn Müllers Büro hingen fast dreißig_____ Bilder.
5. Fünf_____ Beispielsätze sind genug.

Derivations from Cardinal Numbers

196   The adjectives **zweifach** *double, twofold,* **dreifach** *triple, threefold,* etc., are formed by adding **-fach** to the corresponding cardinals. All cardinals can be used.

Er trägt eine dreifache Krone.   *He wears a triple crown.*

---

197   The adverbs **einmal** *once,* **zweimal** *twice,* **dreimal** *three times,* etc., are formed by adding **-mal** to the corresponding cardinals.

Wir haben Deutsch fünfmal die Woche.   *We have German five times a week.*

CHECK AND PRACTICE

Give the German equivalent for the words in parentheses.

1. Sie geht jeden Monat _____ ins Kino. *(four times)*
2. Schreiben Sie bitte die Antwort in _____ Ausfertigung. *(in triplicate)*
3. Herr Schmidt tat alles _____. *(fourfold)*
4. _____ die Woche ißt er Fleisch, _____ Fisch und _____ Nudeln. *(four times/once/twice)*
5. Dieses Mikroskop hat eine _____ Vergrößerung. *(thousandfold)*

Ordinal Numbers

198   Ordinal numbers are formed from cardinal numbers by adding the suffix
   -t for the numbers **zwei** to **neunzehn:**   zweit-
   OR **-st** for all other numbers: zwanzig**st**-
   The ordinals **erste, dritte, siebte,** and **achte** are irregular.

1. **erst-**	2. zweit-	3. **dritt-**
4. viert-	5. fünft-	6. sechst-
7. **siebt-**	8. **acht-**	9. neunt-
10. zehnt-	11. elft-	12. zwölft-
13. dreizehnt-	19. neunzehnt-	20. zwanzig**st**-
21. einundzwanzig**st**-	30. dreißig**st**-	100. (ein)hundert**st**-
101. hundert(und)**erst**-	102. hundert(und)zweit-	1000. (ein)tausend**st**-

199   A period following a numeral designates it as an ordinal number.

der 1. (erste) Juni   *June 1st*

200   Ordinal numbers are adjectives and follow weak or strong declension, depending on whether or not they are preceded by articles.

Peters **erster** Tag im Kindergarten war sehr aufregend.   *Peter's first day in kindergarten was very exciting.*

Er bekam **seinen ersten** Schulranzen.   *He got his first schoolbag.*

201   In compound ordinals, only the last element is declined.

Sie suchte den vierundachtzigst**en** Band von Goethes Werken.
She looked for the 84th volume of Goethe's works.

CHECK AND PRACTICE

Give the missing suffixes and the correct endings.
Use the clues for the irregular ordinals and complete the words.

Example

Jedes zehn_____ Kind erhielt ein Geschenk.
Jedes zehn**te** Kind erhielt ein Geschenk.
Am e_____ Tag seines Urlaubs war Peter besonders faul.
Am **ersten** Tag seines Urlaubs war Peter besonders faul.

1. Der Herr arbeitete sechs Tage und ruhte am sieb_____.
2. Das ist schon die fünf_____ Hose, die ich waschen muß.
3. Der fünfzig_____ Geburtstag ist ein sehr wichtiger Tag.
4. Kennst du den Film "Der dr_____ Mann"?
5. Sein e_____ Auto war das schönste.
6. Ich sage dir das jetzt zum hundert_____ Male.
7. Der acht_____ Tag eines Radrennens ist der schwerste.
8. Fridolins fünfunddreißig_____ Freundin hieß wie seine e_____.
9. Nach dem fünf_____ Stück Kuchen war er wirklich satt.
10. Paul verlor den zwei_____ Satz des Tennisspiels.

DATES

202 Dates are expressed with ordinal numbers. The sequence is always from the smallest to the largest unit: DAY   MONTH   YEAR

Der wievielte ist heute? *What is the date?*	Heute ist der 5. (fünfte) Juni.
	Heute ist Mittwoch, der 5. Juni. *Today is Wednesday, June 5th.*
Den wievielten haben wir heute?	
	Heute haben wir den 5. (fünften) Juni. Heute haben wir Mittwoch, den 5. Juni.
Ich bin am 24. September 1942 geboren. Ich bin am 24.9.1942 geboren.	*I was born September 24, 1942.*

203 1. When the date appears in a letterhead or diary entry, the accusative case is used.

Frankfurt, den 25. Januar	Donnerstag, den 12. März

2. Roman numerals may be used

   a. for months

   b. with the names of rulers

19.XI.1938
Georg III. (Georg der Dritte)

CHECK AND PRACTICE

Give the German equivalents of these dates.

Example

6/18/87
18. Juni (19)87
18.6.87 (der achtzehnte sechste siebenundachtzig)

1. 12/25/86	2. 5/8/45	3. 1/26/11	4. 6/15/1888	5. 9/1/39
6. 11/9/18	7. 7/28/14	8. 2/18/1871	9. 3/13/1848	10. 10/17/1832

FRACTIONS

204   Fractions are considered neuter nouns in German. From one-third on, they are formed by adding **-el** to the ordinal number.

---

ein Drittel   *one-third*   ein Zehntel   *one-tenth*
das letzte Viertel   *the last quarter*   3/100 (drei Hundertstel) 0.3   *three one-hundredths*

---

205   Fractions are not capitalized before measurements.

---

ein drittel Zentner Mehl   *a third of a centner (= 50 kilograms) of flour*
ein viertel Kilo Zucker   *a fourth of a kilo of sugar*
ein achtel Kilo Salz   *an eighth of a kilo of salt*
drei zehntel Sekunden   *three tenths of a second*
vier tausendstel Sekunden   *four thousandths of a second*

---

206   1. German uses two forms for *half*: the noun **die Hälfte** *the half of* and the adjective **halb** *half a*.

---

die bessere **Hälfte**   *the better half*   ein **halbes** Pfund   *half a pound*

Er hat einen **halben** Apfel gegessen. Die andere **Hälfte** gab er mir.
*He ate **half** an apple. The other **half** he gave to me.*

---

2. The form **anderthalb** *one and a half* is undeclined and always followed by a plural noun; the same applies to the forms **zwei(und)einhalb** *two and a half*, etc.

Ich wartete **anderthalb** Stunden.   *I waited **an hour and a half**.*
In **acht(und)einhalb** Jahren kehrt er zurück.   *In **eight and a half** years he will return.*

CHECK AND PRACTICE

Give the correct fractions. Cases are indicated in parentheses.

1. Nach _____ des Wegs war er schon müde. (1/3) (D)
2. Ich möchte _____ Pfund Schinken. (1/4)
3. Du erhälst _____ dieser Summe. (1/9)
4. Paul hatte _____ seines Gewichts abgenommen. (5/100)
5. In _____ Stunde müssen wir weggehen. (1/4) (D)
6. Inge lief _____ Sekunden schneller als Frank. (6/10)
7. Sie sollten _____ der Strecke mit dem Zug fahren. (1/2)
8. Die Steuer betrug _____ ihres Verdienstes. (1/20)
9. Bitte geben Sie mir _____ Pfund Wurst. (1/2)
10. _____ aller Studenten bestanden die Prüfung nicht. (5/8)
11. _____ kann viel oder wenig sein. (1/1000)

TIME

207   Fractions are also used for telling time in German. Portions of an hour, especially the half hour, are usually expressed in terms of the following full hour. Quarter hours are often indicated in the same manner, especially in Southern Germany, Austria, and Switzerland.

THE FIVE O'CLOCK GLASS

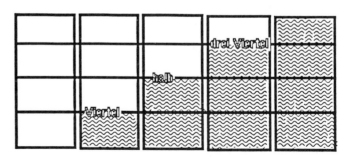

fünf (Uhr)

drei Viertel fünf

halb fünf

Viertel fünf
vier (Uhr)

208   Alternate forms are also used frequently, employing the same system as English for quarter hours but *not* for half hours.

Es ist (ein) Viertel **nach** eins.   *It's a quarter **past** one.*
Es ist (ein) Viertel **vor** zwei.   *It's a quarter **to** two.*

---

209 In addition, time may be specified in hours and minutes, similar to English.

Es ist ein Uhr fünfzehn. *It's one fifteen.*
Es ist fünfzehn Minuten nach eins. *It's fifteen minutes past one.*
Es ist ein Uhr fünfundzwanzig. *It's one forty-five.*
Es ist fünfzehn Minuten vor zwei. *It's fifteen minutes to two.*

---

210 The most usual forms of five-minute intervals are:

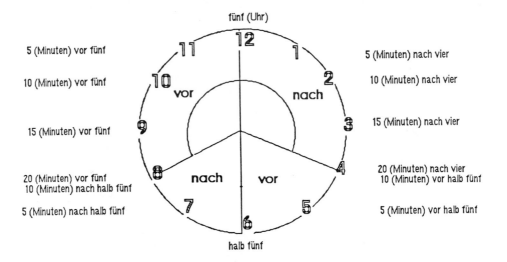

211 In German-speaking countries, time is often told by the 24-hour system, especially in official announcements: railroad, airline, and bus schedules; theater, concert, and movie programs; and university course schedules. Fractions and **vor** and **nach** are not used in the 24-hour system.

13.00 Uhr dreizehn Uhr	14.00 Uhr vierzehn Uhr
= *1 p.m.*	= *2 p.m.*
15.10 Uhr fünfzehn Uhr zehn	16.30 Uhr sechzehn Uhr dreißig
= *3:10 p.m.*	= *4:30 p.m.*

CHECK AND PRACTICE

Tell the time. There are several different ways to do it.

1. 5.20   2. 11.05   3. 12.35   4. 9.45   5. 7.30

DECLENSION OF INDEFINITE NUMERICAL ADJECTIVES

Survey

212   Whereas the before-mentioned numerical adjectives have no adjective endings (with the exception of **eins**), some of the *indefinite numerical adjectives* can be declined.

WITH ADJECTIVE ENDINGS	**Viele** Studenten fahren am Wochenende zu einem Fußballspiel. *Many students are going to a soccer match this weekend.*
WITHOUT ADJECTIVE ENDINGS	Paul hatte **wenig** Geld. *Paul had little money.*

213   Like the other numerical adjectives, the indefinite numerical adjectives are usually *not* preceded by an article. They then have strong endings if they are declined. They always stand *before* descriptive adjectives which also have strong endings.

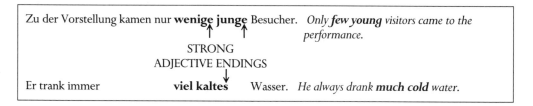

Zu der Vorstellung kamen nur **wenige junge** Besucher.   *Only **few young** visitors came to the performance.*

STRONG ADJECTIVE ENDINGS

Er trank immer   **viel kaltes**   Wasser.   *He always drank **much cold** water.*

214   1. If a numerical adjective is preceded by an article, it has a weak adjective ending.

Die **vielen älteren** Zuschauer applaudierten laut.   *The many older spectators applauded loudly.*

WEAK ADJECTIVE ENDINGS

2. In this group belong:

OFTEN NOT PRECEDED BY AN ARTICLE	**andere**	*other*	**wenige**	*few*
			viele	*many*
NEVER PRECEDED BY AN ARTICLE	**einige**	*some*	**mehrere**	*several*
UNDECLINED AND NEVER PRECEDED BY AN ARTICLE	**etwas**	*some*	**wenig**	*little*
	genug	*enough*	**viel**	*much*

CHECK AND PRACTICE

Insert the appropriate endings. If the nouns appear in the singular, the gender is given in parentheses.

1. Ich esse viel frisch_____ Obst. (das)
2. Lisa hat viel_____ schön_____ Geschenke bekommen.
3. Die viel_____ dumm_____ Fehler, die Paul gemacht hat, haben ihn geärgert.
4. Meine wenig_____ Freunde sind in den Ferien.
5. Es kamen nur wenig_____ Zuschauer.
6. Einig_____ ausländisch_____ Studenten wohnen in Studentenwohnheimen.
7. Die ander_____ ausländisch_____ Studenten wohnen in der Stadt.
8. Er gab mehrer_____ Schülern eine gute Note.
9. Es gab nur wenig gut_____ Essen. (das)

Numerical Adjectives in Detail

215   **andere** *other*

andere often drops the first **e**, especially in the neuter: **and(e)res**. Before **-n** and **-m**, either the first or the second **e** may be dropped: **and(e)ren** or **ander(e)n**.

Andere Länder, **andere** Sitten.   *Other countries, other customs.*
Du fährst heute schon wieder ein **andres** Auto?!   *You are driving yet another car today?!*
Die **andern** Jungen waren stärker.   *The **other** boys were stronger.*

---

216   **wenige** *few,* **viele** *many;* **wenig** *little,* **viel** *much*

1. The declined forms of these indefinite numerical adjectives are predominantly used with nouns in the plural.

DECLINED   Heute gingen nur **wenige** alte Leute im Park spazieren.
               Today, only a few old people strolled in the park.

---

2. The undeclined forms are used with nouns in the singular and especially abstract and mass nouns.

UNDECLINED   Paul hat immer **viel** Zeit.   *Paul has always **a lot** of time.*
                 Viel Geschrei und **wenig** Wolle.   ***Much** ado about **nothing.***
                 (literally: ***much** noise and **little** wool.)*

---

3. Whereas the uninflected forms have a more general and collective meaning, stressing sheer quantity, the inflected forms preceded by articles have a more particular and distributive meaning.

Viel Geld war verloren. ***Much*** *money was lost.*
Das viele schöne Geld war verloren. ***All that*** *nice money was lost.*

---

4. Inflected forms not preceded by articles are possible with nouns in the singular, but are less common (with the exception of the expression **Vielen Dank**).

| LESS COMMON | STANDARD |
Ich habe es mit **vieler** Mühe erreicht.   Ich habe es mit **viel** Mühe erreicht.
*I achieved it with **much** trouble.*

CHECK AND PRACTICE

Translate. The gender of the nouns in the singular is given in parentheses although it is in most cases of no importance to the ending.

1. Sie zog jeden Tag *(another)* Kleid an. *(n.)*
2. *(Other)* Essen mag er nicht. *(n.)*
3. Er kennt *(no other)* Lieder.
4. Nur *(few)* Wagen nahmen an dem Rennen teil.
5. *(The many)* Menschen machen mich nervös.
6. Mein Freund hat *(many)* *(great:* toll) Schallplatten.
7. *(The few)* Zuschauer, die kamen, waren enttäuscht.
8. Das hat mich wirklich *(little)* Mühe gekostet. *(f.)*
9. Mit ganz *(few)* Ausnahmen.
10. Ich habe *(little)* Hoffnung. *(f.)*
11. Dazu gehört *(much)* Mut. *(m.)*

217 einige *some*

1. Usually, **einige** is used with plural nouns, but it might also occur with singular nouns (abstract nouns or mass nouns).

Gestern haben wir **einige** alte Damen getroffen. *Yesterday, we met **some** old ladies.*
Dort drüben, in **einiger** Entfernung, war die Schule. *Over there, at **some** distance, was the school.*

---

218   **mehrere** *several*

Ich war **mehrere** Stunden dort.   *I was there for **several** hours.* Sie unternahmen **mehrere** lange Reisen.   *They took **several** long trips together.*

219   **etwas** *some, a little bit of something*

As an indefinite numerical adjective, **etwas** is used only with mass nouns in the nominative and accusative. In this function, the negation of **etwas** is **kein.**
For **etwas** as an indefinite pronoun, see § 241ff.

Kann ich bitte **etwas** Salz haben?   *May I have the salt (**some** salt), please?*

220   **genug** *enough*

For the parallel forms of **genug** as an indefinite pronoun, see § 241. For **genug** as an adverb, see § 502.

Sie waren zufrieden. Sie hatten **genug** Geld.   *They were content. They had **enough** money.*

CHECK AND PRACTICE

Insert the appropriate endings.

1. In einig___ Entfernung sah der Junge d___ jung___ Katzen des Nachbarn.
   [**in** + *Dative*]
2. In einig___ Entfernung sah der Junge mehrer___ jung___ Katzen des Nachbarn.
3. Der Vater gab d___ klein___ Kindern Schokolade.
4. Der Vater gab mehrer___ klein___ Kindern Schokolade.
5. D___ alt___ Tanten kamen zu Onkel Ottos Geburtstag.
6. Einig___ alt___ Tanten kamen zu Onkel Ottos Geburtstag.
7. Inge gefielen besonders d___ grün___ Röcke.
8. Inge gefielen besonders mehrer___ grün___ Röcke.
9. Die Namen d___ älter___ Kinder wurden nicht notiert.
10. Die Namen einig___ älter___ Kinder wurden nicht notiert.
11. Er hatte *(some)* Geld.
12. *(Some)* Glück im Leben ist schon notwendig.

ADJECTIVAL NOUNS

221   When an adjective is used as a noun, it is capitalized and shows gender, but *retains the adjective declension.* It takes strong or weak endings depending upon whether it appears with or without an article. [For declensions, see § 178ff.]

ADJECTIVE	**interessant**
ADJECTIVAL NOUN	Bitte, zeig mir etwas **Interessantes.**
	Was ist da**s Interessante** an dieser Maschine?
	*What is the **interesting aspect** of this machine?*

222   When referring to people, adjectival nouns are masculine or feminine, singular or plural. When referring to things—abstract or concrete—they are neuter nouns which are generally collective or abstract nouns.

ADJECTIVE	ADJECTIVAL NOUNS		
	referring to people		referring to things
alt	der Alte die Alte die Alten		das Alte
	ein Alter eine Alte Alte		ein Altes
			etwas Altes

NOTE   The noun **Junge** is a weak noun [see § 140.2], not an adjectival noun; it does not take adjective endings after the indefinite article.

223   An adjective modifying the adjectival noun has the same ending as the adjectival noun.

> Ein **junger Deutscher** ist heute morgen zu Besuch gekommen.
> *A **young German** came for a visit this morning.*

224   The neuter adjectival nouns are frequently preceded by **etwas, nichts, viel, wenig,** and **alles.**

etwas	Gutes	alles	Gute
↑	↑	↑	↑
UNINFLECTED	STRONG ENDING	INFLECTED	WEAK ENDING

225 German adjectival nouns often have no direct English noun equivalent.

> Das Interessante daran war die Tatsache . . .
> *The interesting thing was the fact . . .*
> *What was interesting about the situation was the fact . . .*
>
> etwas noch nie Dagewesenes *something unheard of*

226 Adjectival nouns should not be confused with adjectives that stand by themselves because a noun just mentioned before (and, therefore, still understood) has been omitted. In English, the omitted noun is usually replaced with the word *one* or *ones*.

> Gib mir bitte den großen Löffel, nicht den kleinen [**Löffel** *implied*].
> *Please, give me the big spoon not the little one.*
>
> BUT   Gib dem Kleinen den großen Löffel.
>   *the little one*
>   *(the little child)*

CHECK AND PRACTICE

Transform the adjectives into nouns, following the cues. Use masculine and feminine articles for persons; das and etwas for things.

Example

arm *(male person)*
der Arme – ein Armer – die Armen
falsch *(thing)*
das Falsche – etwas Falsches

1. teuer *(thing)*	2. klein *(male person)*
3. billig *(thing)*	4. angestellt *(female person)*
5. bitter *(thing)*	6. bekannt *(female person)*
7. blau *(thing)*	8. gefangen *(female person)*
9. schwer *(thing)*	10. böse *(thing)*
11. fett *(thing)*	12. dumm *(male person)*
13. fremd *(female person)*	14. furchtbar *(thing)*
15. verwandt *(male person)*	16. zufrieden *(male person)*
17. klug *(female person)*	18. deutsch *(female person)*
19. weich *(thing)*	20. deutsch *(male person)*
21. wichtig *(thing)*	22. reisend *(male person)*
23. neu *(thing)*	24. schwach *(female person)*
25. leicht *(thing)*	26. stark *(male person)*
27. schön *(female person)*	28. erwachsen *(female person)*

I. VOCABULARY FOR REVIEW (A, B AND C TEXTS FROM READER, CHAPTER V)

Verbs

ein·kaufen	to shop
ein·packen	to wrap
empfangen (ä) i, a	to receive
pflegen	to care for, attend to
schenken	to give a present
sorgen für	to take care of
verderben (i) a, o	to spoil
verpflichten	to oblige
versprechen (i) a, o	to promise

Nouns

das **Amt, ¨-er**	public office
der **Angestellte, -n**	employee
die **Bedingung, -en**	condition
das **Dasein**	existence
die **Freiheit, -en**	freedom
das **Gebet, -e**	prayer
die **Gelegenheit, -en**	occasion
die **Gemeinde, -n**	community, parish
das **Geschenk, -e**	present, gift
der **Grundsatz, ¨-e**	principle
das **Mißtrauen**	mistrust
die **Mühe, -n**	effort
der **Termin, -e**	appointment
die **Verpflichtung, -en**	obligation
das **Vertrauen**	trust
die **Wäsche**	laundry

Others

allgemein	general
eigennützig	selfish
freiwillig	voluntary
gepflegt	cared for
hübsch	nice
nötig	necessary

ADDITIONAL EXERCISES (A, B AND C TEXTS FROM READER)

Über das Schenken

Complete each answer with the adjective from the first sentence (singular form, weak endings).

1. Ursula, deine Geschenkliste ist aber lang. Ja, hast du nicht auch so eine _____ Liste?
2. Glauben Sie, das Schenken kann eigennützig sein? Ja, für manche Leute ist es eine _____ Aktivität.
3. Sind Geschenke in eurer Familie allgemein? Ja, Geschenke zu geben ist eine _____ Verpflichtung.
4. Dieser Kasten ist aber hübsch! Möchtest du mir so einen _____ Kasten schenken?
5. Unsere Angestellten sind für jede Mühe dankbar. Interessant! Ich möchte mit so einem _____ Angestellten sprechen.

Complete each answer with the adjective from the first sentence (plural form, weak endings).

6. Die Kinder sehen müde aus. Bitte achten Sie gut auf die _____ Kinder!
7. Glauben Sie, Agathes Verpflichtungen sind schwer? Ja, und ich weiß, daß sie die _____ Verpflichtungen ernst nimmt.
8. Manche Termine sind wichtig; haben Sie sie aufgeschrieben? Ja, die _____ Termine habe ich aufgeschrieben.
9. Sind die Geschenke schon eingepackt? Ja, alle _____ Geschenke sind in diesem Kasten hier.
10. Sind diese Nachrichten neu? Ja, unser Amt hat diese _____ Nachrichten gerade empfangen.

Eine Krankenschwester bei den alten Leuten

Complete each response with the adjective from the first sentence (singular form, strong endings).

11. Das Zimmer hier ist warm, möchten Sie hier wohnen? Nein, ich mag kein _____ Zimmer.
12. Ist sein Hunger wirklich so furchtbar? Ja, die meisten alten Leute haben _____ Hunger.
13. Frau Schmidts Wäsche ist aber schmutzig! Weiß sie denn nicht, wo man _____ Wäsche waschen kann?
14. Ist das Vertrauen der Leute zu der Schwester unbewußt? Ja, ich glaube, sie haben _____ Vertrauen zu ihr.
15. Freut sich die Schwester über das große Vertrauen? Ja, aber so ein _____ Vertrauen verpflichtet sie auch.

Complete each response with the adjective from the first sentence (plural form, strong endings).

16. Kennen Sie die grauen Schwestern? Ja, ein paar _____ Schwestern sorgen für meine Verwandten.

17. Haben sie dir ein besseres Dasein versprochen? Ja, mir und viel__ ander__ alt__ Leuten!

18. Arbeitet diese Schwester freiwillig? Ja, und wir kennen noch andere _____ Schwestern.

19. Hast du ihre hübschen Geschenke gesehen? Ja, sie kaufen immer so _____ Geschenke ein.

20. Warten wir auf eine gute Gelegenheit! _____ Gelegenheiten kommen aber nicht so oft.

Familienfragen

Respond with the cardinal numbers that describe your situation.

21. Wieviele Personen sind in Ihrer Familie?

22. Wieviele von Ihren Großeltern und Urgroßeltern leben noch?

23. Wieviele Menschen machen Sie Geschenke? Wieviel Prozent der ganzen Familie sind das?

24. Ungefähr wieviele Onkel und Tanten haben Sie in Ihrer größeren Familie?

25. Wieviele empfangen von Ihnen ein Geschenk?

Respond with the ordinal numbers that describe your situation.

26. Das wievielte Kind sind Sie in Ihrer Familie?

27. An welchem Tag, im wievielten Monat sind Sie geboren?

28. Welches Datum haben wir heute?

29. Der wievielte Tag des Jahres ist heute?

30. An welchem Tag, in welchem Monat und Jahr sind Sie das erste Mal zur Schule gegangen?

Respond with the time that fits your situation (use fractions).

31. Wie spät ist es in diesem Moment?

32. Um wieviel Uhr sind Sie heute aufgestanden?

33. Wann essen Sie zu Mittag?

34. Wie lange dauert ein Mittagessen in Ihrer Familie?

35. Um wieviel Uhr gehen Sie schlafen?

Complete the answer with the indefinite adjective given. Adjust the ending of the descriptive adjective.

Example

Dieses alte Mißtrauen kommt immer wieder. (viel-, genug)
Viel altes Mißtrauen kommt immer wieder.
Genug altes Mißtrauen kommt immer wieder.

36. Bitte achte auf **diese** kleinen Kinder. Ich muß schon auf ____ ____ Kinder achten. (mehrer-, ander-)

37. Hier parken **die** gepflegten Autos. Ja, ich kann ____ ____ Autos sehen! (genug, ein paar, einig-)

38. Sie hat **einen** wichtigen Termin. Sie hat jeden Tag ____ ____ Termine. (viel-, mehrer-)

39. Pflegen die Schwestern **alle** kranken Menschen? Natürlich nicht alle, aber sie sorgen für ____ Krank-. (viel-, einig-, mehrer-)

40. **Manche** alten Leute haben Grundsätze. Muß man denn auf die Grundsätze von ____ ____ Leute hören? (ein paar, mehrer-, viel-)

Respond with adjectival nouns.

Example

Alles, was wichtig ist.
Ja, alles Wichtige.

41. Kauf ein, was nötig ist. Gut, ich kaufe alles ____ ein.

42. Was frisch war, ist jetzt verdorben. Nein, nichts ____ ist verdorben.

43. Kommen dir neue Sachen in den Sinn? O ja, viel ____!

44. Dieses Mädchen arbeitet freiwillig. Ja, wir haben auch noch andere ____.

45. Ist Erika mit dir verwandt? Nein, sie ist keine ____.

II. VOCABULARY FOR REVIEW (D TEXT FROM READER, CHAPTER V)

Verbs

aus·steigen ie, ie (+ sein)	to get out
ein·steigen ie, ie (+ sein)	to get in
bemerken	to notice
bremsen	to brake
entdecken	to discover
sich ereignen	to happen
Gas geben (i) a, e	to accelerate

melden	to report
vergehen i, a (+ sein)	to pass away
verunglücken (+ sein)	to have an accident
zittern	to tremble

Nouns

der **Ärger**	annoyance, trouble
die **Nummer, -n**	number
der **Reifen, -**	tire
der **Stamm, ̈-e**	trunk
das **Steuer, -**	steering wheel
der **Tote, -n**	dead
der **Unfall, ̈-e**	accident
der **Zeuge, -n**	witness

Others

alltäglich	everyday
feucht	damp
unterwegs	on the way
verärgert	annoyed

ADDITIONAL EXERCISES (D TEXT FROM READER)

Auf der Polizei nach einem Unfall

Complete each answer with the adjective from the first sentence (singular form, weak endings).

1. War die Nummer richtig? Natürlich! Ich entdecke immer die _____ Nummer.

2. Hast du gesehen, wie scheu die Zeugin war? Ja, hast du denn dieses _____ Mädchen noch nicht bemerkt?

3. Der andere Zeuge sieht ziemlich alltäglich aus. Was ist der Unterschied zwischen einem _____ und einem besonderen Zeugen?

4. Ihr linker Reifen ist ziemlich abgefahren, Herr Hauck. Mit diesem _____ Reifen sollten Sie nicht fahren!

5. Die Straße war sehr feucht. Richtig, auf der _____ Straße darf man nicht Gas geben.

Complete each answer with the adjective from the first sentence (plural form, weak endings).

6. Diese Menschen sind tot. Diesen _____ Menschen kann man nicht mehr helfen.

7. Meine Lage ist ärgerlich. Du bist ja oft in solchen _____ Lagen, nicht wahr?

8. Unsere Autopapiere sind ganz korrekt. Na ja, solche _____ Papiere kennen wir schon.

9. Dein Auto ist aber sehr schmutzig. In solche _____ Autos steige ich nicht ein.

10. Herr Meyer ist ganz normal. Nein, die _____ Bürger sind bessere Autofahrer als er.

Ärger beim Autofahren

Complete each response with the adjective from the first sentence (singular form, strong endings.)

11. Das Wetter diesen Winter ist wirklich nicht normal! Doch, für Dezember finde ich das _____ Wetter.

12. Ist es für dich alltäglich, solchen Ärger mit dem Auto zu haben? Ja, aber ein _____ Ärger vergeht schnell.

13. Dieses Auto ist doch ziemlich alt, nicht wahr? Ein _____ Auto ist besser als gar keins.

14. Ist dieses Steuerrad auch sicher? Natürlich, das ist ein _____ Steuerrad.

15. Du hast zu langsam gebremst. _____ Bremsen ist manchmal besser.

Arztbesuch

Complete each response with the adjective from the first sentence (plural form, strong endings).

16. Der Besuch des Arztes war dringend. Natürlich, Dr. Krause macht nur _____ Besuche.

17. Weißt du Dr. Krauses private Telefonnummer? _____ Telefonnummern gehen mich nichts an.

18. Glaubst du, das Auto von Dr. Krause war billig? Nein, Dr. Krause fährt nie _____ Autos.

19. Bemerkst du, wie verärgert der Arzt aussieht? Mit _____ Ärzten kann man nicht so gut sprechen.

20. War er verärgert, weil die Straßen so feucht waren? Ja, denn auf _____ Straßen kann man verunglücken.

Answer with cardinal numbers.

21. Wieviele Stunden hat eine Woche?

22. Wieviele Wochen hat ein Jahr? und wieviele Tage?

23. Was kostet ein Mercedes ungefähr?

24. Wieviele Stockwerke hat das Empire State Building?

25. Ungefähr wieviele Bürger und Bürgerinnen leben in den Vereinigten Staaten?

Respond with ordinal numbers.

26. Welcher Tag der Wocht ist Sonntag?

27. Wer war Adam?

28. In welchem Jahrhundert leben wir?

29. Auf welcher Straße steht das Empire State Building?

30. Zu welcher Welt gehört Afrika?

Respond with non-official time expressions.

31. Um wieviel Uhr steht die Sonne am höchsten?

32. Sagen Sie ein anderes Wort für 12 Uhr nachts.

33. Von wann bis wann arbeiten die meisten Leute im Büro?

34. Wann passierte der Unfall im Text?

35. Um wieviel Uhr kam endlich der Polizeiwagen?

Nach dem Autounfall

Respond with the same adjective, ending adjusted, after the indefinite numerical adjective given.

36. Um Gotteswillen, hier liegt ein Toter! Na und? Ich habe schon viel__ Tot__ gesehen. Ich sehe jeden Tag mehrer__ Tot__ auf der Autobahn.

37. Ein schrecklicher Unfall hat sich ereignet. Ich habe gestern einen ander__ schrecklich__ Unfall bemerkt.

38. Wir melden alle schweren Unfälle, die sich ereignen. Es gibt nur wenig__ schwer__ Unfälle, nicht wahr? Jede Woche entdecken wir mehrer__ schwer__ Unfälle.

39. Behandelt dieser Arzt alle Kranken? Ja, morgens hat er einig__ krank__ Leute in der Praxis; nachmittags muß er die ander__ krank__ Leute besuchen; und abends kommen auch noch krank__ Menschen zu ihm.

Respond with adjectival nouns.

Example

Hier steht so ein **scheuer** Zeuge.
Ja wirklich, ein ganz **Scheuer**.

40. Habt ihr unterwegs **interessante** Dinge bemerkt? Leider nur wenig I_____.

41. Ihr habt aber den **schrecklichen** Unfall gesehen? Ja, so etwas S_____ sollte nie vorkommen.

42. Hast du die **jungen** Zeugen gehört? Ja, J_____ sind oft oft gute Zeugen.

43. War der Herr dir **bekannt**? Ja, er ist ein guter B_____ von mir.

PRONOUNS

FUNCTION OF PRONOUNS

227   Pronouns are words that replace nouns and noun phrases in sentences and clauses. They often signal relationships to other elements within or outside of their own clause. Because of their different functions, pronouns are grouped into seven categories:

PERSONAL	INTERROGATIVE	REFLEXIVE AND RECIPROCAL	RELATIVE
INDEFINITE	POSSESSIVE	DEMONSTRATIVE	

PERSONAL PRONOUNS

228

	SINGULAR					PLURAL		
Nominative	ich	du Sie	er	sie	es	wir	ihr Sie	sie
Accusative	mich	dich Sie	ihn	sie	es	uns	euch Sie	sie
Dative	mir	dir Ihnen	ihm	ihr	ihm	uns	euch Ihnen	ihnen
Genitive	meiner	deiner Ihrer	seiner	ihrer	seiner	unser	euer Ihrer	ihrer

NOTE 1   The genitive of the personal pronoun is quite rare. It is still required, however, after certain verbs and after certain prepositions [see 171 and 442ff.].

NOTE 2   All cases of the formal address **Sie** are capitalized. The forms are the same as those of the 3rd person plural **sie** except for the capitalization.

NOTE 3   English *it* may be **es, er,** or **sie** in German.

229   Normally, personal pronouns must be in the same gender as the nouns to which they refer; however, for the nouns **das Mädchen** and **das Fräulein** the feminine **sie** is often used instead. When the name of the person that **das Mädchen** or **das Fräulein** refers to is mentioned, the natural gender dominates and the feminine form *has to be used.*

Das blonde Mädchen in meiner Klasse ist sehr klug.   Es / Sie hat mir bei den Hausaufgaben geholfen.
Das fremde Mädchen heißt Erika Buntschuh. Sie studierte in Freiburg.

---

230 The third person **es** appears very frequently as a contraction with other parts of speech.

Wie geht's dir denn?	*How are you?*
Gab sie's ihm sofort?	*Did she give it to him at once?*

CHECK AND PRACTICE

Replace the underlined nouns with pronouns.

1. Peter sieht das Kind.
2. Paul liebt Marie.
3. Marie liebt Paul.
4. Marie und Paul lieben ihre Eltern.
5. Paul gibt Marie ein Geschenk.
6. Marie gibt Paul ebenfalls ein Geschenk.
7. Die Eltern geben Marie und Paul ein Geschenk.
8. Marie und Paul geben dem kleinen Kind ein Geschenk.
9. Peter hilft seinem Großvater.
10. Hans ißt ein Butterbrot.
11. Der Wagen ist kaputt.

Da-Compounds

231 In combination with prepositions (**bei, mit, von**, etc.), 3rd person pronouns referring to inanimate antecedents (singular and plural) or whole clauses are replaced by **da(r)**-compounds.

Ich habe **einen Freund.** Ich gehe **mit ihm** spazieren.
ANTECEDENT IS PERSON   NO DA-COMPOUND
Ich habe **einen Blcistift.** Ich schreibe **damit.** (**damit** *can refer to a singular or a plural.*)
Ich habe **ein paar Bleistifte.** Ich schreibe **damit.**
ANTECEDENT IS OBJECT   DA-COMPOUND
Fahrt ihr nach Europa? — Nein, **dafür** haben wir leider keine Zeit.
ANTECEDENT IS CLAUSE   DA-COMPOUND
*Are you going to Europe? No, unfortunately we don't have time **for that.***

232   **da-** is used with prepositions that begin with a consonant; **dar-** is used with prepositions that begin with a vowel.

bei	⟩	dabei	gegen	⟩	dagegen	nach	⟩	danach	vor	⟩	davor
durch	⟩	dadurch	hinter	⟩	dahinter	neben	⟩	daneben	zu	⟩	dazu
für	⟩	dafür	mit	⟩	damit	von	⟩	davon	zwischen	⟩	dazwischen

an	⟩	daran	in	⟩	darin	über	⟩	darüber
auf	⟩	darauf				unter	⟩	darunter

CHECK AND PRACTICE

Replace the underlined words with a pronoun, preposition plus pronoun, or *da(r)*-**compound.**

1. Frau Meyer arbeitet zusammen mit einem Kollegen.
2. Frau Meyer fährt jeden Tag mit ihrem Auto zur Arbeit.
3. Herr Kühn geht sonntags mit seiner Mutter im Park spazieren.
4. Gestern ging Peter mit seinen Freunden ins Kino.
5. Marie wollte mit verschiedenen Materialien eine Kollage machen.

233   **da(r)**-compounds are often used to introduce infinitive clauses as well as **daß**-clauses.

	Ich freue mich **darauf**, nach Deutschland zu reisen.
	*I'm looking **forward to** going to Germany.*
Instead of	Ich freue mich auf eine Reise nach Deutschland.
	I'm looking forward to a trip to Germany.

	Ich freue mich **darüber**, daß du so viele Geschenke bekommen hast.
	*I'm **happy that** you've got so many gifts.*
Instead of	Ich freue mich über deine vielen Geschenke.
	I'm happy about your many gifts.

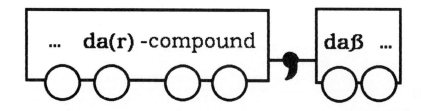

CHECK AND PRACTICE

Fill in the missing parts of speech.

1. Er ist sehr _____, ein neues Auto _____. *He is very much in favor of buying a new car.* (*to be in favor of something* = für etwas sein)

2. Marie sprach _____, daß du viel Arbeit hast. *Marie talked about you having so much work.*

3. Herr Meyer warnte Frau Müller _____, zu schnell _____. *Mr. Meyer warned Mrs. Müller about driving too fast.* (*to warn about something* = vor etwas warnen)

234 If the antecedents are stressed, **da(r)**-compounds can be replaced by a preposition plus demonstrative pronoun.

> Du hast ja hier **einen Hammer.** Was machst du denn **damit**?
> Was machst du denn **mit dem**?
> *You've got **a hammer** here. What are you doing **with it**?*

235 Prepositions such as **ohne**, **außer**, **seit**, and prepositions that require genitive objects do not form **da**-compounds. But in some instances, the preposition plus noun can be replaced by an adverb that is a close equivalent to a **da**-compound.

> Ich habe **einen Sturzhelm.** Ich fahre aber immer **ohne (ihn)**.
> *I have **a crash helmet**. But I always ride **without it**.*
>
> Peter hat **einen Computer. Trotz des Computers** konnte er aber die Aufgabe nicht schneller lösen.
> *Peter has **a computer. In spite of it**, he couldn't solve the problem any faster.*
>
> | ADVERBS | trotzdem *in spite of this* | währenddessen *during this time* |
> |---|---|---|
> | | deshalb, deswegen *for this reason* | seitdem *since then* |
>
> Peter hat **einen Computer. Trotzdem** konnte er aber die Aufgabe nicht schneller lösen.
> **Deswegen** konnte er die Aufgabe schneller lösen.
>
> Inge hatte **eine Deutschstunde.** Paul ging **währenddessen** spazieren.
> *Inge had **a German lesson. During this time**, Paul took a walk.*
>
> Karl hatte **einen Unfall.** Er fuhr **seitdem** immer sehr vorsichtig.
> *Karl had **an accident. Since then** he has been driving very carefully.*

INDEFINITE PRONOUNS

236 Indefinite pronouns stand in a general sense for someone or something unknown.

REFERRING TO PERSONS		
man	**jemand**	**niemand**
one, you, they, people	*someone, anyone*	*no one, not anyone*

REFERRING TO QUANTITIES		
etwas	**nichts**	**genug**
something	*nothing*	*enough*

REFERRING TO PERSONS (masculine and feminine singular)
REFERRING TO QUANTITIES (neuter singular)
REFERRING TO BOTH (plural)

einer	**keiner**	**mancher**	**welcher**	**jeder**	**ein anderer**
eine	**keine**	**manche**	**welche**	**jede**	**eine andere**
one	*no one*	*many (a one)*	*one*	*everyone, each one*	*another one, someone else*
ein(e)s	**kein(e)s**	**manches**	**welches**	**jedes**	**etwas anderes**
one	*none*	*many (a thing)*	*any*	*everything, each*	*something else*
—	**keine**	**manche**	**welche**	**alle**	**andere**
	none	*some*	*some*	*all*	*others*
einiges	**mehreres**			**vieles**	**weniges**
einige	**mehrere**			**viele** **viel**	**wenige** **wenig**
some	*several*			*many* *much*	*few* *little*

man	**jemand**	**niemand**
one, you, they, people	*someone, anyone*	*no one, not anyone*

237 **man**, which is used very frequently in German, appears only in the nominative form.

> Wie sagt **man** das auf deutsch? *How do **you** say that in German?*
> **Man** spielt Fußball in Deutschland. ***They** play soccer in Germany.*

238   Consistent use of **man** is required throughout a German sentence.

> Wenn **man** etwas nicht weiß, soll **man** nichts sagen.
> *If **one** doesn't know, **one (he)** should say nothing.*

REMEMBER: **er** *is not a substitute for* **man** *as* he *in English is a substitute for* one.

239   1. **einen** and **einem** are used as the accusative and dative.

> Je älter **man** wird, um so rätselhafter wird **einem** das Leben.
> *The older **one** gets the more mysterious life becomes.*

2. The genitive does not exist; **sein** is used instead.

> **Man** tut **seine** Pflicht.   *One does **one's** duty.*

240   1. In all cases but the nominative, **jemand** and its negative counterpart **niemand** are declined like the masculine form of the definite article [for declensions, see § 132]. In the accusative and the dative they may be also used undeclined. In the accusative the undeclined form is preferred.

> Es hat **jemand** geklingelt, aber **niemand** steht vor der Tür.
> ***Someone** rang the doorbell but **no one** is there.*
> Ich habe **niemand** getroffen.   SELDOM   Ich habe **niemanden** getroffen.
> Sie sprach mit **niemand.**   OR   Sie sprach mit **niemandem.**

2. Combinations with **irgend-** occur occasionally in German for emphasis.

> **Irgendjemand** kam gestern vorbei, um dich zu sprechen.   ***Someone** came by yesterday to talk to you.*

CHECK AND PRACTICE

Translate.

1. *(You)* kann hier Zigaretten kaufen.
2. Ich *(haven't seen anyone)*.
3. *(One)* sollte nicht rauchen.
4. Er spricht mit *(someone)*.
5. Ist *(someone)* zu Hause?
6. Sie sah *(one)* sehr nervös an.
7. Nein, *(nobody)* ist hier.
8. So viele Dinge können *(to you)* geschehen.
9. Willst du noch *(something)*?
10. Er wollte *(nothing)* more.

etwas	**nichts**	**genug**
something	*nothing*	*enough*

241 **etwas,** its negation **nichts,** and **genug** remain unchanged, regardless of case, person or number.

Hat sie **etwas** gesagt?	Nein, sie hat **nichts** gesagt.
*Did she say **something?***	*No, she didn't say **anything.***
Sein Wort gilt **etwas.** *His word **counts.***	Sein Wort gilt **nichts.** *His word **doesn't count.***
Hast du **genug**? *Do you have **enough?***	

einer, eine, ein(e)s	**keiner, keine, kein(e)s, keine**
one	*no one, none*

242 With a few exceptions, **einer** and **keiner** have the same forms as the indefinite article [for declension, see § 132]. The differences are: a) the genitive is missing; b) in the nominative masculine and neuter, and the accusative neuter, the endings have *not* been dropped.

	MASCULINE	**FEMININE**	**NEUTER**	**ALL GENDERS**
		Singular		**Plural**
Nominative	**einer**	eine	**ein(e)s**	
	keiner	keine	**kein(e)s**	keine
Accusative	einen	eine	**ein(e)s**	
	keinen	keine	**kein(e)s**	keine
Dative	einem	einer	einem	
	keinem	keiner	keinem	keinen

Kennen Sie **ein Mittel** dagegen?   Ja, ich kenne **eins.**
*Do you know **a remedy** for it?   Yes, I know **one.***

Inge hatte **einen eleganten Wagen.** Hans hatte **keinen.**
*Inge had **an elegant car.** Hans had **none.***

Eins noch: Stell dir vor, plötzlich kam **einer.**
***One** more thing; just imagine, suddenly **someone** appeared.*

Mir kann **keiner** helfen.   ***Nobody** can help me.*

243 The indefinite pronouns **einer** and **keiner** are often modified by a genitive.

Der Wagen gehört **einem unserer Nachbarn.** *The car belongs to **one of our neighbors.***
Er kannte **keins der Kinder.** *He didn't know **any of the children.***

REMEMBER [see § 127.2] Er kannte **nicht eins** der Kinder.
*He knew **not a single one** of the children.*

CHECK AND PRACTICE

In the second sentence, use indefinite pronouns which refer back to the underlined noun of the first sentence.

Example

Herr Kühn hat sich einen neuen VW gekauft. Frau Müller besitzt auch _____, aber Frau Schulz hat noch _____.
Herr Kühn hat sich einen neuen VW gekauft. Frau Müller besitzt auch **einen**, aber Frau Schulz hat noch **keinen.**

1. Der Lehrer stellte eine Frage. Peter gab ihm eine Antwort und Barbara gab ihm _____. Paul aber gab ihm _____.

2. Paul und seine Freunde gingen auf eine Reise. Er nahm einen Fotoapparat mit. Peter hatte auch _____, aber Barbara hatte _____.

3. Sie hatten großen Durst und Barbara trank ein Glas Cola. Peter trank auch _____, aber Paul wollte _____.

mancher, manche, manches, manche   **welcher, welche, welches, welche**
many (a one), (plural: many, some)   *one, any (plural: some)*

244 The forms of **mancher** are identical with those of the **der**-words. They are often combined with a genitive or **von**-construction. **manches**, the neuter singular, can also have a plural meaning, referring to *some things*.

Die Studenten machten eine Reise. Aber **manchen (von ihnen)** gefiel es überhaupt nicht.
***The students** went on a journey. But **many of them** didn't like it at all.*
Die Jungen aßen viel scharfe Wurst. Davon bekam **mancher (von ihnen)** großen Durst.
***The boys** ate lots of hot sausage. **Many of them** got really thirsty from it.*

Manche lernen das nie. *Some will never learn that.*
Manches werde ich nie verstehen. ***Some things** I'll never understand.*

---

245 1. To stress the meaning *many a one,* **manch einer** can be used instead of **mancher.**

> **Die Soldaten** marschieren in den Krieg. **Manch einer (von ihnen)** wird nicht mehr zurückkommen. *The soldiers are marching to war. Many a one (of them) will never return.*

2. **So** and **gar** can be used as stress markers.

> So mancher vergißt, was er gelernt hat. *Many a one forgets what he has learned.*

CHECK AND PRACTICE

1. Ich kenne (*many*), die gern in Europa leben würden.
2. Nach ihrer Reise hat die Frau (*many things*) zu erzählen?

246 The forms of **welcher** are identical with those of the **der**-words (the genitive singular is avoided). The use of **welcher** is colloquial. In standard German some other indefinite pronoun (often **einige** in the plural, **etwas** and **einer** in the singular) is used instead.

> Manchmal waren gar keine **Zigaretten** im Haus, Albert mußte am Automaten **welche** ziehen. *Sometimes there were no **cigarettes** in the house at all; Albert had to get **some** from the vending machine.*
>
> Da gibt es **welche,** die das nicht einsehen können. *There are **some** who can't comprehend that.*

jeder, jede, jedes, alle
everyone, everything, each, all

247 These two sets of pronouns are closely related, **alle** serving as the plural of **jeder.** The forms of **jeder** and **alle** are identical with those of the **der**-words [for declension, see § 132].

> **Die Kinder** spielten im Zimmer. **Jedes** hatte ein Spielzeug.
>   *The children played in the room. **Each one** had a toy.*
> **Die Jugendlichen** tanzten. **Alle** waren lustig.
>   *The girls and boys were dancing. **All** were happy.*
> **Jeder** kehre vor seiner Tür! *Mind your own business!* (proverb)
>   *(literally: **Each** person sweep before his own door.)*

248 **alle** refers usually to people; it can refer to things only if these things have just been mentioned.

> **Alle** sind heute krank. *All (people) are sick today.*
> **Diese Übungen** sind nicht gut; **alle** haben Fehler.
> *These exercises are not good; all have mistakes in them.*

249 Colloquially, the neuter singular **alles** can also refer to people in the plural.

> **Alles** mal herhören! *Everyone listen.*

ein anderer, eine andere, etwas anderes, andere
another one, someone else, something else, others

250 In the singular, the masculine and feminine forms of **anderer** are usually used with the indefinite article **ein. anderes,** the neuter singular, is usually used together with **etwas.**

> Er gab einem ein Glas Bier und **einem anderen** ein Glas Wein.
> *He gave a glass of beer to one, and a glass of wine **to another one.***
> Hast du noch **etwas anderes** mitgebracht? *Did you bring **something else?***
> Einige ältere Leute gingen im Park spazieren, **andere** saßen am Ufer des Sees.
> *A few older people took a stroll in the park, **others** sat at the side of the lake.*

einiges, einige   mehreres, mehrere   vieles, viele/viel   weniges, wenige/wenig
some   *several*   *many, much*   *few, little*

251 The forms of these indefinite pronouns are limited to the plural and neuter singular.

> Herr Wendt sammelte **Antiquitäten.** Davon waren **einige** sehr schön. Peter kaufte **mehrere. Viele** konnte er reparieren, nur **wenige** waren vollkommen unbrauchbar.
> Herr Wendt sammelte **Antiquitäten.** Davon war **einiges** sehr schön. Peter kaufte **mehreres. Vieles** konnte er reparieren, nur **weniges** war vollkommen unbrauchbar.
> *Mr. Wendt collected **antiques. Some of them** were very nice. Peter bought **several.** He could repair **many;** only a **few** were completely useless.*
> Denn **viele** sind berufen, aber **wenige** sind auserwählt. *Many are called, but few are chosen. (Matt. 20:16)*
>
> Wer **vieles** beginnt, gar **wenig** zustande bringt.
> *Whoever begins **many things** (at one time), will achieve **very little.** (proverb)*

POSSESSIVE PRONOUNS, CONT.

	ICH	DU	ER	SIE	ES	WIR	IHR	SIE
Dative								
Masc	meinem	deinem Ihrem	seinem	ihrem	seinem	unserem	eurem Ihrem	ihrem
Fem	meiner	deiner Ihrer	seiner	ihrer	seiner	unserer	eurer Ihrer	ihrer
Neut	meinem	deinem Ihrem	seinem	ihrem	seinem	unserem	eurem Ihrem	ihrem
Plural	meinen	deinen Ihren	seinen	ihren	seinen	unseren	euren Ihren	ihren

2. Before the endings **-e, -er,** and **-es, euer** *usually* drops the **e, unser** may drop the **e.**

Wessen Lampe ist das?	Das ist uns(e)re / eu(e)re.
Wessen Schrank ist das?	Das ist uns(e)rer / eu(e)rer.
Wessen Haus ist das?	Das ist uns(e)res / eu(e)res.

3. With the endings **-en** or **-em,** the first or the second **e** is *usually* dropped with **euer** and may be dropped with **unser.**

Welchen Wagen nimmst du? Ich nehme uns(e)ren / unser(e)n.
Ich nehme eu(e)ren / euer(e)n.
Welchem Fahrer gibst du das Geld? Ich gebe es uns(e)rem / unser(e)m.
Ich gebe es eu(e)rem / euer(e)m.

260 The possessive pronoun takes the place of an **ein**-word plus noun. The endings of the possessive pronouns depend on the gender of the nouns they refer to.

Mein Wagen ist kaputt. *My car is broken down.*
Meiner   auch. *Mine, too.*
Sein Wagen ist kaputt. *His car is broken down.*
Wirklich? **Seiner** auch? *Really? His, too?*
Ihr Wagen ist kaputt. *Her car is broken down.*
Wirklich? **Ihrer** auch? *Really? Hers, too?*

261   Used predicatively, the possessive pronoun is often undeclined.

Der Bleistift ist **mein.**	Das ist **mein** Hund.
Die Tasche ist **mein.**	Das ist **meiner.**
Das Buch ist **mein.**	Der Hund ist **mein.**

CHECK AND PRACTICE

Use a possessive pronoun in the second sentence, taking the underlined words of the first sentence as a cue.

Example

Mein Hund ist gestorben. _____ auch.
Meiner auch.
Paul gab seiner Freundin ein Geschenk. – Ich gab _____ auch eins.
Ich gab **meiner** auch eins.

1. Gestern sah ich euren Sohn. – Wirklich? Wir trafen _____ auch.
2. Wo sind Ihre Kinder jetzt? – In Griechenland. Und _____?
3. Paul ging mit seiner Freundin im Park spazieren. – Ich ging mit _____ ins Kino.
4. Herr Müller mußte seine Wohnung streichen. – Herr Kühn strich _____ auch.
5. Wir tranken mit unseren Kollegen ein Bier. Und ihr? – Wir tranken mit _____ einen Schnaps.
6. Herr und Frau Dietz haben in ihrem Garten viel Gemüse. Wir haben in _____ viele Blumen.
7. Erika verlor gestern ihren Schlüssel. – Die Müllers verloren vorgestern _____.
8. Hast du noch deine Briefmarkensammlung? – Ja. _____ ist jetzt wirklich toll. Und _____?
9. Der Verkehr in eurer Stadt ist fürchterlich. In _____ ist es wenigstens am Wochenende still.
10. Mein Kopf tut weh. _____ auch?

262   Primarily in written German, a combination of a definite article and a possessive pronoun is found, very often with the suffix **-ig**. When an article precedes, the possessive pronoun follows the weak adjective declension. To use a genitive, these double forms *must* be used since there is no genitive of the possessive pronoun.

Das ist **mein** Buch.	Das Buch ist **das mein(ig)e.**
	Das Buch ist **meins.**
Das Auto **meines Mannes** ist kaputt.	Das Auto **des mein(ig)en** auch.

REFLEXIVE PRONOUNS

263   Reflexive pronouns are used when the subject and the pronoun object of a verb are the same. Many verbs can be used reflexively.

NON-REFLEXIVE USE	REFLEXIVE USE
Er wäscht **den Hund.** *He is washing **the dog.*** SUBJECT → DIRECT OBJECT	Er wäscht **sich.** *He is washing **himself.*** SUBJECT = DIRECT OBJECT
Er kaufte **seinem Bruder** eine Krawatte. *He bought a tie for his brother.* SUBJECT → INDIRECT OBJECT	Er kaufte **sich** eine Krawatte. *He bought a tie for himself.* SUBJECT = INDIRECT OBJECT

[For the position of reflexive pronouns, see § 301]

264   Reflexive pronouns in German have the same form as personal pronouns except that the third person form, in both singular and plural, is **sich.**

ACCUSATIVE				DATIVE			
Personal	Reflexive	Personal	Reflexive	Personal	Reflexive	Personal	Reflexive
Singular		Plural		Singular		Plural	
mich	mich	uns	uns	mir	mir	uns	uns
dich	dich	euch	euch	dir	dir	euch	euch
Sie	**sich**	Sie	**sich**	Ihnen	**sich**	Ihnen	**sich**
ihn				ihm			
sie	**sich**	sie	**sich**	ihr	**sich**	ihnen	**sich**
es				ihm			

265 When the subject and a prepositional object are the same, the reflexive construction uses the case required by the preposition [see § 346ff.].

NON-REFLEXIVE USE	REFLEXIVE USE	
Ich spreche **über** meinen Freund. *I talk **about** my friend.*	Ich spreche **über** mich. *I talk **about** myself.*	ACCUSATIVE
Er spricht **über** seinen Freund. *He talks **about** his friend.*	Er spricht **über** sich. *He talks **about** himself.*	
Ich spreche **von** meinem Freund. *I talk **about** my friend.*	Ich spreche **von** mir. *I talk **about** myself.*	DATIVE
Er spricht **von** seinem Freund. *He talks **about** his friend.*	Er spricht **von** sich. *He talks **about** himself.*	

266 Verbs are used reflexively in sentences where the direct objects are parts of the body or articles of clothing. Possessive adjectives are used in English.

	INDIRECT OBJECT Dative Reflexive	DIRECT OBJECT Accusative	
Ich wasche	**mir**	die Hände.	*I'm washing **my** hands.*
Sie wäscht	**sich**	die Hände.	*She's washing **her** hands.*
Zieh	**dir**	den Mantel aus.	*Take off **your** coat.*
Sie zieht	**sich**	den Mantel aus.	*She's taking off **her** coat.*

CHECK AND PRACTICE

Change the non-reflexive sentence into a reflexive sentence. Use a reflexive pronoun in place of the underlined noun phrase.

Example

Der Vater zieht das Kind an.
Der Vater zieht **sich** an.

1. Ich kämme meinen Sohn.
2. Wir retten den Vogel.
3. Leg das Baby ins Bett.
4. Sie schützen das Dorf.
5. Schneide das Brot nicht!
6. Haben Sie den Jungen verletzt?
7. Er wäscht die Kleider.
8. Ich verbinde die Wunde.

267 A few verbs, called reflexive verbs, are always accompanied by a reflexive pronoun. The reflexive pronoun is an *obligatory part* of these verbs and is listed as part of the verb in the dictionary. Most often the verbal action is not reflexive. The most common reflexive verbs are:

sich ärgern *to be annoyed*	sich bedanken *to express one's thanks*
sich beeilen *to hurry*	sich besinnen *to remember*
sich beschweren *to complain*	sich entschuldigen *to apologize*
sich entspannen *to relax*	sich ereignen *to take place*
sich entschließen *to decide*	sich erkälten *to catch cold*
sich erinnern *to remember*	sich fragen *to wonder, to ask oneself*
sich erkundigen (nach) *to inquire (about)*	sich freuen auf *to look forward to*
sich freuen (über) *to be happy (about)*	sich fürchten *to be afraid*
sich gewöhnen an *to get used to*	sich irren *to be mistaken*
sich interessieren für *to be interested in*	sich umsehen *to look around*
sich verbeugen *to bow*	sich verspäten *to be late*
sich wehren *to resist*	sich weigern *to refuse*
sich (nicht) wohl fühlen *to feel (not) well*	

Ich beeile mich, um nicht zu spät zu kommen.   *I hurry so as not to be late.*
Er beeilt sich, um nicht zu spät zu kommen.   *He hurries so as not to be late.*

268 A few reflexive verbs can omit the reflexive pronoun without change of meaning.

(sich) ausruhen *to rest*	(sich) ausschlafen *to sleep one's fill*
(sich) duschen *to take a shower*	(sich) davonschleichen *to sneak away*

Er hat (sich) kalt geduscht.   *He took a cold shower.*

269 In a few verbs, the reflexive pronoun follows a preposition and is in the case required by the preposition.

DATIVE	**ACCUSATIVE**
außer sich sein *to be beside yourself*	in sich gehen *to repent*
etwas von sich weisen *to repudiate something*	an sich halten *to contain oneself*
zu sich kommen *to come to (to recover) one's senses*	
vor sich gehen *(only used in the 3rd person) to occur*	

CHECK AND PRACTICE

Translate.

1. I try to remember.
2. She decided to go home.
3. She is in a hurry.
4. They were happy about the grades.

5. They resisted.

6. We were interested in tennis.

7. I bowed.

8. He complained about the food.

9. She expressed her thanks.

10. We inquired about the results of the football game.

270 Like all other transitive verbs, the reflexive verbs always form the perfect with **haben**, even if the non-reflexive verb uses **sein** in the perfect tense.

> Er **hat sich** davongeschlichen. BUT Er **ist** davongeschlichen. *He sneaked away.*

271 If a reflexive verb demands a direct object, the reflexive pronoun is in the dative.

sich **etwas** einbilden	*to imagine **something***
sich **etwas** aneignen	*to take possession of **something***
sich **etwas** anmaßen	*to claim **something** (unduly) for oneself, to usurp **something***
sich **etwas** ausbitten	*to request **something***
sich **etwas** ausdenken	*to conceive **something***
sich **etwas** verbitten	*to refuse to tolerate **something***

Ich	bilde	**mir**	das	nicht nur ein.	*I am not just imagining that.*
SUBJECT		*REFLEXIVE*	*DIRECT OBJECT*		

CHECK AND PRACTICE

Give the perfect tense.

1. Er fährt sich mit der Hand über das Gesicht.

2. Inge fährt mit dem Auto nach Köln.

3. Sie läßt sich in den Sessel fallen.

4. Inge fiel gestern vom Pferd.

5. Der Motor des Autos läuft sich heiß.

6. Paul und Erika laufen jeden Tag eine Stunde.

7. Familie Körner zieht nach Berlin um.

8. Klause zieht sich gerade um.

Add the reflexive pronoun.

9. Wir dachten _____ ein schönes Spiel aus.

10. Ich verbitte _____ diese frechen Bemerkungen.

11. Was wünscht ihr _____ zu Weihnachten?

12. Sie bildete _____ ein, eine Künstlerin zu sein.

RECIPROCAL PRONOUNS

272   1. To indicate a reciprocal rather than a reflexive action (English *each other* or *one another*), German has the reciprocal pronoun **einander**. However, modern German often uses instead the reflexive pronoun **sich**, thereby obscuring the reflexive and the reciprocal meanings. To avoid misunderstanding, German then emphasizes the purely reflexive action in ambiguous sentences with the addition of **selbst** after the reflexive pronoun.

Peter und Paul schlugen **einander**. *Peter and Paul beat each other.*

Peter und Paul schlugen **sich**.   *Peter and Paul beat each other.*
                                            OR: *Peter and Paul beat themselves.*
Peter und Paul schlugen **sich selbst.** *Peter and Paul beat themselves.*

---

2. The pronouns **selbst** and **selber**, which do not change form, are used for emphasis also in non-reflexive sentences; they always follow the noun.

Peter hat diesen Drachen **selbst** gebastelt.   *Peter made this kite by **himself.***
                          selber

NOTE   Do not confuse the pronoun **selbst** with the adverb **selbst**, which stands *before* the noun:
                 Selbst Peter hat einen Drachen gebastelt.
                 ***Even** Peter had made a kite.* [See § 502]

---

273   After a preposition, only **einander** can be used. The preposition and **einander** are written as one word.

Fünf Autos standen **hintereinander**.   *Five cars were standing **behind one another.***

CHECK AND PRACTICE

Translate.

1. I met him. We met each other (by prior arrangement).
2. I'll see her again tomorrow. We'll see each other again tomorrow.
3. I helped them with their homework. They helped each other with their homework.
4. They praised them. They praised each other. They praised themselves.

DEMONSTRATIVE PRONOUNS

274 There are four demonstrative pronouns in German: **der, dieser, jener,** and **ein solcher.**
It is important not to confuse these with the similar articles [see § 119ff.]. Demonstrative
pronouns refer in an emphatic way directly or indirectly to a previously mentioned noun
phrase. They have the same gender and number as their antecedents, but their case is
determined by their function in their own sentence. Usually they stand at the beginning
of a sentence.

> Gestern besuchte uns **Herr Meyer. Den** bewunderst du doch so sehr.
> *Yesterday, **Mr. Meyer** came for a visit. **The very man** you admire so much.*

275 The demonstrative pronouns **dieser, jener,** and **ein solcher** are declined like **der-**
words [for declension of articles, see § 132]. Only the demonstrative **der** varies slightly
from the article declension: it receives syntactical stress and adds **-en** in the dative plural
and the genitive (**denen** instead of **den**). In addition, the genitive of the demonstrative
pronouns **der, die,** and **das** has two forms in the plural and feminine singular: the regular
form **deren,** and **derer.** The latter is used (for persons) as an antecedent of a relative
clause that follows. The genitive forms of **dieser** and the other demonstratives are regular, but are used today only in very stilted official language.

| | SINGULAR | | | | | PLURAL | |
	Masculine		Feminine		Neuter		
Nominative	der	dieser	die	diese	das	dieses	die	diese
Accusative	den	diesen	die	diese	das	dieses	die	diese
Dative	dem	diesem	der	dieser	dem	diesem	**denen**	diesen
Genitive	**dessen**	dieses	**deren**	dieser	**dessen**	dieses	**deren**	dieser
			derer				**derer**	

Kennst du seine neueste Freundin? Nein, **die** kenne ich nicht.
*Do you know his newest girl friend? No, I don't know **her** (but I know the former one).*
Welches Bild gefällt dir? **Dieses.**   *Which picture do you like? **This one.***
Mein Buch und **das** meiner Schwester.   *My book and **the one** of my sister.*
Ich schreibe an meine Eltern. **Denen** geht es nicht gut.   *I'm writing to my parents. **They** are not feeling well.*
Ich kenne meine Nachbarin gut. **Deren** Kinder kenne ich aber nicht.
*I know my neighbor pretty well. But I don't know **her** children (actually: the children of hers).*
Derer, die vor uns kamen, entsinnen wir uns selten.   *We seldom think of **those** who came before us.*
Das Schreiben ist an Sie gerichtet. Der Überbringer **dieses** wurde gebeten, es Ihnen zu übergeben.
*The letter is addressed to you. The bearer of **it** was asked to deliver it to you.*

285 When preceded by a preposition, the relative pronoun **was** must be replaced by a **wo-**compound [see also § 255.2].

Hier ist etwas, **worüber** Paul sich immer sehr gefreut hat.

---

wo

286 **wo** must be used when referring to place nouns, and may be used when referring to other expressions of place and time (instead of a preposition and a regular relative pronoun).

WITH PLACE NOUN

Er fuhr nach **Wien, wo** er seine Tante besuchte.
*He drove to **Vienna, where** he visited his aunt.*

OTHER EXPRESSIONS OF PLACE AND TIME

Ist das **das Restaurant, wo** du gearbeitet hast?
  *Is that **the restaurant where** you worked?*

Sie kam gerade **zu dem Zeitpunkt** an, **wo** das Unglück geschah.
  *She arrived just **at the moment when** the accident happened.*

---

wie

287 **wie** is used to introduce a relative clause referring to expressions of manner.

Die Art, wie er sich benahm, war sehr unschön.
***The way** he behaved was very unpleasant.*

CHECK AND PRACTICE

Give the correct relative pronoun.

1. Karl will nicht ins Kino gehen, _____ uns überrascht.
2. Frau Meyer weiß alles, _____ wir sie fragen.
3. Das Schönste, _____ ich gesehen habe, ist das Meer am Abend.
4. Sie besuchte auch in diesem Jahr den Ort, _____ sie einst zur Schule gegangen war.
5. Es war phantastisch, _____ er mit kleinen Kindern umgehen konnte.

Translate.

6. Do you know what he was asking about?

7. Everything that she said was interesting.

8. I'm not sure whose book that is.

9. He is in Berlin visiting friends.

Relative Pronouns without Antecedents

288 1. Indefinite relative pronouns without antecedents can introduce a clause and have a general meaning: **wer** *whoever, who, he who;* **was** *whatever, what, that which.*

> **Wer** nicht wagt, nicht gewinnt.   *Nothing ventured, nothing gained.*
>   (literally: *He who doesn't dare anything, won't win anything.*)
> **Was** er auch sagte, war falsch. ***Whatever*** *he said was wrong.*

2. The main clause which follows the relative clause introduced by an indefinite relative pronoun is usually introduced by a demonstrative. If the cases of the indefinite relative pronoun and the demonstrative pronoun are identical, the demonstrative can be omitted.

> **Wer** kein Auto besitzt, (**der**) muß zu Fuß gehen.   ***He who*** *owns no car has to walk.*
> **Wer** oft verschläft, **dem** sollte man einen Wecker schenken.
> ***He who*** *oversleeps often should be given an alarm clock.*
>   (literally: *one should give him an alarm clock.*)

3. The other cases of **wer** and **was** are used rarely as an indefinite relative pronoun; they are primarily found in literary speech and proverbs.

> **Wem** das Glück nicht hold, hat selten Gold.
> ***Whom*** *fortune doesn't smile on is seldom wealthy.*
>
> **Wes** (= wessen) das Herz voll ist, des geht der Mund über. (Luther)
> *Out of abundance of the heart the mouth speaketh.*

I. VOCABULARY FOR REVIEW (A TEXT FROM READER, CHAPTER VI)

Verbs

enthalten (ä) ie, a	to contain
entstehen (aus) a, a (+ sein)	to originate (from)
sich langweilen	to be bored
malen	to paint
spiegeln	to reflect
verwechseln	to mix up
wählen	to dial, select, elect
zerstören	to destroy

Nouns

der **Gegensatz**, ⁻e	contrast
die **Gegenwart**	present time
die **Gestalt**, -en	figure
die **Handlung**, -en	plot
das **Mißverständnis**, -se	misunderstanding
die **Puppe**, -n	puppet, doll
die **Semmel**, -n	bread roll
der **Spaß**, ⁻e	fun
der **Stimmung**, -en	mood
der **Versuch**, -e	attempt
das **Vorurteil**, -e	prejudice
das **Zentrum**, **Zentren**	center

Others

bequem	lazy, indolent; comfortable
eilig	hurried
ernst	serious
geistig	intellectual
notwendig	necessary
nüchtern	sober

ADDITIONAL EXERCISES (A TEXT FROM THE READER)

Respond with the personal pronoun.

1. Wer möchte einen Witz erzählen, möchtest _____ das tun, Joachim? Nein, _____ kenne keine Witze.
2. Ist hier jemand aus Köln, sind _____ von dort, Frau Schäl? Ja, _____ komme von dort.
3. Herr Maurer, können _____ mir Ihre Vorurteile erklären? Gern, ich erkläre _____, Fräulein Schmitt.
4. Max und Moritz, kommt _____ mit ins Zentrum? Na klar, _____ kommen mit.
5. Kommt Bernd auch mit? Nein, _____ muß sich beeilen, _____ muß Semmeln kaufen.
6. Hier ist unser Pfarrer. Kennst _____ _____ schon?
7. Ihr macht täglich neue Versuche. Findet _____ _____ notwendig?
8. Meine alte Mutter kann die Menschen nicht mehr erkennen; _____ verwechselt _____ immer.
9. Alte Leute brauchen Hilfe. Was können _____ denn für _____ tun?
10. Unser Pfarrer ist immer bereit, _____ zu dienen.

Respond with *ja* and personal pronouns.

Example

Hören Sie gern etwas über diese Leute?
Ja, ich höre gern etwas über sie.

11. Arbeiten Sie gern mit dem Pfarrer?
12. Hat er sich an seine Gemeinde gewöhnt?
13. Möchtet ihr die Versuche durchführen?
14. Langweilt ihr euch manchmal mit diesen Gestalten?
15. Hast du Frau Meyer mit ihrer Tochter verwechselt?

Respond with *ja* and personal pronouns or *da(r)*-compounds.

Example

Besteht Humor manchmal aus frechen Geschichten?
Ja, Humor besteht manchmal **daraus.**

16. Interessieren Sie sich für die Gegenwartsliteratur?
17. Habt ihr euch an die Gegensätze gewöhnt?
18. Entstehen viele Mißverständnisse aus solchen Gegensätzen?
19. Arbeiten die Autoren mit den notwendigen Pointen?

20. Spiegelt diese Literatur auch ernste Probleme?
21. Solche Pointen können die Stimmung zerstören, nicht wahr?
22. Hast du früher mit Puppen gespielt?
23. Diese Späße entstehen aus Mißverständnissen, nicht wahr?
24. Möchten Sie gern bei der notwendigen Diskussion mitmachen?

Respond with *nein* and the appropriate indefinite pronoun.

Example

Hast du etwas gewählt?
Nein, **nichts.** Nein, ich habe **nichts** gewählt.)

25. Hat man dir etwas erzählt? Nein,
26. Hat jemand über ernste Dinge gesprochen? Nein,
27. Hast du von einem eine Puppe bekommen? Nein,
28. Hat einer deine fröhliche Stimmung zerstört? Nein,
29. Hat jemand ein Bild von euch gemalt? Nein,

Respond with the correct forms of the indefinite pronoun.

Example

Enthalten diese Witze viele gute Pointen?
Nein, **wenige.**/Ja, **mehrere.**

30. Kennst du viele Leute hier? Nein, _____./Ja, _____.
31. Sind Sie Ärztin? Ja, ich _____./Nein, ich _____.
32. Brauchen wir ein neues Gesetz? Nein, wir _____./Ja, wir _____.
33. Habt ihr noch Semmeln? Ja, wir _____./Nein, wir _____.
34. Kommt keiner mit ins Zentrum? Doch, _____ kommt mit.

Ask questions using interrogative pronouns or compounds.

Example

Hannelore braucht eine neue Puppe.
Was braucht sie? **Wer** braucht eine neue Puppe?

35. Wir haben Inge mit Frau Tünnes verwechselt.
36. Diese Witze enthalten viele Mißverständnisse.
37. Die nüchterne Gegenwart gefällt Frau Braun nicht.
38. Du kannst dem Pfarrer die Handlung erzählen.
39. Wir sollten über diese Gestalt nachdenken.

Respond with possessive pronouns.

40. Ist das deine Puppe? Nein, *(hers)*

41. Sind neue Gesetze notwendig? Ja, *(ours)*

42. Wessen Puppe ist das, die von Helga? Ja, das ist *(hers)*

43. Habt ihr über unsere Probleme nachgedacht? Ja, nur über *(yours)*

44. Kannst du über deine Versuche sprechen? Ich spreche nie über *(mine)*

45. Unser Pfarrer spricht von ernsten Dingen. _____ auch? *(yours)*

46. Ist dein Stuhl bequem? Nicht so bequem wie _____ *(yours)*

47. Besprecht ihr die Handlung von meinem Drama? Nein, sondern die von *(ours)*

48. Wessen Ideen vertreten Sie, *(his or hers or your own)*?

49. Unser Lehrer hat es immer eilig, _____ auch? *(yours)*

Respond with the demonstrative pronoun.

Example

Was sagen Sie über diesen Versuch? (notwendig)
Der war notwendig.

50. Möchten Sie dieser Frau dienen? Nein, _____ nicht.

51. Kennen Sie den Pfarrer? Natürlich, kenne ich _____.

52. Verstehen Sie diese neuen Gesetze? Und ob ich _____ verstehe!

53. Möchtest du mit diesen Puppen spielen? Nein, mit _____ nicht.

54. Haben Sie schon von den bekannten Witz-Gestalten gesprochen? Ja, von _____ sprechen wir oft.

Restate the information in a relative clause following the cue.

Example

Sie haben sich zu einem Ausflug entschlossen. (Wann beginnt der Ausflug?)
Wann beginnt der Ausflug, zu dem sie sich entschlossen haben?

55. Ich habe die Handlung dieses Dramas nicht verstanden. Wie heißt denn das Drama, _____.

56. Dieser Mann hat meine gute Stimmung zerstört. Weißt du etwas über den Mann, _____.

57. Die Kinder malen auf weißes Papier. Kannst du das Papier sehen, auf _____.

58. Man darf diese Vorurteile nicht entschuldigen. Erklären Sie bitte die Vorurteile, _____.

59. Der Spaß enstand aus Mißverständnissen. Wissen Sie etwas über die Mißverständnisse, aus _____.

60. Das Leben <u>vieler Menschen</u> enthält schwere Probleme. Was kann man denn für solche Menschen tun, _____.

61. Man wird <u>diesen Leuten</u> ihre gute Stimmung zerstören. Was haben denn die Leute getan, _____.

Complete the statement with a relative pronoun and the information given in the first clause.

Example

Heute hatten wir ein interessantes Erlebnis.
Es war das Interessanteste, **was** wir erlebt haben.

62. Meine Eltern sagen mir alles. Aber ich glaube nichts, _____

63. Wir müssen viel tun. Und was ist das Notwendigste, _____?

64. (Ein Mensch), der dein Freund ist, ist auch mein Freund. _____ dein Freund ist, ist auch mein Freund.

65. (Eine Person), die eine Erziehung hat, steht der Gegenwart nüchtern gegenüber. _____, steht der Gegenwart nüchtern gegenüber.

66. Es freut uns sehr, (daß ihr unsere gute Stimmung nicht zerstört habt). Ihr habt unsere gute Stimmung nicht zerstört, _____.

II. VOCABULARY FOR REVIEW (B TEXT FROM READER, CHAPTER VI)

Verbs

auf·passen (auf)	to pay attention to
erwischen	to catch
probieren	to try
treffen (i) a, o	to hit

Nouns

der **Dummkopf, ··e**	blockhead, jerk
das **Erlebnis, -se**	adventure
der **Esel, -**	ass

das **Gedicht, -e**   poem
die **Kurzgeschichte, -n**   short story
das **Schauspiel, -e**   play

Others

eifrig   eager
ordentlich   decent, respectable
zornig   angry

ADDITIONAL EXERCISES (B TEXT FROM THE READER)

Respond with personal pronouns.

1. Gefällt die Geschichte deinen Kindern? Ja, _____ gefällt _____.
2. Paßt der Onkel gut auf den Neffen auf? Ja, _____ paßt gut auf _____ auf.
3. Mögen Kinder Gedichte? Nein, _____ mögen _____ überhaupt nicht.
4. Diesem Autor fallen oft kindische Dinge ein, nicht wahr? Ja, _____ fallen _____ manchmal ein.
5. Hast du mit diesem Dummkopf gesprochen? Ja, _____ habe mit _____ gesprochen.
6. Haben Sie ein Frühstück bestellt? Ja, _____ habe _____ bestellt.
7. Hat dein Vater den Jungen wirklich nicht erwischt? Doch, _____ hat _____ erwischt.
8. Müssen Sie den Studenten das Gedicht erklären? Ja, ich muß _____ _____ erklären.

Respond with *ja* and personal pronouns or *da(r)*-compounds.

Example

Du möchtest ihm bei dem Versuch helfen, nicht wahr?
Ja, ich möchte ihm **dabei** helfen.

9. Ihr wartet wohl schon lange auf eure Aufträge?
10. Kannst du die Teller schnell auf den Tisch setzen?
11. Bezahlt der Mann jetzt endlich für die Dienstleistungen?
12. Muß ich genau auf korrektes Verhalten aufpassen?
13. Soll ich die Witze wirklich vor einem Publikum erzählen?
14. Können wir uns vor dem Schauspielhaus treffen?
15. Sollte er mit einem Freund über das Erlebnis sprechen?

Respond with *nein* and the appropriate indefinite pronoun.

Example

Hat jemand den Wein probiert?
Nein, **niemand** hat den Wein probiert.

16. Weiß jemand, was ein Witz ist?
17. Ist hier einer, der diese Kurzgeschichte kennt?
18. Hat hier denn niemand aufgeräumt? Doch,
19. Will der Wirt von seinem Geld etwas abgeben?
20. Will denn niemand seinen Anteil mitnehmen?

Respond with *ja* and the correct form of the indefinite pronoun.

Example

Habt ihr Kurzgeschichten gelesen?
Ja, wir haben **welche** gelesen.

21. Gab es bei der Diskussion Mißverständnisse? Ja, es gab _____.
22. Bekam der Putzmann einen guten Stundenlohn? Nein, er bekam _____.
23. Wollte er alle seine Freunde einladen? Nein, nur _____.
24. Er mußte wohl an vielen Türen warten? Nein, nur an _____.
25. Haben Sie interessante Erlebnisse gehabt? Ja, _____.

Respond with interrogative pronouns or compounds.

Example

Harold paßt auf die Kinder auf.
Auf **wen**?

26. Ich habe die Worte des Dummkopfs nicht gehört. _____ Worte?
27. Der Wirt hat etwas Zorniges gesagt. _____ denn?
28. Der Wirt hat schon viele Gäste beschimpft. _____ beschimpft er?
29. Der Kaufmann wollte von seinen Erlebnissen erzählen. _____?
30. Ich gehe mit meinem Bruder ins Schauspielhaus. Mit _____?

Respond with possessive pronouns.

Example

Ist das Ihre Mütze, Herr Schulz? Nein, (*yours*), Herr Kühn.
Nein, das ist **Ihre**, Herr Kühn.

31. Passen Sie auf meine Worte auf oder auf die von Barbara? Auf (*hers*).
32. Wem gehören alle diese Puppen? Das sind (*ours*).

33. Sind das <u>die Entscheidungen des Richters</u>? Ja, das sind (*his*).

34. Arbeitet <u>Ihr Sohn</u> eifrig, Herr Thoma? Ja, (*yours*) auch?

35. Kann <u>dein Esel</u> ein Kind tragen? Ja, (*mine*) kann das.

36. Ist <u>ihr Dorf</u> sehr einsam? Ja, aber (*his*) ist noch einsamer.

37. Habt ihr wieder über <u>eure Erlebnisse</u> gesprochen? Ja, und über (*yours*), liebe Geschwister.

38. Mein Sohn ist ein Dummkopf. Ja, (*mine*) auch.

39. Kinder, unser Wagen ist kaputt. Dürfen wir mit (*yours*) fahren?

Respond with the demonstrative pronoun.

Example

Könnten Sie heute auf <u>meine Kinder</u> aufpassen? Nein,
Nein, auf **die** passe ich nicht auf.

40. Kennst du den Autor dieser spannenden Kurzgeschichte? Nein, ＿＿＿ kenne ich nicht.

41. Wie fanden Sie das Schauspiel? ＿＿＿ fand ich wunderschön.

42. Wem gehört denn dieser Esel? ＿＿＿ gehört einem reichen Mann.

43. Möchten Sie vielleicht bei ihm arbeiten? Bei ＿＿＿ würde ich gern arbeiten.

44. Der reiche Mann ist gestern gestorben. ＿＿＿ Witwe besuchen wir jetzt.

Complete the relative clause with the information from the first clause.

Example

Meine Kinder <u>sind alle so ordentlich</u>.
Wie danke ich meinen Kindern, **die alle so ordentlich sind?**

45. Herr Thoma hat diesem Mann ein schönes Bild gemalt. Wie heißt denn der Mann, ＿＿＿?

46. Viele Studenten lesen gern Gedichte. Zeigen Sie mir ein paar Studenten, ＿＿＿!

47. Ein Esel kam die Straße entlang. Wem gehört der Esel, ＿＿＿?

48. Der Esel ging zu einem Gasthaus. Wissen Sie, wo das Gasthaus liegt, zu ＿＿＿?

49. Man verstand kein Wort von der Diskussion. Warum hören Sie denn einer Diskussion zu, von ＿＿＿.

50. Die Ingenieurin hatte einen guten Job, einen netten Ehemann aber keine Kinder. Ich muß immer an die Ingenieurin denken, ＿＿＿.

Complete each statement with a relative pronoun and the information given in the first clause.

Example

Es machte uns zornig, daß er nie ordentlich sein kann.
Er kann nie ordentlich sein, _____
Er kann nie ordentlich sein, **was** uns zornig machte.

51. Er wollte mir etwas sagen. Ich begriff aber nicht, _____.

52. Es ist nett, daß er eifrig arbeitet. Er arbeitet so eifrig, _____.

53. Heute fällt mir nichts ein, _____ dich interessieren könnte.

54. Ihm gehörte ein großer Besitz. Aber seine Kinder waren das Teuerste, _____.

55. Einer wird dich erwischen! _____, dem danken wir.

7

BASIC WORD ORDER
CONJUNCTIONS
SENTENCE EQUIVALENTS
INTERJECTIONS

294 The front field can only be filled with *one* syntactical element. Of course, this syntactical element may consist of several words, a whole clause, or even a phrase modified by another clause.

FRONT FIELD	
Gestern	kam Onkel Otto zu Besuch.
Yesterday, Uncle Otto came for a visit.	
Am Ende der Woche	kam Onkel Otto zu Besuch.
At the end of the week, Uncle Otto came for a visit.	
Früh am Morgen, als die Sonne aufging,	kam Onkel Otto zu Besuch.
Early in the morning, when the sun rose, Uncle Otto came for a visit.	

CHECK AND PRACTICE

Reduce the elements in the front field to an accepted number. Place the extra elements in the inner field.

1. Heute wir besuchen unsere Freunde.
2. Vielleicht morgen wir gehen ins Theater.
3. Gestern abend um 8 Uhr Marie und Erika sind zu einer Party gegangen.
4. Nachdem Frau Meyer gegessen hatte, sie ist eingeschlafen.

295 Words such as **ja, nein, bitte,** or **danke** which are considered equivalents to a sentence [see § 342ff.] are not part of the front field. They are therefore separated from the front field by a comma.

	FRONT FIELD	**INFLECTED VERB**	
Ja,	Anna	**spielt**	am Morgen.

296 In **wenn**-sentences the front field is occupied by more than one element: the **wenn**-clause and either **dann** or **so.** But this **dann** or **so** contains *no new* information; it merely sums up the **wenn**-clause. Therefore, it cannot be regarded as a new independent element. [For the word order in the **wenn**-clause, see § 308f.]

FRONT FIELD	INFLECTED VERB	INNER FIELD
Wenn er nicht bald kommt, dann	gehen	wir ohne ihn.
Wenn er nicht bald kommt, so	gehen	wir ohne ihn.
If he does not come soon, then we will go without him.		

CHECK AND PRACTICE

Give the correct word order.

1. Ja, spazierengehen wir.
2. Nein, haben die Studenten die Prüfung nicht bestanden.
3. Wenn es zu spät wird, dann die Geschäfte sind zu.

INNER FIELD

297   The inner field is occupied primarily by the indirect and direct objects and the adverbs of time, cause, manner, and place. The sequence of these elements in a German sentence does *not* often correspond to the sequence in English. The sequence in German is:

1. The indirect object (usually a person) precedes the direct object (usually a thing), unless the latter is a personal pronoun. [See § 299]

FRONT FIELD	INFLECTED VERB	INNER FIELD	
Karl	*gave*	***the child***	*the ball.*
Karl	*gave*	*the ball*	***to the child.***
Karl	gab	**dem Kind**	den Ball.
		INDIRECT OBJECT	DIRECT OBJECT

2. Normally, **nicht** follows the objects. [See § 292]

Karl	gab	dem Kind	den Ball	**nicht.**

3. Adverb of time (**wann?**) is followed by adverb of cause (**warum?**), adverb of manner (**wie?**) and adverb of place (**wo?**).
   NOTE: The corresponding interrogatives are in alphabetical order.

For my sake, she sat patiently in the classroom yesterday.			
Sie saß gestern meinetwegen geduldig im Klassenzimmer.			
Adverbs of			
Time	**Cause**	**Manner**	**Place**

4. Normally, **nicht** follows specific time expressions and precedes all other adverbs and adverbial phrases.

Er	ging	heute **nicht**		in die Schule.

*He **didn't** go to school today.*

Sie	ging	diese Woche **nicht** oft		ins Kino.

*She **didn't** go to the movies very often this week.*

Sie	ist	**nicht** deinetwegen	weggegangen.

*She **didn't** leave because of you. (She left, but not because of you.)*

5. Stress can change regular word order:
   a. if the indirect object is to be emphasized, it can follow the direct object:

		DIRECT OBJECT	INDIRECT OBJECT	
Er	hat	sein ganzes Vermögen	seinem Neffen	vermacht.

He left his whole fortune to his nephew.

   b. if the negated part of speech is to be emphasized, **nicht** may precede almost any word. [See also § 315].

Er gab ihm **nicht** den Ball.
*He **didn't** give him the ball.* IMPLIED: *He didn't give him the ball although he promised he would.*

Sie wird **nicht** morgen kommen.
*She **won't** come tomorrow.* IMPLIED: *She won't come tomorrow (that is certain) but perhaps after tomorrow.*

Sie ist deinetwegen **nicht** weggegangen.
*She **didn't** leave because of you.* IMPLIED: *She is still here because of you.*

CHECK AND PRACTICE

Give the most common sequence of the parts of speech in parentheses.

1. Der Lehrer hat (dem Schüler / die Arbeit) zurückgegeben.
2. Der Schüler hat (seinem Vater / sie) gezeigt.
3. Ich komme (mit dem Autobus / in die Stadt / jeden Morgen).
4. Habt ihr (im Garten / heute / bei der Hitze) gegessen?
5. Ist Marie (nach Berlin / gestern / mit dem Zug) gefahren?

Add *nicht* without stress.

6. Lisa hat ihre Hausaufgaben heute gemacht.
7. Leider ist Erika gestern mit dem Auto gekommen.
8. Sie müssen morgen nach Berlin fahren.
9. Nächstes Jahr wird er oft ins Ausland reisen müssen.
10. Sie möchte ihre Tante besuchen.

Rule of Increasing News Value

298 Besides the basic rules given in § 297, the parts of speech in the inner field are arranged according to *increasing news value:* for the sequence of adverbs of the same type, the more general precedes the more specific.

> Paul rief **gestern abend um 10 Uhr** an.
> *Paul called **yesterday evening at 10 o'clock**.*

CHECK AND PRACTICE

Give the most likely sequence of the adverbial modifiers.

1. Er möchte (um 10 Uhr / nächsten Dienstag) ins Kino gehen.
2. Sie kommt (um 5 Uhr / montags) nach Hause.
3. Klaus und Inge waren (im September / letztes Jahr) an der See.

299 According to the rule of increasing news value, objects are arranged in accordance with their grammatical forms; i.e., whether they are nouns with a definite or indefinite article, or whether they are pronouns.

Since nouns have more news value than pronouns, pronouns are position-fixed at the beginning of the inner field. Since nouns with an indefinite article have the greatest news value, they are position-fixed at the end of the inner field.

FRONT FIELD	INFLECTED VERB	INNER FIELD Position-fixed Pronouns		Position-fixed ein-Nouns
Paul	gab	es	seinem Freund heute.	
Paul	gab		seinem Freund heute	ein Buch.

300 Nouns with **der**-words carry somewhat less news value than nouns with possessives. Therefore, direct objects with **der**-words may precede indirect objects with possessives.

> Kannst du heute dem Studenten seine Prüfung   zurückgeben?
> *Could you return his exam to the student today?*
> Kannst du heute dieses Buch   meinem Kollegen geben?
> *Could you give this book to my colleague today?*

301 The sequence of pronouns in the inner field is: subject, reflexive pronoun, direct object, indirect object.

FRONT FIELD	INFLECTED VERB	INNER FIELD			
		Subject	Reflexive Pronoun	Direct Object	Indirect Object
Er	gab			es	ihm.
Dann	gab	er		es	ihm.
Er	fürchtete		sich.		
Dann	fürchtete	er	sich.		

NOTE: The rule applies only to *personal pronouns*. Indefinite pronouns such as **alles** *everything*, **etwas** *something*, and **nichts** *nothing*, as well as the demonstrative pronouns, such as **das**, behave—as far as word order is concerned—like nouns. They come *after* an indirect object.

> Ich zeige dir **etwas.** *I'll show you **something.***
> Ich zeige dir **alles.** *I'll show you **everything.***
> Ich zeige dir **nichts.** *I'll show you **nothing.***
> Ich zeige dir **das.** *I'll show you **that.***

302 Subject nouns usually follow directly after the inflected verb if they stand in the inner field, but an object pronoun (which has less news value) can precede a noun subject.

FRONT FIELD	INFLECTED VERB	INNER FIELD Subject + Position-fixed Pronouns	
Paul	gab		dem Kind den Ball.
Gestern	gab	Paul	dem Kind den Ball.
Gestern	gab	Paul ihm	den Ball.
Gestern	gab	ihm Paul	den Ball.

303 The sequence of objects and adverbs between the beginning of the inner field (reserved for the subject and the position-fixed pronouns) and the end of the inner field (reserved for the **ein**-nouns) are interchangeable. Possible variations include:

FRONT FIELD	INFLECTED VERB	Position-fixed Pronouns	INNER FIELD Interchangeable Elements	Position-fixed ein-nouns
Lisa	gab		dem Kind den Ball heute in der Schule.	
Lisa	gab		heute dem Kind in der Schule den Ball.	
Lisa	gab	ihm	heute in der Schule den Ball.	
Lisa	gab	ihm	den Ball heute in der Schule.	
Lisa	gab	ihn ihm	heute in der Schule.	
Lisa	gab	ihm	heute in der Schule	einen Ball.

304 Prepositional objects and **da**-compounds usually tend to go toward the end of the inner field.

> Peter arbeitet schon lange **an seiner schriftlichen Arbeit.**
> *Peter has been working **on his paper** for a long time.*
> Peter arbeitet schon lange **daran.**

CHECK AND PRACTICE

Give the correct sequence of the parts of speech in parentheses.

1. Paula schreibt (einen Brief / ihrem Freund).
2. Karl schenkt (ein Buch / seinem Vater).

3. Er gibt (es / ihm / nach dem Frühstück / am Morgen).

4. Der Großvater erzählt (eine Geschichte / dem Kind).

5. Frau Meyer stellte (ihren Sohn / dem Pfarrer) vor.

6. Und dann stellte sie (ihn / dem Lehrer) vor.

7. Sie hat schon (von Franz Kafka / viele Bücher).

8. Frau Meyer schenkte (auf dem Spielplatz / heute / einem Kind / ein Plätzchen).

9. Er wartete (am Bahnhof / auf seinen Onkel / gegen Abend).

END FIELD

305 Most German sentences end with the verbal complement and therefore have no end field. If the end field is used, it is reserved for specifications (e.g., the **als-** and **wie-**phrases in comparisons), amplifications, or an afterthought, especially if these additional elements contain a preposition.

FRONT FIELD	INFLECTED VERB	INNER FIELD	VERBAL COMPLEMENT	END FIELD
Paul	kann	schneller	laufen	als Peter.
Paul can run faster than Peter.				
Inge	spielt	so schön	Klavier	wie Ulla.
Inge plays the piano as well as Ulla.				
Es	ist	im Sommer	wirklich schön	hier im Schwarzwald.
In summer, it is really beautiful here in the Black Forest.				

Questions and Commands

306 *Questions* with interrogatives follow the word order pattern found in assertions. The inflected verb part is in *second position*: the subject is forced out of the front field by the interrogative and moves to a position after the inflected verb part.

Paul	spielt	morgen Tennis.
Wann	spielt Paul	morgen Tennis?

307 In yes-or-no questions, which have no interrogative, and in commands [see § 55ff.] the front field remains unoccupied. Again, the subject moves to a position after the inflected verb part. Informal commands, singular and plural, have no explicit subject.

Paul	spielt	morgen Tennis.			
☐	Spielt Paul	morgen Tennis?			
Wir	spielen	jetzt Tennis.	Sie	spielen	jetzt Tennis.
☐	Spielen wir	jetzt Tennis!	☐	Spielen Sie	jetzt Tennis!
Du	spielst	jetzt Tennis.	Ihr	spielt	jetzt Tennis.
☐	Spiel	jetzt Tennis!	☐	Spielt	jetzt Tennis!

NOTE There is no German equivalent for the English auxiliary *do* in questions.

Do you understand me?   Verstehen Sie mich?

CHECK AND PRACTICE

Change the following assertions into questions (replace the underlined cues with an interrogative) and yes-or-no questions.

1. Die Erziehung seiner Kinder war Herrn Müller sehr wichtig.
2. Die Fabrik muß an Feiertagen geschlossen bleiben.
3. Die Eltern fuhren ohne ihre Kinder nach Berlin.
4. Paula freute sich über das Geschenk.
5. Er verbeugte sich an der Tür vor ihr.

BASIC WORD ORDER IN DEPENDENT CLAUSES

308 Dependent clauses are always connected with a main clause; they cannot stand alone. Most dependent clauses are introduced by a subordinating conjunction [see § 316ff.], relative pronouns [see § 279ff.], **wo(r)**-compounds [see § 255f.], or interrogatives [see § 283].

309　Generally, the subject stands immediately after the subordinating conjunction; the inflected verb appears *at the very end* of the clause after the verbal complement, if any. A separable prefix will rejoin its verb stem [see also § 71]. A reflexive pronoun follows the subject.

Ich glaube,	daß	Barbara	heute zu Hause	**ist.**
Ich glaube,	daß	Barbara	heute zu Hause sein	**muß.**
	CONJUNCTION	SUBJECT		INFLECTED VERB PART

| Er sah nach, ob Peter | | Bilder | **auf**hängte. | |
| | | | SEPARABLE PREFIX | |

| Er merkte, daß Peter | **sich** | | vor dem Wolf | fürchtet. |
| | REFLEXIVE | | | |

CHECK AND PRACTICE

Change the clause in parentheses into a dependent clause.

1. Die Nacht schien ihm sehr lang, weil ＿＿＿. (Er hatte Schmerzen.)
2. Ich muß sparen, damit ＿＿＿. (Ich kann ein Haus kaufen.)
3. Er arbeitete, während ＿＿＿. (Sie ging spazieren.)
4. Sie sah, daß ＿＿＿. (Er hat sich an der Tür vor ihr verbeugt.)
5. Er fragte, warum ＿＿＿. (Sie ist so müde.)
6. Sie sagte, daß ＿＿＿. (Sie hat die ganze Nacht gearbeitet.)

310　When a double infinitive occurs in a dependent clause, the principle of inflected verb-last position does not apply. Instead, in this one exception, *the inflected verb precedes the double infinitive.* The inflected verb can be in any of three positions before the infinitives and after the subject. However, as a rule, *the simple past of the modals is preferred to the perfect,* and the double infinitive construction [see § 48] is avoided.

	Ich nehme an, daß Peter		gestern		in den Zoo	**hat**	gehen dürfen.
OR	Ich nehme an, daß Peter		gestern	**hat**	in den Zoo		gehen dürfen.
OR	Ich nehme an, daß Peter	**hat**	gestern		in den Zoo		gehen dürfen.
	Ich nehme an, daß Peter		gestern		in den Zoo		gehen **durfte.**
	*I guess that Peter **was allowed to** go to the zoo yesterday.*						

311　In both English and German, dependent clauses are occasionally inserted into main clauses, but English and German patterns vary.

1. In English and German, *a relative clause* referring to the subject must follow its antecedent immediately.

2. Other dependent clauses referring to the subject appear in German *after the inflected verb part*. In English, these dependent clauses occupy the same position as the relative clauses.

	RELATIVE CLAUSE	INFLECTED VERB PART	
Lisa,	**die sehr müde war,**	ging	noch nicht ins Bett.
Lisa,	*who was very tired,*	*did not go to bed yet.*	

	INFLECTED VERB PART	DEPENDENT CLAUSE	
Lisa	ging,	**obwohl sie sehr müde war,**	noch nicht ins Bett.
Lisa,		*though she was very tired,*	*did not go to bed yet.*

CONJUNCTIONS

312   Conjunctions, as the name implies, join units of speech. Whereas the joining of words and phrases is a lexical question (choosing the correct conjunction to define the relationship), the joining of clauses is also a question of structure: subordinating conjunctions affect the word order [see § 308f.].

Words	Peter <u>und</u> Paul sind Freunde.
Phrases	Sie fahren oft <u>mit dem Fahrrad</u> **oder** <u>mit dem Motorrad.</u>
Clauses	<u>Werktags fahren sie gemeinsam zur Arbeit,</u> **und** <u>sonntags gehen sie zusammen ins Kino.</u>

Coordinating Conjunctions

313   If coordinating conjunctions connect two independent sentences, they do not affect word order.

und	*and*	**denn**	*because, since, for (causal)*	**aber**	*but*
				doch	*but*
oder	*or*			**sondern**	*but, rather, on the contrary*

Peter kann heute nicht kommen, **denn** er muß arbeiten.
   *Peter can't come today, **because** he has to work.*
Wir wollten ihn besuchen, **doch** er war nicht zu Hause.
   *He wanted to visit him, **but** he wasn't at home.*

314   In German, as in English, elements common to both clauses of a compound sentence can be omitted from the second clause. This is often the case in clauses introduced by **und**, **oder**, and **sondern**. But ellipsis is not found after **denn**, and it is rare after **aber** and **doch**. Before elliptical clauses, the comma is omitted before **und** and **oder** but not before **sondern**, **aber**, and **doch**.

FREQUENT USE OF ELLIPSIS

Sonntags geht sie ins Theater,	**und** freitags geht sie ins Kino.	
Sonntags geht sie ins Theater	**und** freitags ins Kino.	NO COMMA

*On Sundays she goes to the theater **and** on Fridays to the movies.*

Peter geht heute abend ins Theater,	**oder** er geht ins Kino.	
Peter geht heute abend ins Theater	**oder** ins Kino.	NO COMMA

*Peter will go to the theater **or** to the movies tonight.*

Monika wollte **nicht** spazierengehen,   **sondern** sie wollte radfahren.
Monika wollte **nicht** spazierengehen,   **sondern**   radfahren.
*Monika **didn't** want to go for a walk **but** wanted to bicycle.*

NO USE OF ELLIPSIS

Peter geht heute abend ins Konzert, **denn** er liebt Musik.
*Peter will go to the concert tonight **because** he likes music.*

RARE USE OF ELLIPSIS

Paul wollte mit Marie ins Kino gehen, **aber** er hatte keine Zeit.
Paul wollte mit Marie ins Kino gehen, **aber**   hatte keine Zeit.
Paul wollte mit Marie ins Kino gehen, **doch** er hatte keine Ziet.
Paul wollte mit Marie ins Kino gehen, **doch**   hatte keine Zeit.
*Paul wanted to go to the movies with Marie **but** he had no time.*

CHECK AND PRACTICE

Join the two sentences (omit any redundant elements).

1. Peter mußte das Auto reparieren. Inge wollte den Rasen mähen. (*and*)
2. Frau Meyer fährt im Sommer nach Österreich. Sie fliegt im Herbst nach Italien. (*or*)
3. Er hatte großen Hunger. Er hatte seit zwei Tagen nichts gegessen. (*because, since, for*)
4. Peter wollte seine blaue Jacke anziehen. Er konnte sie nicht finden. (*but*)
5. Das Kind wollte Schokolade kaufen. Die Mutter hatte ihm kein Geld gegeben. (*but*)

315 **aber** contradicts both positive and negative statements; **sondern** is used *only after a negative* clause or phrase. The element following **sondern** replaces the negated element before **sondern**, whereas the element following **aber** only modifies the first element, giving additional information.

Sie singt nicht schön, **aber** sehr laut.
*She does not sing beautifully **but** she does sing very loud.*

Sie singt nicht leise, **sondern** sehr laut.
*She does not sing softly, **rather (on the contrary)** she sings very loud.*

CHECK AND PRACTICE

Join the two sentences. Use *sondern* or *aber*.

1. Inge wollte nicht wandern. Sie wollte radfahren.
2. Bob spricht Deutsch nicht sehr schnell. Er spricht gut.

Subordinating Conjunctions

316

daß *that*	**während** *while*
damit *in order that, so that*	**indem** *while, by (do)ing (something)*
so daß *so that, thus, hence*	
	nachdem *after*
als *(at the time) when*	**bevor** *before*
als ob, als wenn *as if, as though*	**ehe** *before*
wenn *when(ever), if*	
falls *in (case)*	**bis** *until*
	seit(dem) *since (temporal)*
ob *whether*	
obwohl, obgleich, obschon *although*	**solange** *as long as*
trotzdem *(al)though*	**sobald** *as soon as*
	sooft *as often as*
da *since (causal)*	
weil *because*	

INTERROGATIVES (in indirect questions)

wer *who*	**wann** *when*
wen *whom*	**wie** *how*
wem *to whom*	**wieviel** *how much*
wessen *whose*	**wo** *where*
was *what*	**wohin** *to where*
	woher *from where*

[For relative pronouns, see § 279ff; for **wo**-compounds, see § 255f.]

317 In clauses introduced by subordinating conjunctions, the inflected verb stands at *the end* of the clause [see § 308f.].

> **Als** der Inspektor ins Zimmer <u>kam</u>, klingelte das Telefon.
> *When the inspector came into the room, the telephone rang.*

CHECK AND PRACTICE

Add the suggested subordinate conjunction to the clause in parentheses, and make the necessary adjustments in word order.

1. "Weißt du, _____." (wann) (Paul besucht Inge)

2. _____, gehen wir spazieren. (sobald) (die Sonne scheint)

3. _____, machte er seine Hausaufgaben. (obwohl) (er war sehr müde)

4. Herr Meyer muß zu Fuß gehen, _____. (weil) (sein Wagen ist kaputt)

5. „Bitte komme noch einmal in mein Büro, _____." (bevor) (du gehst weg)

6. _____, ist er viel stiller geworden. (seitdem) (er geht auf die Universität)

7. Lerne deine Vokabeln, _____. (damit) (du kannst bald gut Deutsch)

8. _____, feierte sie. (nachdem) (sie hatte das Spiel gewonnen)

9. Sie hörte immer klassische Musik, _____. (während) (sie lernte)

SPECIAL PROBLEMS

---

daß *that;* **damit** *in order that, so that;* **so daß** *so that, thus, hence*

---

318 Whereas **daß** poses no problem (it means *that*), **damit** and **so daß** can both be translated *so that* and have to be differentiated.

1. A dependent clause introduced by **damit** *in order that, so that* expresses a goal while the main clause gives the basis for achieving this goal.

2. A dependent clause introduced by **so daß** *so that, thus, hence* gives the consequence or result of the action expressed in the main clause.

> Er fühlte, **daß** er alt wurde.
> *He felt **that** he was getting old.*
> Der Lehrer wiederholte alles nochmals, **damit** die Schüler keine Fehler machen würden.
> *The teacher repeated everything again **so that** the students wouldn't make any mistakes.*
> Sie wurde plötzlich krank, **so daß** sie im Bett bleiben mußte.
> *She was suddenly ill, **so** she had to stay in bed.*

CHECK AND PRACTICE

Choose *daß*, *damit*, or *so daß*.

1. Es freut uns, _____ er kommt.

2. Das Kind aß den Teller leer, _____ die Mutter nicht schimpfen würde.

3. Sie mußte soviel arbeiten, _____ sie keine Zeit hatte, ins Kino zu gehen.

als *(at the time) when;* **wenn** *when(ever), if;* **wann** *when (at what time)*
[als/als ob, see § 472]

319   **als** is used in narrating *past events* and events in the historic present [see § 42]. It refers to a point in time or to an uninterrupted period.

Point **In Time**	**Als** der Inspektor ins Zimmer kam, klingelte das Telefon. **Als** der Inspektor ins Zimmer kommt, klingelt das Telefon.
Time **Period**	**Als** sie in Frankfurt wohnte, hatte sie kein Telefon.

320   1. **wenn** is used a. for *future events*,
                          b. to express recurrence, and
                          c. to express *if*.

a.	**Wenn** er morgen nach Hause kommt, werden wir ihn überraschen. ***When*** *he comes home tomorrow, we are going to surprise him.*
b.	**Wenn** die Lehrerin ins Klassenzimmer kommt, sind alle Studenten still. ***When(ever)*** *the teacher comes into the classroom, the students are quiet.* **Wenn** die Lehrerin ins Klassenzimmer kam, waren alle Studenten still.
c.	**Wenn** man auf diesen Knopf drückt, öffnet sich die Tür. *The door will open **if** you push this button.*

   2. **wenn** can be omitted where the understood meaning is *if*, but the verb must be in first place.

Drückt man auf diesen Knopf, öffnet sich die Tür. ***If*** *you **push** this button, the door will open.*

321   **wann** means *at what time* and is only used with questions. It is an interrogative with direct questions and functions as a subordinate conjunction with indirect questions, i.e., it influences word order and causes the inflected verb to move to end position.

Direct Question	**Wann kommt er?** *When is he coming?*
Indirect Question	Ich fragte ihn, **wann er kommt.**
	I asked him when (at what time) he would arrive.

CHECK AND PRACTICE

Choose *als, wenn,* or *wann,* or omit the conjunction and change the word order.

1. _____ sie im Park bummelten, begegneten sie einem alten Freund.
2. _____ der Polizist an der Ecke steht, fahren alle Autos langsam.
3. _____ die Prüfungen schon um acht Uhr begannen, fehlten meist einige Studenten.
4. _____ die Partei ihren Kurs nicht ändert, gewinnt sie die nächsten Wahlen.
5. _____ die Vorlesung beginnt, hat er uns nicht gesagt.
6. _____ er mich fragt, so sage ich es ihm.

weil *because, since (causal)*; **da** *since (causal), because*

322   **weil** indicates a strong causal connection. It is therefore *always* used in an answer to the question: "**Warum . . . ?**" and when the importance of a cause is emphasized by words such as **darum/deshalb/deswegen** *because of it,* **besonders, vor allem** *especially.*

> Ich arbeite, **weil** ich Geld verdienen muß.
> *I work **because** I have to earn money.*
>
> Er mußte schon **deshalb** Deutsch lernen, **weil** er Kant im Original lesen wollte.
> *He had to study German, **because** he wanted to read Kant in the original.*

323   1. **da** indicates a weaker causal connection or none at all.

> **Da** Paul noch Zeit hatte, trank er noch eine Tasse Kaffee.
> ***Since** Paul had some time left, he had another cup of coffee.*

2. Often, **da** is accompanied by **sowieso** *anyway* to further deemphasize the causal connection.

Da Paul **sowieso** zur Post geht, kann er auch uns zwei Briefmarken mitbringen.
*Since Paul is going to the post office **anyway**, he might as well bring us two stamps.*

---

324   **da** can be an adverb meaning *there* or *then*. In that use it occupies the front field and is followed by the verb.

Conjunction	**Da** der schlechtgelaunte Onkel am Tisch **saß**, waren alle still.
	*Since the cross uncle **was sitting** at the table, all were quiet.*
Adverb	**Da saß** sie am Tisch und unterhielt die ganze Tischrunde.
	*There she **was sitting** at the table, entertaining everybody.*

CHECK AND PRACTICE

Choose *da* **or** *weil*. **If both are possible, give first the more probable.**

1. Warum fährst du in die Staaten? _____ ich zu einer Konferenz muß.
2. Anna setzte sich auf den Sessel, _____ er bequemer war als das Sofa.
3. Er wußte deshalb soviel über Medizin, _____ seine Frau Ärztin war.
4. Es war schon spät. _____ kam er endlich nach Hause.

während *while;* **während** *during;* **indem** *while, as, by*

325   **während** *while* is a subordinating conjunction; it introduces a dependent clause. Do not confuse it with **während** *during* which is a preposition with the genitive case [see § 447] and stands before a noun.

DEPENDENT CLAUSE

Der Vater kochte,   **während** die Kinder den Tisch deckten.
*The father cooked **while** the children were setting the table.*

PREPOSITIONAL PHRASE

Während des Essens   kam Besuch. ***During** dinner a visitor came.*

---

326 **indem** *as* expresses simultaneous events; **indem** *by* instrumentality. Whereas in both instances **indem** is followed in German by a regular dependent clause, in English, *by* is followed by an incomplete clause with *-ing*.

> Sie sprach die letzten Worte, **indem** sie aufstand.
>   *She spoke the last words **as** she rose.*
> Sie brachte das Gespräch zum Abschluß, **indem** sie aufstand.
>   *She terminated the conversation **by** ris**ing**.*

CHECK AND PRACTICE

Translate.

1. Anna fell asleep during the lesson.
2. While Paul was doing his homework, Monika played tennis.
3. As she said that, she smiled.
4. By solving the problem, he showed that he was a good student.

nachdem *after;* **nach** *after*

327 **nachdem** and **nach** both mean *after.* But **nachdem** is a subordinating conjunction; it introduces a dependent clause. **nach** is a dative preposition [see § 391] and stands before a noun.

> **Nachdem** man gegessen hat, soll man ruhn.
> ***After** one has eaten, one should take a rest.*
> **Nach** dem Essen sollst du ruh'n oder tausend Schritte tun. *(proverb)*
> ***After** dinner sit awhile, after supper walk a mile.*

328 **nachdem** may be used only with the perfect and past perfect tenses. If the dependent clause is in the past perfect, the main clause must be in the past tense; if the dependent clause is in the perfect, the main clause can be in the present tense or the future tense.

PAST PERFECT	PAST TENSE
Nachdem er seine Arbeit beendet hatte,	fuhr er nach Hause.
After he had finished his work, he drove home.	

PERFECT	PRESENT
Nachdem er ein Bier getrunken hat,	geht er ins Bett.
After he has drunk his beer, he goes to bed.	

PERFECT	FUTURE
Nachdem er geschlafen hat,	wird er ausgehen.
After he has slept, he will go out.	

CHECK AND PRACTICE

Give the correct tense of the *nachdem*-clause.

1. Nachdem (der Besuch geht weg), werden wir es uns gemütlich machen.
2. Nachdem (wir essen das Eis), gehen wir in ein Museum.
3. Nachdem (der Löwe frißt das Fleisch), schlief er.

Fill in *nach* or *nachdem*.

4. *(After)* der Klasse gehen wir in die Bibliothek.
5. *(After)* wir unsere Aufgaben gemacht haben, gehen wir ins Kino.

bevor / ehe *before;* **vor** *before, ago*

329 Both conjunctions **bevor** and **ehe** mean *before*, but **ehe** is less common.

> **Bevor/Ehe** der Inspektor nach Hause ging, schloß er das Büro zu.
> *Before the inspector went home, he locked the office.*

330 **vor** is a preposition; in its temporal use (governing the dative), it can mean *before* or *ago*. [See § 437f.]

> Er geht nie **vor** zwölf Uhr ins Bett. *He never goes to bed **before** 12 o'clock.*
> Sie hatte **vor** zwei Jahren einen Unfall. *She had an accident two years **ago**.*

CHECK AND PRACTICE

Translate.

1. She came before dinner.
2. He came before she had cooked dinner.
3. Two days ago, he came to dinner too early.

bis *until*

331   **bis** *until* can be a subordinating conjunction or a preposition (governing the accusative). [See § 350ff.]

Conjunction	Warten Sie, **bis** ich zurückkomme! *Wait **until** I come back.*
Preposition	Warten Sie **bis** nächsten Monat. *Wait **until** next month.*

CHECK AND PRACTICE

Which *bis* is a conjunction? Which is a preposition?

1. Er ging spazieren, bis er müde war.
2. Wir müssen noch warten, bis der Kaffee kocht.
3. Die Arbeit muß bis nächste Woche fertig sein.

seitdem *since, ever since;* **seitdem** *since then;* **seit** *since*

332   When the conjunction **seitdem** *since* refers to a one-time past action, German uses the perfect tense (whereas English uses the past tense). [See also § 46].

Perfect	**Seitdem** sie mich belogen hat, glaube ich ihr nicht mehr.
Past Tense	*Ever since she lied to me, I don't believe her any more.*

333   When the conjunction **seitdem** *since* refers to a continuing or repeated action, German uses the present tense (whereas English uses the perfect progressive). [See also § 40].

Present Tense	**Seitdem** der Inspektor weniger raucht, ist er nervöser geworden.
Perfect Progressive	*Ever since the inspector has been smoking less, he has become more nervous.*

334 **seitdem** *since then* is an adverb [See § 496]. It can occupy the front field, followed by the inflected verb, or it can occupy a position in the inner field.

> **Seitdem** arbeitet er immer in seinem Büro.
> Er arbeitet **seitdem** immer in seinem Büro. ***Since then** he's always been working in his office.*

335 **seit** *since* is a dative preposition [see § 394f.].

> **Seit** der letzten Prüfung hatte er keine Vokabeln mehr gelernt.
> ***Since** the last exam, he had not learned any new vocabulary words.*

CHECK AND PRACTICE

Translate into English.

1. Seitdem sie im Lotto gewonnen hat, ist sie ein anderer Mensch.
2. Seitdem er im Orchester spielt, sehe ich ihn nur selten.
3. Seitdem ist sie fast nie zu Hause.

Choose *seit* **or** *seitdem.*

4. Sie arbeitet schon _____ sechs Wochen an ihrer schriftlichen Arbeit.
5. _____ sie in der Bibliothek arbeitet, geht es ihr viel besser.

Two-Part Conjunctions

336 The most frequently used two-part conjunctions are:

entweder . . . oder	*either . . . or*
weder . . . noch	*neither . . . nor*
nicht nur . . . sondern auch	*not only . . . but also*
sowohl . . . als auch	*both . . . and, as well as*

POSITION OF THE TWO ELEMENTS

337 In joining words and phrases, the two parts of the two-part conjunctions always stand before their respective elements. In joining clauses, the position of the first part varies.

entweder . . . oder   *either . . . or*

338   As a coordinating conjunction, **entweder** shares the front field with the subject, not affecting word order; or it occupies the front field alone; or it occupies a place in the inner field. **oder** always introduces the second clause.

FRONT FIELD		INNER FIELD	SECOND CLAUSE
Entweder ich	reise	heute noch,	**oder** ich bleibe eine weitere Woche.
Entweder	reise	ich heute noch,	**oder** ich bleibe eine weitere Woche.
Ich	reise	**entweder** heute noch,	**oder** ich bleibe eine weitere Woche.
*Either I'm going to leave today **or** I'm going to stay another week.*			

weder . . . noch   *neither . . . nor*

339   **weder** may occur either in the inner field, or, less frequently, it may occupy the front field alone. **noch** always introduces the second clause; it occupies the front field.

FRONT FIELD		INNER FIELD		SECOND CLAUSE
Er	hat	**weder** viel	getrunken,	**noch** hat er viel gegessen.
Weder	hat	er viel	getrunken,	**noch** hat er viel gegessen.
*Neither did he drink much **nor** did he eat much.*				

nicht nur . . . sondern auch   *not only . . . but also*

340   Referring to the subject, **nicht nur** and **sondern auch** occupy the front field before their respective subjects. Referring to other parts of speech, **nicht nur** appears within the inner field, while **sondern** introduces the second clause, and **auch** follows the inflected verb.

FRONT FIELD	INNER FIELD
Nicht nur Paul, **sondern auch** Anna hatte wenig Zeit.	
*Not only Paul **but also** Anna had little time.*	

FRONT FIELD	INNER FIELD	SECOND CLAUSE
Paul	spielte	**nicht nur** gut Tennis,	**sondern** er war **auch** ein guter Läufer.
*Paul **not only** played tennis well, **but** was **also** a good runner.*		

sowohl . . . als auch   *both . . . and, as well as*

341   These conjunctions connect words or phrases, not clauses.

> **Sowohl** Herr Huber **als auch** der Inspektor waren ratlos.
>   *Both Herr Huber **and** the inspector were helpless.*
> Er ist **sowohl** dumm **als auch** arrogant.
>   *He is stupid **as well as** arrogant.*

SENTENCE EQUIVALENTS

342   A sentence equivalent is a word which is not part of a sentence but takes the place of one. Three groups can be differentiated:

a. **ja, nein, doch**

b. **bitte, danke**

c. interjections

343   **ja, nein,** and **doch** are answers to yes-or-no questions: **ja** confirms the yes-or-no question; **nein** negates it. **doch** is used as an affirmative answer to a negative question or statement.

> Fährst du nach Hause? **Ja** (, ich fahre nach Hause).
>   **Nein** (, ich fahre nicht nach Hause).
>
> Fährst du **nicht** nach Hause? **Doch,** (ich fahre nach Hause).
> Ist das **keine** gute Antwort? **Doch,** (das ist eine gute Antwort).
>
> Mein Herr, Sie sind kein Student. **Doch,** (ich bin Student).   *Yes I am!*

Nein!   Doch!

344 bitte is also a polite way of saying **ja; danke,** a polite way of saying **nein.** Whereas **danke** appears solely as a reaction to a question or statement, **bitte** can be part of a request.

Ich danke Ihnen für Ihre Bemühungen. *Thank you for all your help.*
Bitte (, gern geschehen). *You are welcome./I was happy to do it.*

Ich habe das Buch für Sie mitgebracht. *I brought this book along for you.*
Danke (, das war sehr nett von Ihnen). *That was very nice of you.*

Möchten Sie noch eine Tasse Tee? *Do you want another cup of tea?*
Bitte (, aber nur halb voll). (= Ja.) *Yes, please (but only half a cup).*
Danke (, ich möchte nichts mehr). (= Nein.) *No, thank you (, I had enough).*
Nein, **danke.** *No, thank you.*

Darf ich hier Platz nehmen? *May I take a seat?*
Bitte (, der Platz ist noch frei). (= Ja.) *Yes, the seat has not been taken.*
Nein (, der Platz ist leider besetzt). *Sorry, the seat has been taken.*

Bitte, treten Sie ein! *Please, come in.*
Bitte, nehmen Sie Platz! *Please, have a seat.*

---

345 Interjections express joy, pain, doubt, etc. The meaning of some is obvious; the meaning of others can be determined only by the context. They are usually followed by an exclamation mark.

Joy	**heisa, hurrá, juchhé** *heigh-ho, hurrah*
Disgust	**äks, pfui, puh** *pooh, fie, for shame; how disgusting*
Fear	**uh, hu(hu)**
Pain	**au(a), (o) weh** *ouch*
Mockery	**ätsch** *shame on you, serves you right*
Surprise	**hoho, nanu** *well, I declare; what next*
Regret, Pain, Longing, Surprise	**ach** *oh, alas* **ach was** *oh, nonsense* **ach so** *(oh) I see* **ach wo** *oh, not at all*
Admiration, Joy, Surprise	**ah**
Enjoyment, Reflection, Surprise, Agreement	**hm**
Expressions of Challenge and Request	**hella, halloh, pst, sch . . .**

I. VOCABULARY FOR REVIEW (A AND B TEXTS FROM READER, CHAPTER VII)

Verbs

sich ärgern (über)	to get angry (about)
streicheln	to caress, stroke
unterstützen	to support
verändern	to change
verwöhnen	to spoil
sich zanken	to quarrel

Nouns

die **Eigenschaft, -en**	characteristic
die **Einstellung, -en**	attitude
die **Geduld**	patience
die **Gleichberechtigung**	equality
der **Haß**	hatred
die **Laune, -n**	mood
die **Pflicht, -en**	duty
die **Rücksicht, -en**	consideration
Rücksicht nehmen	to be considerate
die **Treue**	fidelity
der **Trost**	consolation

Others

einsam	lonely, alone
geduldig	patient
gleichgültig	indifferent
gutmütig	good-natured
häuslich	domestic
leidenschaftlich	passionate
liebevoll	loving
selbstsicher	self-assured
sparsam	frugal
verliebt	in love
wütend	furious
zärtlich	tender
zuverlässig	reliable
zu zweit	two together, by twos

44. Du mußt aufpassen, (du/dein Kind/nicht verwöhnen)

45. Er hatte eine so gute Anzeige geschrieben, (er/zu viele Antworten/bekommen)

46. Er schreibt eine gute Anzeige, (er/nette Antworten/bekommen)

Answer the questions as suggested, beginning with *als* or *wenn* as required.

47. Warst du jemals unglücklich? Ja, (einsam sein)

48. Bist du manchmal unglücklich? Ja, (sich einsam fühlen)

49. Hast du schon mal die Geduld verloren? Ja, (mein Partner/Launen haben)

50. Verlierst du manchmal die Geduld? Ja, (meine Kinder/sich zanken)

51. Bist du manchmal wütend auf deinen Partner? Ja, (aber nur/er/schlechte Laune/haben)

52. Warst du schon einmal wütend auf deine Partnerin? Ja, (sie/schlechte Laune haben)

Answer the questions twice: first with *weil*, then with *denn*, making the necessary syntactical changes.

53. Warum geht Ihre Frau so selten aus? (sie/viele häusliche Pflichten/haben)

54. Warum sind Ihre Kinder so selbstsicher? (wir/sie unterstützen)

55. Warum sind Meyers so glücklich? (sie/aufeinander Rücksicht nehmen)

56. Warum sagst du nichts? (ich Geduld/zeigen wollen)

II. VOCABULARY FOR REVIEW (C TEXT FROM READER, CHAPTER VII)

Verbs

atmen	to breathe
erkältet sein (+ sein)	to have a cold
ertragen (ä) u, a	to endure, put up with
flüstern	to whisper
heizen	to heat
schade sein (um) (+ sein)	to be too bad (about)
schlucken	to swallow
seufzen	to sigh
wachen (bei)	to keep watch (at)

Nouns

die **Decke, -n**	blanket
das **Fieber**	fever
der **Kampf, ⁻e**	struggle
der **Schnupfen, -**	head cold
der **Widerstand, ⁻e**	resistance

Others

kühl	cool
sachlich	objective
seltsam	strange
stumm	silent
ungerecht	unfair

ADDITIONAL EXERCISES (C TEXT FROM THE READER)

Ein paar Fragen über die Autorin Luise Rinser

Restate as questions using the interrogatives given (observe verb position).

1. Sie war **von 1934–39** Volksschullehrerin in München. (wann)

2. Von 1934–39 war sie **Volksschullehrerin**. (was)

3. Sie heiratete **einen Mann aus der Opposition**. (wen)

4. Rinsers Mann fiel 1943 **in Rußland**. (wo)

5. **Wegen ihres politischen Widerstands** mußte sie ins Gefängnis. (warum)

Besuch beim kranken Onkel

Answer as suggested (observe verb position).

6. Erwartet sie ein Kind? (Ja, und die junge Frau will ihren Onkel besuchen, obwohl)
7. Ist das ihr erstes Baby? (Ja, sie kann unmöglich fahren, weil)
8. Hat der Kranke noch hohes Fieber? (Ich weiß nicht, ob)
9. Er will sie wohl noch einmal sehen? (Ja, und sie fährt zu ihm, wenn)
10. Starb der Onkel bei ihrem Besuch? (Ja, es war schade, daß)

Im Krankenzimmer

Restate the questions as dependent clauses, following the given introduction.

"Der Arzt fragte, . . ."

11. War der Onkel lange erkältet?
12. Wann hat sein Schnupfen angefangen?
13. Wer wird bei dem Kranken wachen?
14. Kann er schlecht schlucken?
15. Atmet er langsam oder schnell?
16. Erträgt er diese Krankheit stumm?
17. Haben Sie noch eine Decke für den Kranken?

Am Krankenbett

Restate the sentences as dependent clauses, following the given introduction.

"Man konnte sehen, daß . . ."

18. Er sah seltsam aus.
19. Der Onkel möchte seine Nichte noch einmal sehen.
20. Onkel Gottfried konnte nur schwer schlucken.
21. Er konnte seinen Schnupfen nicht gut ertragen.
22. Sein Widerstand wurde immer weniger.
23. Er seufzte nur noch.

Eine Ehegeschichte

Tell the story, using the given elements introduced by coordinating conjunctions.

24. Mein Onkel tat mir leid. (es/um seine Ehe/schade sein)

25. Er liebte seine Frau. (er/alles für sie/tun)

26. Zum Beispiel heizte er den Herd. (er/seiner Frau/das Frühstück bringen)

27. Er sagte immer: „Entweder liebt man sich, (man/wie fremde Leute/nebeneinander leben)"

28. Die Eheleute hatten keine Kinder. (die Frau/keine/wollen)

29. Es gab keinen Kampf zwischen ihnen. (es/nur seinen Widerstand/geben)

30. Wir baten ihn, über seine Ehe zu sprechen. (er/stumm bleiben)

31. Der Neffe wurde wütend. (der Onkel/ganz sachlich/bleiben)

Connect the two statements with *daß, so daß* or *damit* as required.

32. Meine Tante blieb tagelang im Bett. Sie wurde dick.

33. Er flüsterte so leise mit uns. Sie konnte uns nicht hören.

34. Er heizte den Herd. Sie brauchte es nicht zu tun.

35. Sie lebten so kühl nebeneinander. Es war schade um ihr ganzes Leben.

Respond as suggested, beginning with *als* or *wenn* as required.

36. Wann erkältete sich denn der Onkel? (er/bei kaltem Wetter/ausgehen)

37. Er braucht eine Decke. (er/Schnupfen haben)

38. Wann beginnt der Kampf in einer Ehe? (einer den anderen/betrügen)

39. Sollen sie sich scheiden lassen? (Ja/sie/nur nebeneinander/leben)

40. Und wann ging der Konflikt zu Ende? (einer/Sieger/werden)

Answer the questions twice: first with *weil*, then with *denn*. Make the necessary syntactical changes.

41. Warum betrank sich Gottfried jeden Abend? (er/in seiner Ehe/unglücklich sein)

42. Warum seufzte er so tief? (er/das Leben/ungerecht finden)

43. Warum ließen sie sich scheiden? (sie/ihn betrügen)

44. Warum erscheint die Krankheit so gefährlich? (das Fieber/sehr hoch sein)

Eine Krankengeschichte

Tell the story, using the given elements introduced by subordinating conjunctions.

45. Die Frau des Kranken seufzte leise. (sie/die Tür/öffnen)
46. Er hatte sie geheiratet. (sie/fast noch ein junges Mädchen/sein)
47. Man konnte sehen. (es/jetzt/nur noch Kampf zwischen ihnen/geben)
48. Sie hatte ihn einkaufen geschickt. (er/erkältet/sein)
49. Dann wurde er immer kränker. (er/nicht mehr/schlucken können)
50. Die Nichte kam, um allein beim Onkel zu wachen. (sie/große Angst/haben)
51. Der Blick des Kranken war so kühl. (die junge Frau/es nicht ertragen können)
52. Später kam noch der Arzt. (es/für den Kranken/zu spät sein)

PREPOSITIONS

FUNCTION OF PREPOSITIONS

346 A *preposition* is a part of speech that relates words or word groups to each other. As the name indicates, a *pre*position is usually found in front of the word it governs (the word whose case it determines). But a few follow the word governed (e.g., **entlang**), and in some cases a double preposition embraces the word governed (e.g., **um . . . willen**).

der Mann	der Tisch	der Mann **hinter** dem Tisch
the man	*the table*	*the man **behind** the table*

347 1. Often prepositions and the definite article are contracted. The most common contractions are:

am = an dem	aufs = auf das	im = in dem	zum = zu dem
ans = an das	beim = bei dem	ins = in das	zur = zu der
		vom = von dem	

2. Other contractions occur in colloquial speech. **fürs = für das, vorm = vor dem,** and **vors = vor das** are on the border between formal and colloquial.

348 We can differentiate four groups of prepositions by the case they govern.

ACCUSATIVE   DATIVE   ACCUSATIVE OR DATIVE   GENITIVE
see § 349ff.   see § 371ff.   see § 413ff.   see § 442ff.

Although general meaning and usage patterns exist and are described below, these patterns can give only a partial understanding. The use of prepositions is very idiomatic in both German and English.

PREPOSITIONS THAT GOVERN THE ACCUSATIVE

349 The following prepositions govern the accusative:

bis	für	ohne
durch	gegen	um

bis + ACCUSATIVE

LITERAL USE

350 *until, by; as far as, to*   **bis** indicates duration or a distance, and gives the point of termination. It usually stands by itself.

> Ich warte **bis 12 Uhr.** *I'm going to wait **until 12 o'clock.***
> Ich fahre nur **bis Freiburg.** *I'm only going **as far as Freiburg.***

351 1. When **bis** governs a noun which requires an article, *a second preposition must be used* with **bis**. The second preposition determines the case of the object.

> **Bis zu den Ferien** muß ich noch viel lesen. *I still have a lot to read **until vacation time.***
> Das Auto fuhr **bis vor das Hotel.** *The car drove **right up to the hotel.***
> Der Bus fuhr **bis in das Stadion.** *The bus drove **right into the stadium.***
> Von hier **bis zur Kirche** sind es zu Fuß etwa fünf Minuten. *It's about a 5-minute walk from here **to the church.***
> Er kam mit **bis an die Tür.** *He accompanied me **(right) up to the door.***

2. A second preposition is *optional* with:
   a. time phrases like **Woche, Monat, Jahr** modified by **Anfang, Ende, Mitte, vorig-, nächst-,** and with names of weekdays, months, and dates. If **bis** stands by itself, no article follows; if the optional preposition follows, the article of the noun object has to be used.

> **Bis nächstes (Bis zum nächsten) Jahr** will er mit seiner Arbeit fertig sein.
> *He wants to be finished with his project **by next year.***

   b. names of places.

> Er fuhr von Leipzig **bis (nach) Weimar.** *He drove from Leipzig **to Weimar.***

CHECK AND PRACTICE

Give *bis* or *bis zu*. Pay attention to articles and cases. Gender is given in parentheses.

1. _____ heute abend muß Peter noch fünf Briefe schreiben.
2. _____ Urlaub wird Herr Meyer noch viel arbeiten müssen. *(m)*
3. Inge wird noch _____ 1994 bei ihren Eltern wohnen.

Give *bis* and then restate the sentence with *bis zu*.

4. _____ September haben die Kinder Schulferien. *(m)*
5. _____ Donnerstag will ich noch warten. *(m)*
6. _____ 5. Juli muß die Arbeit geschrieben sein. *(m)*
7. _____ Mitte der Woche hat Paula Zeit. *(f)*

Choose the correct answer. Sometimes two answers are possible.

8. Familie Meyer fuhr mit dem Zug _____ München. (bis) (bis zu) (bis nach)

9. Paul lief vom Stadion _____ Schwimmbad. (bis) (bis zum) (bis nach dem)

10. Sie kam _____ hierher, aber nicht weiter. (bis) (bis zu) (bis nach)

11. Frau Schmidt fuhr mit dem Taxi _____ Theater. (bis) (bis vor das) (bis nach dem)

FIGURATIVE USE

352 *till, up to* **bis** (in conjunction with a second preposition) can indicate the utmost degree of an expressed state.

> Sie marschierten **bis zur Erschöpfung.**   *They marched **till exhaustion.***

353 In temporal and modal usage **bis** can be used to indicate uncertainty.
[See also **zwischen**, § 441]

> Die Operation dauerte **zwei bis drei Stunden.**   *The operation took **between two and three hours.***

durch + ACCUSATIVE

354 *through* **durch** indicates a movement through a specified area (also in a more abstract sense) or movement within that area.

> Er geht **durch den Garten.**   *He walks **through the garden.***
> Wir bummeln **durch die Innenstadt.**   *We stroll **through the inner city.***

355 *by, by means of* **durch** indicates the means by which an action is caused. [See passive, § 523].

> Dresden wurde **durch Bomben** zerstört.   *Dresden was destroyed **by bombs.***

CHECK AND PRACTICE

Translate the preposition and give the correct case of the article or omit the article.

1. Er ging *(through)* (das Eßzimmer) in die Küche.

2. Heinz und Gerda spazierten *(through)* (der Park).

3. Der Vortrag wurde *(by)* (der Lärm) gestört.

4. *(By)* (vieles Üben) wurde er ein guter Klavierspieler.

für + ACCUSATIVE

356 *for, to, of*

> Anna war **für** Pressefreiheit. *Anna was for freedom of the press.*
> Seine Krankheit war **für** den Arzt neu. *His sickness was new to the doctor.*
> Er war Direktor **für** Internationale Studien. *He was the director of International Studies.*

CHECK AND PRACTICE

Translate.

1. She'll translate the book for us.
2. Paul has to study tonight for his exam.
3. For all his work he received really very little money.
4. Here is the key to the door.

357 With a twin-noun-construction, **für** can also be used for emphasis. [See also § 370.]

> **Tag für Tag** ging sie ins Büro. *She went to her office day after day.*

ENGLISH *FOR* IN TIME PHRASES

358 *for* in English time phrases implying a duration can be translated into German by
a. **seit;** b. an accusative alone or with optional **lang;** c. **für.**

359 **seit** is used for a period of time beginning in the past and still continuing in the present. [See § 394f.]

> Er ist **seit** drei Wochen hier. *He has been here for three weeks.*

360 1. An accusative without a preposition is usually used for a period of time lying *completely in the past or future*. The addition of **lang** is optional.

> Wir waren drei Wochen **(lang)** in Deutschland. *We were in Germany for three weeks.*

FIGURATIVE USE

369 *for* **um** is used when acquisition of something is expressed.

> Frau Meyer bewarb sich **um** diese Stelle. *Ms. Meyer applied **for** this position.*

370 With a twin-noun-construction, **um** can also be used for emphasis (like **für**).

> **Tag um Tag** wartet er auf Antwort. **Day in and day out,** *he waits for an answer.*

PREPOSITIONS THAT GOVERN THE DATIVE

371

aus	mit	seit
außer	nach	von
bei		zu
gegenüber		

aus + DATIVE

372 *out of; from (a place of origin)*

> Der Sohn nimmt die Wäsche **aus** dem Korb. *The son takes the wash **out of** the basket.*
> Ich stamme **aus** Hamburg. *I'm **from** Hamburg. (I come **from** Hamburg.)*

373 *made out of*   [See also **von**, § 404]

> Der Hammer ist **aus** Eisen. *The hammer is **made out of** iron.*

CHECK AND PRACTICE

Translate.

1. Peter came out of the house.
2. Inge is from Freiburg.
3. This ring is made of gold.
4. He took a pencil out of his pocket.

374   *out of, because of, for (motivation or reason)*   The article is omitted.

> Er half ihr **aus** Mitleid. *He helped her **out of** pity.*

NOTE   **aus** precedes nouns expressing a subjective emotion which is the motivation for a consciously planned action; **vor** [see § 439] precedes nouns whose effect is expressed in the verb: **vor Kälte zittern** *to shiver with cold*

außer + DATIVE

375   *but, except for, besides, aside from, in addition to*

> Alle **außer** Peter waren gekommen.   ***Except for** Peter everyone had come.*
> **Außer** seinem Gehalt erhielt er ein Geschenk.   ***In addition to** his salary he received a present.*

376   *out of*   Used without the article.

> Nach wenigen Minuten war das Boot **außer** Sichtweite.   *In a few minutes the boat was **out of** sight.*

CHECK AND PRACTICE

Translate.

1. All but one girl had taken the exam.
2. No one of my colleagues except Mr. Müller drove a sports car.
3. Besides tennis, I like to play soccer and golf.
4. Aside from the terrible weather, we had a good vacation.

bei + DATIVE

SPATIAL AND FIGURATIVE USE

377   *near, next to, at, by*   **bei** is used to express physical proximity.

> Er saß **bei** der Tür. *He sat **at** the door.*
> In Brühl **bei** Bonn steht ein bekanntes Schloß. *In Brühl, **near** Bonn, is a well-known palace.*

378   *with (someone; in someone's house or home),* **at,** *for (with a job),* **with** *or* **on** *(one's person)*

> Sie wohnt **bei** ihren Eltern. *She is living **with** her parents.*
> Er ist **beim** Bäcker. *He is **at** the baker's.*
> Sie arbeitet **bei** der Firma Wendt. *She works **for** (the firm) Wendt.*
> Ich habe kein Geld **bei** mir. *I have no money **with/on** me.*

CHECK AND PRACTICE

Translate.

1. Paul sat by the window.
2. The school is next to the church.
3. She works for IBM.

TEMPORAL USE

379   ***while, in the process of***   bei is primarily used in the meaning of *while* in combination with nouns derived from verbs (e.g., **essen — das Essen**).

> **Beim** Essen soll man nicht sprechen. *You are not supposed to speak **while** eating.*

380   *at, during, upon*

> **Bei** ihrer Ankunft regnete es. *It was raining **at** her arrival.*

CHECK AND PRACTICE

1. (*During the lesson*) sollst du dich konzentrieren.
2. (*At*) (die Neuigkeit) wurde er bleich.

381   *if, in case of*

> **Bei** Gefahr Notbremse ziehen. ***In case of** danger, pull the emergency brake.*

382   IDIOMATIC USE

> Er war **bei** guter / schlechter Laune. *He was **in** a good / bad mood.*
> Sie nahm mich **beim** Wort. *She took me **at** my word.*
> Er nahm mich **bei** der Hand. *He took me **by** the hand.*

gegenüber + DATIVE

383   *across from, opposite*   **gegenüber** may precede or follow a noun, but when used with a pronoun, the pronoun *must* precede it.

> Der Schule **gegenüber** befindet sich ein Krankenhaus.   ***Opposite** the school, there is a hospital.*
> OR **Gegenüber** der Schule befindet sich ein Krankenhaus.
> BUT ALWAYS Paul saß ihm **gegenüber.**

CHECK AND PRACTICE

Translate.

1. Each Monday, Mr. Meyer visits the restaurant opposite the church.
2. She sat opposite the window.
3. Paul came and sat down across from her.

384   *to; (as) compared to*

> Sie war mir **gegenüber** sehr freundlich. *She was very polite **to** me.*
> Einem Bus **gegenüber** hat ein Zug viele Vorzüge. ***Compared to** a bus, a train has many advantages.*

mit + DATIVE

385   *(together)* **with, in the company of**

> Die Kinder gehen **mit** ihren Eltern ins Theater.   *The children are going to the theater **with** their parents.*

386   *with (the help of),* **by means of**   [See also passive, § 523]

> Er schreibt den Brief **mit** der Schreibmaschine.   *He is writing the letter **with** a typewriter.*

387   *by (means of transportation)*   Note the use of the definite article. [See § 128.9]

> Er ist **mit** dem Zug gekommen. *He came **by** train.*

388   *to*

> Ich muß mal **mit** meinem Sohn über seine schlechten Noten sprechen.
> *I have to talk **to** my son about his bad grades.*

CHECK AND PRACTICE

Translate.

1. Peter traveled with Inge to Spain.
2. She locked the door with a key.
3. Mr. Meyer came by car.
4. The teacher spoke to the student.

389   *at (the time of),* **by, upon**

> **Mit** Beginn des Sommers wird es wieder wärmer. ***By** summer it will become warmer again.*
> In Deutschland kommen die Kinder **mit** sechs Jahren in die Schule.
> *In Germany children start school **at** the age of six.*
> SET PHRASES: **mit** der Zeit *by and by.*

nach + DATIVE

SPATIAL USE

390   *to*   Used before names of towns, countries, islands, continents, and in adverbial expressions (such as geographical directions), usually without an article.

> Sie reisten **nach Indien.** *They traveled **to India.***
> Gehen Sie bitte **nach rechts!** *Please go **to the right.***
> Wir flogen **nach Süden.** *We flew **South.***
> AND Ich gehe **nach Hause.** *I'm going home (= **to** my **house**).*

NOTE   A few names of countries are used with an article [see 128.6]. In these cases, the preposition **in** is preferred.

> Sie reisten **in die Schweiz.**

TEMPORAL USE

391 *after*

Wir sind **nach Mitternacht** in Leipzig angekommen. *We arrived in Leipzig **after midnight**.*
Nach dem Essen gehen sie immer spazieren. ***After dinner** they always take a walk.*

CHECK AND PRACTICE

Translate.

1. Turn to the left and then to the right.
2. Our friends traveled to Italy.
3. After the movies, we'll go to a restaurant.

FIGURATIVE USE

392 *about, for, after* Used with verbs of inquiry and desire.

Er **fragte nach** dem Examen. *He **asked about** the exam.*
Sie **sehnte sich nach** Ruhe. *She was **longing for** peace and quiet.*
Sie **forschte nach** der Wahrheit. *She **sought after** the truth.*

---

393 *according to* Pre- or post-position is possible.

Die Waren wurden **nach** der Qualität sortiert.
Die Waren wurden der Qualität **nach** sortiert. *The goods were sorted **according to** quality.*

---

seit + DATIVE

394 *since* Used with a point in the past covering time up to the present.

Seine Frau liegt **seit letztem Sonntag** im Krankenhaus.
*His wife has been in the hospital **since last Sunday**.*

---

395 *for* Used with a time period.

Seit drei Monaten liegt seine Frau im Krankenhaus.
*His wife has been in the hospital **for three months**.*

CHECK AND PRACTICE

Translate. Use the present tense in German.

REMEMBER   English uses present perfect and German uses present tense. [See § 40.]

1. We've been waiting now for three hours.
2. Today, I've been studying German since three o'clock.
3. He has been waiting here since this morning.
4. They have been in the theater for five hours.

von + DATIVE

396 *from*   **von** with persons, but **aus** with places.

> Ich habe einen Brief **von** Thomas bekommen.   *I got a letter **from** Thomas.*
> Ich habe einen Brief **aus** Mainz bekommen.   *I got a letter **from** Mainz.*

397 *from . . . to*   Combined with a second preposition, **von** is also used with places.

> Der Zug fährt **von** Frankfurt **bis** Heidelberg.   *The train runs **from** Frankfurt **to** Heidelberg.*
> Wir fliegen **von** Berlin **nach** Moskau.   *We'll fly **from** Berlin **to** Moscow.*
> Das Kind läuft **vom** Haus **zum** Spielplatz.   *The child runs **from** the house **to** the playground.*

398 *from, off*

> Der Apfel fällt **vom** Baum.   *The apple falls **from** the tree.*

NOTE If the point of departure is emphasized, a second preposition is added.

> **Von** der Brücke **an** fuhr das Auto langsamer.   ***Starting at** the bridge, the car went more slowly.*
> Er sprang **von** der Straßenbahn **(ab)**.   *He jumped **off** the tram.*

CHECK AND PRACTICE

Translate the phrase in parentheses.

1. Ich bin gerade (*from*) Paul gekommen.
2. Sie fuhren (*from*) Berlin nach Basel.
3. Die Flasche fiel (*off the table*).

399 *by (an author, composer, agent in a passive sentence)* [See passive, § 522]

> Die Studenten haben ein Stück **von** Brecht gelesen.   *The students read a play **by** Brecht.*

400 *of*   Used in a possessive sense as an alternative to the genitive.

> Das Auto **von** Herrn Schulz ist neu.   *Mr. Schultz's car is new.*

401 *of*   Used in a partitive sense (part of a whole).

> Gib dem Kind ein Stück **von** dem Kuchen.   *Give the child a piece **of** this cake.*

NOTE **von** is *not* used to express English *of* in the following situations:
  a. with the names of towns, months, and dates;
  b. with units of measure. [See § 168]

402 *from (a person or institution)*

> Erich hat dieses Geschenk **von** seiner Tante bekommen.   *Erich received this gift **from** his aunt.*

CHECK AND PRACTICE

1. Minna hatte die Gedichte (*by*) Goethe sehr gern.
2. Peter erhielt einen Brief (*from the university*).
3. Inge war die beste Studentin (*of all*).

403 **von**   is used to express time in conjunction with a second preposition to emphasize the starting point or give the end point.

> **Von** acht Uhr **ab** bin ich wieder zu Hause.   ***From** eight o'clock **on**, I'll be home again.*

404 *of*   **von** is used to denote a characteristic, quality or material.

> Hier sehen Sie nur Juwelen **von** hoher Qualität.   *Here you see only jewels **of** high quality.*

zu + DATIVE

405 *to*

> Wir gehen **zum** Bahnhof. *We are going **to** the train station.*   BUT   Ich bin **zu Hause.** *I'm **at home.***

NOTE   The preposition **nach** is used before geographic names. [See § 390]

406 *for*

> Was gibt's **zum** Abendessen? *What's **for** dinner?*

CHECK AND PRACTICE

Translate.

1. I am at home.
2. Our friends went to the bank.
3. For lunch we'll eat frankfurters.

407 *for*   **zu** can be used to give the result or reason for the action implied in the verb phrase.

> **Zum** Gelingen des Festes waren viele Vorbereitungen nötig.
> ***For** the party to succeed, many preparations were necessary.*

408 *at, for*   Used with prices.

> Sie kauften zwei Kilo Äpfel **zu** einer Mark.   *They bought two kilos of apples **for** one mark.*

409 **zu** can be used to specify part of a whole.

> Er hat das Buch **zur** Hälfte gelesen.   *He read half **of** the book.*

410 *by*   With dates a second preposition is optional. [See § 351.2]

> Die Arbeit muß **(bis) zum** 1. September fertig sein.   *The work has to be done **by** September 1.*

411 *at*   With religious holidays **zu** is optional. The article is omitted.

> Er will **(zu)** Ostern verreisen.   *He wants to leave **at** Easter.*

über

DATIVE OR ACCUSATIVE WITH SPATIAL EXPRESSIONS

DATIVE	*ACCUSATIVE*

427 *over, above*   *over, across*

Das Bild **hängt** über seinem Schreibtisch.	Sie **hängte** das Bild über den Schreibtisch.
*The picture **hangs** over his desk.*	*She **hung** the picture over the desk.*
Das Flugzeug **kreist** über der Stadt.	Das Flugzeug **fliegt** über den Ozean.
*The airplane **is circling** over the city.*	*The airplane **flies** across the ocean.*

CHECK AND PRACTICE

Translate the phrases in parentheses. The nouns are given with their article.

1. Die Lampe hängt *(over the table).* (der Tisch)
2. Herr Müller hängt eine Lampe *(over the table).*
3. Der Ballon ist jetzt *(over the forest).* (der Wald)
4. Der Hund springt *(over the fence).* (der Zaun)

ACCUSATIVE WITH FIGURATIVE USE

428 *over*   **über** can mean *more than.*

Das Schiff ist **über hundert Meter** lang. *The boat is **over (more than) a hundred meters** long.*

429 *via*

Die Maschine fliegt **über** Prag nach Sofia. *The airplane flies to Sofia **via** Prague.*

430 *during*   Used in post-position.

Die Nacht **über** hat es geregnet. *It rained **during** the night.*

431   **über** is used in twin forms for emphasis.

> Sie stellte Fragen **über** Fragen. *She asked question **after** question.*

unter

DATIVE OR ACCUSATIVE WITH SPATIAL EXPRESSIONS

DATIVE	*ACCUSATIVE*

432   *under*   *under*

> Unter dem Tisch **liegt** ein Teppich.   Sie **legte** den Teppich unter den Tisch.
> *A carpet **is** under the table.*   *She **put** the carpet under the table.*

433   *among*   *among*

> Unter den Steinen **befindet** sich ein Diamant.   Ich **mischte** mich unter die Zuschauer.
> *There's a diamond **among** the stones.*   *I went **among** the spectators.*

CHECK AND PRACTICE

Translate the phrases in parentheses.

1. Der Hund liegt *(under the table)*.
2. Der Hund legt sich *(under the table)*.
3. *(Among the books on the table,)* findest du einen Roman von Grass.
4. Er mischte sich *(with the other politicians)*. (der Politiker)

DATIVE WITH FIGURATIVE USE

434   *under*   **unter** can mean *less than*.

> Er suchte ein Hotelzimmer **unter 30 Mark.** *He looked for a hotel room **under 30 marks.***

435 *under*

> Der Roman handelt von den Verhältnissen **unter** Friedrich dem Großen.
> *The novel deals with the conditions **under** Frederick the Great.*

vor

DATIVE OR ACCUSATIVE WITH SPATIAL EXPRESSIONS

DATIVE	*ACCUSATIVE*

436 *before, in front of*   *to the front of, up to*

> Das Taxi **steht** vor dem Hoteleingang.   Das Taxi **fährt** vor den Hoteleingang.
> *The taxi **is standing** in front of the hotel entrance.*   *The taxi **is driving** up to the hotel entrance.*

CHECK AND PRACTICE

Translate.

1. Peter is sitting on a bench in front of the library.
2. Some workmen are carrying a bench to the front of the library.

DATIVE WITH TEMPORAL USE

437 *ago*   [See also **seit**, § 394]

> **Vor** einer Woche haben die Ferien begonnen. *A week **ago**, vacation started.*

438 *before*   [opposite: **nach,** see § 391]

> **Vor** dem Einschlafen soll der Patient nicht lesen.   *The patient should not read **before** falling asleep.*

CHECK AND PRACTICE

Translate the phrases in parentheses.

1. Frau Kühn beantwortete diesen Brief *(one month ago).*
2. *(Before dinner,)* muß Peter seine Hausaufgaben beenden.
3. *(A year ago,)* kam unsere Tante aus Deutschland zu Besuch.

439   *because of*

Vor Lärm konnte man nichts verstehen.   ***Because of*** *the noise, we couldn't understand anything.*

---

zwischen

DATIVE OR ACCUSATIVE WITH SPATIAL EXPRESSIONS

	DATIVE	*ACCUSATIVE*

440   *between*   *between*

Zwischen dem Schrank und dem Bett **steht** ein Tisch.
*There **is** a table **between** the cupboard and the bed.*

Sie haben den Tisch **zwischen** den Schrank und das Bett **gestellt.**
*They **put** the table **between** the cupboard and the bed.*

CHECK AND PRACTICE

Translate.

1. Our car is standing between two red cars.
2. Let's park our car between these two red cars.

DATIVE WITH FIGURATIVE USE

441   *between*

In diesem Geschäft kosten Geschenke **zwischen** einer und zwanzig Mark.
*Gifts cost **between** one and twenty marks in this store.*

Less Freq

449 anläßlich *o*

> **Anläßlich** uns
> *On the occasio*

450 außerhalb *o*

> Der Lehrer woh
> *The teacher lives*

451 diesseits *on*

> Weil keine Brü
> **diesseits** des
> *Because no bridg*
> *this side of th*

452 unterhalb *b*

> Sie stand **unter**
> *She stood below*

453 The above geni
sition **von** whi

> **Unterhalb** vo

VERBS R

454 Most verbs are
many verbs, in
tions. If the pr

> Ich freue mich
> Ich freue mich

CHECK AND PRACTICE

1. *(Between today and tomorrow,)* können viele Dinge geschehen.
2. Der Preis dieses Mantels liegt *(between 100 and 150 marks)*.

PREPOSITIONS THAT GOVERN THE GENITIVE

442

FREQUENTLY USED	LESS FREQUENTLY USED
(an) statt *instead of*	anläßlich *on the occasion of*
trotz *in spite of*	anstelle *instead of*
um . . . willen *for the sake of*	diesseits *on this side of*
während *during*	jenseits *on the other side of*
wegen *because of*	außerhalb *outside of*
	innerhalb *inside of*
	oberhalb *above*
	unterhalb *below*

Frequently used prepositions

443 **(an)statt** *instead of*

> **(An)statt** des Huts hättest du lieber eine warme Mütze aufsetzen sollen.
> *Instead of the hat, you should have put on a warm cap.*

444 **anstelle** *in place of, instead of*

> **Anstelle** des Bruders kam die Schwester. *The sister came **instead of** the brother.*

445 **trotz** *in spite of*

> **Trotz** des schlechten Wetters gingen wir spazieren. *In spite of the bad weather, we took a walk.*

CHECK AND PRACTICE

1. Wir brauchen einen Arzt *(instead of a policeman)*.
2. Du bist rechts *(instead of left)* abgebogen.
3. *(In spite of his warm coat,)* war es ihm kalt.

446 um . . . willen

Um der Kinder w
divorce.

NOTE **willen** fo
meiner

447 während *duri*

Während der Ark

448 wegen *becaus*

Wegen des schlec
Des schlechten We
Because of the bac

NOTE **wegen** i
meiner

deiner

Ich hoffe, Sie tun c

CHECK AND

1. *(For the sake c*
2. *(During the w*
3. *(Because of ra*

---

455 Because the use of prepositions in fixed combinations is figurative, English and German combinations seldom correspond. To understand and use these correctly, they must be learned.

Ich warte **auf** Frau Meyer.	*I'm waiting for Ms. Meyer.*
Ich spreche **von** Herrn Dietz.	*I'm talking about Mr. Dietz.*
Ich bin **in** sie verliebt.	*I'm in love with her.*
Ich bin **mit** ihr verlobt.	*I'm engaged to her.*
Ich bin **mit** ihr böse.	*I'm mad at her.*
Ich bin verrückt **nach** ihr.	*I'm mad about her.*
Ich habe Angst **vor** ihr.	*I'm afraid of her.*
Ich bin stolz **auf** sie.	*I'm proud of her.*
Ich halte es **für** gut.	*I consider it good.*

456 Frequently used verbs with prepositional objects:

Angst haben vor *(dat.)*	*to be afraid of*
antworten auf *(acc.)*	*to reply to*
bitten um *(acc.)*	*to ask for*
danken für *(acc.)*	*to thank (someone) for*
denken an *(acc.)*	*to think of, to remember*
nachdenken über *(acc.)*	*to think (meditate) about*
einladen zu *(dat.)*	*to invite to*
fragen nach *(dat.)*	*to ask about, to inquire about*
sich freuen auf *(acc.)*	*to look forward to*
sich freuen über *(acc.)*	*to be happy about*
gehören zu *(dat.)*	*to be part or a member of, to belong to*
glauben an *(acc.)*	*to believe in*
halten von *(dat.)*	*to have an opinion about, to think (highly, a great deal, not much, etc.) of*
halten für *(acc.)*	*to consider (as), to take for*
hoffen auf *(acc.)*	*to hope for, to trust in, to look forward to*
hören von *(dat.)*	*to hear from (somebody) or about (something)*
sich interessieren für *(acc.)*	*to be interested in*
lachen über *(acc.)*	*to laugh about*
reagieren auf *(acc.)*	*to react to*
sein für *or* sein gegen *(acc.)*	*to be for or against*
sprechen von *(dat.)*	*to talk of, to mention*
stolz sein auf *(acc.)*	*to be proud of*
trinken auf *(acc.)*	*to (drink a) toast to*
verstehen von *(dat.)*	*to know (understand) about*
warten auf *(acc.)*	*to wait for*
Wert legen auf *(acc.)*	*to value*
wissen von *(dat.)*	*to know about*
zufrieden sein mit *(dat.)*	*to be satisfied with*

I. VOCABULARY FOR REVIEW (A TEXT FROM READER, CHAPTER VIII)

Verbs

an·greifen i, i	to attack
besetzen	to occupy
herrschen (über)	to rule
scheitern (+ sein)	to fail
übernehmen (i) a, o	to take over
vernichten	to annihilate
verwalten	to administer

Nouns

der **Angriff, -e**	attack
die **Einheit, -en**	unity, unit
das **Ereignis, -se**	event
der **Feind, -e**	enemy
der **Flüchtling, -e**	refugee
das **Gebiet, -e**	territory
die **Macht, ⸚e**	power
die **Niederlage, -n**	defeat
der **Sieg, -e**	victory
der **Überfall, ⸚e**	invasion
das **Urteil, -e**	judgment, verdict
die **Verfassung, -en**	constitution
die **Verhandlung, -en**	negotiation
der **Widerspruch, ⸚e**	contradiction
der **Zusammenbruch, ⸚e**	collapse

Others

bedingungslos	unconditional
verantwortlich	responsible
wirtschaftlich	economic

ADDITIONAL EXERCISES (A TEXT FROM THE READER)

Fragen über den zweiten Weltkrieg.

Answer the questions with the given phrases after *bis*.

1. Wie lange wartet ihr mit dem Angriff? *(next week)*
2. Wie weit gingen die Sowjets vor? *(to the German boundary)*
3. War euer ganzes Land besetzt? Ja, *(to the last village)*
4. Wie lange dauerte die Potsdamer Konferenz? *(into the month of August)*

Answer the questions with the given phrases after accusative prepositions.

5. Wie wurde Dresden vernichtet? *(by bombs)*
6. Für wen war Hitler der schlimmste Feind? *(for every Jew* [der Jude]*)*
7. Wofür waren die Alliierten verantwortlich? *(for the administration of Germany)*
8. Wie verwalteten die Alliierten Deutschland? *(through the AAC* [der Alliierte Kontrollrat]*)*
9. Wo lief die Grenze zwischen der russischen Zone und Polen? *(along the Oder)*
10. Was sagte man über das Urteil von Nürnberg? *(Nobody was against it.)*
11. Wann begann die Berliner Blockade? *(toward the end of spring)*
12. Worum geht die Diskussion heute? *(about the solution of the German question)*
13. Was für eine Verfassung sucht man? *(a constitution without contradictions)*
14. Wie wollen die meisten Menschen leben? *(without a war)*
15. Wie kann man der Öffentlichkeit dienen? *(through responsible actions* [die Handlung]*)*

Respond with the given phrases after dative prepositions.

16. Wie begann der Krieg? *(with the invasion of Poland)*
17. Wann griffen die Deutschen Polen an? *(after the pact with Stalin)*
18. Wie endete der Krieg? *(with the total collapse)*
19. Wer hat Deutschland besetzt? *(nobody except the Allied powers)*
20. Wann haben sie die Verantwortung übernommen? *(at* [bei] *the Potsdam negotiations)*
21. Wann bildeten die Alliierten die Besatzungszonen? *(after the war)*
22. Wie lange hat Deutschland neue Verfassungen? *(since the year 1949)*
23. Wo wohnten Sie am Ende des Krieges? *(across from a destroyed church)*
24. Woher kommen Sie jetzt? *(from the territory around Berlin)*
25. Wohin fahren Sie morgen? *(to the peace negotiations)*

Answer with the preposition given, followed by a dative or accusative as required.

26. Wann war der Krieg in Europa zu Ende? (an/der 8. Mai 1945)

27. Wieviel Tote gab es im zweiten Weltkrieg? (über/54 000 000)

28. Wo gab es die meisten Toten? (unter/die Zivilbevölkerung)

29. Wohin flohen die Feinde? (hinter/die Grenze)

30. Wo wohnen die Flüchtlinge jetzt? (auf/das Land)

31. Wo ist die Ostgrenze der DDR? (an/die Oder)

32. Wo gab es nach dem Krieg Konflikte? (unter/die Siegernationen)

33. Wo sitzen die ostdeutschen Politiker? (auf/die Volkskammer *[People's Chamber]*)

34. Wohin gehören ihre Parteien? (zu/der antifaschistische Block)

35. Wann wurde die Bundesrepublik gebildet? (vor/über 40 Jahre)

36. Wo wurde die neue Verfassung diskutiert? (auf/viele Verhandlungen)

37. Wo liegen heute die beiden deutschen Staaten? (zwischen/der Osten und der Westen)

38. Wo steht die Weltöffentlichkeit? (hinter/die Friedensinitiative)

39. Wo hat dieser Soldat gedient? (in/die amerikanische Armee)

40. Wohin stellt sich ein guter Offizier? (vor/seine Soldaten)

Answer with prepositions requiring the genitive, followed by the phrases suggested.

41. Wann besetzten die Russen Berlin? *(during the last days of the war)*

42. Haben die Deutschen den Krieg verloren? Ja, *(in spite of their early victories)*

43. Deutschland erlebte eine schwere Niederlage, nicht wahr? Ja, *(instead of a victory)*

44. Warum scheiterte der Versuch, Deutschland zu einer wirtschaftlichen Einheit zu machen? *(because of the French veto* [das Veto])

45. Warum sollten die Nationen zusammenarbeiten? *(for the sake of peace)*

Respond with an appropriate preposition followed by the phrase given.

46. Wo konnte man über Hitlers Pläne nachlesen? *(his book* Mein Kampf)

47. Wann war Hitlers Macht am größten? (die Jahre 1938–1941)

48. Wie wurde der Krieg zum Weltkrieg? *(the invasion of the USSR)*

49. Wo erlebte die deutsche Armee ihre größte Niederlage? (Stalingrad)

50. Woher kamen die meisten Flüchtlinge? *(the lost territories* [das verlorene Gebiet])

51. Woraus entwickelte sich der Kalte Krieg? *(contradictions between the winners* [der Sieger])

52. Sollte die UdSSR über das gesamte Land Berlin herrschen? *(no circumstances* [der Umstand])

53. Welche Parteien nahmen an den östlichen Verhandlungen teil? *(no parties/the KPD)*

54. Wo verläuft die Grenze zwischen der DDR und Polen? *(the Oder and then/the Neiße)*

II. VOCABULARY FOR REVIEW (B TEXT FROM READER, CHAPTER VIII)

Verbs

hamstern	to hoard (food)
schleichen i, i (+ sein)	to sneak
unter·tauchen (+ sein)	to go underground
vernehmen (i) a, o	to interrogate
verstecken	to hide

Nouns

die **Aufregung, -en**	excitement
der **Beamte, -n**	official
die **Siedlung, -en**	(housing) development
der **Unsinn**	nonsense
der **Zuhörer, -**	listener

Others

aufgeregt	excited
rasch	quickly
schrecklich	fearful
ungeschickt	clumsy
verzweifelt	desperate
vollkommen	complete

ADDITIONAL EXERCISES (B TEXT FROM THE READER)

Answer the questions with prepositions requiring the accusative, followed by the phrases given.

1. Wie lange wollen wir auf den Zug warten? *(until this evening)*
2. Sollten wir Karotten hamstern? Ja, *(for our children)*

3. Können wir das leicht tun? Ja, *(without any excitement)*

4. Wie kommen wir zu eurer Siedlung? *(Go along our street.)*

5. Und wie fährt der Zug? *(through the whole city)*

6. Wann soll der nächste Hamsterzug kommen? *(toward 7 o'clock)*

7. Und wann kam der Zug wirklich? *(at midnight)*

8. Wie weit fährt der Zug? *(until the mountains)*

Answer with prepositions requiring the dative, followed by the given phrases.

9. Wie lange gehen Sie schon hamstern? *(since the beginning of the war)*

10. Wohin gehen Sie, wenn Sie etwas zu essen brauchen? *(to my friends)*

11. Kann man dort etwas zu essen kaufen? Ja, *(at the farmers'* [die Bauern])

12. Woher haben die ihre Karotten? *(from their garden)*

13. Und Sie bekommen auch welche? Ja, *(from my friends)*

14. Fahren Sie allein dorthin? Nein, *(with my husband)*

15. Ist ein Bahnhof in der Nähe? Ja, *(across from their house)*

16. Wer weiß etwas über die Hamsterreisen? Niemand, *(except one official)*

17. Sind Sie aufgeregt? Natürlich, *(after such a trip)*

Respond with prepositional phrases in the dative or accusative as required.

18. Wo leben Sie mit Ihrem Mann? *(in a city)*

19. Haben Sie dort einen Garten? Ja, *(in front of our house)*

20. Wohnen andere Leute in der Nähe? Ja, *(next to our house)*

21. Sitzen Sie oft vor der Tür? Ja, *(in the garden between the house and the street)*

22. Setzt sich Ihr Mann oft zu Ihnen? Nein, er setzt sich *(next to the house)*

23. Wann ist er denn zu hause? *(on Sunday)*

24. Man sieht ihn nicht oft, denn er versteckt sich. Wohin? *(under the table)*

25. War er einmal untergetaucht? Ja, *(among his friends)*

26. Darf man darüber sprechen? Nein, nicht *(about this nonsense)*

27. Dann schleiche ich mich jetzt weg. Ja, *(into the smallest room)*

28. Darf ich mich dort hinlegen? Ja, *(onto the bed)*

Respond with prepositional phrases in the genitive.

29. Wo liegt das Konzentrationslager? *(beyond our village)*

30. Liegt es in der Stadt? Nein, *(outside of the city)*

31. Wurden dort Menschen ermordet? Ja, *(inside of the camp)*

32. Wann war Ihr Mann im Konzentrationslager? *(during the war)*

33. Warum war er in Gefahr? *(because of a clumsy comrade* [der Kamerad])

34. Warum hat er sich in schreckliche Gefahr gebracht? *(for the sake of justice* [die Gerechtigkeit])

35. Wurde er oft vernommen? Ja, *(despite his desperate situation)*

36. Wie lebt er jetzt? Er liebt die Ruhe *(instead of the excitement)*

Respond with prepositional phrases in the correct case.

37. Wo haben Sie gewohnt? *(during the war? on the Rhine)*

38. Und Ihre Eltern? *(after the war? in the country)*

39. Warum wurden sie von der Partei vernommen? *(because of their demonstrations)*

40. Wie lange mußten sie untertauchen? *(for several years)*

41. Wo konnten sie sich denn verstecken? *(at their friends')*

42. Wohnen sie jetzt in Oberbayern? Ja, *(directly below the mountains)*

43. Können sie dort etwas zu essen finden? *(only from their garden)*

44. Wovon sprechen sie am meisten? *(of the fearful problems)*

45. Gehen sie noch aus dem Haus? Ja, aber nur *(to their work)*

46. Und Sie? Studieren Sie? Ja, *(at an American university)*

VERBS (Part Three)

SUBJUNCTIVE

457 Both English and German possess two sets of verb forms which indicate the speaker's attitude toward what he is saying.

INDICATIVE	SUBJUNCTIVE

The indicative is used for statements that the speaker regards as factual or relatively likely. The subjunctive indicates that a statement is relatively unlikely, implausible, conjectural, or simply contrary-to-fact.

Ach wie schön ist es, hier in der Sonne zu liegen. *It is so nice to lie here in the sun.*	WISHFUL THINKING! *It won't happen!*
A FACT Wenn ich Zeit habe, liege ich immer in der Sonne. *If I find the time (AND I DO FIND THE TIME), I always lie in the sun.*	Ach wie schön **wäre** es, in der Sonne zu liegen. Wenn ich Zeit **hätte, würde** ich immer in der Sonne liegen. *It **would be** so nice to lie in the sun. If I **had** the time (BUT I DON'T AND WON'T) I **would** always lie in the sun.*

Forms

PERSONAL ENDINGS IN THE SUBJUNCTIVE

458 1. In German, there are two subjunctive moods: the *general subjunctive* and
the *special subjunctive,*
which is less common

2. Both sets of subjunctive use the same personal endings for all verbs and all tenses. They are:

	SINGULAR		PLURAL
ich	-e	wir	-en
du	-est	ihr	-et
Sie	-en	Sie	-en
er sie es	-e	sie	-en

459 The two subjunctive forms differ in regard to their stem.

1. The *general subjunctive* uses the *past tense stem.*

Past Tense	Er **wohnte** in Bonn. *He **lived** in Bonn.*
General Subjunctive	**Wohnte** er doch in Bonn! ***Would** he only **live** in Bonn.*

2. The *special subjunctive* uses the *present tense stem.*

Present Tense	Er **wohnt** in Bonn. *He **lives** in Bonn.*
Special Subjunctive	Er sagt, er **wohne** in Bonn. *He says he **lives** in Bonn.*

CHECK AND PRACTICE

Add the correct personal ending for the subjunctive or give the correct a. general, b. special subjunctive forms for the infinitives.

1. ich lern-
2. er spielt-
3. wir (bauen)
4. ich lernt-
5. er spiel-
6. sie *(pl.)* (erklären)

VERB STEMS OF THE GENERAL SUBJUNCTIVE

460 1. In the case of *weak verbs* and the modals **sollen** and **wollen,** the *present tense* of the general subjunctive is identical to the *past tense of the indicative.*

GENERAL SUBJUNCTIVE PRESENT TENSE			INDICATIVE PAST TENSE		
ich	wohnte	sollte	wollte	ich	wohnte	sollte	wollte
du	wohntest	solltest	wolltest	du	wohntest	sollest	wolltest
er	wohnte	sollte	wollte	er	wohnte	sollte	wollte
wir	wohnten	sollten	wollten	wir	wohnten	sollten	wollten
ihr	wohntet	solltet	wolltet	ihr	wohntet	solltet	wolltet
sie	wohnten	sollten	wollten	sie	wohnten	sollten	wollten

461 1. All strong verbs and the special weak verbs **bringen** and **denken** add an umlaut where possible **(ä, ö, ü)**. The modals **können, müssen, dürfen, mögen** keep their umlaut in the *present tense* of the general subjunctive.

INFINITIVE	INDICATIVE PAST TENSE	GENERAL SUBJUNCTIVE
sehen	er sah	er sähe
denken	er dachte	er dächte
haben	er hatte	er hätte
werden	er wurde	er würde
sein	er war	er wäre
müssen	er mußte	er müßte

2. The general subjunctive forms of **kennen, nennen, brennen, rennen** are spelled with an **e** instead of an **ä: kennte, nennte, brennte, rennte.** (The past tense stem is: **kannt-, nannt-, brannt-, rannt-.)** These forms go back to regular weak forms.

VERB STEMS OF THE SPECIAL SUBJUNCTIVE

462 1. Many forms of the special subjunctive of weak and strong verbs are identical to present tense indicative forms. The main differences occur in the forms of the second and third person singular. [See vowel change for some strong verbs, § 27]

SPECIAL SUBJUNCTIVE PRESENT TENSE				INDICATIVE PRESENT TENSE			
ich	wohne	singe	spreche	ich	wohne	singe	spreche
du	wohnest	singest	sprechest	du	wohnst	singst	sprichst
er	wohne	singe	spreche	er	wohnt	singt	spricht
wir	wohnen	singen	sprechen	wir	wohnen	singen	sprechen
ihr	wohnet	singet	sprechet	ihr	wohnt	singt	sprecht
sie	wohnen	singen	sprechen	sie	wohnen	singen	sprechen

2. The forms of the special subjunctive of the modals **wissen** and **sein** differ more from their present tense indicative forms because the latter are irregular. [See § 28f.]

SPECIAL SUBJUNCTIVE PRESENT TENSE					INDICATIVE PRESENT TENSE				
ich	müsse	solle	wisse	sei	ich	muß	soll	weiß	bin
du	müssest	sollest	wissest	seiest	du	mußt	sollst	weißt	bist
er	müsse	solle	wisse	sei	er	muß	soll	weiß	ist
wir	müssen	sollen	wissen	seien	wir	müssen	sollen	wissen	sind
ihr	müsset	sollet	wisset	seiet	ihr	müßt	sollt	wißt	seid
sie	müssen	sollen	wissen	seien	sie	müssen	sollen	wissen	sind

NOTE   The forms **ich sei** and **er sei** have no **-e** ending.

ALTERNATE FORMS OF THE GENERAL AND THE SPECIAL SUBJUNCTIVE

463 1. Because the present tense of the general subjunctive and the past tense indicative forms of regular weak verbs are identical in German, the **würde** construction is often preferred, except in **wenn**-clauses. [See § 466]

    ich würde lernen   INSTEAD OF **ich lernte**

2. In colloquial German, the **würde** construction is usually used with all verbs except the auxiliaries **(sein, haben, werden),** the modals, and a few frequently used verbs like **kommen.**

464 Because many special subjunctive forms are identical or similar to the indicative [see § 23ff.], only the special subjunctive forms of **sein,** the three singular forms of the modals and **wissen,** the third person singular of **haben, werden,** and weak and strong verbs are used (see table below). These forms are all clearly distinct from the present indicative. In the other instances, general subjunctive forms are used instead of special subjunctive forms.

	sein	MODALS	haben	werden	WEAK VERBS	STRONG VERBS
ich	**sei**	**wolle**	hätte	würde	lernte	ginge
du	**seiest**	**wollest**	hättest	würdest	lerntest	gingest
er	**sei**	**wolle**	**habe**	**werde**	**lerne**	**gehe**
wir	**seien**	wollten	hätten	würden	lernten	gingen
ihr	**seiet**	wolltet	hättet	würdet	lerntet	ginget
sie	**seien**	wollten	hätten	würden	lernten	gingen

CHECK AND PRACTICE

Give the general subjunctive forms, present tense. Use a *würde*-form if the subjunctive form is identical with the past tense indicative.

1. sie *(pl.)* (bauen)
2. ich (fahren)
3. es (anfangen)
4. du (singen)
5. wir (antworten)
6. ihr (können)
7. wir (ziehen)
8. ihr (bekommen)
9. du (bringen)
10. sie *(sg.)* (müssen)
11. sie *(pl.)* baden
12. ich (erklären)

Give the special subjunctive forms, present tense. Use a general subjunctive if the special subjunctive is identical with the present tense indicative.

13. es (sein)
14. sie *(pl.)* (sollen)
15. du (haben)
16. ihr (werden)
17. er (studieren)
18. wir (schreiben)
19. ich (laufen)
20. sie *(sg.)* (denken)
21. du (besuchen)
22. ihr (dürfen)
23. wir (wandern)
24. ich (wissen)

Ich _____ gern.

TENSES OF THE GENERAL AND THE SPECIAL SUBJUNCTIVE

465   The indicative has six tenses [See § 1]. The subjunctive mood, however, has only *four.*

INDICATIVE	GENERAL SUBJUNCTIVE	SPECIAL SUBJUNCTIVE
Present Tense er spricht er reist	**Present Tense** er spräche er reiste	er spreche er reise
Past Tense er sprach er reiste	**Past Tense** er hätte gesprochen er wäre gereist	er habe gesprochen er sei gereist
Perfect Tense er hat gesprochen er ist gereist		
Past Perfect Tense er hatte gesprochen er war gereist		
Future Tense er wird sprechen er wird reisen	**Future Tense** er würde sprechen er würde reisen	er werde sprechen er werde reisen
Future Perfect Tense er wird gesprochen haben er wird gereist sein	**Future Perfect Tense** er würde gesprochen haben er würde gereist sein	er werde gesprochen haben er werde gereist sein

CHECK AND PRACTICE

Give the general subjunctive form. (Tenses: PR, PA, F)

1. ich (nehmen) PR
2. es (haben) PA
3. sie *(pl.)* (reisen) F
4. er (sein) PA
5. wir (können) PR
6. ihr (essen) PA
7. sie *(sg.)* (ändern) F
8. ich (wissen) PR
9. er (grüßen) PA
10. wir (heiraten) F
11. ihr (schlagen) PR
12. sie *(pl.)* (öffnen) PA

Give the special subjunctive form for the same verbs and the same tenses (use the general subjunctive if the special subjunctive is identical to the indicative forms).

Usage

UNREAL CONDITIONS

466 The general subjunctive is used to express hypothetical (unreal) conditions which are generally accompanied by equally hypothetical conclusions. The sequence of the clauses and the use of **wenn, dann,** and **so** can vary.

PRESENT TENSE

Condition	Conclusion	
Wenn ich Zeit hätte,	(so / dann) käme ich.	*If I had time, I would come.*
Hätte ich Zeit,	(so / dann) käme ich.	

Conclusion	Condition
Ich käme,	wenn ich Zeit hätte.

PAST TENSE

Condition	Conclusion	
Wenn ich Zeit gehabt hätte,	(so / dann) wäre ich gekommen.	*If I had had time I would have come.*
Hätte ich Zeit gehabt,	(so / dann) wäre ich gekommen.	

Conclusion	Condition
Ich wäre gekommen,	wenn ich Zeit gehabt hätte.

NOTE Although **würde**-forms are used very frequently in colloquial German, they are avoided in formal German in **wenn**-clauses.

FORMAL

Wenn ich in Berlin wohnte, würde ich oft ins Theater gehen.
If I lived in Berlin, I would go to the theater frequently.

COLLOQUIAL

Wenn ich in Berlin wohnen würde, würde ich oft ins Theater gehen.

CHECK AND PRACTICE

Express unreal conditions and conclusions. Answer the questions with: Nein, aber...

Example

Bist du nach Frankfurt gefahren und ins Museum gegangen?
Nein, aber **wenn ich** nach Frankfurt gefahren **wäre, dann wäre ich** bestimmt ins Museum gegangen.

1. Wart ihr in Bonn, und habt ihr den Bundestag besucht?
2. Haben Klaus und Inge genug Geld bekommen und ihr neues Haus gebaut?
3. Hast du einen Hammer und kannst das Bild aufhängen?
4. Bekam Peter letzte Woche eine Freikarte und ging mit euch ins Kino?

Translate.

5. Paul would have studied German last night if he had had his textbook.
6. I would give you a cigarette if I had one.

467   Unreal conditions may follow questions.

Was würdest du tun, wenn du an seiner Stelle wärest?   *What would you do if you were in his place?*

468   Sometimes the conclusion stands alone. The unreal condition is only implied.

Das wäre großartig!   *That would be great.*   IMPLIED   *if we could do that.*

UNREAL WISHES

469   In German as in English, unreal wishes *("If only...!")* consist of a subordinate clause without a main clause, i.e., they are conditional clauses without a conclusion. Emphatic modifiers such as **doch, nur,** and **bloß** are obligatory. These wishes have the intonation of an exclamation. They can employ or omit **wenn.**

Wenn ich nur Zeit hätte!   *If only I had time.* Hätte ich nur Zeit!

470 Unreal wishes can also be introduced by **wünschte / wollte** followed by a main clause in general subjunctive or, more frequently, a **daß**-clause in general subjunctive.

Ich wünschte, er käme heute.   *I wish he could come today.*
Ich wünschte, daß er heute käme.

---

471 In talking about activities, constructions like **es wäre schön** plus infinitive with **zu** or a modal construction in general subjunctive are used frequently instead of the general subjunctive of the main verb.

Es wäre schön, schwimmen zu gehen.   *It would be nice to go swimming.*
Es wäre schön, wenn wir schwimmen gehen könnten.   *It would be nice if we could go swimming.*
INSTEAD OF Es wäre schön, wenn wir schwimmen gingen.

CHECK AND PRACTICE

Express as an unreal wish.

Example

Peter spielt Karten mit mir.
Ich **wünschte, daß** Peter mit mir Karten **spielte / spielen würde.**
Ich wünschte, Peter **spielte** mit mir Karten (**würde** mit mir Karten **spielen**).

1. Inge geht mit mir ins Theater.
2. Herr Dietz zeigt uns seine Briefmarkensammlung.
3. Das Wetter wird besser.
4. Der Weg nach Berlin ist kürzer als der nach Hamburg.

Example

(Ich möchte) mal wieder Schokolade essen.
Es wäre schön, mal wieder Schokolade **zu** essen.
Es wäre schön, wenn man mal wieder Schokolade essen **könnte.**

5. eine große Wanderung machen
6. Freunde treffen
7. Golf spielen
8. zusammen skilaufen

UNREAL COMPARISONS

472 Unreal comparisons consist of an indicative statement followed by an **als ob / als wenn** *as if / as though* dependent clause in the general subjunctive. The double conjunction can be reduced to **als** in which case the verb is in second position.

> Sie sieht aus, **als ob** sie krank **wäre**.   *She looks as if she were sick.*
> Sie sieht aus, **als wäre** sie krank.

ASSUMPTIONS

473 Assumptions are frequently expressed by the general subjunctive in relative clauses, while the main clause is in the indicative.

> Er hat ein Auto, das du vielleicht ausleihen **könntest**.   *He has a car which you **might be able to** borrow.*

DOUBT

474 A doubtful question can be expressed by the general subjunctive and, frequently, a modifier such as **wirklich.**

> **Würden** Sie ihm **wirklich** das Geld **geben?**   *Would you really give him the money?*

POLITENESS AND MODESTY

475
> **Dürfte** ich um Wasser bitten? *May/Might I ask for some water?*
> Und das **sollte** ich gesagt haben? *And I'm **supposed to** have said that?*

POSSIBILITY

476
> Das **dürfte** richtig sein. *That **might** be correct.*

IDIOMATIC EXPRESSIONS

477   In German, subjunctive is used; in English, indicative is usually used.

Sie **hätte** es beinahe vergessen.   *She nearly forgot it.*
Das **wäre** alles.   *That's all.*

CHECK AND PRACTICE

Translate.

1. Sie tat, *(as if she had always known that).*
2. Er wohnt neben dem Theater und *(could buy you your tickets).*
3. *(Would you be so kind as to)* nicht zu rauchen? (die Güte haben)
4. *May I ask you a favor?*
5. *I would know how to get money.*
6. *Would you please open the books.*

INDIRECT SPEECH

478   In indirect speech, the German speaker can choose one of three verb forms, depending on his attitude toward the original quotation:

INDICATIVE
SPECIAL SUBJUNCTIVE
GENERAL SUBJUNCTIVE

479   The *indicative* implies that the speaker is reporting a fact. Therefore, verbs such as **wissen** *to know,* **sehen** *to see,* and phrases such as **es ist klar** *it is clear,* and **es ist nicht zu leugnen** *it cannot be denied* are followed by the indicative. Even verbs such as **sagen** are also frequently followed by the indicative if they are used in the present tense first person.

Wir **wissen** alle, daß die Entscheidungen des Präsidenten wichtig **sind.**
*We all **know** that the decisions by the president **are** important.*
Ich **sage** Ihnen nochmals, ich **bin** furchtbar müde.   *I'm **telling** you again **I'm** terribly tired.*

---

480   The *special subjunctive* is used in recipes, directions, and in impartial reporting. It is usually introduced by neutral verbs of saying, thinking, and feeling such as: **sagen** *to say, to tell,* **erzählen** *to tell, to relate,* **schreiben** *to write,* **antworten** *to answer,* **berichten** *to report,* **fürchten** *to fear,* **feststellen** *to declare,* and **bemerken** *to remark.*

Man **nehme:** Dr. Oetker.
Use Dr. Oetker (a brand name for puddings and cake mixes).

Er **sagte,** er **werde** mich um acht Uhr besuchen.
He said he would call on me at 8 o'clock.

Sie **schrieb** mir, die ganze Familie **habe** einen Ausflug ins Gebirge gemacht.
She wrote me that the whole family had taken a trip to the mountains.

Die Zeitung **berichtete,** daß ein berühmter europäischer Schauspieler angekommen **sei.**
The newspaper reported that a famous European actor had arrived.

---

481   The use of the *general subjunctive,* on the other hand, implies skepticism or doubt on the speaker's part. In addition, it is used in everyday conversation instead of the special subjunctive.

Er behauptete, daß er krank **gewesen wäre.**   Er sagt, sein Vater **hätte** sehr viel Geld.
He said he had been sick (but I doubt it).   *He says his father is very rich (but I doubt it).*

CHECK AND PRACTICE

Give the special subjunctive forms.

Man _____ das Paket, indem man die Verpackung	öffnen
entlang der punktierten Linie _____. Zuerst _____	aufschneiden
man die Gebrauchsanweisung _____ und _____	herausnehmen lesen
sie gründlich. Dann _____ man den Inhalt in	schütten
eine Schüssel, _____ zwei Tassen heißes Wasser	hinzufügen
_____, _____ einen Löffel und _____ heftig. Nun	nehmen rühren
_____ man es in einem Topf, _____ es anschließend	erhitzen gießen
in eine Schüssel und _____ es heiß. Guten Appetit!	servieren

482   In changing questions from direct to indirect speech, care must be taken to change not only the verb but also the pronouns and possessives.

Direct Quotation	Karl sagte:	"Ich	habe	mein	Buch verloren."
Indirect Quotation	Karl sagte,	er	habe	sein	Buch verloren.
	Karl said he had lost his book.				
Direct Quotation	Sie schrieb mir:	"Ich	bin	bei	meiner	Tante."
Indirect Quotation	Sie schrieb mir,	sie	sei	bei	ihrer	Tante.
	She wrote me that she was at her aunt's house.				
Direct Quotation	Er sagte zu mir:	"Ich	kann	es	mir	nicht leisten."
Indirect Quotation	Er sagte mir,	er	könne	es	sich	nicht leisten.
	He told me that he could not afford it.				

CHECK AND PRACTICE

Change into indirect speech.

1. Der Künstler schrieb mir: "Ich habe alle meine Bilder verkauft."
2. Die Gärtnerin sagte: "Ich bin in meinen Garten gegangen und habe meinen Blumen Wasser gegeben."
3. Der Briefträger antwortete mir: "Sie haben recht, ich habe mich geirrt und Ihre Briefe gestern Ihrem Nachbarn gegeben."
4. Mein Bruder schrieb mir: "Wir haben unsere Ferien hier in Bayern verbracht."
5. Meine Schwester berichtete aus dem Urlaub: "Ich und meine Freundin haben uns gut erholt, doch Dein Freund Karl ist krank geworden."

Indirect Statements in Subordinate Clauses

483   The tense used in the subordinate clause of an indirect statement is dependent upon the tense used in the direct quotation that underlies it. But remember that the special subjunctive (like the general subjunctive) has only one form for the past, perfect, and past perfect tense indicative. [See § 465]

INDICATIVE	SPECIAL SUBJUNCTIVE
Present Tense	**Present Tense**
"Es **ist** notwendig."	Er sagte, es **sei** notwendig.
Past Tenses	**Past Tenses**
"Es **war** notwendig."	
"Es **ist** notwendig **gewesen.**"	Er sagte, es **sei** notwendig **gewesen.**
"Es **war** notwendig **gewesen.**"	
Future	**Future**
"Es **wird** notwendig **sein.**"	Er sagte, es **werde** notwendig **sein.**

484 If the original quotation is in the general subjunctive, the indirect quotation will also be in the general subjunctive.

"Ich **wäre** damit zufrieden."	Er sagte, er **wäre** damit zufrieden.
*I **would be** satisfied with that.*	*He said he **would be** satisfied with that.*

485 Dependent clauses in a direct statement become subjunctive in the indirect statement.

Der Reporter berichtete: "Der Politiker, **der in der Vergangenheit in viele Skandale verwickelt war,** wird sicherlich morgen mit großer Mehrheit zum Parteivorsitzenden gewählt."
Der Reporter berichtete, daß der Politiker, **der in der Vergangenheit in viele Skandale verwikkelt gewesen sei,** sicherlich morgen mit großer Mehrheit zum Parteivorsitzenden gewählt werde.
*The reporter remarked that the politician **who had been involved in many scandals in the past** would certainly be elected chairman of his party tomorrow by a large majority.*

CHECK AND PRACTICE

Change into indirect speech. Pay attention to tenses.

"Einmal ist eine Maus nachts in einen Laden gelaufen. Sie wollte vom Käse und der Wurst fressen. Sie ist schnell zum Käse gerannt, aber da hat sie auf der anderen Seite einen Kuchen gesehen und ist schnell dorthin gelaufen. Da hat sie Äpfel und Schokolade gerochen. Zuerst wollte sie jetzt diese fressen. Aber. . .
Ja, sie läuft noch immer dort herum und morgen wird man sie fangen."
Der Großvater erzählte, einmal. . . .

Indirect Questions

486 In the transformation from direct to indirect question, not only does mood change but the word order changes also. Indirect questions are always dependent clauses. [See § 308ff.]

Ich fragte ihn:	"Was haben	Sie	in der Hand?"
Ich fragte ihn,	was	er	in der Hand habe.
I asked him what he had in his hand.			
Ich fragte ihn:	"Wo waren	Sie	heute morgen?"
Ich fragte ihn,	wo	er	heute morgen gewesen sei.
I asked him where he had been this morning.			

487 If the direct question has no interrogative word, the subordinating conjunction **ob** must be supplied. [See § 316]

Er fragte:	"War	sie krank?"
Er fragte,	**ob**	sie krank gewesen sei. *He asked whether she had been sick.*

488 After an imperative, the indirect question is in the indicative.

Erzählen Sie mir, was geschehen ist! *Tell me what happened.*
Imperative

Indirect Commands

489 An indirect command is usually expressed by the present tense of the special or general subjunctive of **sollen** and a dependent infinitive. Whereas most direct commands have an exclamation mark in German, indirect commands have a period.

Er sagte	zu	mir:	"Stehen Sie auf!"
Er sagte		mir,	ich **solle** aufstehen.
Er sagte		mir,	daß ich aufstehen **solle**. *He told me to get up.*

CHECK AND PRACTICE

Change the text into indirect speech.

Einmal hat ein Mädchen, das viele ältere Brüder besaß, ihr Schwesterchen in einem Kinderwagen, in dem sie auch schon gelegen hatte, spazierengefahren. Das Schwesterchen war müde und gähnte. Eine Verkäuferin eines Blumengeschäfts, in dessen Schaufenster viele Blumen standen, hat das gesehen, und gleich hat sie mitgegähnt. "Warum gähnen Sie?" hat ihr Chef gefragt und unter Gähnen noch hinzugefügt: "Haben Sie heute zuviel gearbeitet?"

Die Leute im Blumengeschäft und dann alle Leute, die außerhalb des Blumengeschäfts waren, mußten auch gähnen. Ein Vater, der gerade mit seinem Sohn vorbeiging, fragte seinen Sohn: "Hast du schon einmal so viele offene Münder gesehen?" Und er und sein Sohn gähnten ebenfalls.

"Gähnen Sie nicht!" befahl ein Polizist einem Autofahrer. Aber umsonst. Bald haben alle Leute, alle Hunde, Katzen und Mäuse in der Stadt gegähnt. Und alle sind an diesem Abend früher schlafen gegangen.

Der Urgroßvater erzählte, einmal. . . .

Special Subjunctive and Imperative

490   1. There is a relationship between the special subjunctive and the imperative, as the formal imperative and first-person plural imperative forms show [see § 56 and § 61]. In addition to these forms, which are thought of and listed as imperatives, a few other special subjunctive forms (also imperatives) are considered archaic today. They are usually found in proverbs, official documents, and stereotyped phrases. The third person singular may have either normal or inverted word order.

Er **trete ein.** / **Trete** er **ein.**   *Let him **enter.***
Jeder **kehre** vor seiner Tür!   *Mind your own business. (literally: Let each person **sweep** in front of his own door.*

Man **beachte** die Vorschriften!   ***Observe** the rules.*
Edel **sei** der Mensch.   *Let man **be** noble.*

---

2. The third person plural is even less frequently used.

Alle **setzen sich!**   *(May) all **be seated.***

---

491   The special subjunctive is also found in set phrases, prayers, and formal greetings.

Es **lebe** die Freiheit!   *May freedom **live.***
Er **lebe** glücklich.   *May he **live** happily.*
Gott **sei** Dank!   *Thank God!*
Seine Seele **ruhe** in Frieden.   *May his soul **rest** in peace.*
Möge das neue Jahr Ihnen viel Glück bringen.   ***May** the new year bring you much good fortune.*
Gott **gebe** es.   *May God **grant** it.*
Der Himmel **gebe** es.   *May the heavens **grant** it.*

I. VOCABULARY FOR REVIEW (A AND B TEXTS FROM READER, CHAPTER IX)

Verbs

bauen	to build
erhalten (ä) ie, a	to preserve, maintain
ernähren	to feed
mähen	to mow
rad·fahren (ä) u, a (+ sein)	to bicycle

Nouns

die **Ernte, -n**	harvest
das **Gewerbe, -**	trade
das **Huhn, ¨er**	chicken
die **Kuh, ¨e**	cow
die **Lebensmittel** *(pl.)*	groceries
das **Pferd, -e**	horse
der **Pflug, ¨e**	plow
die **Schürze, -n**	apron
der **Stall, ¨e**	barn, stable
die **Stille**	silence
die **Wiese, -n**	meadow

Others

herrlich	magnificent
ländlich	rural

ADDITIONAL EXERCISES (A AND B TEXTS FROM THE READER)

Put the questions and answers into the present tense of the general subjunctive.

Wann werden Sie in einer Kleinstadt wohnen?

1. Wenn uns ein Stück Land gehört.
2. Wenn wir ein schönes Haus bauen.

3. Wenn ich einen kleinen Laden kaufe.

4. Wenn du mir einen Garten schenkst.

5. Wenn ihr uns eine nette Kleinstadt zeigt.

Glaubst du, dir wird das Dorfleben gefallen? Vielleicht, . . .

6. Wenn wir einen Bauernhof finden.

7. Wenn du uns ein paar Hühner gibst.

8. Wenn ich der Pastor im Dorf werde.

9. Wenn mein Vater dort ein Gewerbe findet.

10. Wenn ein Schnellzug dorthin fährt.

Put the answers into the past tense of the general subjunctive.

Hättet ihr eure Ferien auf dem Land verbracht? Ja, . . .

11. Wenn ihr uns eingeladen habt.

12. Wenn wir Stille gebraucht haben.

13. Wenn wir dort Freunde hatten.

14. Wenn man uns ein stilles Dorf zeigte.

15. Wenn wir dort bei der Ernte geholfen haben.

Wärt ihr gern in die Großstadt gezogen? Ja, . . .

16. Weil wir dort reicher waren.

17. Weil mein Bruder dort Bürgermeister wurde.

18. Weil das Leben dort interessanter war.

19. Weil meine Großeltern auch dorthin gezogen sind.

20. Weil viele Besucher zu uns kamen.

Answer in the negative, using the future tense of the general subjunctive.

Example

Ulrich kauft einen neuen Pflug. Und der alte Bauer?
Der alte Bauer würde keinen neuen Pflug kaufen.

21. Mein Vater wird Bürgermeister. Und Sie, Herr Hauck?

22. Meine Familie geht oft in diese Weinstube. Deine auch?

23. Meyers kaufen einen Bauernhof. Und Müllers?

24. Wir fahren jeden Tag Rad. Und ihr?

25. Ich sitze gern auf dieser Wiese. Und du?

Answer in the negative, using the future perfect tense of the general subjunctive.

Example

Meine Eltern haben immer auf dem Land gewohnt. Und deine?
Meine würden nicht immer auf dem Land gewohnt haben.

26. Ich habe mich für die Großstadt entschieden. Und Sie?
27. Wir haben zu viele Lebensmittel gekauft. Ihr auch?
28. Meine Kinder halfen bei der Ernte. Und Ihre?
29. Die Bauersfrau trug immer eine lange Schürze. Und Sie?
30. Meine Eltern ernähren die ganze Familie. Deine auch?

Answer with the present tense of the general subjunctive.

Was hat dein Vater bestimmt? Daß...

31. Ich kann hier radfahren.
32. Meine Kinder dürfen auf dem Pferd reiten.
33. Er will die Sache mit uns besprechen.
34. Wir müssen einen neuen Stall bauen.
35. Robert soll die Wiese mähen.

Answer with the past tense of the general subjunctive.

Warum seid ihr nie in die Großstadt gezogen? Weil...

36. Wir konnten den Autoverkehr nicht ertragen.
37. Unsere Kinder durften dort nicht radfahren.
38. Wir mußten dort jeden Tag im Park spazierengehen.
39. Wir wollten auf unseren Bauernhof zurückgehen.
40. Mein Mann sollte dort Bürgermeister werden.

Answer with the passive statements given, in the present tense of the general subjunctive.

Möchten Sie auf dieser ländlichen Straße wohnen? Warum nicht,...

41. Wenn hier kein Laden gebaut wird.
42. Wenn mir ein gutes Haus angeboten wird.
43. Wenn meine Hühner gut ernährt werden.
44. Wenn das Gras jede Woche gemäht wird.
45. Wenn diese Straße gut erhalten wird.

Answer with the passive statements given, in the past tense of the general subjunctive.

Was für Dinge wären vom Staat für die Bürger getan worden?

Example

Viele Kühe wurden vom Staat gekauft.
Viele Kühe wären vom Staat gekauft worden.

46. Viele alte Häuser wurden vom Staat erhalten.
47. Die Opfer des Faschismus wurden nicht vergessen.
48. Die meisten alten Leute wurden unterstützt.
49. Viele Städte sind rekonstruiert worden.
50. Alle Bewohner sind gut ernährt worden.

Use the general subjunctive to reject the statements. Retain the given tense.

Example

Wenn du Hühner hast, kannst du jeden Tag Eier essen. Nein,
Nein, wenn ich Hühner hätte, könnte ich nicht jeden Tag Eier essen.

51. Wenn du Lebensmittel verkaufst, verdienst du viel Geld. Nein,
52. Wenn Hans Bürgermeister ist, wird er alles bestimmen.
53. Wenn meine Kinder auf dem Dorf wohnen, fahren sie den ganzen Tag Rad.
54. Wenn wir in dieses Restaurant gingen, gab uns der Wirt immer die Hand.
55. Wenn die Ernte gut war, konnten wir die ganze Welt ernähren.

Inquire about the statements by repeating them in the special subjunctive.

Example

Meine Eltern haben geschrieben: "Das Leben in der Stadt ist herrlich."
Haben deine Eltern wirklich geschrieben, daß das Leben in der Stadt herrlich sei.

56. Der Bauer meldete: "Wir haben jetzt drei Kühe im Stall."
57. Unser Pfarrer sagt: "Die Menschen müssen manchmal schwere Opfer bringen."
58. Wir fragten den Bürgermeister: "Sollen wir eine Bürgerinitiative gründen?"
59. Der Bauer telefonierte: "Unser Stall muß repariert werden."
60. Sie wollte wissen: "Gibt es auf jedem Bauernhof Pferde und Kühe?"

Change into indirect commands after: Er bestimmte, daß...

61. "Kinder, mäht die Wiese noch heute!"
62. "Genießt die ländliche Stille!"
63. "Kauf heute keine Lebensmittel mehr ein, Irmtraut!"
64. "Martin, werde entweder Pastor oder Bürgermeister!"
65. "Erhalten Sie die herrliche Landschaft, meine Herren!"

II. VOCABULARY FOR REVIEW (C TEXT FROM READER, CHAPTER IX)

Verbs

ab·nehmen (i) a, o	to remove
an·sprechen (i) a, o	to approach, address
auf·setzen	to put on
bluten	to bleed
Feuer an·machen	to light a fire
heilen	to heal
schießen, o, o	to shoot
stammen aus	to come from
sich trennen (von)	to separate (from)
um·fallen (ä) ie, a (+ sein)	to fall over
sich um·sehen (ie) a, e	to look around
verbieten, o, o	to forbid
weg·nehmen (i) a, o	to take away

Nouns

der **Bauch,** ··e	belly
das **Fell, -e**	fleece
das **Frühjahr, -e**	spring
der **Geruch,** ··e	smell
die **Grube, -n**	ditch
das **Kinn, -e**	chin
die **Mütze, -n**	cap
das **Schaf, -e**	sheep
die **Stirn, -en**	forehead

Others

mager	skinny
vernünftig	reasonable
zäh	tough

ADDITIONAL EXERCISES (C TEXT FROM THE READER)

Complete each question with the suggested phrase in the present tense of the general subjunctive.

Was würdest du machen, wenn . . .

1. Der Mann spricht dich an.
2. Das Schaf blutet.
3. Die Kinder machen Feuer an.
4. Ich stamme auch aus dem Osten.
5. Ich nehme die Mütze nicht ab.
6. Heute beginnt das Frühjahr.
7. Der Geruch gefällt dir nicht.
8. Ich setze den Hut auf.
9. Ein Schaf fällt in eine Grube.
10. Die Regierung verbietet das.

Complete each question with the suggested phrase in the past tense of the general subjunctive.

Was hättest du gemacht, wenn . . .

11. Wir haben uns getrennt.
12. Der Arzt hat das Schaf schon geheilt.
13. Er hat die Hauptsache nicht verstanden.
14. Sie haben auf dich geschossen.
15. Sie hat sich nicht umgesehen.
16. Ich bin eingeschlafen.
17. Wir waren betrunken.
18. Der Tisch fiel um.
19. Sie haben dir die Schafe weggenommen.
20. Dein Kinn tat weh.

Recommend against each order by using the future tense of the general subjunctive.

Was sagen Sie dazu?

Example

"Mach Feuer an!" (Ich . . . nicht . . . !)
Ich würde nicht Feuer anmachen!

21. "Nimm die Mütze ab!"
22. "Sprechen Sie den fremden Mann nicht an!"

23. "Schießt auf die Schafe!"
24. "Trenn dich nicht von deinem Freund!"
25. "Seht euch nicht um!"

Reject each statement by using the future perfect of the general subjunctive.

Wer würde das auch getan haben?

Example

Die Frau hat sich nicht umgesehen. Ihr Mann
Ihr Mann würde sich umgesehen haben.

26. Der Schäfer hat den Hund erschossen. Ich (nicht)
27. Walter hat das Schaf losgelassen. Du (nicht)
28. Ihr habt die Hauptsache nicht verstanden. Meine Freunde
29. Sie haben sich über ihn lustig gemacht. Ihr (nicht)
30. Wir blieben zäh. Die anderen (nicht)

Answer with *Ja*, followed by the present tense of the general subjunctive.

31. Können Sie das Schaf heilen?
32. Im Restaurant muß er die Mütze abnehmen, nicht wahr?
33. Sollt ihr auf die Schafe aufpassen?
34. Darf ich den Boxer ansprechen?
35. Müssen wir das verbieten?

Put each statement in the past tense of the general subjunctive after the suggested introduction.

Ja, nach einer Weile . . .

Example

Mußte er sich umsehen?
Ja, nach einer Weile hätte er sich umsehen müssen.

36. Durftest du die Mütze abnehmen?
37. Wolltest du dich von deiner Freudin trennen?
38. Sollten wir ihm das Fell waschen?
39. Konnte er magerer werden?
40. Mußtet ihr euch umsehen?

Answer by putting each passive statement into the present tense of the general subjunctive after the suggested introduction.

Diesmal nicht, aber das nächste Mal...

Example

Wurde die Sache vernünftig diskutiert?
Diesmal nicht, aber das nächste Mal würde sie vernüftig diskutiert.

41. Ist Feuer angemacht worden?
42. Wurden unsere Fragen verboten?
43. Ist sie angesprochen worden?
44. Ist seine Stirn verwundet worden?
45. Seid ihr eingeladen worden?

Answer by putting each statement into the past tense of the general subjunctive after the suggested introduction.

Früher oder später...

Example

Glaubt er, sie schießen auf ihn?
Früher oder später hätten sie auf ihn geschossen.

46. Glaubst du, du wirst einmal vernünftig werden?
47. Glauben Sie, sein Bauch blutet?
48. Glaubt ihr, euer Geld wurde weggenommen?
49. Glauben Sie, die Felle sind eingepackt worden?
50. Glaubst du, das Schaf wurde geheilt?

Repeat each statement affirmatively in the general subjunctive. Retain the given tense.

Example

Wenn du dich umsiehst, lachen wir.
Ja, wenn du dich umsähest, lachten wir.

51. Wenn das Schaf blutet, heilen wir es.
52. Wenn die Frau aus Pommern stammt, setzen wir uns zu ihr.
53. Wenn du so mager bleibst, siehst du nicht gut aus.
54. Wenn wir tranken, habt ihr immer mit uns angestoßen.
55. Wenn das Frühjahr kam, merkten wir es hauptsächlich am Geruch.

Repeat each direct statement as indirect speech by using the special subjunctive. Retain the given tense.

Example

„Tut ihm der Bauch weh?"
Sie fragte, ob ihm der Bauch weh tue.

56. „Kannst du das einsehen?"

57. „Bald kommt das Frühjahr."

58. „Manfred wollte das besorgen."

59. „Kannst du nicht besser aufpassen?"

60. „Ich will mich von ihm trennen."

Change into indirect commands.

Mein Vater sagte, . . .

61. „Fall nicht um!"

62. „Bleibt nüchtern!"

63. „Trenn dich von deiner Freundin!"

64. „Lassen Sie meine Hand los!"

65. „Setz die Mütze auf!"

66. „Laß dir nichts verbieten!"

10 ADVERBS AND ADJECTIVES
(Part Two)

BUNDESREPUBLIK
DEUTSCHLAND

DEUTSCHE
DEMOKRATISCHE
REPUBLIK

Kiel
SCHLESWIG-
HOLSTEIN

Rostock

HAMBURG

Schwerin

Neubrandenburg

BREMEN • Bremen

NIEDERSACHSEN

West
Berlin • Berlin

Frankfurt
(Oder)

• Hannover

Potsdam

Magdeburg

NORDRHEIN-

Cottbus

• Düsseldorf

WESTFALEN

Halle •

• Leipzig

Dresden

Bonn •

HESSEN

Erfurt •

Karl-
Marx-Stadt

Suhl •

Gera •

• Wiesbaden

RHEINLAND-
PFALZ
Mainz

SAARLAND
• Saarbrücken

BAYERN

• Stuttgart

BADEN-
WÜRTTEMBERG

• München

ADVERBS

492   Adverbs are used to modify verbs, adjectives, and other adverbs, as well as the sentence as a whole. Their purpose is to enhance meaning.

Er sprach **leise.**	**leise** modifies the verb **sprach.**
*He spoke **quietly.***	
Er sprach **sehr** leise.	**sehr** modifies the adverb **leise.**
*He spoke **very** quietly.*	
Leider sprach er leise.	**leider** modifies the whole sentence; it expresses
Unfortunately, *he spoke quietly.*	the attitude of the speaker.

493   Adverbs never show case endings. Some of the mose frequent adverbial endings are:

-e	lang**e** *long*	**-erweise**	glücklich**erweise** *fortunately*
-s	morgen**s** *in the morning*	**-maßen**	einiger**maßen** *somewhat*
-lich	neu**lich** *recently*	**-wärts**	heim**wärts** *homeward*
-falls	jeden**falls** *in any case*	**-mal(s)**	mehr**mal(s)** *frequently*
-nd	schweig**end** *silently*	**-t**	begeister**t** *enthusiastically*

CHECK AND PRACTICE

Find the adverbs. There may be more than one in a sentence.

1. Ich habe heute besonders an dich gedacht.
2. Endlich weiß ich, warum er gestern mehrmals angerufen hat.
3. Er kommt manchmal zu mir.
4. Mindestens dreißig Studenten kamen zu dem Vortrag.
5. Mittags geht er immer nach Hause.
6. Sie blickten westwärts.
7. Das Unglück war folgendermaßen geschehen:...
8. Paul aß davon löffelweise.
9. Plötzlich war es still.
10. Anna muß abends arbeiten.

Adverb Classification

ADVERBS OF TIME

494

DEFINITE TIME   **wann?** *when? at what time?*

DAYS   and their additions to specify a TIME OF DAY
Kommst Du **morgen?**   Ja, **morgen abend!**

vorgestern	**morgen**	**vormittag**	**mittag**	**nachmittag**	**abend**	**nacht**
the day before yesterday	*morning*	*mid morning*	*noon*	*afternoon*	*evening*	*night*
gestern	morgen	vormittag	mittag	nachmittag	abend	nacht
yesterday						
heute	morgen	vormittag	mittag	nachmittag	abend	nacht
today						
morgen	**früh**	vormittag	mittag	nachmittag	abend	nacht
tomorrow						
übermorgen	früh	vormittag	mittag	nachmittag	abend	nacht
the day after tomorrow						

bald *soon*	**gleichzeitig** *at the same time*	**sonst** *formerly, always*
damals, dann *then, at*	**jetzt, nun** *now*	**vorher** *previously*
that time	**nachher** *afterwards, later*	**vorhin** *before, a short time ago*
eben *just now*	**neulich** *the other day, quite recently*	**zugleich** *at the same time, together*

Morgen früh haben wir wieder Deutschunterricht.
Tomorrow morning we'll have a German class again.

Sonst war er immer fröhlich, aber **jetzt** lacht er kaum noch.
*He **always** used to be cheerful, but **now** he rarely laughs anymore.*

495

FREQUENCY   **wie oft?** *how often?*

oft *often*	**niemals, nie** *never, at no time*	**zweimal** *twice*
manchmal *sometimes*	**einmal** *one time*	**täglich** *daily*
selten *seldom*	**nochmals/wieder** *once more, again*	**wöchentlich** *weekly*
häufig *frequently*	**mehrmals** *again and again, several times*	**monatlich** *monthly*
immer *always*	**vielmals** *often, frequently*	**dreimal** *three times, etc.*

The **-s** forms of the parts of day and the days of the week such as:

morgens *in the morning*	**sonntags** *on Sundays*
vormittags *in the mid morning*	**montags** *on Mondays*
mittags *at noon*	**dienstags** *on Tuesdays*
nachmittags *in the afternoon*	**mittwochs** *on Wednesdays*
abends *in the evening*	**donnerstags** *on Thursdays*
nachts *in the night*	**freitags** *on Fridays*
	samstags *on Saturdays*

Nachmittags geht Frau Schmidt **immer** in ein Cafe.
*In the afternoon Mrs. Schmidt **always** goes to a coffeehouse.*

ADVERBS OF PLACE

500

> FIXED PLACE *wo?* *where?*
> DIRECTION ***woher?*** *from where?* ***wohin?*** *to where?*

hier *here*
hierher *to this place, this way*
nach hier *to this place*
von hier *from this place*
hier und dort *here and there*

da *there*
dahin *to that place*
von da *from there*
da drüben *over there*
daher *from that place*

dort *there, over there*
dorthin *there*
nach dort *to that place*
dorther *from there*
dort oben *up there*

außen *outside*
von außen *from the outside*
draußen *outside, out of doors*
nach draußen *(to the) outside*
von draußen *from the outside*

innen *inside*
von innen *from within*
drinnen *inside, there within*
von drinnen *from the inside*

oben *above*
nach oben *up, up to*
von oben *from above*
droben *up there*

unten *below, at the bottom*
nach unten *down, downwards*
von unten *from below*
von oben bis unten *from head to toe*
drunten *down there, below*

vorn(e) *in front, at the beginning*
nach vorn *forward, to the front*
von vorn *from the front*

hinten *behind, in the rear*
nach hinten *towards the rear*
von hinten *from behind*

links *to the left, on the left*
von links *from the left*
nach links *to the left*

rechts *to the right, on the right*
von rechts *from the right*
nach rechts *to the right*

drüben *over there*
nach drüben *towards over there*
von drüben *from over there*

-wärts *-ward*
abwärts *downward*
von auswärts *from abroad*
vorwärts *forward, in front*
rückwärts *back, backwards*
seitwärts *sideways, laterally*

her *to this place*
hin *to that place, away*
hin und her *back and forth, to and fro*
herab, hinab *down*
herauf, hinauf *up*
heraus, hinaus *out*
herein, hinein *in*
herüber, hinüber *over*
herunter, hinunter *down*

CHECK AND PRACTICE

Complete with adverbs.

1. Komm _____! *(here, to this place)*
2. Ist Hans schon _____? *(here)*
3. Von wo fährt der Zug ab? _____. *(from here)*
4. _____ will ich nicht gehen! *(there)*
5. _____ komme ich auch. *(from there)*
6. Wo ist Inge? _____. *(over there)*
7. Kommen Sie aus Berlin? Ich habe Verwandte _____. *(there)*
8. Sehen Sie den Turm? _____ ist es windig. *(there)*
9. Wie ist das Wetter _____? *(outside)*
10. Es ist kalt, gehen wir nicht _____. *([to the] outside)*
11. _____ sieht alles besser aus. *(inside)*
12. Ist der Knopf _____? Nein, außen. *(inside)*
13. Es ist spät, geht _____ in euer Zimmer, Kinder. *(up to)*
14. _____ habt ihr Ruhe. *(above)*
15. Wir bleiben noch _____ im Wohnzimmer. *(below)*
16. Gehen wir _____ in den Keller! *(down)*
17. Er sah mich von _____ bis _____ an. *(from head to toe)*
18. Der Lehrer ging _____ an die Tafel. *(to the front)*
19. _____ stand der Filmprojektor. *(in front)*
20. In der Klasse sitze ich _____. *(in the rear)*
21. _____ kann man alles sehen. *(from behind)*
22. Komm doch auch _____! *(towards the rear)*
23. Gehen wir _____. *(to the left)*
24. _____, wo das Herz ist. *(left)*
25. Ein Auto kam _____. *(from the right)*
26. _____ stand der Polizist. *(on the right)*
27. Kommen diese Leute _____? *(from abroad)*
28. Lassen Sie den Film _____ laufen. *(backward)*
29. Die Zeit bewegt sich nur _____. *(forward)*
30. Man kann die Maschine _____ schieben. *(sideways)*

ADVERBS OF QUANTITY, DEGREE AND NUANCE, AND SENTENCE ADVERBS

501   *Adverbs of quantity and degree* modify individual parts of speech in an objective way. The *adverbs of nuance,* on the other hand, give the language its idiomatic flavor; they imply the subjective opinion of the speaker and are primarily used in colloquial German. They are in many ways related to the *sentence adverbs* but, in contrast to them, refer only to individual parts of speech.

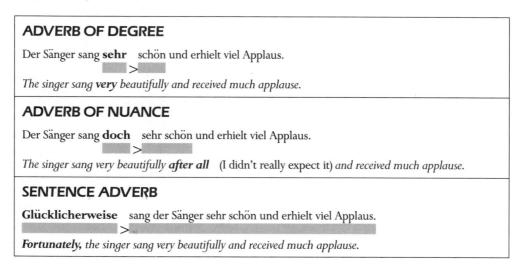

> **ADVERB OF DEGREE**
>
> Der Sänger sang **sehr**   schön und erhielt viel Applaus.
>
> ■■■ > ■■■
>
> *The singer sang **very** beautifully and received much applause.*
>
> **ADVERB OF NUANCE**
>
> Der Sänger sang **doch**   sehr schön und erhielt viel Applaus.
>
> ■■■ > ■■■
>
> *The singer sang very beautifully **after all**   (I didn't really expect it) and received much applause.*
>
> **SENTENCE ADVERB**
>
> **Glücklicherweise**   sang der Sänger sehr schön und erhielt viel Applaus.
>
> ■■■ > ■■■
>
> ***Fortunately,** the singer sang very beautifully and received much applause.*

With the help of the *adverb of nuance,* the speaker emphasizes that the singer sang very beautifully; but apparently it was contrary to the expectations of the listeners, or of somebody who had expressed a doubt beforehand. The *sentence adverb* shows that the speaker is emotionally bound to the singer and what he does.

502   Adverbs of quantity and degree

beinahe *almost*	**höchst** *very, (most) highly, extremely*	**ganz** *(with stress) completely*
fast *almost*	**äußerst** *extremely*	**ganz** *(without stress) rather, quite*
etwa *approximately*	**sehr** *very*	**zu** *too*
etwas *somewhat*	**viel** *much*	**genug** *(with post-position) enough*
ziemlich *pretty, rather*	**besonders** *especially*	**selbst** *even*
höchstens *at the most*	**weitaus** *by far*	

CHECK AND PRACTICE

Complete the sentence.

1. Frau Körner arbeitet _____ _____. *(too much)*
2. Sie singt am besten, _____ besser als die anderen. *(by far)*
3. Er hat _____ viel getan. *(especially)*

4. Paul hätte _____ seinen Paß vergessen. *(almost)*

5. Das Geschenk war _____ teuer. *(rather)*

6. Das Bild ist dem Maler _____ gut gelungen. *(quite)*

7. Er hat die Aufgabe _____ unvollkommen gelöst. *(pretty)*

8. Sie warteten _____ drei Stunden. *(almost)*

9. _____ zehn Schüler dürfen ins Ausland fahren. *(at the most)*

10. Das ist etwas _____ anderes. *(completely)*

Adverbs of nuance and sentence adverbs

503

Adverbs of Assertion and Emphasis	**bestimmt** *decidedly, certainly* **doch** *(use of "do"-construction)* **gewiß** *certainly* **ja** *really* **natürlich** *naturally* **noch** *yet*	**nun** *well* **schon** *certainly* **selbstverständlich** *of course* **sicher, sicherlich** *surely, certainly* **tatsächlich** *actually* **wirklich** *really*
of Limitation and Reduction	**allerdings** *to be sure, indeed* **eigentlich** *strictly speaking, to tell the truth* **freilich** *to be sure, certainly, I admit, however* **zwar** *it is true (but)*	
of Supposition and Doubt	**anscheinend** *apparently* **offenbar** *evidently* **offensichtlich** *obviously* **scheinbar** *seemingly*	**vielleicht** *perhaps* **vermutlich** *supposedly* **möglicherweise** *possibly* **wahrscheinlich** *probably*
of Interest or Impatience	**denn** *well*	
of Emphatic Negation	**keinesfalls** *in no case* **keineswegs** *by no means, not at all* **mitnichten** *by no means (very literary)*	
of Positive Emotions	**glücklicherweise** *fortunately* **hoffentlich** *hopefully* **lieber** *preferably*	**erstaunlicherweise** *surprisingly* **gottlob** *thank God (old-fashioned)*
of Negative Emotions	**leider** *unfortunately* **unglücklicherweise** *unfortunately* **bedauerlicherweise** *regretfully*	

Bedauerlicherweise starb er zu früh.   ***Unfortunately*** *he died too young.*
Natürlich war Paul nicht zu Hause.   ***Naturally,*** *Paul wasn't at home.*
Inge war **offensichtlich** nicht dumm.   *Inge was **obviously** not stupid.*
Leider muß ich morgen arbeiten.   ***Unfortunately,*** *I'll have to work tomorrow.*
Eigentlich sollte ich jetzt nach Hause gehen.   ***To tell the truth,*** *I should go home now.*

504 Sentence adverbs do not modify a single word or phrase but the whole sentence. Some may also function as adverbs of a different category.

Anna spricht **bestimmt** mit Herrn Meyer. *Anna speaks to Mr. Meyer **with certainty.*** *(How does she talk to him? **With certainty.** **spricht** is modified by **bestimmt.**)*	ADVERB OF MANNER
Anna spricht **bestimmt** mit Herrn Meyer. OR: **Bestimmt** spricht Anna mit Herrn Meyer. *Anna will **certainly** speak to Mr. Meyer.* *(Will Anna speak to Mr. Meyer? **Certainly.** **bestimmt** gives the speaker's opinion about the sentence; that is, he believes Anna is going to speak to Mr. Meyer.)*	SENTENCE ADVERB

COMPARISON OF ADJECTIVES AND ADVERBS

505 Almost all adjectives and adverbs derived from adjectives and the primary adverbs **bald, gern, oft,** can have comparative forms:

POSITIVE   COMPARATIVE   SUPERLATIVE

Predicate Adjectives and Adverbs

REGULAR FORMS

506 *Predicate adjectives* [see § 290.1.e] and *adverbs* add **-(e)r** for the comparative, and form their superlative with **am** and **-sten.** The English comparison with *more* and *most* does not exist in German.

Positive	leise	*quiet*	wichtig	*important*
Comparative	leis**er**	*quieter*	wichtig**er**	*more important*
Superlative	am leise**sten**	*quietest*	am wichtig**sten**	*most important*

507 Adjectives and adverbs ending in **-el, -en,** and **-er,** drop the **-e** of the stem ending in the comparative.

Positive	dunkel	*dark*	trocken	*dry*	teuer	*expensive*
Comparative	dunkl**er**		trockn**er**		teur**er**	
Superlative	am dunkelsten		am trockensten		am teuersten	

508   In the superlative, an **e** is added to words ending in **d, t,** or **s, ß, z.**

Positive	solid *solid*	laut *loud*	heiß *hot*
Comparitive	solider	lauter	heißer
Superlative	am solid**e**sten	am laut**e**sten	am heiß**e**sten

COMPARATIVE AND SUPERLATIVE FORMS WITH UMLAUT

509   Many *one-syllable* adjectives and adverbs with the stem vowel **a** or **u** will take an *umlaut* in the comparative and superlative. The stem vowel **o** is occasionally umlauted.

MANDATORY UMLAUT			NO UMLAUT	
alt	jung	groß	zart	toll
älter	j**ü**nger	gr**ö**ßer	zarter	toller
am **ä**ltesten	am j**ü**ngsten	am gr**ö**ßten	am zartesten	am tollsten

alt *old*	dumm *stupid*	grob *coarse*	flach *flat*	froh *glad*
arm *poor*	jung *young*	groß *large*	klar *clear*	roh *raw*
hart *hard*	klug *clever*		rasch *quick*	stolz *proud*
kalt *cold*	kurz *short*		schlank *slender*	toll *fantastic*
lang *long*			zart *tender*	voll *full*
scharf *sharp*				
schwach *weak*				
stark *strong*				
warm *warm*				

IRREGULAR FORMS

510   Some comparatives and superlatives have irregular forms.

POSITIVE	COMPARATIVE	SUPERLATIVE	
bald	eher	am ehesten	*soon*
gern	lieber	am liebsten	*gladly, willingly*
groß	größer	am größten	*large*
gut	besser	am besten	*good*
hoch	höher	am höchsten	*high*
nah(e)	näher	am nächsten	*near*
viel	mehr	am meisten	*much*

NOTE 1.   **hoch** is also irregular in the positive. When endings are added, the **c** drops from the stem:

| Das sind **hohe** Preise.   *These are **high** prices.* |

2. **wenig** has two comparative and superlative forms:

Positive	wenig	wenig	*little*
Comparative	weniger	minder	
Superlative	am wenigsten	am mindesten	

3. The superlative of **oft** *often* is not used very frequently. Usually the superlative of **häufig** is used instead.

Positive	oft	häufig
Comparative	öfter	häufiger
Superlative	am häufigsten	am häufigsten

Attributive Adjectives

511 *Attributive adjectives* add **-(e)r** for the comparative and **-(e)st** for the superlative forms. The definite article always precedes the superlative.

In addition to the comparative suffixes, attributive adjectives add case endings. [See 178ff.]

	PREDICATE ADJECTIVES + ADVERBS		ATTRIBUTIVE ADJECTIVES	
Positive	Anna ist	**schön.**	Anna ist eine **schöne**	Frau.
	Anna singt	**schön.**		
Comparative	Ute ist	**schöner.**	Ute ist eine **schönere**	Frau.
	Ute singt	**schöner.**		
Superlative	Ulla ist	**am schönsten.**	Ulla ist die **schönste**	Frau.
	Ulla singt	**am schönsten.**		
	*Ulla sings **most** beautifully.*			

512 The prefix **aller-** may be added to any superlative form to mean *of all*.

In dieser Klasse ist Paula die **aller**klügste Studentin.	*Paula is the smartest student **of all** in this class.*
Peter spielt Tennis am **aller**besten.	*Peter plays tennis best **of all**.*

CHECK AND PRACTICE

Replace the underlined adjective with each of the suggested adjectives.

A. Das ist ein billiges Auto.
    Das ist ein billigeres Auto.
    Das ist das billigste Auto, das ich je gesehen habe.
    Das rote Auto ist billiger als das blaue, das grüne ist am billigsten.

1.	klein	3.	praktisch	5.	schnell
2.	neu	4.	teuer	6.	langsam

B. Das sind kluge Hunde.
    Das sind klügere Hunde.
    Das sind die klügsten Hunde, die ich je gesehen habe.
    Die kleinen Hunde sind klüger als die großen, die ganz kleinen Hunde sind am klügsten.

7.	jung	9.	schmutzig	11.	selten
8.	nett	10.	treu	12.	alt

C. Paul erzählte eine kurze Geschichte.
    Inge erzählte eine kürzere Geschichte.
    Monika erzählte die kürzeste Geschichte, die ich je gehört habe.
    Paul erzählte kurze Geschichten.
    Inge erzählte kürzere Geschichten.
    Monika erzählte die kürzesten Geschichten, die ich je gehört habe.

13.	lang	15.	traurig	17.	interessant
14.	schön	16.	toll	18.	lustig

Phrases of Comparison

513 Comparisons can also be expressed by using **(nicht) so . . . wie, ebenso/genauso . . . wie** and **als, je . . . desto/umso, immer.**

Positive Form	Die Reproduktion war **(nicht) so** gut **wie** das Original. *The reproduction was (not) as good as the original.* Paul ist **genauso / ebenso** geschickt **wie** seine Schwester. *Paul is **just as** skillful as his sister.*
Comparative Form	Das Unglück war schlimmer **als** befürchtet. *The accident was worse **than** feared.* **Je** später der Abend, **desto** netter die Gäste. ***The** later the evening, **the** nicer the guests.* Es kamen **immer** weniger Besucher. *Fewer and fewer visitors came.*

CHECK AND PRACTICE

Answer the following questions, using the cues (= equal; ≠ unequal; < increasing under the given condition).

Example

Wer ist älter — Paul oder Peter? (=)
Paul ist **so alt wie** Peter.

Was ist billiger — ein Motorrad oder ein Auto? (≠)
Ein Motorrad ist billiger **als** ein Auto.

Läuft Peter schnell? (<, mehr)
Je mehr Peter läuft, **desto schneller** läuft er.

1. Was ist schwerer — ein Pfund Äpfel oder ein Pfund Bananen? (=)
2. Welches Bild ist schöner — das von Paul oder das von Peter? (≠)
3. Ist der Wein gut? (<, älter)
4. Welches Gebäude ist höher — der Kölner Dom oder die Frauenkirche in München? (≠)
5. Wo ist der Winter kälter — in Frankreich oder in Deutschland? (=)
6. Gibt Paul noch immer viel Geld aus? (<, mehr haben)
7. Wer schreibt weniger Briefe — Inge oder Monika? (=)
8. Welche Ferien sind länger — die Sommerferien oder die Herbstferien? (≠)
9. Wo ist es wärmer — in Italien oder in Deutschland? (≠)
10. Welche Stadt ist größer — Frankfurt oder Düsseldorf? (=)

Absolute Comparative

514   There are forms which function as an *absolute comparative* . They do not compare two things but indicate a comparatively higher degree. Most absolute comparatives occur in set expressions.

A **höhere Schule,** the equivalent of the American high school, for example, is a school that is "higher" than the **Grundschule** *elementary school,* but "lower" than a **Hochschule** *university.*

> eine **ältere** Dame   *an elderly (rather old) lady*   ein **längerer** Brief   *a lengthy (rather long) letter*

Absolute Superlative

515 There is also an *absolute superlative* of adjectives. It indicates a very high degree — but not the highest degree — of a given attribute. It does not intend a comparison. With attributive adjectives, it usually occurs without an article but with the appropriate inflectional ending.

Hier gibt es nur **beste** Weine.	Die Firma arbeitet mit **modernsten** Maschinen.
*Only the **best** wines are served here.*	*The factory works with the **most modern** machines.*

516 1. The absolute superlative of adverbs is formed in three ways:

    a. **-st**
    b. **-stens**
    c. **aufs -ste**

Er grüßte ihn **freundlichst.** *He greeted him in **a very friendly way.***
Rauchen ist **strengstens** verboten. *Smoking is **strictly** prohibited.*
Lisa hat gestern **aufs fleißigste** gearbeitet. *Lisa worked **most diligently** yesterday.*

    2. The forms with **-st** are used in salutatory and complimentary expressions with adverbs ending in **-ig** and **-lich.**

gefälligst *(if you) please*	herzlichst *most cordially*	gehorsamst *most obedient*
gütigst *kindly*	freundlichst *sincerely*	ergebenst *sincerely*
baldigst *without delay*	höflichst *politely*	möglichst *possibly*

I. VOCABULARY FOR REVIEW (A, B AND C TEXTS FROM READER, CHAPTER X)

Verbs

ab·sperren	to close off
auf·reißen, i, i	to tear open
betreten (i) a, e	to enter
fliehen, o, o (+ sein)	to flee
gestatten	to permit

sichern	to safeguard, secure
töten	to kill
trennen	to divide
unter·gehen, i, a (+ sein)	to perish
zielen (auf)	to aim (at)
zwingen	to force

Nouns

der **Befehl, -e**	order, command
die **Bewachung**	surveillance
die **Flucht**	escape
die **Genehmigung, -en**	permission
der **Graben, ¨-**	ditch
die **Herrschaft**	rule
die **Maßnahme, -n**	measure
der **Personalausweis, -e**	identification card
der **Posten, -**	guard
der **Stacheldraht, ¨-e**	barbed wire
die **Trennung, -en**	division
die **Übergangsstelle, -n**	crossing point
die **Unterdrückung, -en**	suppression
der **Vertrag, ¨-e**	treaty
das **Visum, die Visa**	visa
die **Wiedervereinigung, -en**	reunification

ADDITIONAL EXERCISES (A, B AND C TEXTS FROM THE READER)

Identify the adverb(s) in each sentence.

1. Heute geht traurigerweise eine Grenze durch Deutschland.
2. Die Politiker haben diese Maßnahme nicht genau erklärt.
3. Früher konnten alle Bürger leicht nach Osten oder Westen reisen.
4. Manchmal fuhren sie vielleicht einigermaßen unglücklich nach Hause.
5. Vermutlich blicken die Jugendlichen in der DDR oft westwärts.

Repeat each statement, adding an adverb of time in the proper place.

6. Die DDR ist das Deutschland der 50er Jahre. *(today, still, since then)*

7. Reisen in die DDR ohne Visum sind nicht gestattet. *(always, just now)*

8. Jugendliche demonstrieren gegen die Trennung. *(sometimes, frequently, monthly, in the night)*

9. Viele sprechen über die Wiedervereinigung. *(now, daily, up to now)*

Repeat each statement adding an adverb of cause in the proper position.

10. Der Vertrag sichert die Herrschaft des Proletariats. *(therefore)*

11. Viele Menschen fliehen vor der Unterdrückung. *(consequently, for that reason)*

12. Die DDR ändert ihren politischen Kurs nicht. *(in spite of it)*

Repeat each statement, adding an adverb of place in the proper position.

13. Man braucht eine Genehmigung für die Reise. *(to this place, to that place)*

14. Der Posten hörte seinen Kollegen rufen. *(outside, from the outside)*

15. Der Befehl eines Postens gilt nicht. *(here, there, up there)*

16. Viele Flüchtlinge kamen aus dem Wald. *(from the left, from the right)*

Answer each statement, adding an adverb of quantity or degree next to an adverb of manner.

17. Sind alle Übergangsstellen streng gesichert? *(very, especially)*

18. Hat der Posten langsam auf den Mann gezielt? *(somewhat, quite)*

19. Wird die Bevölkerung unmenschlich unterdrückt? *(completely, extremely)*

Answer each question with the predicate adjective in its comparative form, preceded by *noch*.

20. Sind Reisen nach Dresden beliebt? Ja, aber die Reisen nach Weimar sind _____

21. Ein Visum ist wohl schwer zu bekommen? Ja, aber eine Aufenthaltsgenehmigung ist _____

22. Sind die Gefängnisse dort drüben gefährlich? Ja, aber die Flucht ist _____

23. Die Sportler in der Bundesrepublik sind wohl sehr gut? Ja, aber die in der DDR sind _____

24. Finden Sie die wirtschaftliche Konkurrenz im Westen störend? Ja, aber staatliche Kontrolle ist _____

Answer by repeating each question with the adverb in its comparative form, preceded by *noch*.

Example

Fahren Sie <u>schnell</u>? Nein, (mein Mann)
Nein, mein Mann fährt **schneller**.

25. Reisen Sie <u>gern</u>? Nein, ich (zu Hause bleiben)
26. Brauchen Sie die Fahrkarte <u>dringend</u>? Nein, ich (ein Visum/brauchen)
27. Ist ein Visum <u>schwer</u> zu bekommen? Ja, aber (eine Aufenthaltsgenehmigung/zu bekommen sein)
28. Kann man den Graben <u>gut</u> sehen? Nein, man (den Posten sehen können)
29. Wurde der Graben <u>schnell</u> gezogen? Ja, aber (der Stacheldraht wurde)

Answer with the predicate or attributive adjective in its superlative form.

Example

Welcher Posten ist <u>gefährlich</u>? (am Stacheldraht)
Der Posten am Stacheldraht ist **am gefährlichsten**.
Wo sind die **neuen** Personalausweise? Hans hat (in seinem Büro)
Hans hat die **neusten** Personalausweise in seinem Büro.

30. Welche Reisen sind jetzt <u>beliebt</u>? (die Reisen nach Europa)
31. Wie kann man denn <u>sichere</u> Bewachung garantieren? (durch Soldaten)
32. Finden Sie oft <u>scharfe</u> Konkurrenz? Ja, (auf dem Nachrichtenmarkt)
33. Sind alle Übergangsstellen <u>gefährlich</u>? (die mit Stacheldraht)
34. Wissen Sie, wo in Deutschland das Essen <u>gut</u> ist? (in München)
35. Woher kommen die <u>armen</u> Flüchtlinge? (aus Osteuropa)

Answer with the adverb in its superlative form.

Example

Hat man alle Straßen <u>schnell</u> aufgerissen? (die Bernauer Straße)
Die Bernauer Straße hat man **am schnellsten** aufgerissen.

36. Welche Konkurrenz halten Sie für <u>gefährlich</u>? Ich finde (die vom Fernsehen)
37. Wie kann man zwei Stadtteile <u>gut</u> trennen? (mit Stacheldraht)
38. Reisen Sie <u>gern</u> in die DDR? Ja, ich reise (nach Dresden und Weimar)
39. Wie kann man die Menschen <u>sicher</u> zum Bleiben zwingen? Man kann sie (mit vielen Maßnahmen)
40. Wie komme ich <u>schnell</u> von Bonn nach Berlin? Sie kommen (mit dem Flugzeug)

Answer, using the cues.

Example

Sperrt man Flüchtlinge strenger ein als andere Menschen? (genauso)
Man sperrt sie **genauso streng** ein **wie** andere Menschen.

41. Ist die Flucht gefährlicher als das Gefängnis? (genauso)
42. Was ist schwerer für die Deutschen, die Trennung oder die Wiedervereinigung? (ebenso)
43. Wo arbeiten die Jugendlichen schwerer, im Osten oder im Westen? (im Westen nicht so)
44. Wo ist die Friedensbewegung aktiver, in der DDR oder in der Bundesrepublik? (in der DDR nicht so)
45. Welche Stadt finden Sie interessanter, Berlin oder Bonn? (Bonn nicht so)

Answer with the comparative of the adjective or adverb, preceded by *immer* where required.

Example

Ist es schwer, ein Visum zu bekommen? Ja, und es wird
Ja, und es wird **immer schwerer**.
Sind die Maßnahmen hier so streng wie drüben? Nein, drüben
Nein, die Maßnahmen sind drüben **strenger**.

46. Ist eure Bewachung jetzt weniger scharf? Nein, sie wird
47. Ist ein Personalausweis bei euch wichtig? Ja, er wird täglich
48. Ist der Graben hier so breit wie der dort? Nein, der dort ist
49. Zielt dieser Posten genau? Nein, der im Graben zielt
50. Sind die Sportler hier gut? In anderen Ländern sind sie

II. VOCABULARY FOR REVIEW (D AND E TEXTS FROM THE READER, CHAPTER X)

Verbs

aus·packen	to unpack
sich befinden, a, u	to be
sich begeben (i) a, e	to go, proceed
sich beherrschen	to control oneself
davon·kommen, a, o (+ sein)	to get off

entlassen (ä) ie, a	to release
sich erhängen	to hang oneself
erschießen, o, o	to shoot dead
gestehen, a, a	to confess
recht behalten (ä) ie, a	to prove (to be) right
das Recht haben	to have the right
unterschreiben, ie, ie	to sign
sich weigern	to refuse

Nouns

die **Drohung, -en**	threat
die **Fahne, -n**	flag
der **Hauptmann, -leute**	captain
der **Lehrling, -e**	apprentice
die **Träne, -n**	tear
die **Unterhose, -n**	underpants
die **Unterschrift, -en**	signature
das **Wohnheim, -e**	dormitory

ADDITIONAL EXERCISES (D AND E TEXTS FROM THE READER)

Identify the adverbs in each statement.

1. Seit langem lebt er hauptsächlich im Ausland.
2. Er weigerte sich deshalb, schnell nach Hause zurückzukommen.
3. Glücklicherweise beherrscht er sich immer sofort.
4. Er hat den Vertrag freundlicherweise sofort unterschrieben.
5. Wir gestanden ungern, daß er wieder recht behalten hatte.

Answer each question with *Ja* or *Nein* followed by an adverb of time in the proper place.

6. Hat er das Recht, sich ins Wohnheim zu begeben? *(since then, today)*
7. Hat dir deine Mutter dieses Spielzeug gekauft? *(just now, this morning)*
8. Gehen dir meine Tränen auf die Nerven? *(never, sometimes)*
9. Behält dein Vater recht? *(always, frequently)*
10. Hast du deine Unterschrift gegeben? *(a short time ago, the other day)*

Repeat each statement, adding an adverb of cause in the proper place.

11. Ich habe dem Hauptmann nichts gestanden. *(for that reason, nevertheless)*
12. Ich habe mich geweigert. *(for your sake, in any case)*
13. Er hat versucht, sich zu erhängen. *(accordingly, therefore)*

Answer each question affirmatively with an adverb of manner in the proper place.

14. Mußtest du den Koffer auspacken? *(very quickly, slowly)*

15. Hat der Herr dir geholfen? *(with pleasure)*

16. Hat er dich zur Unterschrift aufgefordert? *(politely, nervously)*

17. Wie schreibt dein neuer Kugelschreiber? *(clearly, well)*

Repeat each statement, adding an adverb of place in its proper position.

18. Sie hatten ihn erwischt? *(over there, out of doors)*

19. Gestern wollte man ihn entlassen. *(from there, to this place)*

20. Er hat sich erhängt. *(here, up there)*

Answer each question with the predicate adjective or adverb in its comparative form, preceded by *noch*.

Example

Diese Unterhosen sind teuer. Die Cordhosen
Die Cordhosen sind **noch teurer**.

21. Fühlst du dich oft müde? Ja, aber der junge Lehrling

22. Wohnen Sie weit von hier? Nicht sehr weit, viele Angestellte

23. Ist dieses Spielzeug nicht gefährlich? Doch, aber richtige Waffen

24. Dieser Revolver ist ziemlich schwer, ja? Nicht sehr, die Pistole

25. Ist die Fahne für euch wichtig? Ja, aber unsere Partei

26. Dieser Junge ist leicht davongekommen. Die anderen Lehrlinge sind sogar

27. Warum sprichst du so laut? Du selbst sprichst

28. Deine Kameraden behalten wohl oft recht? Nein, unser Hauptmann behält

29. Klingen meine Worte zu scharf? Manche Propaganda klingt

Answer with the attributive or predicate adjective in its superlative form.

Example

Ein Lehrling weigerte sich lange, das zu unterschreiben. Wer
Wer weigerte sich **am längsten**?

30. Gibt hier jemand guten Rat? Der Pfarrer

31. Bist du immer schnell mit der Arbeit fertig? Meine Geschwister

32. Befindet sich deine Familie weit von hier? Meine Großeltern

33. Gibt es bei euch viele nette Wohnheime? Das Lehrlingswohnheim

34. Sind deine neuen Unterhosen elegant? Meine alten

Answer with the adverb in its superlative form.

Example

Möchten Sie gern jemand erschießen? (niemand)
Ich möchte **am liebsten** niemand erschießen.

35. Welche Festspiele finden bald statt? (die Weltfestspiele)
36. Die Lehrlinge arbeiten wohl viel? Ja,
37. Womit kann man gut unterschreiben? (mit dem Kugelschreiber)
38. Ihr mußtet euch lange beherrschen, nicht wahr? Ja, (aber meine Eltern)
39. Arbeiten alle gern für den Sozialismus? (die Jugendlichen)
40. Hast du deine Sachen schnell ausgepackt? Ja, (und mein Spielzeug)

Answer *Ja* or *Nein*, using the cues.

41. Ist eure Fahne blauer als eure Uniform? Nein, (genauso)
42. Ist eine Drohung schlimmer als eine Unterschrift? (ebenso)
43. Hat die Mutter so viel Angst gehabt wie der Junge? (nicht so)
44. Wurde dir der Personalausweis schneller als das Visum weggenommen? (nicht so)
45. Weigert sich Hans energischer als du? Nein, (genauso)

Answer with the comparative of the adjective or adverb, preceded by *immer* where required.

Example

Befinden Sie sich gern im Ausland? Ja, mit der Zeit
Ja, mit der Zeit **immer lieber**.

46. Kannst du mich weit begleiten? Jeden Tag
47. Klingen diese Drohungen gefährlich? Sie werden
48. Müßt ihr viel arbeiten? Jedes Semester
49. Hast du dich gut beherrscht? Ja, aber meine Schwester
50. Könnt ihr denn verantwortliche Lehrlinge finden? Lehrlinge werden

11 VERBS (Part Four)

PASSIVE

Passive versus Active

517   The *passive voice* is distinguished from the *active voice* by the relationship of the grammatical subject to the verb. In the active voice the grammatical subject performs or causes the action, whereas in the passive voice the grammatical subject is being *acted upon.*

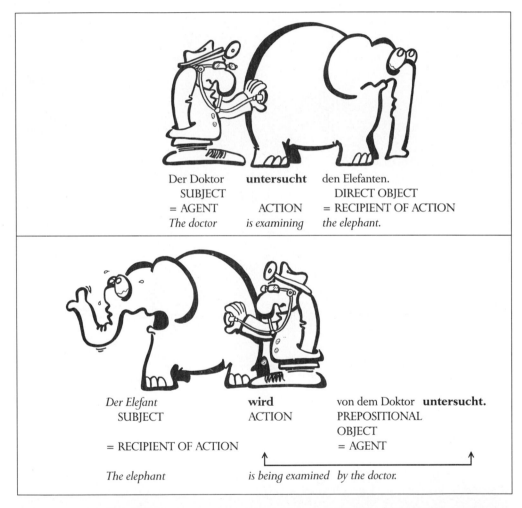

Der Doktor **untersucht** den Elefanten.
SUBJECT   DIRECT OBJECT
= AGENT   ACTION   = RECIPIENT OF ACTION
The doctor   is examining   the elephant.

Der Elefant **wird** von dem Doktor **untersucht.**
SUBJECT   ACTION   PREPOSITIONAL
                                 OBJECT
= RECIPIENT OF ACTION   = AGENT

The elephant   is being examined by the doctor.

518   When active verb forms are used *with a direct object*, such active sentences can be transformed into the passive. Then the direct (accusative) object of the active sentence becomes the subject (nominative) of the passive sentence. The subject of the active sentence becomes a prepositional object. In English the preposition is *by,* while in German it is usually **von.** [See § 522]

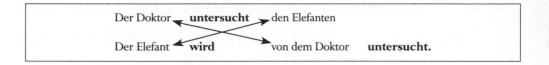

Verb Forms in the Passive

519 German and English passive verb forms resemble each other: In English, the passive voice is formed with the auxiliary "*to be*" plus *a past principle;* in German with the auxiliary **werden** plus *a past participle.* The infinitive **werden** preceded by the past participle is called the *passive infinitive.*

ACTIVE INFINITIVE	PASSIVE INFINITIVE
schlagen *to beat*	geschlagen werden *to be beaten*

520 In the passive, in both languages only the auxiliary (**werden** in German, *to be, get, become* in English) is inflected; the past participle remains unchanged.

Present Tense	ich **werde** gelobt	*I am being* praised
Past Tense	ich **wurde** gelobt	*I was being* praised
Future Tense	ich **werde** gelobt **werden**	*I will be* praised

521 The auxiliary **werden** forms the perfect tenses with **sein (ich bin geworden).** But the passive uses **worden** instead of the normal past participle **geworden.**

Perfect	ich **bin**	gelobt	**worden**	*I have*	*been* praised
Past Perfect	ich **war**	gelobt	**worden**	*I had*	*been* praised
Future Perfect	ich **werde**	gelobt	**worden sein**	*I will have*	*been* praised

CHECK AND PRACTICE

Give the missing forms of *werden* **in these passive sentences.**

1. das Examen _____ begonnen _____ (PE)
2. die Geschenke _____ ausgepackt _____ (F)
3. die Schokolade _____ gegessen _____ (PE)
4. ich _____ beobachtet _____ (PE)
5. der Kuchen _____ gebacken (PA)
6. er _____ gebadet (PR)

The Agent in Passive Sentences

522   1. Most transitive verbs followed by an accusative object can be used in the passive. The passive sentences may or may not contain an agent indicating who or what is performing the action. The agent is usually introduced by the dative preposition **von** if it is a person.

> Der Schüler wird **von dem Lehrer** gelobt.   *The student is being praised **by the teacher**.*

2. The agent is usually a person but a "non-personal" agent such as rain can be used figuratively.

> Zwei Männer sind **vom Regen** überrascht worden.   *Two men were surprised **by the rain**.*

523   1. When the agent is an impersonal force (i.e., the means), the accusative preposition **durch** is used. The dative preposition **mit** is used to express the instrument with which an action is being performed.

> Er wurde **durch** einen Stich ins Herz getötet.   *He was killed **by** a stab in his heart.*
> **Mit** einem Messer.   ***With** a knife.*   Sehr richtig! Aber **von** wem?   *Quite right! But **by** whom?*

2. The means are usually "non-personal," but a person might also function in the role of means; for example, soldiers who act on orders.

> Die Brücke wurde **durch** Soldaten zerstört.   *The bridge was destroyed **by** soldiers.*

CHECK AND PRACTICE

Choose *von*, *durch*, or *mit*. Give the correct case ending.

1. Das erste Spiel wurde _____ Ursula gewonnen.
2. Der Brief wurde _____ d_____ Hand geschrieben, aber der Aufsatz _____ d_____ Schreibmaschine.
3. Das Auto ist _____ ein_____ Fremden gefahren worden.
4. Die Not war _____ d_____ Hilfe vieler Menschen gemildert worden.
5. Die Hausaufgaben dürfen _____ d_____ Computer gemacht werden.
6. Der Kuchen war _____ mein_____ Tochter gebacken worden.
7. Die Stadt ist _____ Bomben zerstört worden.

8. Dieses Lied wird _____ alten und jungen Leuten gesungen.

9. Unser Interesse ist _____ dein_____ Rede geweckt worden.

10. Der Fisch darf nicht _____ d_____ Messer geschnitten werden.

11. Wurde das Bild _____ Ölfarbe gemalt?

524 The agent is omitted in a passive sentence if it is a pronoun, or if mentioning it is unnecessary or awkward. The pronoun **man** is never used as an agent in a passive sentence.

> Sicherlich werden **wir** den Schlüssel finden. *Certainly we will find the key.*
> Der Schlüssel wird sicherlich gefunden werden. *The key will certainly be found.*
>
> Faulen Studenten sollte **man** nicht helfen. *You shouldn't help lazy students.*
> Faulen Studenten sollte nicht geholfen werden.

Das Museum
wird
um 5 Uhr
geschlossen

CHECK AND PRACTICE

Complete the passive sentence. Omit the agent if possible.

1. Sie hatten den Grund ihres Besuchs nicht erklärt.
   _____ war _____ nicht erklärt worden.

2. Den Brief schreiben wir erst morgen.
   _____ wird _____ erst morgen geschrieben.

3. Kann man irgendetwas tun?
   Kann _____ _____ getan werden?

4. Man stellt den Flugverkehr oft ein.
   _____ wird _____ oft eingestellt.

525 Reflexive verbs [see § 267] cannot form a passive. Yet for verbs used reflexively, a passive transformation is possible under certain cirumstances:

1. in emphatic commands in which the subject is omitted:

> Jetzt wird sich gewaschen! *Now wash yourself.*

2. in cases in which the subject is not mentioned:

> Da wurde in zitternder Angst sich verkrochen. *They hid in trembling fear.*

Passive of Intransitive Verbs

526 Intransitive verbs followed by a dative object can also be used in a passive sentence, but the dative object must be preserved. If it is placed in front position, the passive sentence has no subject. If it is placed after the verb, the pronoun **es** is introduced as a stylistic subject at the beginning of the clause. Usually in such sentences the agent is omitted.

Active	Der Sohn	dankte	dem Vater.	*The son thanked his father.*	
Passive					
SELDOM	Dem Vater	wurde	von dem Sohn	gedankt.	*The father was thanked by his son.*
USUALLY	Dem Vater	wurde		gedankt.	
	Es STYLISTIC SUBJECT	wurde	dem Vater	gedankt.	

527 The stylistic role of **es** is seen in a passive transformation of a sentence with a direct as well as an indirect object. The ending of the verb is determined by the grammatical subject, not by **es.**

Sein Freund SUBJECT	gab	ihm INDIRECT OBJECT		die Geschenke. DIRECT OBJECT
The gifts were given to him by his friend. Die Geschenke SUBJECT	wurden	ihm INDIRECT OBJECT		von seinem Freund gegeben.
Ihm INDIRECT OBJECT	wurden	die Geschenke SUBJECT		von seinem Freund gegeben.
Es STYLISTIC SUBJECT	wurden	ihm INDIRECT OBJECT	die Geschenke GRAMMATICAL SUBJECT	von seinem Freund gegeben.

Pay attention to the difference between German and English.

GERMAN	**ENGLISH**
Sein Freund gab **ihm** die Geschenke.	*His friend gave **him** the gifts.*
Die Geschenke wurden **ihm** von seinem Freund gegeben.	*The gifts were given **to him** by his friend.*
Ihm wurden die Geschenke von seinem Freund gegeben.	***He** was given the gifts by his friend.*

In the English sentence, the indirect object of the active sentence becomes the *subject* of the passive sentence.

CHECK AND PRACTICE

Fill in the missing element.

1. Ein Freund half dem neuen Schüler bei den Hausaufgaben.
   _____ wurde bei den Hausaufgaben geholfen.
2. Man gehorcht dem General. (gehorchen *to obey*)
   _____ wird gehorcht.
3. Wir haben dem Großvater zum Geburtstag gratuliert.
   _____ ist zum Geburtstag gratuliert worden.

Translate.

4. She was sent a ring by her boy friend.
5. The best student was given a book.

528   Certain verbs which are followed by a genitive object or a prepositional object can also be used in the passive. Again, as with the indirect object, the genitive or prepositional object is preserved, the passive construction has no grammatical subject, and the agent is usually omitted.

Active	Wir gedachten **der Toten.** *We remembered **the dead.***
Passive	**Der Toten** wurde (von uns) gedacht.
	Es wurde (von uns) **der Toten** gedacht. *The dead were remembered (by us).*
Active	Wir bleiben **bei dieser Meinung.** *We hold **to this opinion.***
Passive	**Bei dieser Meinung** wird geblieben.
	Es wird **bei dieser Meinung** geblieben.

529   When an activity is to be stressed for which the agent is unknown or inconsequential, German uses impersonal passive sentences, with or without **es.** There is generally no direct English equivalent.

Es wird hier nicht geraucht.   *No smoking here.*
Hier wird nicht geraucht.
Es wird heute nicht gearbeitet.   *There's no work being done today.*
Heute wird nicht gearbeitet.
Es wird gesagt . . .   *It is said*
Es wurde viel über ihn geredet.   *He was much talked about.*

Passive with Modal Auxiliaries

530   Modals are followed by an infinitive [see § 94ff.]. In a passive construction the modal verb is followed by the passive infinitive.

		MODAL		**INFINITIVE**	
Active	Ich	**muß**	es	lesen.	*I have to read it.*
				PASSIVE INFINITIVE	
Passive	Es	**muß**		gelesen werden.	*It has to be read.*

531   As in the active voice, only the modal verb is inflected. The perfect tenses with their double infinitives are usually avoided.

Present Tense	es **muß**	gelesen werden	*it has to be read*
Past Tense	es **mußte**	gelesen werden	*it had to be read*
Future Tense	es **wird**	gelesen werden **müssen**	*it will have to be read*

CHECK AND PRACTICE

Form passive sentences in the suggested tense.

1. Die Rechnungen _____ (müssen / bezahlen) (FUTURE TENSE)
2. Die Musik _____ (dürfen / spielen) (PAST TENSE)
3. Die Preise _____ (können / erhöhen) (PAST TENSE)
4. Das Volk _____ (müssen / informieren) (FUTURE TENSE)
5. Der Bericht _____ (sollen / schreiben) (PAST TENSE)
6. Jeder Mensch _____ (wollen / loben) (PRESENT TENSE)
7. Späße _____ (dürfen / machen) (PRESENT TENSE)
8. Der Wagen _____ (sollen / waschen) (PAST TENSE)

Use of Passive

532   In German, the passive voice is primarily used:

1. whenever the action as such is the topic of conversation and the "agent"-subject is of no importance;
2. when the speaker wants to conceal the agent's identity without being too obvious about it;
3. as a rhetorical means for emphasis.

Warst du auf der Party von Helga?	Ja. Dort wurde viel getanzt.
Were you at Helga's party?	*Yes. There was a lot of dancing.*

Der Ankläger: *prosecutor*	Der Verteidiger: *defense*
Der Angeklagte ermordete Herrn Meyer im Juni letzten Jahres.	Herr Meyer wurde im Juni letzten Jahres ermordet.
The accused murdered Mr. Meyer last June.	*Herr Meyer was murdered last June.*
Agent is mentioned in prominent position.	Agent is not mentioned.

Ruhe! Jetzt wird aber geschlafen! *Silence. Go to sleep.*

CHECK AND PRACTICE

Change into a passive construction.

1. Man bereitet das Experiment vor.
2. Schlafen Sie nicht in der Klasse!
3. Hier müssen Sie deutsch sprechen.

Alternates to the Passive

533 Since German usage prefers the active voice, the passive is frequently circumscribed. The following patterns, which would be passive voice in English, are used as alternates for the passive construction in German.

534 **man** plus a verb in the active voice

	Man sagt heute, daß. . . ***It is said*** *today that* . . .
INSTEAD OF	Es wird heute gesagt, daß . . .

535 **sein** plus infinitive with **zu**

This passive equivalent shows that the action implied in the infinitive has a modal meaning (**können** or **müssen** is used, depending on the context).

	Diese Worte **sind** gut **zu verstehen.** *These words **are (can be)** easily **understood.***
	Das Rauchen **ist** sofort **einzustellen.** *The smoking **must be stopped*** *right away.*
INSTEAD OF	Diese Worte können gut verstanden werden.
	Das Rauchen muß sofort eingestellt werden.

536   bleiben, stehen, geben, gehen plus infinitive with **zu**

The use of these verbs expresses the possibility or necessity of a future action. The use of **gehen** is colloquial. English translations retain the passive.

	Das Ergebnis **bleibt abzuwarten.** *The result **remains to be seen.***
INSTEAD OF	Das Ergebnis muß abgewartet werden.
	Es **steht zu befürchten,** daß. . . *It **is to be feared** that. . .*
INSTEAD OF	Es muß befürchtet werden, daß. . .
	Es **gibt** viel **zu tun.** *There's much **to be done.***
INSTEAD OF	Es muß viel getan werden.
	Das Bild **geht** nicht **zu befestigen.** *The picture **can't be fastened.***
INSTEAD OF	Das Bild kann nicht befestigt werden.

537   Reflexive **lassen** plus infinitive

The action implied has a modal meaning (in most cases, **können**).

	Das **läßt sich machen.** *That **can be done.***
INSTEAD OF	Das kann gemacht werden.

538   Reflexive use of the verb

1. When the subject is "non-personal" and the agent cannot be named (in contrast to the above passive alternates in which the agent is usually omitted but may be named):

	Die Tür **öffnete sich.** *The door **opened.***
INSTEAD OF	Die Tür wurde geöffnet.

2. If the reflexive constructions are modified by adverbs, the modal meaning **können** is implied.

Die Tür **öffnet sich** leicht.   *The door **can be opened** easily.*
Die Tür kann leicht geöffnet werden.

So etwas **erklärt sich** schwer.   *Such things are difficult **to explain.***
So etwas kann schwer erklärt werden.

Das Buch **liest sich** schnell.   *The book **can be read** fast.*
Das Buch kann schnell gelesen werden.

CHECK AND PRACTICE

Give a passive alternate.

1. Es wird hier immer viel getrunken.
2. In diesem Geschäft ist wenig gekauft worden.
3. Die Erlaubnis war ihnen gegeben worden.
4. Die Erlaubnis muß ihnen gegeben werden.
5. Die Musik konnte sogar ganz hinten im Saal gut gehört werden.
6. Kann das Auto noch repariert werden?
7. Wie viele Briefe müssen noch geschrieben werden?
8. Die Situation kann leicht erklärt werden.
9. Das kann nicht mehr geändert werden.
10. Der Name wird leicht vergessen.

GERMAN VERBS WITH PASSIVE MEANING IN ENGLISH

539 **dürfen** *to be allowed to* [see § 80], **sollen** *to be supposed to, to be said to* [see § 91], **heißen** *to be called*

Das Kind **darf** nicht auf der Straße spielen. *The child is not **allowed to** play in the street.*
Er **soll** sehr klug sein. *He **is said to be** very clever.*
Wie **heißt** es? *What is it **called**?*

CHECK AND PRACTICE

1. I'm not allowed to go out.
2. What am I supposed to do?

3. He's called Jonathan.

STATAL PASSIVE

540 The passive voice describes an activity or process: the *statal passive* (or apparent passive) denotes a condition, or state of being. The past participle of the verb functions as a predicate adjective [see § 174] of the verb **sein**. In modern usage only the present and past tenses of the statal passive occur.

PASSIVE	STATAL PASSIVE
werden + past participle	**sein** + past participle
Die Tür **wird geschlossen.**	Die Tür **ist geschlossen.**
*The door **is being closed.***	*The door **is closed.***
Die Tür **wurde geschlossen.**	Die Tür **war geschlossen.**
*The door **was being closed.***	*The door **was closed.***

CHECK AND PRACTICE

Give the statal passive.

1. Der Bericht wird geschrieben.
2. Die Rechnung wird bezahlt.
3. Die Wäsche wird gewaschen.
4. Das Fenster wurde geschlossen, jetzt ist es aber wieder offen.
5. Das Auto wird repariert.

I. VOCABULARY FOR REVIEW (A AND B TEXTS FROM READER, CHAPTER XI)

Verbs

auf·nehmen (i) a, o	to receive
begrüßen	to greet, acclaim
inszenieren	to stage
regieren	to reign, rule

Nouns

die **Aufführung, -en**	performance
die **Ausstellung, -en**	exhibition
der **Empfänger, -**	recipient
die **Fußgängerzone, -n**	pedestrian mall
der **Hintergrund, ⁻e**	background
der **König, -e**	king
das **Märchen, -**	fairy tale
das **Plakat, -e**	poster
der **Saal, Säle**	auditorium, hall

das **Schauspiel, -e**	play
die **Spannung**	suspense
der **Standpunkt, -e**	point of view
die **Vorstellung, -en**	performance
der **Zuschauer, -**	spectator

ADDITIONAL EXERCISES (A AND B TEXTS FROM THE READER)

Classify the statements as active or passive.

1. Die Ausstellung wurde wirklich gut.
2. Die Kinder wurden freundlich begrüßt.
3. Täglich werden viele Gäste aufgenommen.
4. Dieser Standpunkt muß energisch vertreten werden.
5. Der Saal wurde im vorigen Winter gebaut.

Select the appropriate elements to form passive statements.

6. Theater: im Freien spielen/im Freien gespielt werden
7. Die Kinder: nicht langweilen/nicht gelangweilt werden; die Vorstellung/von der Vorstellung
8. Die Vorstellung: freundlich aufnehmen/freundlich aufgenommen werden; die Zuschauer/von den Zuschauern
9. Das Wörterbuch: herausgeben/herausgegeben werden; die Brüder Grimm/von den Brüdern Grimm
10. Das Schauspiel: inszenieren/inszeniert werden; eine gute Truppe/von einer guten Truppe

Answer the questions by stating the agent.

Example

Dieser Standpunkt wird doch heute nicht mehr vertreten? Doch (mehrere Leute)
Doch, dieser Standpunkt wird **von mehreren Leuten** vertreten.

11. Von wem wird das Land jetzt regiert? (ein alter König)
12. Ist der Saal denn geschlossen worden? Ja, (die Einwohner)
13. Von wem wurde das Theater gebaut? (der Bürgermeister)
14. Sind die Meldungen schon aufgenommen worden? Ja, (wir selbst)
15. Glauben Sie, diese Aufführung wird begrüßt werden? (unsere Zuschauer/bestimmt)
16. Wie werden die Zuschauer am Schauspiel interessiert? (durch Spannung)
17. Kann dieses Land überhaupt regiert werden? Doch, (ein intelligenter Minister)
18. Wie kann dieses Programm am schnellsten gesendet werden? (das Radio)
19. Dieser Saal kann wohl nicht geöffnet werden? Doch, (ein besonderer Schlüssel)
20. Wie können diese Zuschauer denn noch erreicht werden? Vielleicht (vieles Lesen)

Answer in the passive voice, observing the subject, stating or omitting the agent, and keeping the tense given.

Example

Haben wir das Land gut regiert?
Ja, das Land **ist** gut **regiert worden**.

21. Glauben Sie, wir haben die Szenen zu lang gemacht? Ja, mehrere
22. Wieviele Aufführungen haben Sie gegeben? Rund 26 000
23. Wer kann denn die kleinen Gäste begrüßen? (die Schauspieler)
24. Wer schrieb denn das Libretto? (eine unbekannte Autorin)
25. Glauben Sie auch, daß niemand den König liebt? Doch, (die jüngste Tochter)
26. Wann geben wir die Aufführung? Um sieben Uhr
27. Wird jemand die Plakate aufhängen? (viele Helfer)
28. Wer dient denn jetzt dem Vater? (niemand)
29. Planen Sie Ihre Lesezeit gut? Nein,
30. Wer liest heute Bücher und Zeitschriften? (Leute mit höherer Bildung)

Ein Schauspiel wird diskutiert.

Respond using the modal verb given.

Example

Wurde dieses Märchen schon erzählt? Nein, (nicht dürfen)
Nein, dieses Märchen **darf** nicht **erzählt werden**.

31. Ist er artig begrüßt worden? (wollen)
32. Wird er von allen verstanden? (können)
33. Wird das Stück morgen aufgeführt? (sollen)
34. Wird dieses Drama inszeniert? (dürfen)
35. Wird es vom Direktor akzeptiert? (müssen)
36. Wird das neue Plakat rechtzeitig fertigemacht? (können)

Straßentheater wird geplant.

Respond in the passive voice, keeping the tense.

Example

Dürfen wir mit den Schauspielern sprechen?
Ja, mit den Schauspielern **darf gesprochen werden**.

37. Können wir heute abend mal unsere Müdigkeit vergessen? Ja,
38. Sollen wir also das Straßentheater planen? Ja,

39. Wir dürfen auf der Fußgängerzone spielen, nicht wahr? Nein,

40. Wollen wir den berühmten Autor einladen? Nein,

41. Müssen wir viele Plakate machen? Natürlich,

42. Glauben Sie, wir können die geplante Spannung erreichen? Sicher,

43. Und werden alle große Spannung empfinden können? Bestimmt,

44. Man muß immer den Zuschauern dienen, nicht wahr? Ja leider,

45. Wird das Publikum so eine Aufführung vergessen? (nicht können)

Touristen unterhalten sich über das Straßentheater.

Restate each question, using the given substitute for the passive.

Example

Muß der Hintergrund genau erklärt werden? Ja, (sich lassen)
Ja, der Hintergrund **läßt sich** genau **erklären**.

46. Unter den Studenten wird wohl viel über Straßentheater gesprochen? Ja, (man)

47. Kann so eine Vorstellung wiederholt werden? Ja, (sich lassen)

48. Muß der Saal von jemand geöffnet werden? (sein + *infinitive with* zu)

49. Werden solche Aufführungen leicht inszeniert? (sich)

50. Kann diese Art Theater auch auf einer Bühne gegeben werden? Nein, (sich nicht lassen)

51. Ein Schauspiel kann doch erzählt werden, nicht wahr? Nein, (sich nur schwer lassen)

52. Die Fußgängerzone kann wohl gut als Bühne gebraucht werden? Ja, (sein + *infinitive with* zu)

53. Wird Straßentheater von den Zuschauern positiv aufgenommen? Ja, (man)

II. VOCABULARY FOR REVIEW (C, D AND E TEXTS FROM READER, CHAPTER XI)

Verbs

ab·lehnen	to reject
auf·fallen (ä) ie, a	to attract attention
erraten (ä) ie, a	to guess
jammern	to lament
verlangen	to demand, desire
versichern	to assure

sich **wehren**	to defend oneself
zu·schließen, o, o	to lock
sich **zurück·ziehen**, o, o	to withdraw

Nouns

der **Anblick**, -e	view
die **Brücke**, -n	bridge
die **Dienerin**, -nen	servant
der **Gang**, ˙-e	hall
der **Geist**, -er	spirit, genius
die **Hochzeit**, -en	wedding, marriage
die **Schlange**, -n	snake
das **Stroh**	straw
die **Ungeduld**	impatience
das **Unrecht**	wrong
die **Wut**	rage
der **Zorn**	fury

Others

ausgezeichnet	distinguished
geschickt	skillful
reizend	delightful
zierlich	delicate

ADDITIONAL EXERCISES (C, D AND E TEXTS FROM THE READER)

Classify the statements as active or passive.

1. Lessing wird als Vater der modernen deutschen Literatur angesehen.
2. In seiner Hamburger Dramaturgie werden Schauspiele diskutiert.
3. Goethe wurde Theaterdirektor in Weimar.
4. Eine ganze literararische Periode wurde nach ihm gennant.
5. Grimms Märchen wurden in aller Welt berühmt.

Select the appropriate elements to form a passive statement.

6. Die Hausmärchen, herausgeben/herausgegeben werden, die Brüder Grimm/von den Brüdern Grimm
7. Märchen, erzählen/erzählt werden, eine Märchentante/von einer Märchentante
8. Das Stroh, zu Gold spinnen/zu Gold gesponnen werden, die Müllerstochter/von der Müllerstochter

9. Giftige *poisonous* Schlangen, hassen/gehaßt werden, die anderen Tiere/von den anderen Tieren

10. Kein Unrecht, tun/getan werden, das Schaf/von dem Schaf

Fragen aus der Literatur

Answer in the passive, stating the agent.

Example

Wurde der Name wirklich erraten? Ja, (die Müllerstochter)
Ja, der Name wurde **von der Müllerstochter** erraten.

11. Werden giftige Schlangen wirklich gehaßt? Ja, (alle Tiere)

12. Wie wurde dem frommen Schaf geholfen? (die Worte von Zeus)

13. Wurde dem König viel von der schönen Müllerstochter erzählt? Ja, (ihr Vater)

14. Das Stroh wurde doch nicht zu Gold gesponnen? Doch, (das Männlein)

15. Wie wurde das denn gemacht? (eine Spule *a spool*)

16. Ist dann Hochzeit gehalten worden? Ja, (der König und die Müllerin)

17. Und dann ist das Männchen getötet worden? Ja, (sein eigener Zorn)

18. Werden Goethes Dramen heute noch gelesen? Ja, (viele Menschen)

19. Wie wird Unrecht im allgemeinen erwidert? (neues Unrecht)

Complete the answer with the same verb in the passive, incorporating the agent suggested.

Example

Wer verlangt das? (alle)
Das wird **von allen** verlangt.

20. Hast du den Bogen angesehen? Nein, der Bogen (nur der Besitzer)

21. Wie kann man denn dem frommen Schaf helfen? Dem frommen Schaf (nicht mit schrecklichen Zähnen)

22. Das ganze Volk sammelte die Märchen, nicht wahr? Nein, die Märchen (die Brüder Grimm)

23. Wie machte man das Unrecht wieder gut? Das Unrecht (geschickte Worte)

24. Wer lehnt solche Literatur ab? Solche Literatur (viele ausgezeichnete Kritiker)

25. Haben Sie schon Fabeln geschrieben? Nein, Fabeln (Künstler)

26. Hat der König Rumpelstilzchen getötet? Nein, Rumpelstilzchen (sein Zorn und seine Wut)

27. Glauben Sie, Kinder lieben Märchen? Ja, Märchen (die meisten Kinder)

28. Wer erzählt abends spannende Geschichten? Spannende Geschichten (Eltern oder Großeltern)

Respond in the passive, using the modal verb suggested.

Example

Werden Märchen abends erzählt? (müssen)
Ja, Märchen **müssen** abends **erzählt werden**.

29. Werden Zeus' Worte von allen interpretiert? Ja, (können)
30. Die Flüchtlinge wurden mit Neuigkeiten unterhalten, nicht wahr? Nein, (nicht mögen)
31. Waren sie von dem "Heer der Franken" bedroht worden? Ja, aber (nicht / wollen)
32. Ist die Brücke schon gebaut worden? Nein, (erst/müssen)
33. Wurde von den Leuten viel gejammert? Ja, aber (eigentlich nicht/dürfen)
34. Wann wird die Tür zum Gang zugeschlossen? In der Nacht (sollen)

Answer in the passive voice, keeping the tense. Use the new subject where given.

Example

Kann man jetzt den Geist sehen? Nein,
Nein, der Geist **kann** nicht **gesehen werden**.

35. Sollen wir die Schlange jetzt hassen? Nein,
36. Wen müssen wir dem König zeigen? (eine geschickte Spinnerin)
37. Muß sie das Stroh zu Gold spinnen? Ja, noch heute
38. Konnte das Männlein ihr denn helfen? Ja,
39. Sie sollte dem Männlein sicher etwas versprechen, nicht wahr? Ja, (ihre zierlichen Schuhe)
40. Darf das Männlein denn alles verlangen? Nein, (nur der Ring)
41. Wie kann man den Namen erraten? (überhaupt nicht)
42. Durfte sie endlich das Kind behalten? Ja,
43. Müssen wir jetzt über diese Sammlung sprechen? Ja,

Restate each question, using the given substitute for the passive.

Example

Kann hier schnell eine Brücke gebaut werden? Ja, (man)
Ja, hier **kann man** schnell eine Brücke **bauen**.

44. Kann diese Interpretation hier angewendet werden? (sich lassen)
45. Darf diese Neuigkeit erwähnt werden? (sein + *infinitive with* zu)
46. Die richtige Bedeutung wird bestimmt gefunden. (sich)
47. Geschickte Arbeit muß verlangt werden. (sein + *infinitive with* zu)
48. Kann man dieses Zeug noch verkaufen? (sich lassen)
49. Das Männlein wird Rumpelstilzchen genannt. (sich)
50. Dann wurde Hochzeit gehalten. (man)

12 SPECIAL PROBLEMS

INFINITIVE CLAUSES

541 English and German treat infinitive clauses in essentially the same manner. The infinitive may take an object, or it may be found with prepositional phrases or expressions of time, manner, and place. The basic difference is that the German infinitive must stand *at the end* of its phrase, preceded by the preposition **zu**. If the verb in the infinitive phrase has a separable prefix, then the **zu** is inserted between the prefix and the verb stem (just like the **ge-** prefix of the past participle).

Peter bat mich, ihm **zu helfen.** *Peter asked me* **to help** him.	
1 **2** **2** 1	
Peter versprach, bald **zurückzukommen.** *Peter promised* **to come back** *soon.*	

542 Infinitive phrases are separated from the main clause by a comma. When the infinitive construction consists only of the infinitive with **zu**, the comma is omitted. It is also omitted if the infinitive construction is incorporated into the main clause.

Peter fing sehr früh an, an seiner Dissertation **zu arbeiten.**	
Peter began **to work** *very early on his dissertation.*	
Peter fing sehr früh an **zu arbeiten.**	
Peter fing sehr früh **zu arbeiten** an. *Peter began* **to work** *very early.*	
Peter fing sehr früh an seiner Dissertation **zu arbeiten** an.	

CHECK AND PRACTICE

Translate.

1. We began to understand the problem.
2. It began to rain.
3. It's too late to go to the movies.
4. She asked me to come back.
5. She asked me to come back tomorrow.

543 A few verbs are followed by an infinitive construction in which the infinitive is preceded by a modifier *without* a comma separating the main clause and the infinitive phrase. The most frequently used verbs of this group are: **brauchen** *to need,* **haben, pflegen** *to usually do something,* **scheinen** *to appear, to seem,* **sein.**

Das scheint richtig **zu sein.** *That appears* **to be** *correct.* Er hat viel **zu tun.** *He has much* **to do.**	

544   As in English, a sentence in German may contain a series of infinitive constructions.

> Es ist schön, **Gelegenheit zu haben, Sie wiederzusehen.**
> *It is nice **to have the opportunity to see you again.***

545   As in English, the infinitive construction may express a past time with the help of a *past infinitive*.

	PAST PARTICIPLE OF THE MAIN VERB	INFINITIVE OF THE AUXILIARY
Er behauptet, ein guter Tennisspieler *He claims **to have been** a good tennis player.*	**gewesen**	**zu sein.**
Er behauptet, den Weltmeister *He claims **to have known** the world champion.*	**gekannt**	**zu haben.**

CHECK AND PRACTICE

Translate.

1. This book is easy to understand.
2. It is difficult to get a chance to visit him.
3. (Er versicherte uns,) to have been a good swimmer.

English and German usage differ:

546   When a dependent clause is introduced by an interrogative, English has a choice between an infinitive construction and a modal phrase. German *must* use a modal phrase.

ENGLISH	GERMAN
*I don't know **when to come.*** *I don't know **when I'm supposed to come.***	Ich weiß nicht, **wann ich kommen soll.**

547   1. The verbs **sagen** and **erwarten**, plus the modals **wollen** and **mögen (möchte)** always require a dependent clause; their English equivalents have the choice between an infinitive construction and a dependent clause.

> *He told me **to do it.***
> *He told me **that I should do it.***   Er sagte mir, **daß ich es tun soll.**

2. When another verb is substituted for **sagen**, an infinitive phrase may be used.

> Sie befahl mir, **das zu tun.**   *She ordered me **to do it.***
> Sie bat mich, **das zu tun.**   *She asked me **to do it.***

CHECK AND PRACTICE

Translate.

1. She showed us where to park the car.
2. Can you tell me where to go?
3. (Die Firma) expects you to sell more.
4. I don't want you to go home now.
5. He told her to visit her aunt in the afternoon.
6. Do you expect me to play the piano now?
7. Do you know how to write a report?

548   With modal auxiliaries, the verb **lassen**, and with verbs of perception (such as **hören, sehen, fühlen**), German never uses **zu** before infinitives.

> Er will mitkommen.   *He wants **to** come along.*

549   The verb **brauchen** can occur in combination with a dependent infinitive with or without **zu**. The standard form is still with **zu**, but the trend is to the form without **zu** because **brauchen** is frequently used as the negation of the modal **müssen**.

> Du **brauchst** das nicht (zu) **tun.**   *You **don't have/need to** do that.*
> A: **Muß** es gleich sein?   *Does it have to be right now?*
> B: Nein, es **braucht nicht** gleich sein.   *No, it **doesn't have** to be right away.*

550 The verbs **heißen, helfen, lehren,** and **lernen** occur in combination with a dependent infinitive without **zu**, if there is no additional object.

Er **heißt** mich **kommen.**	*He is **asking** me **to come.***
Er hilft ihr **aufräumen.**	*He is **helping** her **to clean up.***
Sie **lehrt** ihn **schreiben.**	*She is **teaching** him **to write.***
Er **lernt schreiben.**	*He is **learning to write.***

551 The usage varies if the infinitive is extended, i.e., if other parts of speech are added to the infinitive construction:

Er **hieß**	ihn	**den Raum**	**verlassen.**	*He **asked** him **to leave the room.***
Er **hieß**	ihn,	**den Raum** **zu**	**verlassen.**	
Er **hilft**	ihr	**das Zimmer**	**putzen.**	*He is **helping** her **to clean the room.***
Er **hilft**	ihr,	**das Zimmer** **zu**	**putzen.**	
Er **lehrt**	ihn	**die Maschine**	**bedienen.**	*He is **teaching** him **to run the machine.***
Er **lehrt**	ihn,	**die Maschine zu**	**bedienen.**	
Er **lernt**		**die Maschine**	**bedienen.**	*He is **learning to run the machine.***
Er **lernt**		**die Maschine zu**	**bedienen.**	

552 The verb **machen** occurs in combination with a dependent infinitive without **zu** only in set phrases.

Du **machst** mich **lachen.**	*You **make** me **laugh.***

553 The prepositions **um, ohne,** and **(an)statt** may introduce infinitive phrases.

1. **um . . . zu** is used to indicate purpose. It must be used (instead of **zu** alone) when one can sensibly use *in order to* in the equivalent English sentence.

Er eilte sich, **um** nicht zu spät **zu** kommen.	*He hurried (in order) not to come too late.*

2. The English equivalents of **ohne zu** and **(an)statt zu** require a present participle.

Sie sagte es, **ohne** mich an**zu**sehen.   *She said it **without** look**ing** at me.*
(An)statt hier **zu** sitzen, sollten wir ihn suchen.   ***Instead of** sitting here, we should look for him.*

554   If the subject of the main clause and the phrase following **ohne, (an)statt,** and **um** *is not* the same, the infinitive construction has to be replaced by a dependent clause in German introduced by **ohne daß, (an)statt daß,** and **damit/so daß,** respectively.

Er wollte ein Konzert geben, **ohne** vorher geübt **zu** haben.
*He wanted to give a concert **without** having practiced beforehand.*

Er wollte ein Konzert geben, **ohne daß** sein Lehrer darüber informiert war.
*He wanted to give a concert **without** his teacher being informed about it.*
Er   **sein Lehrer**
⬑_____**DIFFERENT SUBJECTS**_____⬏

CHECK AND PRACTICE

Translate.

1. *(She heard mother calling.)*
2. *(I saw him come into the room.)*
3. Oft nimmt er den Wagen, *(without asking his father.)*
4. Karl arbeitete sogar nachts, *(to earn more money).*
5. Karl arbeitete sogar nachts, *(so that his boss could go to Bonn).*
6. *(Instead of flying to Vienna),* blieben wir eine zweite Woche in München.
7. *(We wanted to buy him a present without his knowing it.)*
8. *(She is helping him to do his homework.)*
9. *(Do you learn to speak German, too?)*

EXTENDED ADJECTIVE CONSTRUCTIONS

555   Extended adjective constructions are adjectival or participial phrases that precede a noun. They consist of an article (sometimes omitted) that is separated from its noun by any number of adverbs or adverbial phrases modifying an attributive adjective or participle. The best way to translate such constructions is with a relative clause.

	ARTICLE		ADJECTIVE	NOUN
Sie betrachtete	**ihre**		müden	**Hände.**
*She looked at **her** tired **hands.***				

EXTENDED ADJECTIVE CONSTRUCTION
ADVERBIAL PHRASE(S) MODIFYING THE ADJECTIVE

Sie betrachtete	**ihre**	von der Arbeit	müden	**Hände.**
*She looked at **her hands** which were tired from working.*				
Sie betrachtete	**ihre**	von der Arbeit im Garten	müden	**Hände.**
*She looked at **her hands** which were tired from working in the garden.*				

---

556 The attributive adjective in an extended adjective construction corresponds to the predicate adjective in a relative clause.

Sie betrachtete ihre **von der Arbeit müden** Hände.

Sie betrachtete ihre Hände,
    die **von der Arbeit müde** waren.

---

557 1. A present participle (a verb ending in **-nd**) in an extended adjective construction corresponds to an inflected verb in a relative clause.

Wir sahen die **heute im Klassenzimmer fleißig schreibenden** Schüler.

Wir sahen die Schüler,
    die **heute im Klassenzimmer fleißig schrieben.**

*We saw the students **who wrote diligently in the classroom today.***

---

2. When the present participle is preceded by **zu,** the resulting phrase is a substitute for a passive modal construction in a relative clause which can be changed to a **sein**-plus-infinitive-with-**zu** construction [see § 535].

Die **zu schreibende** Aufgabe war schwer. *The exercise which had to be written was difficult.*
Die Aufgabe, **die gechrieben werden muß,** war schwer.
Die Aufgabe, **die zu schreiben ist,** war schwer.

Es ist ein **deutlich zu hörender** Schrei. *It is a scream clearly to be heard.*
Es ist ein Schrei, **der deutlich gehört werden kann.**
Es ist ein Schrei, **der deutlich zu hören ist.**

558 A past participle in an extended adjective construction corresponds to:

1. a statal passive if a condition is being described;

2. a regular passive construction if a process is being described.

Hier sind alle **noch nicht bezahlten** Rechnungen.

Hier sind alle   Rechnungen,
                    die **noch nicht bezahlt** sind.   *Here are all bills **that have not been paid yet.***

Das **bei der Herstellung von Kunststoff verwendete**   Material ist giftig.

Das   Material ist giftig,

das **bei der Herstellung von Kunststoff verwendet** wird.

*The material which is being used **in the production of plastics** is poisonous.*

---

559 Of course, the extended adjective may be followed by another adjective or participle which also modifies the noun.

	EXTENDED ATTRIBUTE	2ND ATTRIBUTE	
Wir sprachen mit dem	**langsam rauchenden,**	**alten**	Mann.

We talked with the *old* man who was ***smoking slowly.***

PROBLEM VERBS

LASSEN

560 **lassen** is one of the most commonly used verbs in German. Its most frequent meanings are:

1. *to let or allow*

lassen can be followed by *two* accusative objects; in the example, **mich** and **den Brief:**

Laß mich den Brief lesen. *Let me read the letter.*

2. *to leave behind*

> Wo habe ich meinen Schirm **gelassen?**   *Where did I **leave** my umbrella?*

3. *to have (something done); have or make (someone do something)*

lassen often indicates that the subject is not itself performing an action, but causing it to be done. In English, the past participle is used if a person has something done (in example below, *picked up*). If a person is having another person do something (in example below, *my son*), English can use an infinitive instead (in example below, *pick up*). In both cases, German uses the infinitive form after **lassen.**

SUBJECT AS **DIRECT** AGENT The subject performs the action.	Ich **hole** die Post **ab**. *I'm picking up the mail.*
SUBJECT AS **INDIRECT** AGENT The subject causes the action to be performed.	Ich **lasse** die Post **abholen.** *I'm **having** the mail picked up.* Ich **lasse** meinen Sohn die Post **abholen.** *I'm **having** my son **pick up** the mail.* Ich **lasse** die Post von meinem Sohn **abholen.** *I'm **having** the mail **picked up** by my son.*

4. Often a reflexive verb is used to stress that the subject has something done for himself.

> Wir lassen **uns** ein Haus bauen.
> *We're having a house built **(for ourselves)**.*

CHECK AND PRACTICE

Translate.

1. Let me help you.
2. I'll let you drive.
3. Peter left his German book in the library.
4. (Jeden Samstag) he had his car washed.
5. (Jeden Samstag) he had a boy wash his car.
6. (Jeden Morgen) he had the newspaper delivered.

Change the role of the grammatical subject from an active to a causal role.

7. Meine Frau grüßt Sie.
8. Herr Fuchs richtet Ihnen aus, daß er morgen nicht kommen kann.

VERB PAIRS

561   Some verbs in German can be seen as complementary pairs. The first verb is intransitive and expresses a condition or process; the second is transitive and expresses an action. The first verb has strong past tense forms, while the second has weak ones.

Er **setzte** das Kind auf den Stuhl. Es **saß** ganz still.
He sat the child on the chair. She sat there very quietly.

---

erschrecken	erschrak	ist erschrocken	*to be frightened*
erschrecken	erschreckte	hat erschreckt	*to frighten someone*
hängen	hing	hat gehangen	*to hang*
hängen	hängte	hat gehängt	*to hang something*
sitzen	saß	hat gesessen	*to sit*
setzen	setzte	hat gesetzt	*to set someone/something*
sich setzen			*to seat oneself, to sit down*
liegen	lag	hat gelegen	*to lie*
legen	legte	hat gelegt	*to lay*
sich legen			*to lie down*
fallen	fiel	ist gefallen	*to fall*
fällen	fällte	hat gefällt	*to fell (to cause to fall)*
ertrinken	ertrank	ist ertrunken	*to drown*
ertränken	ertränkte	hat ertränkt	*to drown someone*
versinken	versank	ist versunken	*to sink*
versenken	versenkte	hat versenkt	*to sink something*
verschwinden	verschwand	ist verschwunden	*to disappear*
verschwenden	verschwendete	hat verschwendet	*to squander*

CHECK AND PRACTICE

Choose the correct infinitive (if there are two) and give the past tense or present perfect.

1. Paul _____ Inge. (erschrecken)
2. Das Bild _____ an der Wand. (hängen)
3. Die Mutter _____ das Kind auf den Stuhl. (sitzen / setzen)
4. Der Hund _____ auf dem Bett. (liegen / legen)

5. Er _____ gleich nach dem Unfall. (verschwinden / verschwenden)

6. Peter _____ das Buch auf den Tisch _____. (liegen / legen)

7. Herr Meyer _____ all sein Geld. (verschwinden / verschwenden)

8. Das Kind _____ lang auf dem Stuhl _____. (sitzen / setzen)

9. Sie _____ den Mantel auf einen Bügel. (hängen)

10. Ich _____ wirklich _____. (erschrecken)

11. Die Bäume _____ im Sturm. (fallen / fällen)

12. Die Männer _____ die Bäume. (fallen / fällen)

WISSEN, KENNEN, KÖNNEN

562 All three verbs can mean *to know.*

wissen	wußte	gewußt
kennen	kannte	gekannt
können	konnte	gekonnt

563 **kennen** means *to be acquainted with* or *to be familiar with (someone or something).* It is followed by a direct object.

Kennst du Herrn Meyer? *Do you know Mr. Meyer?*

　　　　　DIRECT OBJECT

564 **wissen** is used for facts, concepts, or information. Unlike **kennen,** it is very rarely followed by a direct object (with the exception of nouns such as **das Neueste** and the pronouns **das, es, nichts, alles,** etc.). Usually it is used with clauses.

Wissen Sie, wo die Post ist? *Do you know where the post office is?*

　　　　　CLAUSE

Weißt du **es**? *Do you know it?*
Herr Meyer-Wendt **weiß alles**. *Mr. Meyer-Wendt knows everything.*
Sie **weiß** immer **das Neueste**. *She always knows the latest novelty.*

565 The modal verb **können** is used to mean *to know* in the sense of *to be able to (do something), to know how to, to master.* [See § 82ff.] It is used with languages, things memorized (such as poems), and activities.

Peter **kann** gut skifahren. *Peter knows how to ski well.*

CHECK AND PRACTICE

Translate.

1. Do you know the museum in Cologne?
2. Do you know when she will come?
3. Do you know how to play the piano?

I. VOCABULARY FOR REVIEW (A, B AND C TEXTS FROM THE READER, CHAPTER XII)

Verbs

ab·brechen (i) a, o	to break off
aus·drücken	to express
dar·stellen	to depict
fest·stellen	to identify
gestalten	to form, create
predigen	to preach
preisen, ie, ie	to praise
vor·werfen (i) a, o	to reproach

Nouns

die **Anschauung, -en**	view
die **Aufklärung**	Enlightenment
die **Besserung**	improvement
die **Beteiligung**	participation
die **Ursache, -n**	cause
der **Wahnsinn**	madness, insanity
die **Wahrheit, -en**	truth

Others

gründlich	thoroughly
mit gutem Gewissen	in good conscience
unbequem	irritating
wirksam	effective
unwirksam	ineffective
zerstörend	destructive

ADDITIONAL EXERCISES (A, B AND C TEXTS)

Respond to each statement by completing the suggested phrase.

Example

Er hoffte, diesem Wahnsinn ein Ende zu machen. Aber wer weiß,
Aber wer weiß, wie man diesem Wahnsinn ein Ende machen kann?

1. Wir baten ihn, uns die Wahrheit zu sagen. Aber er wußte nicht, warum
2. Ich versprach, bald für Besserung zu sorgen. Aber ich wußte nicht, wann
3. Wer versucht, die Ursachen zu erklären? Niemand weiß, wie man

Rephrase each introduction, using "Er sagte,"

Example

Er hoffte, nur die Wahrheit zu predigen.
Er sagte, daß er nur die Wahrheit predigen wollte.

4. Er verspricht, die Ursachen zu erklären.
5. Er erlaubte ihr, ihre Anschauungen auszudrücken.
6. Er befahl uns, diesen Wahnsinn abzubrechen.

Rephrase each statement using the suggested modal verb.

Example

Ein Autor ist in der Lage, Aufklärung zu bringen. (können)
Ein Autor kann Aufklärung bringen.

7. Viele Schriftsteller wünschen, die Wahrheit zu preisen. (wollen)
8. Es gelang ihm nicht, diese Anschauung wirksam darzustellen. (können)
9. Wir planten, die Ursache der Krankheit festzustellen. (wollen)
10. Dichter sind nicht fähig, den Lauf der Geschichte darzustellen. (können)
11. Jeder Dichter hat die Verpflichtung, die Probleme seiner Zeit auszudrücken. (müssen)

Answer each question, using *ohne*, *um* or *statt*, as appropriate.

Example

Hat er die Verhandlung abgebrochen?
Ja leider, _____ die Tatsachen festzustellen.
Ja, leider **ohne** die Tatsachen festzustellen.

12. Spricht er immer über diesen Wahnsinn? Ja leider, _____ uns Aufklärung zu geben.
13. Kam der Arzt jeden Tag? Ja, aber _____ dem Kranken zu helfen.
14. Warum hast du so laut geschrieen? _____ dir deine dummen Anschauungen vorzu-werfen.
15. Kann der Arzt eine Diagnose stellen? Nicht _____ den Kranken gründlich zu unter-suchen.
16. Warum muß man die genaue Diagnose feststellen? _____ jemand gesund machen zu können.

Respond by using *lassen* to indicate that the subject is causing someone else (a direct object in the resulting statement) to perform the action.

Example

Sagt er den Menschen die Wahrheit? Nein, er (ein Pfarrer)
Nein, er läßt **einen Pfarrer** den Menschen die Wahrheit sagen.

17. Kaufen Sie ihr Benzin selbst? Nein, ich lasse (der Chauffeur)
18. Spricht der Professor heute über die Aufklärung? Nein, er läßt (sein Kollege)
19. Fährt Ihr Sohn Auto? Ja, wir lassen (unser Sohn)
20. Preist jeder Mensch die Natur? Nein, man läßt (die Dichter)
21. Predigen Sie gern? Nein, wir lassen (der Pfarrer)

Express in English. The translations will differ depending on whether agency is unspecific or named.

22. Die Kirche läßt die Pfarrer nur die Wahrheit predigen.
23. Die Kirche läßt nur die Wahrheit predigen.
24. Lassen wir ihn seine Anschauungen erklären?
25. Müssen wir diese Anschauung erklären lassen?
26. Man läßt einen Dichter die Welt gestalten.
27. Man läßt die Welt gestalten.

Translate into English. Observe German usage of the reflexive with *lassen*.

28. Die Wahrheit läßt sich nicht wirksam gestalten.
29. Das läßt sich nicht mit gutem Gewissen sagen.
30. Die schlechte Beteiligung des Publikums läßt sich nicht erklären.
31. Ich lasse mir nichts vorwerfen.

Complete the statements with the appropriate verb form.

32. Dein Schweigen hat mich erschreckt; ja, davon _____ ich wirklich.

33. Die Katze ist ertrunken. Wer hat sie _____?

34. Legen wir den Kranken ins Bett. Er _____ doch schon seit gestern!

Translate the questions and answer them in German.

35. Do you know his irritating views?

36. Do you know what I want to depict?

37. Do you know the cause of this destructive madness?

38. Who knows the truth?

39. He certainly knows how to express himself.

II. VOCABULARY FOR REVIEW (D TEXT FROM THE READER, CHAPTER XII)

Verbs

brüllen	to yell
täuschen	to deceive
verfluchen	to curse
versäumen	to miss
vertragen (ä) u, a	to endure

Nouns

der **Bart, ⸚e**	beard
das **Gesetz, -e**	law
die **Heimat**	home (-town, -land)
das **Hindernis, -se**	obstacle
der **Koch, ⸚e**	cook
das **Tor, -e**	portal
der **Traum, ⸚e**	dream
der **Zufall, ⸚e**	coincidence, chance

ADDITIONAL EXERCISES (D TEXT FROM THE READER)

Respond to each statement by completing the suggested phrase.

Example

Er half mir, das Tor zu öffnen. Aber ich wußte nicht, warum
Aber ich wußte nicht, warum ich das Tor **öffnen sollte**.

1. Er befahl mir, über den Traum zu sprechen. Aber verstehe nicht, warum ich
2. Er bat mich, in seine Heimat zu fahren. Aber ich weiß nicht, wann ich
3. Der Mann hoffte, das Tor zum Gesetz zu finden. Aber er erklärte nicht, wo er

Replace each introduction with "Er sagte,"

Example

Er zwang die Kinder, laut zu brüllen.
Er sagte, **daß** die Kinder laut **brüllen sollten**.

4. Er bat mich, ihn nicht zu täuschen.
5. Er befahl uns, die Sitzung nicht zu versäumen.
6. Er erlaubte uns, den unglücklichen Zufall zu verfluchen.

Rephrase each statement using the suggested modal verb.

Example

Er war in der Lage, alle Hindernisse zu überwinden. (können)
Er **konnte** alle Hindernisse **überwinden**.

7. Der junge Mann plante, sich zu verloben. (wollen)
8. Man erlaubte ihm nicht, die Sitzung zu versäumen. (nicht dürfen)
9. Er wünscht, sich mit seinem Vater zu verstehen. (wollen)
10. Er war unfähig, uns zu täuschen. (nicht können)

Answer each question, using *ohne*, *um* or *statt*, as appropriate.

Example

Möchtest du Koch werden? Ja, _____ Medizin zu studieren.
Ja, **statt** Medizin zu studieren.

11. Warum kommst du in mein Zimmer? _____ deinen Bart zu rasieren.
12. Werden deine Probleme wirklich immer größer? Ja, _____ nachzulassen, wie ich hoffte.

13. Ich soll dir wohl Glück wünschen? Ja, _____ so unfreundlich zu sein.

14. Verfluchst du immer noch seinen schlimmen Tod? Leider, _____ Trost zu finden.

15. Du möchtest also in die Heimat zurückkehren? Ja, _____ mich endlich auszuruhen.

Respond by using *lassen* to indicate that the subject is causing someone else (unspecified) to perform the action.

Example

Täuscht dieser Mann seinen Chef? Nicht direkt, aber er läßt
Nicht direkt, aber er läßt seinen Chef täuschen.

16. Schreibst du den Brief selbst? Nein, ich lasse

17. Habt ihr euren Koch schon angestellt? Nein, wir lassen (erst morgen)

18. Öffnet er das Tor selbst? Nein, er

19. Ihr sucht jetzt wohl ein geeignetes Haus? Ja, wir lassen

20. Will der Mann das Tor zum Gesetz selbst finden? Nein, er läßt

Observe whether agency is unspecific or named. Translate into English accordingly.

21. Wir lassen unseren Vater nichts tun.

22. Im Geschäft lassen wir nichts tun.

23. Lassen wir die Träume erklären.

24. Wir lassen den Psychologen die Träume erklären.

25. Er läßt das Essen machen.

26. Er läßt den Koch das Essen machen.

27. Meine Mutter läßt das Zimmer aufräumen.

28. Meine Mutter läßt uns Kinder das Zimmer aufräumen.

Translate into English. Observe the German use of the reflexive with *lassen*.

29. Der Türhüter ließ sich Geschenke geben.

30. Aber der Mann läßt sich nichts erklären.

31. Er ließ sich nie etwas sagen.

32. Er sagte: „Ich lasse mich nicht täuschen."

Fill in the appropriate verb form.

33. Liegt er im Bett? Wer hat ihn dahin _____?

34. Warum erschrakst du? Ein Traum hat mich _____.

35. Das Bild hing über dem Sofa. Wer hat es dahin _____?

36. Er setzte sich auf den Stuhl. _____ er jetzt noch dort?

Translate the questions and answer them in German.

37. Do you know Kafka's parables?

38. Did he know German?

39. Do you know whether he wrote in German?

40. Do you know the various interpretations of this text?

41. Do you know anybody who does?

Vocabulary

For articles, **ein-** and **der-**words, basic adverbs, adjectival nouns, numerical adjectives, conjunctions, modals, prepositions, and pronouns, see the INDEX and/or the respective grammar chapters. For more detailed information about verbs, adverbs, and adjectives, see the cross listings in the INDEX. Omitted are the days of the week, the months, most proper names, and self-explanatory compounds. Many noun cognates are included in order to show plural forms and grammatical gender. Verbs with separable prefixes are indicated by a dot (·) between the prefix and the stem.

	ab·brechen (i), a, o	to break off, to stop
der	**Abend, -s, -e**	evening
das	**Abendessen, -s, -**	supper
	ab·fahren (ä), u, a	to leave, to drive off
	ab·fliegen, o, o	to take off
	ab·geben (i), a, e	to turn in
der	**Abgeordnete, -n, -n**	representative
die	**Abgeschiedenheit, -**	seclusion
der	**Abhang, -s, ̈e**	slope
	ab·holen	to pick up
	ab·legen	to lay down, to take off
	ab·lehnen	to refuse, to reject
	ab·nehmen (i), a, o	to remove
	ab·reisen	to leave
der	**Abschluß, -sses, ̈sse**	closure, end, conclusion
die	**Absicht, -, -en**	intention
	ab·sperren	to close off
	ab·warten	to wait and see
die	**Abwesenheit, -**	absence
	achten auf	to watch for
die	**Adresse, -, -en**	address
die	**Agentur, -, -en**	agency
	ähnlich	similar
die	**Akademie, -, -n**	academy
der	**Akademiker, -s, -**	academically trained person
die	**Akte, -, -n**	file
die	**Aktentasche, -, -n**	briefcase
die	**Aktivität, -, -en**	activity
	akzeptabel	acceptable

	akzeptieren	to accept
das	**Album, -s, . . . ben**	album
	allerdings	to be sure, indeed
	allgemein	general
der	**Alliierte, -n, -n**	ally
	alltäglich	everyday
das	**Alphabet, -s, -e**	alphabet
	alt	old
das	**Alter, -s**	age
der	**Amerikaner, -s, -**	American
das	**Amt, -s, ̈er**	public office
	sich amüsieren	to amuse oneself
	analysieren	to analyze
	an·bieten, o, o	to offer
der	**Anblick, -s, -e**	view
	an·blicken	to look at
	ändern	to change
	sich etwas aneignen	to take possession of something
die	**Anerkennung, -**	recognition
der	**Anfang, -s, ̈e**	beginning
	an·fangen (ä), i, a	to start, to begin
das	**Angebot, -s, -e**	offer
die	**Angelegenheit, -, -en**	matter, concern
	angenehm	pleasant
	angestellt	employed
der	**Angestellte, -n, -n**	employee
der	**Angler, -s, -**	fisherman
	an·greifen, i, i	to attack
der	**Angriff, -s, -e**	attack
die	**Angst, -, ̈e**	fear

an·halten (ä), ie, a   to stop
an·klagen   to accuse
an·kommen, a, o   to arrive
die **Ankunft, -, ̈-e**   arrival
anläßlich   on the occasion of
sich etwas **an·maßen**   to claim something unduly for oneself, to usurp something
an·nehmen (i), a, o   to accept
an·reden   to address, to speak to
an·rufen, ie, u   to telephone
die **Anschauung, -, -en**   view
anscheinend   apparently
anschließend   adjacent, following
an·schreien, ie, ie   to shout at
an·sehen (ie), a, e   to look at
an·sprechen (i), a, o   to approach, to address
an·stellen   to turn on, to employ
die **Anstellung, -, -en**   employment
an·stoßen (ö), ie, o   to nudge, to bump against
sich **an·strengen**   to make an effort
der **Anteil, -s, -e**   share
die **Antenne, -, -n**   antenna
der **Antifaschist, -s, -en**   antifascist
die **Antiquität, -, -en**   antique
die **Antwort, -, -en**   answer
antworten   to answer
an·vertrauen   to entrust
an·wenden auf   to apply to
die **Anzeige, -, -n**   notice
an·zeigen   to notify
sich **an·ziehen, o, o**   to put on, to dress
der **Anzug, -s, ̈-e**   outfit, suit
der **Apfel, -s, ̈-**   apple
applaudieren   to applaud
das **Aquarium, -s, . . . ien**   aquarium
die **Arbeit, -, -en**   work
arbeiten   to work
der **Arbeiter, -s, -**   worker
der **Arbeitgeber, -s, -**   employer
arbeitslos   unemployed
der **Ärger, -s**   annoyance, trouble
ärgerlich   annoying

ärgern   to annoy
das **Argument, -s, -e**   argument
arm   poor
der **Arm, -s, -e**   arm
die **Armee, -, -n**   army
die **Art, -, -en**   kind, manner
artig   well-behaved
der **Artikel, -s, -**   article
der **Arzt, -(e)s, ̈-e**   physician
der **Ast, -(e)s, ̈-e**   branch
der **Athlet, -en, -en**   athlete
atmen   to breathe
die **Atombombe, -, -n**   atomic bomb
der **Aufenthalt, -s, -e**   stay
auf·fallen (ä), ie, a   to attract attention
auf·führen   to perform
die **Aufführung, -, -en**   performance
die **Aufgabe, -, -n**   task
auf·geben (i), a, e   to give up
auf·gehen, i, a   to rise
aufgeregt   excited
auf·halten (ä), ie, a   to delay
auf·hängen   to hang up
die **Aufklärung, -**   Enlightenment
auf·machen   to open up
aufmerksam   attentive
die **Aufmerksamkeit**   attention
auf·nehmen (i), a, o   to receive, to admit
auf·passen   to pay attention
auf·räumen   to tidy up
sich **auf·regen**   to be annoyed
aufregend   exciting
die **Aufregung, -, -en**   excitement
auf·reißen, i, i   to tear open
auf·rufen, ie, u   to call on
der **Aufsatz, -es, ̈-e**   essay
auf·schlagen (ä), u, a   to open
auf·schließen, o, o   to open
auf·schneiden, i, i   to cut open
auf·schreiben, ie, ie   to write down
auf·setzen   to put on
auf·springen, a, u   to jump up
auf·stehen, a, a   to get up
auf·tragen (ä), u, a   to order, to instruct

der **Auftrag, -s, ⸚e** order
auf·wachen to wake up
das **Auge, -s, -n** eye
das **Augenlid, -s, -er** eyelid
aus·bilden to train, to educate
die **Ausbildung, -, -en** education, training
sich etwas aus·bitten, a, e to request something
aus·dehnen to expand
sich etwas aus·denken, a, a to conceive something
der **Ausdruck, -s, ⸚e** expression
sich aus·drücken to express oneself
auserwählt chosen
der **Ausflug, -s, ⸚e** excursion
aus·füllen to fill in
die **Ausgabe, -, -n** expense
aus·geben (i), a, e to spend
ausgezeichnet excellent, distinguished
die **Auskunft, -, ⸚e** information
aus·laden (ä), u, a to unload
das **Ausland, -s** abroad
der **Ausländer, -s, -** foreigner
ausländisch foreign
aus·lasten to work to capacity
aus·leihen, ie, ie to lend out
aus·löschen to put out
aus·machen to agree upon, to arrange
die **Ausnahme, -, -n** exception
ausnahmsweise exceptionally
aus·packen to unpack
aus·probieren to try out
aus·rechnen to calculate
aus·richten to deliver a message
sich aus·ruhen to rest
die **Aussage, -, -n** declaration
aus·schalten to switch off
sich aus·schlafen (ä), ie, a to sleep one's fill
aus·schließen, o, o to expel, to exclude
aus·sehen (ie), a, e to look like
die **Aussicht, -, -en** view
sich aus·sprechen (i), a, o to express
aus·steigen, ie, ie to get out

auswärts abroad
auswendig·lernen to memorize
aus·ziehen, o, o to take off, to undress
das **Auto, -s, -s** car
die **Autobahn, -, -en** highway
der **Autobus, -ses, -se** bus
der **Automat, -s, -en** vending machine
die **Autopapiere (pl.)** car papers
der **Autor, -s, -en** author

der **Bäcker, -s, -** baker
die **Bäckerei, -, -en** bakery
baden to bathe
die **Bahn, -, -en** train
der **Bahnhof, -s, ⸚e** train station
der **Bahnsteig, -s, -e** platform
bald soon
baldigst without delay
der **Ball, -s, ⸚e** ball
der **Ballon, -s, -e** balloon
die **Banane, -, -n** banana
das **Band, -s, ⸚er** ribbon
der **Band, -s, ⸚e** volume
die **Bank, -, ⸚e** bench
die **Bank, -, -en** bank
das **Bankwesen, -s** banking (system)
der **Bart, -s, ⸚e** beard
die **Basis, -, . . . sen** basis
basteln to build, to do handicraft
der **Bauch,-s, ⸚e** belly
bauen to build
der **Bauer, -n, -n** farmer
der **Bauernhof, -s, ⸚e** farm
der **Baum, -s, ⸚e** tree
Bayern Bavaria
der **Beamte, -n, -n** civil servant, official
beantworten to answer
sich bedanken to thank
bedauern to regret
bedecken to cover
die **Bedeutung, -, -en** significance
bedienen to serve
die **Bedingung, -, -en** condition
bedingungslos unconditional

bedrohen   to threaten
bedürfen (a), u, u   to need
sich beeilen   to hurry
beeinflussen   to influence
beenden   to end
der Befehl, -s, -e   order, command
befehlen (ie), a, o   to order
befestigen   to fasten
sich befinden, a, u   to be (present)
sich befleißigen   to apply oneself to
befragen   to ask
befürchten   to fear
sich begeben (i), a, e   to go, to proceed
begegnen   to encounter
die Begegnung, -, -en   encounter
begeistert   enthusiastic
beginnen, a, o   to begin
begleiten   to accompany
begreifen, i, i   to grasp
begrenzt   restricted
der Begriff, -s, -e   concept
begrüßen   to greet, to acclaim
behalten (ä), ie, a   to retain
behandeln   to treat
behaupten   to assert
beherrschen   to master
der Beifall, -s   applause
das Bein, -s, -e   leg
beinahe   almost
das Beispiel, -s, -e   example
beißen, i, i   to bite
bekannt·geben (i), a, e   to announce
der Bekannte, -n, -n   acquaintance
bekommen, a, o   to receive
beliebt   popular
belügen, o, o   to lie to
bemalen   to paint
sich bemächtigen   to get hold of
bemerken   to remark
die Bemerkung, -, -en   remark
benachbart   contiguous
das Benehmen, -s   behavior
sich benehmen (i), a, o   to behave
benutzen   to use

die Benutzung, -   use
beobachten   to observe
die Beobachtung, -, -en   observation
bequem   comfortable, convenient; lazy, indolent
bereit   ready, prepared
der Berg, -s, -e   mountain
berichten   to report
der Beruf, -s, -e   profession
sich beruhigen   to quiet oneself, to calm down
beruhigt   calmed down
berühmt   famous
die Besatzungszone, -, -n   occupied zone
beschäftigen   to employ
der Beschäftigte, -n, -n   employee
die Beschäftigung, -, -en   occupation
sich beschweren   to complain
der Besen, -s, -   broom
besetzen   to occupy
besichtigen   to visit, to inspect
besiegen   to defeat
sich besinnen, a, o   to think about
der Besitz, -es, -e   property, estate
besitzen, a, e   to own
besorgen   to take care of
besprechen (i), a, o   to discuss
die Besserung, -, -en   recovery, improvement
bestehen, a, a, aus   to consist of
bestellen   to order
bestimmen   to determine
bestimmen   to determine
der Besuch, -s, -e   visit
besuchen   to visit
der Besucher, -s, -   visitor
beteiligen   to participate in
die Beteiligung, -, -en   participation
beteuern   to assert
betrachten   to look at, to regard
betreten (i), a, e   to enter
der Betrieb, -s, -e   factory
sich betrinken, a, u   to get drunk
der Betrug, -s   deception, fraud

	betrügen to deceive
der	**Betrunkene, -n, -n** drunk person
das	**Bett, -s, -en** bed
	beugen to bend
die	**Bevölkerung, -, -en** population
die	**Bewachung, -, -en** surveillance
	bewegen to move
die	**Bewegung, -, -en** movement
	beweisen, ie, ie to prove
	sich bewerben (i), a, o to apply for a position
	bewohnen to occupy
	bewußt conscious of
	bewundern to admire
	bezahlen to pay
die	**Bibliothek, -, -en** library
	biegen, o, o to bend
das	**Bier, -s, -e** beer
	bieten, o, o to offer
das	**Bild, -s, -er** picture
	bilden to form, to create, to educate
die	**Bildung, -, -en** education, schooling
	billig cheap
die	**Billion, -, -en** trillion
die	**Binde, -, -n** bow tie
	binden, a, u to bind
der	**Biologe, -n, -n** biologist
die	**Birne, -, -n** pear
	bißchen a little bit
	bitten, a, e (um) to request, to ask for
	bitter bitter
	blasen (ä), ie, a to blow
das	**Blatt, -s, -er** leaf
	blau blue
das	**Blei, -s** lead
	bleiben, ie, ie to remain
der	**Bleistift, -s, -e** pencil
der	**Blick, -s, -e** look, glance
	blicken to look (at)
	blindlings blindly
der	**Block, -s, -e** block
die	**Blockade, -, -n** blockade
	blöd(e) silly
der	**Blödsinn, -s** nonsense

	blühen to bloom, to flower
die	**Blume, -, -n** flower
die	**Bluse, -, -n** blouse
das	**Blut, -s** blood
	bluten to bleed
der	**Bogen, -s, -/:** bow
die	**Bombe, -, -n** bomb
das	**Boot, -s, -e** boat
	böse bad, angry, mad, evil
die	**Boutique, -, -n** boutique
	braten (ä), ie, a to roast
	brauchen to need
	braun brown
die	**Braut, -, -e** bride
der	**Bräutigam, -s, -e** bridegroom
das	**Brautpaar, -s, -e** bride and bridegroom
	brav well-behaved
	brechen (i), a, o to break
	breit broad
	bremsen to brake
	brennen, a, a to burn
der	**Brief, -s, -e** letter
die	**Briefmarke, -, -n** stamp
der	**Briefträger, -s, -** mail carrier
	bringen, a, a to bring
das	**Brot, -s, -e** bread
der	**Bruchteil, -s, -e** fraction
die	**Brücke, -, -n** bridge
der	**Bruder, -s, :** brother
	brüllen to yell
das	**Buch, -s, -er** book
die	**Bücherei, -, -en** library
der	**Buchstabe, -n, -n** letter
	buchstabieren to spell
der	**Bügel, -s, -** clothes hanger
die	**Bühne, -, -n** stage
	bummeln to stroll
der	**Bundesbürger, -s, -** citizen of the Federal Republic
die	**Bundesrepublik** Federal Republic
	bunt colorful
der	**Bürger, -s, -** citizen
der	**Bürgermeister, -s, -** mayor
das	**Büro, -s, -s** office

der **Bus, -ses, -se**   bus
die **Butter, -**   butter

der **Champagner, -s**   champagne
die **Chance, -, -n**   chance, opportunity
der **Chef, -s, -s**   boss
chinesisch   Chinese
das **Chlor, -s**   chlorine
der **Chor, -s, -̈e**   choir, chorus
das **Christentum, -s**   Christianity
die **Cordhose, -, -n**   corduroy pants

das **Dach, -s, -̈er**   roof
die **Dame, -, -n**   lady
der **Dank, -s**   thanks, gratitude
dankbar   grateful
danken   to thank
dar·stellen   to depict
das **Dasein, -s**   existence
das **Datum, -s, . . . ten**   date
die **Dauer, -**   duration
dauern   to last
davon·kommen, a, o   to get off,
   to escape
sich davon·schleichen, i, i   to sneak
   away
die **DDR (Deutsche Demokratische
   Republik)**   German Democratic Republic
die **Decke, -, -n**   blanket, cover
demaskieren   to take off a mask
demnach   therefore, accordingly
die **Demonstration, -, -en**   demonstration
denken, a, a   to think
das **Denken, -s**   thinking
der **Denker, -s, -**   thinker
deutlich   distinct, clear
deutsch   German
der **Deutsche, -n, -n**   German
die **Diagnose, -, -n**   diagnosis
der **Diamant, -en, -en**   diamond
dick   fat
dienen   to serve
der **Diener, -s, -**   servant
die **Dienstleistung, -, -en**   service

der **Dienstmann, -s, -̈er/. . . leute**   porter
diesjährig   of this year
das **Ding, -s, -e**   thing
der **Direktor, -s, -en**   director
der **Dirigent, -en, -en**   conductor
die **Discothek, -, -en**   disco
die **Diskussion, -, -en**   discussion
diskutieren   to discuss
disqualifizieren   to disqualify
der **Doktor, -s, -en**   doctor
das **Dokument, -s, -e**   document
der **Dom, -s, -e**   cathedral
die **Donau, -**   Danube
doof   stupid, foolish
der **Doppelgänger, -s, -**   double
doppelt   double
das **Dorf, -s, -̈er**   village
der **Dorfbewohner, -s, -**   villager
der **Drachen, -s, -**   kite
das **Drama, -s, . . . men**   drama
die **Dramaturgie, -, -n**   dramatic theory,
   dramaturgy
dringend   urgent
drohen   to threaten
die **Drohung, -, -en**   threat
der **Druck, -s, -̈e/-e**   pressure, stress (*pl.*: -̈e);
   print (*pl.*: -e)
drücken   to press, to push
der **Drucker, -s, -**   printer
dumm   stupid
der **Dummkopf, -s, -̈e**   blockhead, jerk
dunkel   dark
dünn   thin
durchbrechen (i), a, o   to violate
durch·brechen (i), a, o   to break through
durchdenken, a, a   to think through
durchfahren (ä), u, a   to pass through,
   to flash through (one's mind)
durch·fahren (ä), u, a   to travel nonstop,
   to pass through
durchschnittlich   average
der **Durst, -s**   thirst
durstig   thirsty
sich duschen   to take a shower

	ebenfalls as well	
die	**Ecke, -, -n** corner	
	edel noble	
der	**Edelmann, -s, . . . leute** noble(man)	
der	**Egoismus, -** egotism	
	ehe before	
die	**Ehe, -, -n** marriage	
die	**Ehefrau, -, -en** wife	
der	**Ehemann, -s, ̈-er** husband	
das	**Ehepaar, -s, -e** couple	
die	**Eheleute** (*pl.*) couple	
das	**Ei, -s, -er** egg	
	eifrig eager	
	eigennützig selfish	
die	**Eigenschaft, -, -en** characteristic	
	eigentlich really, actually	
die	**Eile, -** hurry	
	eilen to hurry	
	eilig hurried	
der	**Eimer, -s, -** bucket	
	sich etwas ein·bilden to imagine something	
	ein·fallen (ä), ie, a to occur to one's mind	
der	**Einfluß, -sses, ̈-sse** influence	
der	**Eingang, -s, ̈-e** entry	
	ein·greifen, i, i intervene	
die	**Einheit, -, -en** unit; unity	
	einigermaßen to a certain extent	
der	**Einkauf, -s, ̈-e** purchase, transaction	
	ein·kaufen to shop	
	ein·laden (ä), u, a to invite	
die	**Einladung, -, -en** invitation	
	ein·packen to wrap	
die	**Einrichtung, -, -en** establishment, arrangement, furniture	
	einsam alone, lonely	
	ein·schalten to turn on	
	ein·schlafen (ä), ie, a to fall asleep	
	ein·schrauben to screw in	
	ein·sehen (ie), a, e to realize	
	ein·stecken to put in	
	ein·steigen, ie, ie to get in	
	ein·stellen to suspend (work); to hire; to adjust	

die	**Einstellung, -, -en** attitude
	ein·treffen (i), a, o to arrive
	ein·treten (i), a, e to enter
der	**Eintritt, -s, -e** entry
das	**Einzelkind, -s, -er** only child
das	**Einzelzimmer, -s, -** single room
das	**Eis, -es** ice, ice cream
das	**Eisen, -s, -** iron
das	**Elend, -s** misery, misfortune
der	**Elefant, -en, -en** elephant
die	**Eltern** (*pl.*) parents
der	**Elternteil, -s, -e** parent
	empfangen (ä), i, a to receive
der	**Empfänger, -s, -** recipient
	empfehlen (ie), a, o to recommend
das	**Ende, -s, -n** end
	enden to end
	endlich finally
die	**Energiequelle, -, -n** energy source
	energisch energetic
der	**Engel, -s, -** angel
der	**Enkel, -s, -** grandchild
	entbehrlich dispensable
	entdecken to discover
die	**Entfernung, -, -en** distance
	entfliehen, o, o to flee from
	enthalten (ä), ie, a to contain
	sich enthalten (ä), ie, a to refrain from
	entlang·gehen, i, a to go along
	entlassen (ä), ie, a to dismiss
	entscheiden, ie, ie to decide
die	**Entscheidung, -, -en** decision
	sich entschließen, o, o to decide
	sich entschuldigen to apologize
	sich entsinnen, a, o to recollect, to remember
	sich entspannen to relax
	entstehen, a, a to originate
	enttäuscht disappointed
	entwickeln to develop
	entziehen, o, o to take away
	sich erbarmen to take pity on
das	**Epos, -, . . . pen** epic (poem)
	erbauen to build

das **Erbe, -s** inheritance
der **Erbe, -n, -n** heir
die **Erde, -, -n** earth; soil (*only sg.*)
    sich ereignen to happen
das **Ereignis, -ses, -se** event
    erfahren (ä), u, a to come to know
die **Erfahrung, -, -en** experience
    erfinden, a, u to invent
der **Erfinder, -s, -** inventor
der **Erfolg, -s, -e** success
    erfolgreich successful
die **Erfrischung, -, -en** refreshment
die **Erfüllung, -, -en** fulfillment
    ergänzen to add, to supplement
    ergebenst sincerely
das **Ergebnis, -ses, -se** result
    erhalten (ä), ie, a to preserve, to maintain
    sich erhängen to hang oneself
    erhitzen to heat
    erhöhen to increase
die **Erhöhung, -, -en** increase
    sich erholen to recover, to rest
die **Erholung, -** recreation
    sich erinnern to remember
    sich erkälten to catch a cold
    erkältet sein to have a cold
    erkennen, a, a to recognize
    erklären to declare, to explain
    sich erkundigen to inquire
die **Erlaubnis,-** permission
    erleben to experience
das **Erlebnis, -ses, -se** experience, adventure
    erlöschen to go out, to expire
    ermorden to murder
    ernähren to feed
    ernst serious
    die Ernte, -, -n harvest
    erraten (ä), ie, a to guess
    erreichen to reach
    erringen, a, u to get, to attain
der **Ersatz, -es** substitute
    erscheinen to appear
    erschießen, o, o to shoot dead

    erschlagen (ä), u, a to kill
    erschöpft exhausted
die **Erschöpfung, -** exhaustion
    erschrecken to frighten
    erschrecken (i), a, o to become frightened
    ersetzen to replace
    erstaunlicherweise surprisingly
    ertränken to drown someone
    ertrinken, a, u to drown
der **Ertrinkende, -n, -n** drowning person
der **Ertrunkene, -n, -n** drowned person
    erwachsen grown-up
der **Erwachsene, -n, -n** grown-up, adult
    erwähnen to mention
    erwarten to expect
    erwidern to reply
    erwischen to catch
    erzählen to narrate, to tell
die **Erzählung, -, -en** narration, tale
    erziehen, o, o to educate
der **Erzieher, -s, -** educator
die **Erziehung, -** education
der **Esel, -s, -** donkey, ass; idiot
    eßbar edible
    essen (i), a, e to eat
das **Essen, -s** food
das **Eßzimmer, -s, -** dining room
    Europa Europe
das **Examen, -s, -** examination
das **Experiment, -s, -e** experiment

die **Fabel, -, -n** fable
die **Fabrik, -, -en** factory
der **Fabrikant, -en, -en** manufacturer
das **Fach, -s, ̈-er** subject, topic
der **Faden, -s, ̈-** thread
    fähig capable of
die **Fähigkeit, -, -en** capability
die **Fahne, -, -n** flag
    fahren (ä), u, a to drive
die **Fahrkarte, -, -n** ticket
der **Fahrplan, -s, ̈-e** schedule
das **Fahrrad, -s, ̈-er** bicycle

die	**Fahrt, -, -en**	trip, drive
	fallen (ä), ie, a	to fall
	fällen	to fell
	falsch	wrong
	familiär	(concerning the) family
	– e Angelegenheiten	family affairs; familiar
die	**Familie, -, -n**	family
	fangen (ä), i, a	to catch
	fassen	to grasp, to reach, to comprehend
	faul	lazy
die	**Faust, -, ¨-e**	fist
	fehlen	to miss, to lack
der	**Fehler, -s, -**	mistake
der	**Feierabend, -s, -e**	after-work hours
	feiern	to celebrate
der	**Feiertag, -s, -e**	holiday
der	**Feind, -s, -e**	enemy
das	**Feld, -s, -er**	field
das	**Fell, -s, -e**	fleece
der	**Felsen, -s, -**	rock
das	**Fenster, -s, -**	window
die	**Ferien** *(pl.)*	vacation, holidays
der	**Fernfahrer, -s, -**	long-distance trucker
	fern·sehen (ie), a, e	to watch TV
das	**Fernsehen, -s**	TV
	fertig	ready
	fertig·bringen, a, a	to accomplish
das	**Fest, -s, -e**	celebration, feast
	sich fest·halten (ä), ie, a	to hold onto
	fest·stellen	to declare; to notice
die	**Festung, -, -en**	fortress
der	**Festzug, -s, ¨-e**	procession, parade
	fett	fat
	feucht	damp
das	**Feuer, -s, -**	fire
der	**Feuerwehrmann, -s, ¨-er**	fire fighter
das	**Fieber, -s**	fever
der	**Film, -s, -e**	film
	filmen	to film
	finden, a, u	to find
der	**Finger, -s, -**	finger
die	**Finanzierung, -, -en**	financing
die	**Firma, -, . . . men**	firm, company
der	**Fisch, -s, -e**	fish
	flach	flat
die	**Flasche, -, -n**	bottle
der	**Fleiß, -es**	diligence
	fleißig	industrious, diligent
das	**Fleisch, -s**	meat
	fliegen, o, o	to fly
	fliehen, o, o	to flee
	fließen, o, o	to flow
die	**Flucht, -**	escape
der	**Flüchtling, -s, -e**	refugee
der	**Flugverkehr, -s**	air traffic
das	**Flugzeug, -s, -e**	airplane
der	**Fluß, -sses, ¨-sse**	river
	flüstern	to whisper
die	**Folge, -, -n**	consequence
	folgen	to follow
	folgendermaßen	as follows
	folglich	consequently
	fordern	to demand
	forschen	to research
der	**Forscher, -s, -**	researcher
	fort·fahren (ä), u, a	to continue
	fort·gehen, i, a	to go away
der	**Fotoapparat, -s, -e**	camera
die	**Fotographie, -, -n**	photograph
die	**Frage, -, -n**	question
	fragen	to ask
	Frankreich	France
der	**Franzose, -n, -n**	French person
	französisch	French
	frech	impertinent
die	**Frechheit, -, -en**	impertinence
	frei	free
	im Freien	outdoors
die	**Freiheit, -, -en**	freedom, liberty
die	**Freikarte, -, -n**	free entry ticket
	freilich	indeed
	freiwillig	voluntary
die	**Freizeit, -, -en**	free time, leisure time
	fremd	strange
der	**Fremde, -n, -n**	stranger
das	**Fremdwort, -s, ¨-er**	foreign word
der	**Fremdling, -s, -e**	stranger
	fressen (i), a, e	to eat (of animals), to devour

die **Freude, -, -n**   joy
sich freuen auf   to look forward to
sich freuen über   to be happy about
der **Freund, -s, -e (die Freundin, -, -nen)**
   friend (girlfriend)
die **Freundlichkeit, -, -en**   kindness
die **Freundschaft, -, -en**   friendship
freundlich   friendly
der **Friede, -ns**   peace
das **Friedenstreffen, -s, -**   peace rally
friedlich   peaceful
frieren, o, o   to freeze, to be cold
frisch   fresh
der **Friseur, -s, -e**   barber
fröhlich   merry
fromm   pious
früh   early
das **Frühjahr, -s, -e**   spring
der **Frühling, -s, -e**   spring
das **Frühstück, -s, -e**   breakfast
(sich) fühlen   to feel
führen   to lead
der **Führer, -s, -**   guide, leader
der **Führerschein, -s, -e**   driver's license
füllen   to fill
furchtbar   horrible
sich fürchten   to fear
fürchterlich   terrible
das **Fürstentum, -s, -̈er**   principality
der **Fuß, -es, -̈e**   foot
der **Fußball, -s, -̈e**   soccer ball; soccer (*only sg.*)
die **Fußgängerzone, -, -n**   pedestrian mall

die **Gabel, -, -n**   fork
gähnen   to yawn
die **Galerie, -, -n**   gallery
der **Gang, -s, -̈e**   hall
die **Gans, -, -̈e**   goose
gar   fully, even, very
der **Garten, -s, -̈**   garden
Gas geben (i), a, e   to accelerate
der **Gast, -s, -̈e**   guest
das **Gasthaus, -es, -̈er**   inn
das **Gebäude, -s,-**   building

geben (i), a, e   to give
das **Gebet, -s, -e**   prayer
das **Gebiet, -s, -e**   territory
gebieten, o, o   to order
das **Gebirge, -s, -**   mountains, mountain range
geboren   born
gebrauchen   to use
die **Gebrauchsanweisung, -, -en**   directions
   for use, instructions
der **Geburtstag, -s, -e**   birthday
der **Gedanke, -en, -en**   thought
gedenken, a, a   to think of
das **Gedicht, -s, -e**   poem
die **Geduld, -**   patience
geduldig   patient
geeignet   suitable
die **Gefahr, -, -en**   danger
gefährlich   dangerous
gefallen (ä), ie, a   to be pleasing to
gefälligst   (if you) please
gefangen   imprisoned
das **Gefängnis, -ses, -se**   prison, jail
das **Gefühl, -s, -e**   feeling
die **Gegend, -, -en**   area
der **Gegensatz, -es, -̈e**   contrast
das **Gegenteil, -s, -e**   contrary, opposite
die **Gegenwart, -**   present time, presence
der **Gegner, -s, -**   opponent
das **Gehalt, -s, -̈er**   salary
der **Gehalt, -s, -e**   content
geheim   secret
das **Geheimnis, -ses, -se**   secret
gehen, i, a   to go
das **Gehirn, -s, -e**   brain
gehorchen   to obey
gehören   to belong to
der **Geist, -s, -er**   spirit, genius, ghost
geistig   intellectual
das **Geld, -s, -er**   money
die **Gelegenheit, -, -en**   occasion
das **Gelingen, -s**   achievement
gelingen, a, u   to achieve, to succeed
gelten (i), a, o   to hold, to apply
die **Gemeinde, -, -n**   community, parish

gemeinsam   common

das Gemüse, -s, -e   vegetable

gemütlich   cozy, homey

genau   exact

die Genehmigung, -, -en   permission

der General, -s, ¨e/-e   general

das Genie, -s, -s   genius

genießen, o, o   to enjoy

der Genosse, -n, -n   comrade, associate

genug   enough

geographisch   geographic

der Geologe,-n, -n   geologist

das Gepäck, -s   luggage

gepflegt   cared for

geradeaus   straight ahead

gerecht   just

die Gerechtigkeit, -   justice

das Gericht, -s, -e   court of law

der Geruch, -s, ¨e   smell

gesamt   total

der Gesang, -s, ¨e   singing

das Geschäft, -s, -e   business

der Geschäftsmann, -s . . . leute   businessman

geschehen (ie), a, e   to happen

das Geschenk, -s, -e   present, gift

die Geschichte, -, -n   story, tale; history
  (only sg.)

die Geschicklichkeit, -   skill, dexterity

geschickt   skillful, dexterous

geschieden   divorced

das Geschirr, -s   dishes

der Geschmack, -s, ¨e/(humorous) ¨er   taste

das Geschrei, -s   yells

geschwind   quick

die Geschwindigkeit, -, -en   speed

die Geschwister (pl.)   siblings

die Gesellschaft, -, -en   society

das Gesetz, -es, -e   law

das Gesicht, -s, -er   face

das Gespräch, -s, -e   discussion, conversation

die Gestalt, -, -en   figure

gestalten   to form, to create

gestatten   to permit

gestehen, a, a   to confess

gesund   healthy

geteilt   divided, separated

das Getränk, -s, -e   drink

getrennt   separated

gewahr werden (i), u, o   to catch sight of

das Gewerbe, -s, -   trade

das Gewicht, -s, -e   weight

gewinnen, a, o   to win

mit guten Gewissen   in good conscience

das Gewitter, -s, -   thunderstorm

sich gewöhnen an   to get used to

gewohnt sein   to be accustomed to

die Gewohnheit, -, -en   habit

gewöhnlich   ordinary

die Gewöhnung, -   habituation, habit
  formation

gießen, o, o   to pour, to water

das Gift, -s, -e   poison

giftig   poisonous

glänzen   to shine

das Glas, -es, ¨er   glass

glätten   to smooth, to flatten

der Glaube, -n, -n   belief

glauben   to believe

gleichen, i, i   to resemble

gleichfalls   likewise

gleichgültig   indifferent

die Gleichberechtigung, -   equality, equal
  rights

gleichzeitig   at the same time

das Glück, -s   luck, fortune, happiness

glücken   to succeed

glücklich   fortunate, happy

die Glückszahl, -, -en   lucky number

der Glückwunsch, -s, ¨e   congratulation

die Glühbirne, -, -n   light bulb

der Gott, -s, ¨er   God

der Gottesdienst, -s, -e   church service

gottlob   thank God

graben (ä), u, a   to dig

der Graben, -s, ¨   ditch, trench

der Graf, -en, -en   count

das Gramm, -s, -e   gram

die Grammatik, -, -en   grammar

	gratulieren to congratulate	
	grau grey	
	greifen, i, i to seize	
die	**Grenze, -, -n** border, boundary	
der	**Grieche, -n, -n** Greek	
	grob rude	
	groß great, big	
	großartig splendid	
die	**Großmutter, -, ̈** grandmother	
der	**Großvater, -s, ̈** grandfather	
die	**Großeltern** (*pl.*) grandparents	
die	**Grube, -, -n** ditch	
	grün green	
der	**Grund, -s, ̈e** reason	
	gründen to found, to organize	
	gründlich thoroughly	
der	**Grundsatz, -es, ̈e** principle	
die	**Grundschule, -, -n** elementary school	
die	**Gruppe, -, -n** group	
der	**Gruß, -es, ̈e** greeting	
	grüßen to greet	
	gut good	
das	**Gut, -s, ̈er** farm, estate	
die	**Güte, -** kindness	
	gütigst kindly	
	gutschreiben, i, i to credit an account	

das	**Haar, -s, -e** hair	
	habhaft in possession of	
der	**Hafen, -s, ̈** harbor	
der	**Hahn, -s, ̈e** rooster	
	halb half	
die	**Hälfte, -, -n** half	
der	**Hals, -es, ̈e** neck, throat	
	halten (ä), ie, a to keep, to hold	
die	**Haltestelle, -, -n** bus (tram) stop	
die	**Haltung, -, -en** attitude	
der	**Hammer, -s, ̈** hammer	
der	**Hampelmann, -s, ̈er** jumping jack	
	hamstern to hoard (food)	
die	**Hand, -, ̈e** hand	
der	**Handel, -s** trade, business	
	handeln to act	
die	**Handtasche, -, -n** handbag	

die	**Handlung, -, -en** plot	
das	**Handtuch, -s, ̈er** towel	
der	**Hang, -s, ̈e** slope	
	hängen, i, a to hang	
	hart hard	
der	**Hase, -n, -n** rabbit	
der	**Haß, -sses** hatred	
	hassen to hate	
	hauen to beat	
	häufig frequent	
der	**Hauptmann, -s, . . . leute** captain	
die	**Hauptsache, -, -n** main thing	
	hauptsächlich mainly	
die	**Hauptstadt, -, ̈e** capital	
das	**Haus, -es, ̈er** house	
die	**Hausaufgabe, -, -n** homework	
die	**Hausfrau, -, -en** housewife	
der	**Hausherr, -n, -en** landlord	
	häuslich domestic	
	heben to lift	
das	**Heer, -s, -e** army	
das	**Heft, -s -e** notebook	
	heftig vigorous	
der	**Heide, -n, -n** heathen	
die	**Heide, -, -n** heath(land), heather	
	heilen to heal	
die	**Heimat, -** home, native country	
	heimwärts homeward	
die	**Heirat, -, -en** marriage	
	heiraten to marry	
	heiß hot	
	sich heiß·laufen to overheat	
	heißen, ie, ei to be called	
	heizen to heat	
	helfen (i), a, o to help	
	hell light, bright	
das	**Hemd, -s, -en** shirt	
die	**Henne, -, -n** hen	
	heraus·geben (i), a, e to publish, to edit	
	heraus·nehmen (i), a, o to take out	
	heraus·werfen (i), a, o to throw out	
	her·bringen, a, a to bring here	
der	**Herbst, -s, -e** autumn	
der	**Herd, -s, -e** stove	

	herein·kommen, a, o to come in	
	her·kommen, a, o to come here	
der	**Herr, -n, -en** gentleman	
	herrlich magnificent	
die	**Herrschaft, -** rule	
	herrschen über to rule over	
	her·stellen to produce	
die	**Herstellung, -** production	
	herum·drehen to turn around	
	herum·laufen, ie, au to run around	
	hervor·zaubern to produce by magic	
das	**Herz, -ens, -en** heart	
	hetzen to hunt	
	herzlich cordial	
die	**Hilfe, -** help	
	hilfreich helpful	
der	**Himmel, -s, -** heaven	
	hinauf·gehen, i, a to go up	
	hin·bringen to take there	
das	**Hindernis, -ses, -se** obstacle	
	hin·gehen, i, a to go there	
	hin·kommen, a, o to come there, to get there	
	hin·legen to lay down	
	hintereinander behind each other	
der	**Hintergrund, -s, -̈e** background	
	hinunter·gehen, i, a to go down	
	hinunter·kommen, a, o to come down	
	hinzu·fügen to add, to attach	
der	**Hirte, -n, -n** shepherd	
die	**Hitze, -** heat	
die	**Hochschule, -, -n** university	
die	**Hochzeit, -, -en** wedding, marriage	
der	**Hochzeitskuchen, -, -** wedding cake	
	hoffen to hope	
die	**Hoffnung, -, -en** hope	
	höflich polite	
die	**Höhe, -, -n** height	
	holen to get, to fetch	
der	**Honig, -s** honey	
	hören to hear	
der	**Horizont, -s, -e** horizon	
die	**Hose, -, -n** trousers	
	hübsch nice	

der	**Hubschrauber, -s, -** helicopter	
das	**Huhn, -s, -̈er** chicken	
	humorvoll humorous	
der	**Hund, -s, -e** dog	
der	**Hunger, -s** hunger	
	hungern to go hungry	
	husten to cough	
der	**Hut, -s, -̈e** hat	
die	**Hut, -** guard	
	hüten to protect	
die	**Hütte, -, -n** hut	
der	**Hymnus, -, . . . nen** hymn	
die	**Idee, -, -n** idea	
	imponieren to impress	
	inakzeptabel unacceptable	
	Indien India	
die	**Industrie, -, -n** industry	
die	**Information, -, -en** information	
	informieren to inform	
der	**Ingenieur, -s, -e** engineer	
die	**Innenstadt, -, -̈e** inner city	
das	**Inserat, -s, -e** advertisement	
der	**Inspektor, -s, -en** inspector	
das	**Institut, -s, -e** institute	
	inszenieren to stage	
	interessant interesting	
das	**Interesse, -s, -n** interest	
	sich interessieren für to be interested in	
	interpretieren to interpret	
	inzwischen in the meantime	
die	**Ironie, -** irony	
	sich irren to err	
der	**Irrtum, -s, -̈er** error	
	Italien Italy	
die	**Jacke, -, -n** jacket	
	jählings abruptly	
das	**Jahr, -s, -e** year	
	jahrelang for years	
die	**Jahreszeit, -, -n** season	
das	**Jahrhundert, -s, -e** century	
	jammern to lament	
	jedenfalls in any case	

jedoch   however
das **Jenseits, -**   hereafter
das **Joghurt, -s**   yogurt
das **Jubiläum, -s . . . äen**   anniversary
die **Jugend, -**   youth
jugendlich   youthful
der **Jugendliche, -n, -n**   youth
jung   young
der **Junge, -n, -n**   boy

der **Kaffee, -s**   coffee
der **Käfig, -s, -e**   cage
der **Kalk, -s**   lime
kalt   cold
das **Kamel, -s, -e**   camel
kämmen   to comb
der **Kampf, -s, ̈-e**   struggle
die **Kanalisation, -, -en**   sewerage
der **Kapitän, -s, -e**   captain
das **Kapitel, -s, -**   chapter
kaputt   broken
kaputt·gehen, i, a   get broken
der **Karneval, -s, -e/-s**   carnival
die **Karotte, -, -n**   carrot
der **Karren, -s, -**   cart, wheelbarrow
die **Karte, -, -n**   card, map, ticket
der **Kartenspieler, -s, -**   card player
die **Kartoffel, -, -n**   potato
der **Käse, -s**   cheese
der **Kassierer, -s, -**   bank teller
der **Kasten, -s, -/ ̈-**   box
der **Katalog, -s, -e**   catalogue
die **Katze, -, -n**   cat
kaufen   to buy
der **Kaufmann, -s, . . . leute**   businessman
kaum   barely
das **Kegeln, -s**   German bowling
der **Kegler, -s, -**   bowler
kehren   to sweep
der **Keil, -s, -e**   wedge
der **Keller, -s, -**   cellar
der **Kellner, -s, -**   waiter
die **Kellnerin, -, -nen**   waitress
kennen, a, a   to know

kennen·lernen   to meet, to become
   acquainted
der **Kerl, -s, -e**   fellow
die **Kerze, -, -n**   candle
kichern   giggle
das **Kilogramm, -s, -e**   kilogram
das **Kind, -s, -er**   child
kinderlos   childless
kinderreich   with many children
der **Kinderwagen, -s, -**   baby carriage
kindisch   childish
das **Kindlein, -s, -**   little child
das **Kinn, -s, -e**   chin
das **Kino, -s, -s**   cinema
die **Kirche, -, -n**   church
das **Kissen, -s, -**   pillow
klagen   to complain
der **Klang, -s, ̈-e**   sound
klar   clear
die **Klarheit, -**   clarity
die **Klasse, -, -n**   class
klassisch   classical
das **Klavier, -s, -e**   piano
das **Kleid, -s, -er**   dress
der **Kleiderschrank, -s, ̈-e**   closet
klein   little
die **Kleinigkeit, -, -en**   little thing (gift), trifle
klettern   to climb
klingeln   to ring a bell
klingen, a,u   to sound
klopfen   to knock
das **Kloster, -s, -**   monastery
klug   intelligent
der **Knopf, -s, ̈-e**   button
der **Koch, -s, ̈-e**   cook
kochen   to cook
der **Koffer, -s, -**   suitcase
die **Kollage, -, -n**   collage
der **Kollege, -n, -n**   colleague
der **Komiker, -s, -**   comedian
komisch   comic(al), funny
das **Komma, -s, -s/-ta**   comma
der **Kommandant, -en, -en**   commandant
kommen, a, o   to come

die **Kommission, -, -en**   commission, committee

die **Konferenz, -, -en**   conference, meeting

die **Konfrontation, -, -en**   confrontation

der **König, -s, -e**   king

die **Königin, -, -nen**   queen

das **Königtum, -s, ̈-er**   kingdom

der **Konsument, -en, -en**   consumer

das **Konzentrationslager, -s, -**   concentration camp

das **Konzert, -s, -e**   concert

der **Kopf, -s, ̈-e**   head

das **Kopftuch, -s, ̈-er**   (head) scarf

das **Kopfweh, -s**   headache

der **Korb, -s, ̈-e**   basket

der **Körper, -s, -**   body

korrigieren   to correct

kosten   to cost

kostbar   precious

kräftig   strong

der **Kragen, -s, -**   collar

krank   sick

der **Kranke, -en, -en**   patient, sick person

das **Krankenhaus, -es, ̈-er**   hospital

der **Krankenpfleger, -s, -**   male nurse

die **Krankheit, -, -en**   sickness, disease

die **Krawatte, -, -n**   tie

kreisen   to circle

kriechen   to crawl

der **Krieg, -s, -e**   war

der **Kritiker, -s, -**   critic

die **Krone, -, -n**   crown

die **Küche, -, -n**   kitchen

der **Kuchen, -s, -**   cake

der **Kugelschreiber, -s, -**   ballpoint pen

die **Kuh, -, ̈-e**   cow

kühl   cool

das **Küken, -s, -**   chick

die **Kultur, -, -en**   culture

sich kümmern um   to take care of

der **Kunde, -n, -n**   customer

die **Kunde, -, -n**   news

kündigen   to give notice

der **Künstler, -s, -**   artist

die **Künstlerin, -, -nen**   female artist

der **Kunststoff, -s, -e**   plastics

der **Kurs, -es, -e**   course, direction

kurz   short

die **Kurzgeschichte, -, -n**   short story

der **Kuß, -es, ̈-e**   kiss

die **Kutsche, -, -n**   carriage

das **Labor, -s, -s**   laboratory

lächeln   to smile

lachen   to laugh

das **Lachen, -s**   laugh

lächerlich   ridiculous

der **Laden, -s, ̈-**   shop, store

die **Lage, -, -n**   situation

das **Lagerfeuer, -s, -**   campfire

die **Lampe, -, -n**   lamp

das **Land, -s, ̈-er**   land

die **Landkarte, -, -n**   map

ländlich   rural

die **Landschaft, -, -en**   landscape

langsam   slow

langweilen   to be bored

langweilig   boring

der **Lärm, -s**   noise

lassen (ä), ie, a   to let, to leave, to allow, to cause

das **Latein, -s**   Latin

der **Lauf, -s, ̈-e**   course, path, orbit; race

laufen (äu), ie, au   to run

der **Läufer, -s, -**   runner

die **Laune, -, -n**   mood

laut   loud

das **Leben, -s, -**   life

der **Lebenslauf, -s, ̈-e**   curriculum vitae

die **Lebensmittel (pl.)**   groceries

ledig   single

leer   empty

legen   to put, to lay

lehren   to teach

der **Lehrer, -s, -**   teacher

die **Lehrerin, -, -nen**   female teacher

der **Lehrling, -s, -e**   apprentice

leicht   easy

das **Leid, -s**   suffering
leid tun, a, a   to be sorry
leiden, i, i   to suffer
leidenschaftlich   passionately
leise   quiet
sich leisten   to afford
die **Leistung, -, -en**   performance
leiten   to direct
der **Leiter, -s, -**   leader
die **Leiter, -, -n**   ladder
lenken   to direct, to steer
lernen   to learn
lesen (ie), a, e   to read
der **Leser, -s, -**   reader
leserlich   legible
leugnen   to deny
die **Leute** (*pl.*)   people
das **Licht, -s, -er**   light
der **Lichtschalter, -s, -**   light switch
lieb   dear
die **Liebe, -**   love
lieben   to love
liebenswürdig   kind
die **Liebesgeschichte, -, -n**   love story
liebevoll   loving
das **Lied, -s, -er**   song
liegen, a, e   to lie
der **Likör, -s, -e**   liqueur
die **Limonade, -, -n**   lemonade
die **Linie, -, -n**   line
die **Liste, -, -n**   list
der **Liter, -s, -**   liter
die **Literatur, -, -en**   literature
loben   to praise
das **Loch, -s, ̈-er**   hole
der **Löffel, -s, -**   spoon
löffelweise   in spoonfuls
der **Lohn, -s, ̈-e**   wages, reward
löschen   to extinguish
lösen   to solve
los·fahren (ä), u, a   to depart, to take off
los·lassen (ä), ie, a   to let go
die **Lösung, -, en**   solution
der **Löwe, -n, -n**   lion
die **Luft, -, ̈-e**   air

lügen, o, o   to lie, to tell a lie
lustig   funny
der **Luxus, -**   luxury

die **Macht, -, ̈-e**   might, power
mächtig   powerful
das **Mädchen, -s, -**   girl
das **Mädel, -s, -**   girl
das **Magazin, -s, -e**   magazine
der **Magen, -s, ̈-/-**   stomach
mager   skinny, thin
mähen   to mow
malen   to paint
der **Maler, -s, -**   painter
der **Mann, -s, ̈-er**   man
das **Männchen (Männlein), -s, -**   little man
die **Mannschaft, -, -en**   team
der **Manschettenknopf, -s, ̈-e**   cuff link
der **Mantel, -s, ̈-**   coat
das **Märchen, -s, -**   fairy tale
der **Marktplatz, -es, ̈-e**   market place
marschieren   to march
der **Marsmensch, -en, -en**   man from Mars
die **Maske, -, -n**   mask
maskieren   to put on a mask
das **Maß, -es, -e**   measure
die **Masse, -, -n**   mass, bulk
die **Maßnahme, -, -n**   measure
das **Material, -s, -ien**   material
die **Mathematik, -**   mathematics
der **Maurer, -s, -**   mason, bricklayer
die **Maus, -, ̈-e**   mouse
der **Mechaniker, -s, -**   mechanic
das **Meer, -s, -e**   sea, ocean
das **Mehl, -s**   flour
mehr   more
mehrmals   repeatedly
die **Mehrheit, -, -en**   majority
meinen   to mean
die **Meinung, -, -en**   opinion
der **Meister, -s, -**   master, champion
die **Meisterschaft, -, -en**   championship
melden   to announce, to report
die **Meldung, -, -en**   report, news item

der **Mensch, -en, -en**   man, person, human being
die **Menschheit, -**   mankind
merken   to notice
merkwürdig   strange
die **Messe, -, -n**   fair; mass
messen   to measure
das **Messer, -s, -**   knife
der **Meter, -s, -**   meter
der **Metzger, -s, -**   butcher
die **Metzgerei, -, -en**   butcher shop
der **Mieter, -s, -**   tenant
das **Mikrophon, -s, -e**   microphone
das **Mikroskop, -s, -e**   microscope
die **Milch, -**   milk
die **Milliarde, -, -n**   billion
die **Million, -, -en**   million
mindestens   at least
der **Minister, -s, -**   minister
die **Minute, -, -n**   minute
mischen   to mix
mißachten   to disregard
mißbrauchen   to misuse
mißglücken   to fail
mißfallen (ä), ie, a   to displease
mißtrauen   to mistrust
das **Mißtrauen, -s**   mistrust
mißtrauisch   suspicious
das **Mißverständnis, -ses, -se**   misunderstanding
mißverstehen, a, a   to misunderstand
der **Mitarbeiter, -s, -**   coworker
mit·bringen, a, a   to bring along
miteinander   with each other, together
das **Mitglied, -s, -er**   member
das **Mitleid, -s**   compassion, pity
der **Mitmensch, -en, -en**   fellow man
mit·nehmen (i), a, o   to take along
mitnichten   by no means
der **Mittag, -s, -e**   noon
das **Mittagessen, -s, -**   lunch
die **Mitte, -, -n**   middle
mit·teilen   to notify, to tell
das **Mittel, -s, -**   means
die **Mitternacht, -, ¨e**   midnight
der **Mohammedaner, -s, -**   muslim

der **Moment, -s, -e**   moment
die **Monarchie, -, -n**   monarchy
der **Monat, -s, -e**   month
der **Mörder, -s, -**   murderer
der **Morgen, -s, -**   morning
das **Motiv, -s, -e**   motive, theme
der **Motor, -s, -en**   motor
müde   tired
die **Müdigkeit, -**   tiredness
die **Mühe, -, -n**   effort, trouble
der **Müller, -s, -**   miller
der **Mund, -s, ¨er**   mouth
das **Museum, -s . . . een**   museum
die **Musik, -**   music
der **Musikant, -en, -en**   musician
der **Musiker, -s, -**   musician
der **Mut, -s**   courage
mutig   brave
die **Mutter, -, ¨**   mother
die **Mütze, -, -n**   cap

der **Nachbar, -s/-n, -n**   neighbor
nach·denken (über), a, a   to think (about), reflect (on)
nach·eilen   to hurry after
nach·kommen, a, o   to come later, to follow
nach·lassen (ä), ie, a   to let up, to slacken off
nach·lesen (ie), a, e   to look up
der **Nachmittag, -s, -e**   afternoon
die **Nachricht, -, -en**   news
die **Nacht, -, ¨e**   night
der **Nachtisch, -s, -e**   dessert
der **Nachteil, -s, -e**   disadvantage
die **Nachtigall, -, -en**   nightingale
der **Nachtzug, -s, ¨e**   night train
der **Nagel, -s, ¨**   nail
nah   near
die **Nähe, -**   proximity
nähen   to sew
der **Name, -ns, -n**   name
die **Nase, -, -n**   nose
das **Nashorn, -s, ¨er**   rhinoceros

die **Nation, -, -en** nation

die **Natur, -** nature

die **Naturwissenschaft, -, -en** natural science

   naturwissenschaftlich scientific

   nebeneinander next to each other

der **Nebensatz, -es, ˬe** dependent clause

der **Neffe, -n, -n** nephew

   nehmen (i), a, o to take

der **Neid, -s** envy

   nennen, a, a to name

der **Nerv, -s, -en** nerve

   nett nice

   neu new

   neugierig curious

die **Neuigkeit, -, -en** news

der **Neuling, -s, -e** beginner

die **Nichte, -, -n** niece

   nicken to nod

   nieder·brennen, a, a to burn down

die **Niederlage, -, -n** defeat

   nieder·schlagen (ä), u, a to knock down

die **Not, -, ˬe** sorrow, need, want, distress, poverty, misery

die **Notbremse, -, -n** emergency brake

die **Note, -, -n** grade, (musical) note

   notieren to take notes, to write down

   nötig necessary

die **Notiz, -, -en** note

   notwendig necessary

die **Novelle, -, -n** novella

   nüchtern sober

die **Nudel, -, -n** noodle

die **Nummer, -, -n** number

die **Nuß, -, ˬsse** nut

   nützlich useful

der **Ober, -s, -** waiter

das **Obst, -(e)s** fruit

   offen open

   öffentlich public

die **Öffentlichkeit, -** public

   offiziell officially

der **Offizier, -s, -e** officer

   öffnen to open

das **Ohr, -s, -en** ear

die **Ohrfeige, -, -n** box on the ear

der **Onkel, -s, -** uncle

die **Oper, -, -n** opera

die **Operation, -, -en** operation

das **Opfer, -s, -** victim, sacrifice

die **Opposition, -, -en** opposition

das **Orchester, -s, -** orchestra

   ordentlich decent, respectable, orderly

die **Ordnung, -, -en** order, rule

das **Original, -s, -e** original

der **Ort, -s, -e** place, town

der **Osten, -s** east

   Ostern Easter

   Österreich Austria

der **Ozean, -s, -e** ocean

das **Paar, -s, -e** pair, couple

   packen to wrap, to pack

das **Paket, -s, -e** package

das **Papier, -s, -e** paper

das **Paradox, -es, -e** paradox

der **Park, -s, -s** park

   parken to park

der **Parkplatz, -es, ˬe** parking lot

der **Partner, -s, -** partner

das **Parlament, -s, -e** parliament

die **Partei, -, -en** (political) party

der **Parteisekretär, -s, -e** secretary of a party

der **Parteivorsitzende, -n, -n** chairman of a party

der **Paß, -sses, ˬsse** passport

der **Passagier, -s, -e** passenger

   passen to fit

   passieren to happen

der **Patient, -en, -en** patient

die **Pause, -, -n** pause, intermission

das **Pech, -s** bad luck

der **Pechvogel, -s, ˬ** unlucky fellow

die **Periode, -, -n** period

die **Peripherie, -, -n** periphery

die **Person, -, -en** person

der **Personalausweis, -es, -e**   identification card

persönlich   personal, private

der **Pfarrer, -s, -**   priest, minister

pfeifen, i, i   to whistle

der **Pfennig, -s, -e**   penny

das **Pferd, -s, -e**   horse

Pfingsten   Whitsun, Pentecost

pflanzen   to plant

das **Pflaster, -s, -**   pavement

die **Pflaume, -, -n**   plum

pflegen   to care for, to attend to

die **Pflicht, -, -en**   duty

der **Pflug, -s, ̈-e**   plow

das **Pfund, -s, -e**   pound

phantastisch   fantastic

die **Philosophie, -, -n**   philosophy

die **Physik, -**   physics

der **Photograph, -en, -en**   photographer

das **Picknick, -s, -s**   picnic

piepsen   to squeak

der **Pilot, -en, -en**   pilot

die **Pistole, -, -n**   pistol

das **Plakat, -s, -e**   poster

der **Plan, -s, ̈-e**   plan

der **Planet, -en, -en**   planet

der **Platz, -es, ̈-e**   place, square

das **Plätzchen, -s, -**   little place

die **Platzkarte, -, -n**   seat reservation ticket

die **Plauderei, -, -en**   chat, small talk

plaudern   to chat, to talk

plötzlich   suddenly

die **Pointe, -, -n**   point (of a joke), punch line

der **Pole, -n, -n (die Polin, -, -nen)**   Pole (Polish woman)

die **Politik, -**   politics

der **Politiker, -s, -**   politician

politisch   political

die **Polizei, -**   police

der **Polizeiwagen, -s, -**   police car

der **Polizist, -en, -en**   policeman

der **Portier, -s, -s**   doorman, porter

die **Position, -, -en**   position

die **Post, -**   mail; *(pl.)* **Postämter**   post office

der **Posten, -s, -**   guard

die **Postkarte, -, -n**   postcard

praktisch   practical

die **Präposition, -, -en**   preposition

der **Präsident, -en, -en**   president

die **Praxis, -**   practice, practical experience

predigen   to preach

der **Preis, -es, -e**   price; prize

preisen, ie, ie   to praise

die **Pressefreiheit, -, -en**   freedom of the press

die **Probe, -, -n**   rehearsal, test

probieren   to try

das **Problem, -s, -e**   problem

der **Professor, -s, -en**   professor

prophezeien   to prophesy, predict

die **Prophezeiung, -, -en**   prophecy, prediction

der **Profit, -s, -e**   profit

das **Prosastück, -s, -e**   prose piece, work of prose

der **Protest, -s, -e**   protest

das **Prozent, -s, -e**   percent

die **Prüfung, -, -en**   exam

der **Psychologe, -n, -n (die Psychologin, -, -nen)**   psychologist

das **Publikum, -s**   public, audience

punktieren   to perforate

pünktlich   punctual

die **Puppe, -, -n**   puppet, doll

putzen   to clean

der **Putzmann, -s, ̈-er**   cleaning man

die **Qualität, -, -en**   quality

qualifizieren   to qualify

das **Rad, -s, ̈-er**   wheel, bicycle

radeln   to bicycle

rad·fahren (ä), u, a   to bicycle

die **Radierung, -, -en**   etching

radieren   to etch, to erase

das **Radrennen, -s, -**   bicycle race

das **Radio, -s, -s**   radio

der **Rand, -s, ̈-er**   border, edge

rasch   quickly

der **Rasen, -s, -**   lawn

rastlos restless
sich rasieren to shave
der **Rat, -s, . . . schläge** advice
raten (ä), ie, a to advise
das **Rätsel, -s, -** puzzle
rätselhaft mysterious
rauchen to smoke
das **Rauchen, -s** smoking
der **Raucher, -s, -** smoker
der **Raum, -s, ̈e** room
reagieren auf to react to
die **Realität, -, -en** reality
rechnen to figure, to calculate
die **Rechnung, -, -en** bill
recht right
recht behalten (ä), ie, a to be right in
the end
recht haben to be right
der **Rechtsanwalt, -s, ̈e (die
Rechtsanwältin, -, -nen)** lawyer
rechtzeitig in time
die **Rede, -, -n** speech
eine Rede halten (ä), ie, a to give a
speech
reden to speak
die **Redewendung, -, -en** phrase,
expression
der **Redner, -s, -** speaker
die **Reduzierung, -, -en** reduction
der **Reflex, -es, -e** reflex
die **Reform, -, -en** reform
die **Reformation, -, -en** reformation
die **Regel, -, -n** rule
regelmäßig regular
der **Regen, -s** rain
regieren to rule, to govern
der **Regisseur, -s, -e** stage manager, director
regnen to rain
reich rich
der **Reichtum, -s, ̈er** wealth
der **Reifen, -s, -** tire, hoop
die **Reihe, -, -n** row
die **Reise, -, -n** trip
das **Reisebüro, -s, -s** travel agency

reisen to travel
das **Reiseland, -s, ̈er** tourist country
der **Reiseplan, -s, ̈e** travel plans
die **Reisestrecke, -, -n** travel route
reißen, i, i to tear
reiten, i, i to ride
reizend charming, delightful
der **Rektor, -s, -en** principal, president of
a university
die **Relativitätstheorie, -, -n** theory of
relativity
rekonstruieren to reconstruct
rennen, a, a to run
renovieren to renovate
reparieren to repair
die **Republik, -, -en** republic
reservieren to reserve
der **Rest, -s, -e** remainder, rest
das **Restaurant, -s, -s** restaurant
das **Resultat, -s, -e** result
retten to save
der **Rettich, -s, -e** radish
die **Rettung, -, -en** salvation
die **Revanche, -, -n** revenge
der **Revolver, -s, -** revolver
der **Rhein** Rhine
der **Rhythmus, -, . . . men** rhythm
richten to direct; to judge
der **Richter, -s, - (die Richterin, -,
-nen)** judge
richtig correct
die **Richtung, -, -en** direction
riechen, o, o to smell
ringen, a, u to wrestle
das **Risiko, -s, . . . ken** risk
der **Rock, -s, ̈e** skirt
roh raw
der **Roman, -s, -e** novel
romantisch romantic
die **Rose, -, -n** rose
die **Rübe, -, -n** turnip
die **Rücksicht, -, -en** consideration
Rücksicht nehmen (i), a, o to pay
heed, to be considerate

der **Rücktritt, -s, -e**   resignation

rufen, ie, u   to call

die **Ruhe, -**   calm, quiet

ruhen   to rest

ruhig   quiet

sich rühmen   to boast

rühren   to stir

der **Saal, -s, Säle**   hall, dance hall

die **Sache, -, -n**   matter

sachlich   objective

der **Sack, -s, -̈e**   bag

der **Saft, -s, -̈e**   juice

sagen   to say

der **Salat, -s, -e**   salad

das **Salz, -es, -e**   salt

sammeln   to collect

der **Sänger, -s, - (die Sängerin, -, -nen)**   singer

satt sein   to be full, to be satisfied

der **Satz, -es, -̈e**   sentence

sauber   clean

sauer   sour

der **Sauerstoff, -s, -e**   oxygen

saufen (äu), o, o   to booze

säugen   to nurse

schade sein   to be too bad

schaden   to harm, to damage

schädlich   harmful

das **Schaf, -s, -e**   sheep

der **Schäfer, -s, -**   shepherd

schaffen, u, a   to create

der **Schal, -s, -e**   shawl, scarf

die **Schallplatte, -, -n**   record

schalten   to switch

sich schämen   to be ashamed

scharf   sharp

der **Schatz, -es, -̈e**   treasure

schauen   to observe

das **Schaufenster, -s, -**   shop window

das **Schauspiel, -s, -e**   play

der **Schauspieler, -s, -**   actor

sich scheiden lassen (ä), ie, a   to get divorced

die **Scheidung, -, -en**   divorce

scheinen, ie, ie   to seem

scheitern   to fail

schenken   to give a present

scheu   shy

der **Schi (Ski), -s, -er/-**   ski

schicken   to send

das **Schicksal, -s, -e**   fate, destiny

schieben, o, o   to push, to shove

der **Schiefer, -s, -**   slate

schießen, o, o   to shoot

schi·fahren (ä), u, a   to ski

der **Schifahrer, -s, - (die Schifahrerin, -, -nen)**   skier

das **Schiff, -s, -e**   ship

schimpfen   to scold, to grumble

der **Schinken, -s, -**   ham, bacon

der **Schirm, -s, -e**   umbrella

schlafen (ä), ie, a   to sleep

schlafen·gehen, i, a   to go to bed

schlagen (ä), u, a   to strike, to beat, to hit

die **Schlange, -, -n**   snake

schlank   slim, slender

schlecht   bad

schlecht·gehen, i, a   to be in a bad way

schlechtgelaunt   ill humored, in a bad mood

schleichen, i, i   to crawl, to sneak

schließen, o, o   to close

der **Schlittschuh, -s, -e**   ice skate

Schlittschuh laufen (äu), ie, au   to ice skate

das **Schloß, -sses, -̈sser**   castle

schlucken   to swallow

der **Schluß, -sses, -̈sse**   ending

der **Schlüssel, -s, -**   key

die **Schlußprüfung, -, -en**   final exam

schmecken   to taste

schmeicheln   to flatter

der **Schmerz, -es, -en**   pain

der **Schmetterling, -s, -e**   butterfly

der **Schmuck -s**   jewelry

schmutzig   dirty

der **Schnaps, -es, -̈e**   hard liquor, brandy

der **Schnee, -s**   snow

der **Schneemann, -s, ¨-er**   snowman
schneiden, i, i   to cut
schneien   to snow
schnell   fast
das **Schnitzel, -s, -**   cutlet
der **Schnupfen, -s, -**   head cold
die **Schokolade, -, -n**   chocolate
schon   already
schön   beautiful
die **Schönheit, -, -en**   beauty
der **Schrank, -s, ¨-e**   cupboard, closet
der **Schreck, -s, -e**   scare, shock
schrecklich   terrible, frightful
der **Schrei, -s, -e**   scream
schreiben, ie, ie   to write
das **Schreiben, -s, -**   letter, writing
der **Schreiber, -s, -**   writer
die **Schreibmaschine, -, -n**   typewriter
der **Schreibtisch, -s, -e**   desk
schreien, ie, ie   to scream
schreiten, i, i   to stride
schriftlich   written
die **schriftliche Arbeit, -, -en**   paper,
   written assignment
der **Schritt, -s, -e**   step
schüchtern   shy
schuften   to work hard, to slave
der **Schuh, -s, -e**   shoe
schuldig   guilty
die **Schule, -, -n**   school
der **Schüler, -s, - (die Schülerin, -, -nen)**
   student, pupil
die **Schulklasse, -, -n**   class, form
der **Schulranzen, -, -**   schoolbag, satchel
die **Schulter, -, -n**   shoulder
die **Schürze, -, -n**   apron
der **Schuß, -sses, ¨-sse**   shot
die **Schüssel, -, -n**   bowl
schütteln   to shake
schützen   to protect
schwach   weak
schwarz   black
der **Schwarzwald, -s**   Black Forest
der **Schwefel, -s**   sulfur

schweigen, ie, ie   to be silent
schweigend   silent, quiet
die **Schweiz, -**   Switzerland
schwer   heavy, severe
die **Schwester, -, -n**   sister
die **Schwierigkeit, -, -en**   difficulty
das **Schwimmbad, -s, ¨-er**   swimming pool
schwimmen, a, o   to swim
der **Schwimmer, -s, -**   swimmer
schwingen, a, u   to swing
schwören, o, o   to swear
der **See, -s, -n**   lake
die **See, -, -n**   sea, ocean
der **Seemann, -s, ¨-er**   seaman, sailor
sehen (ie), a, e   to see
sehnen   to long for, to yearn for
die **Sehnsucht, -, ¨-e**   longing
die **Seite, -, -n**   side, page
der **Sekretär, -s, -e (die Sekretärin, -, -nen)**
   secretary
die **Sekunde, -, -n**   second
selbständig   independent
selbstsicher   self-assured
selbstverständlich   obvious, matter-
   of-course
seltsam   strange
das **Semester, -s, -**   semester
die **Semmel, -, -n**   breakfast roll
senden, a, a   to send
servieren   to serve
der **Sessel, -s, -**   easy chair, arm chair
setzen   to set, to put
seufzen   to sigh
die **Sicherheit, -, -en**   security
sichern   to safeguard
die **Siedlung, -, -en**   settlement
der **Sieg, -s, -e**   victory
siegen   to win
der **Sieger, -s, -**   victor
das **Silber, -s**   silver
singen, a, u   to sing
der **Sinn, -s, -e**   sense
die **Sitte, -, -n**   custom
die **Situation, -, -en**   situation

der **Sitz, -es, -e** seat
sitzen, a, e to sit
sitzen·bleiben, ie, ie to repeat a class in school, fail
die **Sitzung, -, -en** meeting
Sizilien, -s Sicily
der **Skandal, -s, -e** scandal
die **Skulptur, -, -en** sculpture
das **Sofa, -s, -s** sofa
der **Sohn, -s, ¨e** son
die **Solarenergie, -, -n** solar energy
der **Soldat, -en, -en** soldier
der **Sommer, -s, -** summer
die **Sonne, -, -n** sun
die **Sorge, -, -n** worry
sorgen für to take care of
sortieren to sort
der **Spaß, -es, ¨e** fun
die **Sozialwissenschaft, -, -en** social science
spannend suspenseful
die **Spannung, -, -en** suspense
sparen to save
sparsam frugal
spät sein to be late
spazieren (spazieren·gehen, i, a) to stroll, to take a walk
der **Spaziergang, -s, ¨e** walk, stroll
der **Speiseraum, -s, ¨e** dining room
spiegeln to glitter
das **Spiel, -s, -e** game, play
spielen to play
der **Spielplatz, -es, ¨e** playground
das **Spielzeug, -s, -e** toy
spinnen, a, o to spin; to be crazy
spitzen to sharpen
Sport treiben, ie, ie to do sports
die **Sportart, -, -en** type of sport
der **Sportler, -s, - (die Sportlerin, -, -nen)** athlete
der **Sportwagen, -s, -** sports car
die **Sprache, -, -n** language
sprechen (i), a, o to speak
das **Sprichwort, -s, -e** proverb
springen, a, u to jump

spülen to rinse, to wash
das **Spültuch, -s, ¨er** dish cloth
spüren to feel, to sense
der **Staat, -s, -en** state
der **Staatsmann, -s, ¨er** statesman
der **Stacheldraht, -s, ¨e** barbed wire
das **Stadion, -s, . . . ien** stadium
die **Stadt, -, ¨e** city, town
der **Städter, -s, -** town dweller
der **Stadtteil, -s, -e** part of a town, quarter
der **Stall, -s, ¨e** barn, stable
der **Stamm, -s, ¨e** trunk
stammen aus to come from
das **Stammlokal, -s, -e** favorite pub
stark strong
starten to start
statt·finden, a, u to take place
der **Staubsauger, -s, -** vacuum cleaner
stechen (i), a, o to prick
stecken to stick
stehen, a, a to stand
stehlen (ie), a, o to steal
steif stiff
steigen, ie, ie to climb
der **Stein, -s, -e** stone
die **Stelle, -, -n** place, spot
stellen to put, to place
die **Stellung, -, -en** position
der **Stellvertreter, -s, -** deputy
sterben (i), a, o to die
sterblich mortal
der **Stern, -s, -e** star
das **Steuer, -s, -** steering wheel
die **Steuer, -, -n** tax
das **Steurrad, -s, ¨er** steering wheel
der **Stich, -s, -e** stab
still quiet, silent
stimmen to be right
die **Stimmung, -, -en** mood
stinken, a, u to stink
die **Stirne, -, -n** forehead
das **Stockwerk, -s (der Stock, -s), -e** floor
stolz proud
stören to disturb

die **Störung, -, -en** disturbance

stoßen (ö), ie, o to push

die **Straße, -, -n** street

die **Straßenbahn, -, -en** street car

die **Strecke, -, -n** stretch, section, route

streicheln to caress, to stroke

streichen, i, i to paint, to spread, to stroke

streiten, i, i to quarrel, to argue

streng strict

der **Streß, -sses** stress

das **Stroh, -s** straw

der **Strom, -s, ¨e** river

der **Struwwelpeter, -** Shock-headed Peter

das **Stück, -s, -e** piece; play

der **Student, -en, -en (die Studentin, -, -nen)** student

das **Studentenwohnheim, -s, -e** dormitory

die **Studie, -, -n** study

studieren to study

das **Studierzimmer, -s, -** study (room)

das **Studium, -s, . . . ien** studies

der **Stuhl, -s, ¨e** chair

stumm silent

die **Stunde, -, -n** hour

der **Stundenlohn, -s, ¨e** hourly wage

stundenlang for hours

der **Sturm, -s, ¨e** storm

stürzen to fall

der **Sturzhelm, -s, -e** crash helmet

suchen to look for, to search

der **Süden, -s** south

die **Summe, -, -n** sum

die **Suppe, -, -n** soup

süß sweet

das **Symbol, -s, -e** symbol

das **System, -s, -e** system

die **Szene, -, -n** scene

die **Tafel, -, -n** blackboard

der **Tag -s, -e** day

die **Tageszeitung, -, -en** daily newspaper

täglich daily

das **Talent, -s, -e** talent

die **Tanne, -, -n** fir tree

die **Tante, -, -n** aunt

der **Tanz, -es, ¨e** dance

tanzen to dance

die **Tasche, -, -n** pocket, bag

die **Tasse, -, -n** cup

die **Tat, -, -en** action, deed

die **Tatsache, -, -n** fact

der **Tau, -s** dew

das **Tau, -s, -e** rope

tauschen to trade

die **Technik, -, -en** technology

der **Tee, -s** tea

der/das **Teil, -s, -e** part

teilen to share, to divide

teil·nehmen (i), a, o to participate

der **Teilnehmer, -s, -** participant

das **Telefon, -s, -e** telephone

telefonieren to telephone

das **Telegramm, -s, -e** telegram

der **Teller, -s, -** plate

die **Temperatur, -, -en** temperature

der **Teppich, -s, -e** carpet

der **Termin, -s, -e** appointment

teuer expensive

der **Text, -s, -e** text

das **Theater, -s, -** theater

das **Theaterstück, -s, -e** play

das **Thema, -s, . . . men** theme, subject, topic

die **Theorie, -, -n** theory

tief deep

das **Tier, -s, -e** animal

die **Tinte, -, -n** ink

tippen to type

der **Tisch, -s, -e** table

der **Tischler, -s, -** cabinet maker

die **Tischrunde, -, -n** table (i.e., group of people around a table)

der **Thron, -s, -e** throne

der **Titel, -s, -** title

die **Tochter, -, ¨** daughter

toll great

die **Tomate, -, -n** tomato

die **Tonne, -, -n**   ton
der **Topf, -s, ̈-e**   pot
das **Tor, -s, -e**   gate
der **Tor, -s, -en**   fool
die **Torheit, -, -en**   folly
der **Tote, -n, -n**   dead
   töten   to kill
der **Tourist, -en, -en**   tourist
   tragen (ä), u, a   to carry
   trainieren   to train
die **Träne, -, -n**   tear
   trauen   to trust
der **Traum, -s, ̈-e**   dream
   träumen   to dream
   traurig   sad
   treffen (i), a, o   to hit, to meet
das **Treffen, -s, -**   meeting
die **Trennung, -, -en**   division, separation
   treten (i), a, e   to step, to kick
   treu   faithful, loyal
die **Treue, -**   faithfulness, fidelity, loyalty
   trinken, a, u   to drink
   trocken   dry
der **Trost, -s**   comfort
die **Truppe, -, -n**   troop
die **Tschechoslowakei, -**   Czechoslovakia
die **Tulpe, -, -n**   tulip
   tun, a, a   to do
der **Tunnel, -s, -/-s**   tunnel
die **Tür, -, -en**   door
die **Türkei, -**   Turkey
der **Turm, -s, ̈-e**   tower
   turnen   to do gymnastics
der **Turner, -s, -**   athlete
   typisch   typical

   üben   to practice
der **Überbringer, -s, -**   deliverer, bearer
der **Überfall, -s, ̈-e**   invasion, attack
die **Übergangsstelle, -, -n**   crossing point
   über·geben (i), a, e   to hand over
   überhaupt   in general, at all, entirely
   überhören   not to hear, to ignore

   überlaufen (äu), ie, au   to overcome, to be seized with
   über·laufen (äu), ie, au   to flow over
   überleben   to survive
   überlegen   to ponder, to reflect, to consider, to deliberate
   über·legen   to cover
die **Überlegung, -, -en**   consideration, deliberation
   übermorgen   day after tomorrow
   übernachten   to spend the night
   übernehmen (i), a, o   to take over
   überqueren   to cross over
   überraschen   to surprise
   übersetzen   to translate
   über·setzen   to ferry across
   überwinden   to overcome
   überzeugen   to convince, persuade
das **Ufer, -s, -**   shore
die **Übung, -, -en**   exercise
die **Uhr, -, -en**   clock, watch
   um·fallen (ä), ie, a   to fall over
   um·gehen, i, a   to handle (people)
   umschreiben, ie, ie   to outline, to describe
   um·schreiben, ie, ie   to rewrite
   sich um·sehen (ie), a, e   to look around
der **Umstand, -s, ̈-e**   circumstance
die **Umwelt, -**   environment
die **Umweltverschmutzung, -, -en**   environmental pollution
   um·ziehen, o, o   to change clothes, to move
   unbedeutend   unimportant
   unbedingt   absolutely
   unbequem   irritating, uncomfortable
   unbewußt   subconscious
   unbrauchbar   unusable
   unendlich   endless, infinite
   unentbehrlich   indispensable
   unfähig   incapable
der **Unfall, -s, ̈-e**   accident
die **Ungeduld, -**   impatience
   ungefähr   about, approximately

	ungerecht unfair, unjust	das	**Uran, -s** uranium
	ungern unwillingly	die	**Urgroßeltern** (*pl.*) great-grandparents
	ungeschickt clumsy	der	**Urgroßvater, -s, ⸚** great-grandfather
	ungewöhnlich unusual	die	**Urkunde, -, -n** document
das	**Unglück, -s, -e** accident, bad luck	der	**Urlaub, -s, -e** leave, vacation
	unglücklich unlucky	die	**Ursache, -, -n** cause
die	**Unglückszahl, -, -en** unlucky number	das	**Urteil, -s, -e** judgment, verdict
	ungünstig unfavorable		
	unheimlich sinister	der	**Vater, -s, ⸚** father
	unhöflich impolite		**sich verabschieden** to say good-bye, to dismiss oneself
die	**Universität, -, -en** university		**verantwortlich** responsible
	unmenschlich inhuman	die	**Verantwortung, -, -en** responsibility
	unmöglich impossible		**verärgern** to annoy
	unpraktisch impractable	das	**Verb, -s, -en** verb
das	**Unrecht, -s** wrong		**verbannen** to banish
	unregelmäßig irregular		**sich verbeugen** to bow
	unruhig nervous		**verbiegen, o, o** to spoil by bending
	unschön unpleasant		**verbieten, o, o** to forbid
	unschuldig innocent		**verbinden, a, u** to bandage
der	**Unsinn, -s** nonsense		**sich etwas verbitten, a, e** to refuse to tolerate something
	unsterblich immortal		
	unterbrechen (i), a, o to interrupt	der	**Verblichene, -n, -n** departed person, diseased
	unterdrücken to suppress		**verboten** forbidden
	unter·gehen, i, a to perish		**verbrannt** burned
	sich unterhalten (ä), ie, a to converse		**verbrauchen** to consume
die	**Unterhaltung, -, -en** conversation, entertainment		**verbringen, a, a** to spend time
die	**Unterhose, -, -n** underpants		**verderben (i), a, o** to spoil
der	**Unterricht, -s, -e** instruction		**verdeutlichen** to make clear
	unterrichten to instruct, to teach		**verdienen** to earn, to deserve
	unterscheiden, ie, ie to distinguish	der	**Verdienst, (e)s, -e** earnings, income, merit
der	**Unterschied, -s, -e** difference	der	**Verein, -s, -e** club
	unterschlagen (ä), u, a to embezzle	die	**Vereinigten Staaten** (*pl.*) United States
	unter·schlagen (ä), u, a to fold (arms), to cross (legs)	die	**Verfassung, -, -en** condition, constitution
	unterschreiben, ie, ie to sign		**verfluchen** to curse
die	**Unterschrift, -, -en** signature		**vergällen** to embitter
	untersuchen to examine	die	**Vergangenheit, -** past
die	**Untersuchung, -, -en** examination		**vergeben (i), a, e** to forgive
	unter·tauchen to go underground		**vergebens** in vain, to no purpose
	unterwegs on the way		**vergehen, i, a** to pass, to fade
	unwichtig unimportant		**vergessen (i), a, e** to forget
	unwirksam ineffective	die	**Vergeßlichkeit, -** forgetfulness
	unzufrieden dissatisfied		**sich vergewissern** to make sure of

vergleichen, i, i   to compare

das **Vergnügen, -s, -**   amusement, pleasure

die **Vergrößerung, -, -en**   enlargement

das **Verhalten, -s**   behavior

das **Verhältnis, -ses, -se**   relationship

die **Verhandlung, -, -en**   negotiation

verheiratet   married

verhungern   to starve to death

verkaufen   to sell

der **Verkäufer, -s, -**   salesman

der **Verkehr, -s**   traffic

verklingen   to fade away

verkriechen, o, o   to hide

verlangen   to demand

verlassen (ä), ie, a   to leave

verlaufen (äu), ie, au   to lose one's way

verletzen   to hurt

verliebt   in love

verlieren, o, o   to lose

der **Verlierer, -s, -**   loser

verloben   to engage

der **Verlobte (die Verlobte), -en, -en**   fiancé(e)

die **Verlobung, -, -en**   engagement

verloren·gehen, i, a   to get lost

verlöschen   to extinguish

der **Verlust, -s, -e**   loss

vermachen   to bequeath

vermögen   to succeed

vermuten   to surmise

vernichten   to annihilate

verniedlichen   to play something down

vernünftig   reasonable

die **Verpackung, -, -en**   packaging

verpassen   to miss

sich verpflichten   to commit oneself to

die **Verpflichtung, -, -en**   obligation

verreisen   to go on a trip

verrückt   crazy

versammeln   to assemble, to gather, to collect

die **Versammlung, -, -en**   meeting

versäumen   to miss

verschieben, o, o   to postpone

verschieden   different

verschlafen (ä), ie, a   to oversleep

verschollen   missing

verschwenden   to squander

verschwinden, a, u   to disappear

versenken   to sink something

versichern   to assure

versinken, a, u   to sink into

die **Version, -, -en**   version

sich verspäten   to be late

versprechen (i), a, o   to promise

der **Verstand, -s**   reason

verstecken   to hide

verstehen, a, a   to understand

der **Versuch, -s, -e**   attempt

versuchen   to try, to attempt

vertragen (ä), u, a   to endure

der **Vertrag, -s, ̈-e**   treaty

vertrauen   to trust

das **Vertrauen, -s**   trust

vertreten (i), a, e   to represent

der **Vertreter, -s, -**   representative, salesman

verunglücken   to have an accident, to crash

verurteilen   to condemn, to sentence

verwalten   to administer

verwandt   related

der **Verwandte (die Verwandte), -en, -en**   relative

verwechseln   to mix up, to confuse

verwenden   to use

verwickeln   to entangle, to involve

verwitwet   widowed

verwöhnen   to spoil

verzeihen, ie, ie   to forgive

verzichten auf   to renounce, to give up, to do without

verzweifeln   to despair

verzweifelt   desperate

der **Vetter, -s, -n**   cousin

das **Vieh, -s**   cattle

das **Viertel, -s, -**   quarter

der **Virus, -, . . . ren**   virus

das **Visum, -s, . . . sa/ . . . sen**   visa

der **Vogel, -s, ̈-**   bird

die **Vokabel, -, -n**   vocabulary word
die **Volkskammer, -, -n**   People's Chamber (of the GDR)
voll sein   to be full up, to be tight
vollkommen   complete
die **Voraussetzung, -, -en**   condition
vorbei·führen   to lead past
vorbei·gehen, i, a   to go past, to pass by
vorbei·kommen, a, o   to pass by
vor·bereiten   to plan, to prepare
die **Vorbereitung, -, -en**   preparation
vorgestern   day before yesterday
vorig   previous
sich vorkommen, a, o   to consider oneself
vor·lesen (ie), a, e   to read something to someone
die **Vorlesung, -, -en**   lecture
der **Vorname, -n, -n**   first name
der **Vormittag, -s, -e**   morning
der **Vorsatz, -es, ̈-e**   intention
vor·schlagen (ä), u, a   to suggest
die **Vorschrift, -, -en**   instruction, rule, regulation
vorsichtig   careful
sich vor·stellen   to introduce oneself; to imagine
die **Vorstellung, -, -en**   introduction, impression, performance
der **Vortrag, -s, ̈-e**   lecture
vor·werfen (i), a, o   to reproach
der **Vorzug, -s, ̈-e**   advantage

die **Waage, -, -n**   scales
wachen   to be awake
wachsen (ä), u, a   to grow
die **Waffe, -, -n**   weapon
wagen   to dare
der **Wagen, -s, -**   car
der **Wagenheber, -s, -**   jack
die **Wahl, -, -en**   election, choice
wählen   to vote, to elect, to choose; to dial
der **Wahlspruch, -s, ̈-e**   slogan
der **Wahnsinn, -s**   madness, insanity
wahr   true

die **Wahrheit, -, -en**   truth
der **Wald, -s, ̈-er**   wood, forest
das **Wäldchen, -s, -**   little forest
walten   to reign
die **Wand, -, ̈-e**   wall
der **Wanderer, -s, -**   hiker
wandern   to hike
die **Wanderschaft, -**   journeying
die **Wanderung, -, -en**   hike
die **Ware, -, -n**   ware, merchandise
die **Wärme, -**   warmth
warnen   to warn
warten   to wait
die **Wäsche, -**   laundry
waschen (ä), u, a   to wash
das **Wasser, -s**   water
wechseln   to change
der **Wecker, -s, -**   alarm (clock)
der **Weg, -s, -e**   way
weg·fahren (ä), u, a   to drive away
weg·gehen, i, a   to go away
weg·nehmen, i, o   to take away
sich wehren   to defend oneself
weh tun   to hurt
das **Weib, -s, -er**   woman
weich   soft
sich weigern   to refuse
Weihnachten   Christmas
der **Wein, -s, -e**   wine
weinen   to cry
die **Weinstube, -, -n**   wine tavern
weiß   white
weit   wide, far
weitaus   by far
weiter·arbeiten   to keep on working
weiter·gehen, i, a   to go on
weiter·lesen (ie), a, e   to go on reading
weiter·spielen   to keep playing
die **Welt, -, -en**   world
weltberühmt   world famous
der **Weltkrieg, -s, -e**   world war
der **Weltmeister, -s, -**   world champion
wenden   to turn
das **Werbematerial, -s, -ien**   advertising material

	werden (i), u, o to become	
	werfen (i), a, o to throw	
das	**Werk, -s, -e** work	
die	**Werkstatt, -, -̈en** workshop	
	werktags on working days	
	wert worth	
der	**Wert, -s, -e** value	
das	**Wesen, -s, -** creature, being, nature	
der	**Westen, -s** west	
die	**Wette, -, -n** bet	
das	**Wetter, -s, -** weather	
der	**Wettkampf, -s, -̈e** competition	
	wichtig important	
	wickeln to wrap	
	widersprechen (i), a, o to contradict	
der	**Widerspruch, -s, -̈e** contradiction	
der	**Widerstand, -s, -̈e** resistance	
	wiederholen to repeat, to review	
	wieder·holen to get back	
	wieder·sehen (ie), a, e to see again	
die	**Wiedervereinigung, -, -en** reunification	
	wiegen, o, o to weigh	
die	**Wiese, -, -n** meadow	
das	**Wild, -s** game	
der	**Wille, -ns, -n** will	
	willkommen welcome	
der	**Wind, -s, -e** wind	
	windig windy	
	winken to wave	
der	**Winter, -s, -** winter	
	wirksam effective	
der	**Wirt, -s, -e** innkeeper	
die	**Wirtschaft, -, -en** inn, economy	
	wirtschaftlich economic	
die	**Wirtschaftlichkeit, -** thriftiness	
das	**Wirtshaus, -es, -̈er** inn	
die	**Wissenschaft, -, -en** science	
der	**Wissenschaftler, -s, - (die Wissen-schaftlerin, -, -nen)** scientist	
	wissen, u, u to know	
die	**Witwe, -, -n** widow	
der	**Witwer, -s, -** widower	
der	**Witz, -es, -e** joke	
die	**Woche, -, -n** week	

das	**Wochenende, -s, -n** weekend	
	wöchentlich weekly	
	wohl probably	
	sich wohl fühlen to feel well	
	wohnen to live, to dwell	
das	**Wohnheim, -s, -e** dormitory	
die	**Wohnung, -, -en** apartment	
das	**Wohnzimmer, -s, -** living room	
die	**Wolle, -** wool	
das	**Wort, -s, -̈er/-e** word (*pl.* -̈er: vocabulary words; *pl.* -e: text words)	
das	**Wörterbuch, -s, -̈er** dictionary	
	wunderbar wonderful	
	wunderschön marvelous	
	wünschen to wish	
	würdig worthy of	
die	**Wurst, -, -̈e** sausage	
das	**Würstchen, -s, -** little sausage	
die	**Wut, -** rage	
	wütend furious	
	zäh tough	
die	**Zahl, -, -en** number	
	zählen to count	
die	**Zahlung, -, -en** payment	
der	**Zahn, -s, -̈e** tooth	
der	**Zahnarzt, -s, -̈e** dentist	
	zart tender	
	zärtlich tender	
	zeichnen to draw	
der	**Zeichner, -s, -** designer	
die	**Zeichnung, -, -en** drawing	
	zeigen to show	
die	**Zeile, -, -n** line	
die	**Zeit, -, -en** time	
der	**Zeitpunkt, -s, -e** moment, (particular) time	
die	**Zeitschrift, -, -en** journal, periodical	
die	**Zeitung, -, -en** newspaper	
der	**Zentner, -s, -** centner	
das	**Zentrum, -s, . . . ren** center	
	zerreißen, i, i to tear up	
	zerschlagen (ä), u, a to smash	
	zerstören to destroy	
	zerstörend destructive	

das **Zeug, -s** material, stuff
der **Zeuge, -n, -n** witness
das **Zeugnis, -ses, -se** report card, testimony
ziehen, o, o to pull
das **Ziel, -s, -e** aim, goal, destination
zielen to aim
zierlich delicate
die **Zigarette, -, -n** cigarette
das **Zimmer, -s, -** room
die **Zivilbevölkerung, -, -en** civilian population
der **Zirkus, -, -se** circus
das **Zitat, -s, -e** quotation
zitieren to quote
zittern to tremble
zögern to hesitate
die **Zone, -, -n** zone
der **Zoo, -s, -s** zoo
der **Zorn, -s** anger, rage
zornig angry
der **Zucker, -s** sugar
zuerst at first
der **Zufall, -s, ̈-e** coincidence
zufällig by chance, incidental
zufrieden content
der **Zug, -s, ̈-e** train, trait
die **Zugspitze** name of the highest mountain in Germany
zu Hause at home

zu·hören to listen to
der **Zuhörer, -s, -** listener
zu·machen to close
zu·nehmen (i), a, o to increase, to gain weight
zurück·geben (i), a, e to give back, to return
zurück·fahren (ä), u, a to drive back
zurück·kehren to return, to come back
zurück·treten (i), a, e to step back, to resign
zurück·ziehen, o, o to withdraw
zusammen·fahren (ä), u, a to start back in alarm
zusammen·hängen, ie, a to be connected
der **Zusammenbruch, -s, ̈-e** collapse
zu·schauen to watch
der **Zuschauer, -s, -** spectator
zu·schließen, o, o to lock
zu·sehen (ie), a, e to watch
zustande·bringen, a, a to achieve
zu·stimmen to agree
zuverlässig reliable
zuviel too much
zuvor·kommen, a, o to forestall
zu zweit two together, by twos
der **Zweck, -s, -e** purpose
der **Zweifel, -s, -** doubt
zwingen, a, u to force

Index

Numbers refer to the grammar points.